THE CHRISTIAN EDUCATOR'S HANDBOOK ON ADULT EDUCATION

THE CHRISTIAN EDUCATOR'S HANDBOOK ON ADULT EDUCATION

edited by

KENNETH O. GANGEL & JAMES C. WILHOIT

VICTOR BOOKS
A DIVISION OF SCRIPTURE PRESS PUBLICATIONS INC.
USA CANADA ENGLAND

Scripture quotations, unless otherwise indicated, are from the *Holy Bible, New International Version* ®. Copyright © 1973, 1978, 1984 by International Bible Society. Used by permission of Zondervan Publishing House. All rights reserved. Other quotations are from the *New American Standard Bible* (NASB), © the Lockman Foundation 1960, 1962, 1963, 1968, 1971, 1972, 1973, 1975, 1977; *The New King James Version* (NKJV). © 1979, 1980, 1982, Thomas Nelson, Inc., Publishers; *The New Testament in Modern English,* Revised Edition (PH), © J.B. Phillips, 1958, 1960, 1972, permission of Macmillan Publishing Co. and Collins Publishers; the *New Revised Standard Version of the Bible* (NRSV), © 1989 by the Directors of Christian Education of the National Council of the Churches of Christ in the United States of America; and the *Authorized (King James) Version* (KJV).

Copyediting: Robert N. Hosack
Cover Design: Scott Rattray

Library of Congress Cataloging-in-Publication Data

The Christian educator's handbook on adult education / by Kenneth O. Gangel, editor, James C. Wilhoit, editor.
p. cm.
Includes bibliographical references.
ISBN 1-56476-019-7
1. Christian education of adults. I. Gangel, Kenneth O. II. Wilhoit, Jim.
BV1488.C465 1993
268'.434–dc20
92-37338
CIP

1 2 3 4 5 6 7 8 9 10 Printing/Year 97 96 95 94 93

CONTENTS

INTRODUCTION

In 1989 the United Way of America published an outstanding trend analysis handbook entitled *What Lies Ahead: Countdown to the 21st Century*. In the introduction to that volume, the Environmental Scan Committee which prepared the research identified "Changedrivers: Nine Leading Forces Reshaping American Society." Included in their list were such familiar items as globalization, economic restructuring, and the information-based economy. They entitled the first item "The Maturation of America" and dealt with many of the items which make up the fabric of this book. Regarding the maturation of America, the United Way people observe:

> This trend starts with the maturing of the baby boom generation as these individuals move into their prime family-, household-, and asset-formation phrase. It also includes trends pertaining to the "graying of America"—the growth of the age-65-and-over population, a more active, more affluent group than existed in previous generations. Accompanying the aging of the population is the related psychological phenomenon of a maturing and increasing sophistication of tastes. The U.S. is leaving an era obsessed with youth, and moving into one that will be more realistic, more responsible, and more tolerant of diversity.[1]

Specific statistics are offered for every point, but in general the report observes what we already know—that the population will continue to grow older; the median age will continue to rise;

there will be a decline in the proportion of young adults; a sharp increase in the proportion of middle-aged Americans (thirty-five–fifty-four) will occur; a dramatic increase in the proportion of Americans over seventy-five will result; and there will be a political activism which will pragmatically reflect the aging of the society.

We consider it likely that the evangelical community, which has only now begun to reposition itself to minister to 76 million Baby Boomers, will have given very little thought to what happens when those active, young, and middle-age adults move into older age brackets. Already national news magazines have observed that Boomers are returning to church and that more than 80 percent of them consider themselves religious and believe in life after death.

The first Boomers become fifty in 1996 and four years later (to borrow the framework of the United Way report) move into older adulthood. Is it possible that churches which have radically restructured their programs and services to accommodate the external sociological preferences of Baby Boomers will find those very people rejecting the change and opting for more traditional models? Trading in hymnbooks for worship chorus slides; exchanging organs and pianos for worship bands; offering a message of languorous good-will—these have been Band-Aid™ solutions calculated to draw people into public meetings but unproven in meeting their inner needs.

Right now these are radical changes, but what will happen by the end of the decade? One could argue that Busters will replace the Boomers and are likely to want even more radical worship and educational patterns, but we have no clear-cut research to argue that point. We do know, however, that demographers expect as many as 1 million Boomers to reach the age of 100 and to both continue and increase their dominant influence in national institutions—including the church.

Most of the authors contributing to this volume seem to concur that the church has not yet awakened to its responsibilities and potential in adult education. We still live in that youth culture the United Way report insists we are leaving behind. Placement directors in Christian colleges and seminaries regularly find requests for youth directors and, occasionally, a director of children's ministry. Directors of adult education, discipleship, and family life appear only in the mega-church pattern and then well down the line of priority staffing.

Yet Americans over the age of sixty-five have increased their ranks by 50 percent since 1950 and will increase another 75 percent by 2030. Adults make up about 73.9 percent of the population and by the year 2000 should number about 200 million. The 1980 median age of 30 will climb to 38.4 by the end of this decade. Meanwhile, the youth population continues to shrink.

> During the 1990s the 18-25 age group will decrease by 12 percent. In 1980 there were 4.2 million 19 year olds; in 1992 there will be 3.1 million. The fastest growing age group in America is the age group over 85. By 1998 the number of Americans over 85 will have grown by 50 percent. At the same time there will be a 45 percent increase in 45-50 year olds and a 21 percent increase in those 75-84.[2]

Meanwhile, largely because of inadequate philosophies of leadership among pastoral staff members, lay leadership struggles and volunteerism languishes. We desperately need a lay renewal, a new emphasis on the universal priesthood of believers in the ministry of God's people. According to an ETA survey, churches spend six times more for music than for worker training, and 60,000 churches do not report one annual conversion. Yet the genius of the New Testament clearly focused on lay ministry, not the dominance of professional theologians. George Barna puts it this way:

> For more churches to grow, both in numbers and spiritual depth, a major overhaul of our approach to lay leadership must also transpire. Often, pastors complain that there are not enough people willing to be leaders in the church. In actuality, our research has shown that there are more than enough people capable and willing to serve in leadership roles. However, people will refuse to accept the burden of responsibility alone. They must be involved in team ministry, partnering with the clergy and other leaders to make ministry happen.[3]

No book on adult education can complete its task without some focus on family life education. Though we have included only one chapter directly aimed at this crucial ministry, many other authors have dealt with it in the broader sense. The United Way report observes trends we have come to expect—slow growth in the number of single person households; slowing increase in the number of childless married-couple households; a slowing of the baby boomlet (echo boom) in the mid-1990s. But they also are calling for a decline in the divorce rate and an increase in family violence. As the chaotic outside world tries to force the family to be a more stabilizing force, at the same time internal stresses make it less able to fulfill its supportive role. In America over 2.3 million people live together without a marriage bond (POSSLQS), and 700,000 of those households have children. In addition, 92,000 domiciles shared by gay or lesbian couples house children. Mobility is an established fact in American society, and the percentage of women working now stands at 55 and continues to grow.

The *Futurist* magazine lists decline in work ethic as one of the long-term trends affecting the United States, and focus has shifted from remuneration (salary and benefits) to the advantage work provides to the worker. That shift reflects the high priority of time over money as the number one currency of the society. Another demonstration is called "cocooning," the return to the home as the center of all life's activities and relationships, from running a telemarketing program for employment to playing *Trivial Pursuit* or *Pictionary* on Friday night.

Barna cites a trend toward different spouses for different eras of life, claiming, "By 2000, Americans will generally believe that a life spent with the same partner is both unusual and unnecessary. We will continue our current moral transition by accepting sexual relationships with one person at a time—'serial monogamy'—to be the civilized and moral way to behave. But we will not consider it at all unusual to be married two or three times during the course of life."[4]

The tragedy of all this family breakdown is its effect in the lives of children. In 1988, 12.5 million U.S. children lived in poverty. Between 6.6 and 10.6 million kids under twelve go hungry every day in America. Some studies claim this country contains more than 500,000 homeless children.[5]

In this book we have attempted to pull together a coalition of people who work in various areas of adult education, both research and active ministry. Their collective expertise offers the student of adult education a sweeping picture of this crucial dimension of the broader field of church education. The authors come from a wide diversity of confessions and institutions, and we have attempted to include areas of consideration sometimes neglected in earlier works such as gender differentiation and culture consideration. We hope the book will serve as a basic text for Christian colleges and seminaries and as an essential reference handbook for pastors, church staffs, and lay leaders involved with adult ministry.

Even the casual reader will immediately notice the emphasis on the four central andragogical assumptions developed in the research of Malcolm Knowles. While we do not present these as documented fact, we find them consistent both with biblical data and ongoing research in adult education and have chosen to make them the general framework of the book.

In addition, we want to portray a solid commitment to the authority of Scripture. One senses an overwhelming practicality in the Bible's emphasis on adult education. People do not learn just to acquire knowledge, but rather to use it in the service of God. Parents learn so they can teach their children; elders learn so they can serve the church; new converts learn so they can mature in their faith. Though he did not word it exactly as we might, Eugene Trester spells out this learning-for-service motif in *Andragogy in Action*:

> Without a doubt, one of the most significant dynamics emerging in contemporary church life, that has strong implications for Christianity's future, is the growing reassertion by laity in recent decades of their rightful place in the ministry of the church. . . . This is to state that an important recent development concerning Christianity's relationship to society has been the increasingly significant role of adults in the various social undertakings of the churches. Informed adult Christians are indispensable to the challenge of translating Christian values and attitudes into social, political, and economic institutions. . . . [6]

Right. But the need of adults to know Scripture does not by itself provide theological foundation for adult education. In the first two chapters we have attempted to lay a basis, both biblically and theologically, for andragogical process in adult ministry. Though this book deals with education and not theology, we do want our theological commitment to be maintained throughout, a commitment which most of the authors have captured.

We dedicate the effort to the glory of the God who makes that ministry possible and calls us to fulfill it.

Notes

1. *What Lies Ahead: Countdown to the 21st Century* (United Way of America, 1989), 2.

2. Leith Anderson, *Dying for Change* (Minneapolis: Bethany, 1990), 29.
3. George Barna, *The Frog in the Kettle* (Ventura, Calif.: Regal, 1990), 148–49.
4. Ibid., 72.
5. Kim A. Lawton, "The World's Most Vulnerable," *Christianity Today*, 19 Nov. 1990, 48.
6. Eugene Trester, "The Biblical Andragogy Clinic," in *Andragogy in Action*, ed. Malcolm Knowles and Associates (San Francisco: Jossey-Bass, 1984), 344.

ONE
BIBLICAL FOUNDATIONS FOR ADULT EDUCATION

Kenneth O. Gangel

Essentially the Bible is an adult book written by adults for adults and about adults. To be sure, one can find a great deal of biblical information, both biographical and didactic, about the church's ministry to children and young people. Almost all of it, however, falls within the context of the family or congregation in which adults carry out that ministry. Most texts commonly used in describing a biblical approach to youth or children's ministry draw upon passages written to adults, who in turn, communicate God's truth to following generations.

In contrast to an argument from *silence* (God must not be concerned about that because He didn't mention it), biblical support for adult education represents an argument of the *obvious* (God talks about adult responsibilities so frequently He must assume we are equipping people to carry them out). Since neither testament centers on programming or methodology, one hardly expects to find a defined and organized strategy of adult education presented in Scripture. But several questions persist.

How do the Scriptures speak to the principles of adult education? What teaching principles can we discern which may enhance the adult learning process? How do we transfer these concepts to a modern educational setting?

We may keep two things in mind as we approach a biblical study of adult education. First, people are people, no matter when they lived. All have limitations; all are sinners; and all need help for growth. Second, growth in the context of Christian education focuses on the goal of Christlikeness. Adult Christian education aims at the transformation of both mind and life (Rom. 12:1-2).

We will start with a look at the Master Teacher, Jesus Christ. How can we characterize His theology of learning, His teaching methods, His expectations of those who followed Him? Further examples of learning experiences are found in Old Testament narrative literature which describes some profound life-changing moments. What acted as the catalyst for these decisions and actions? Who affected them?

The answers to these questions will help us identify the common threads, the principles and practices, the interpersonal relationships which produced learning experiences. From this foundation, we can formulate a biblical base for a modern philosophy of adult Christian education.

JESUS THE MASTER TEACHER

Where could we find a better model of teaching than in the first four books of the New Testament? Jesus is referred to or addressed as "Teacher" 41 times.[1] In John 1:38, we learn that this approximates the Jewish term "Rabbi."[2] He had gathered around Him a group of disciples[3] so we can observe His teaching methods with a small and intimate group as well as with the larger crowds who followed Him.

As we look at Jesus' teaching encounters, no clear pattern immediately emerges, no way of saying "this is done first" and "that is done next." Instead, flexibility and an intense attention to individual persons color each approach.

When a sinful woman anoints Jesus as He eats in the home of Simon the Pharisee (Luke 7:36-50), He recognizes her great love despite a sinful life and treats her with immense gentleness and compassion. The situation in Matthew 15 stands in contrast. Here Jesus responds to the Pharisees and teachers of the Law. Again recognizing the underlying motivation behind the question, "Why do your disciples break the tradition of the elders? They don't wash their hands before they eat!" (Matt. 15:2-3), Jesus, without a trace of the previously mentioned gentleness or compassion, denounced them as hypocrites. His disciples noted that the response offended the Pharisees.

When asked a direct question, Jesus might reply indirectly, requiring the questioner to think through the issue and come up with the appropriate answer. Messengers came from John the Baptist to ask Him, "Are you the one who was to come, or should we expect someone else?" The answer was not a clear "yes," but an encouragement to look at what they had seen and heard (Luke 7:18-23). When His disciples asked, "Who is the greatest in the kingdom of heaven?" Jesus answered by drawing an object lesson from a child standing nearby (Matt. 18:1-9).

Jesus Approaches Strangers

Clearly Jesus tailored His responses to the particular audience. Look at two situations dealing with accusations of Sabbath violations in Matthew 12. First, the hungry disciples pick and eat heads of grain. The text identifies the accusers as Pharisees. Jesus rejoins by going straight to the Scriptures, using with accuracy the very tool His questioners used against Him. They saw themselves as learned and accomplished in the Law. Jesus based His answer on their self-perception.

The second scene takes place in a synagogue. Although the more educated group would be present, we may also assume a less sophisticated audience from the local agrarian background. Jesus now addresses Himself to them. He prepares to heal a man with a shriveled hand by reminding them of their responsibility as shepherds to a sheep should one fall into a pit on the Sabbath.

A close look at the familiar story of Jesus and the Samaritan woman in John 4 may prove helpful. While this story is often cited as a model for personal evangelism, it is useful for that model precisely because Jesus picks up on the teachable moment and uses it to provide a profound change point for the woman.

Jesus approached the woman on the basis of her experience, namely the drawing of water from the well. Shocked at His approach, she expresses the shock by reminding Him of her position on the societal ladder. He immediately reveals something of His person to her, consistent with His goal of drawing all people to Himself (John 12:32). He begins to paint a metaphor of water, using familiar territory to teach new truths.

Intrigued by this partial revelation of Himself, she questions Him further, seeking to place Him in her hierarchy of important people. Continuing with the water metaphor, the Lord expands it further in a direction she would be unlikely to find on her own. Although she perceives her needs as physical, Jesus discerns the real need running far deeper. He helps her acknowledge this real need by reminding her of her unholy marital situation.

She calls Jesus a prophet and takes another step in recognition of His person. The Lord continues to bring her along by addressing her religious experiences and her insecurity in worshiping as a Samaritan rather than as a Jew. When she finally expressed her belief in a coming Messiah, Jesus more completely revealed Himself as that Promised One. At that point, she makes a giant leap from self-centeredness ("Sir, give me this water so that I won't get thirsty," John 4:15) to other-centeredness ("The woman went back to the town and said to the people, 'Come see a man who told me everything I ever did. Could this be the Christ?' " John 4:29). Jesus knew her, loved her, moved her.

One common denominator in each encounter—Jesus spoke the truth to the people involved. He discerned the reality behind the questions and dealt with actual issues, not superficial ones. He knew His audience, their backgrounds, their interests, the ways in which they perceived themselves. He spoke to this self-perception, whether a sinner recognizing her need for forgiveness or a scholar, comfortable in intimate knowledge of the law. He never ignored the significance of self-concept in the adults He taught.

Jesus spoke to an agrarian society surviving without significant labor-saving devices, oppressed outwardly by Roman taxation and rule and inwardly by pharisaical regulations. To this audience He called, "Come to Me, all you who are weary and burdened, and I will give you rest. Take My yoke upon you and learn from Me, for I am gentle and humble in heart, and you will find rest for your souls. For My yoke is easy and My burden is light" (Matt. 11:28-30).[4] Unquestionably, our Lord saw Himself as the appropriate focus of all learning experiences.

What did Jesus expect of those who accepted the invitation to learn from Him? Here we need to turn from the more general audience to those who formed His intimate circle.

Jesus Activates His Disciples

When He named His disciples, they were chosen first of all to be with Him: "Jesus went up on a mountainside and called to Him those He wanted, and they came to Him. He appointed twelve—designating them apostles—that they might be with Him and that He might send them out to preach" (Mark 3:13-14).

He expected active rather than intellectual assent. To His future disciple: "As Jesus went on from there, He saw a man named Matthew sitting at the tax collector's booth. 'Follow Me,' He told him, and Matthew got up and followed Him" (Matt. 9:9). To the rich ruler who wanted to inherit eternal life: "You still lack one thing. Sell everything you have and give to the poor, and you will have treasure in heaven. Then come, follow Me'' (Luke 18:22). To those whom Jesus identified as His own: "My sheep listen to My voice; I know them, and they follow Me'' (John 10:27). To those who understood that He was the Christ: "Then He called the crowd to Him along with His disciples and said: 'If anyone would come after Me, he must deny himself and take up his cross and follow Me' " (Mark 8:34). The key word jumps out: "follow,"[5] an action-oriented word touching.

Jesus Applies Strategy in Teaching

He gave His followers the opportunity to practice what they had seen by sending them out to preach and to heal (Luke 9:1-6). After the practice session, He made them answer for themselves the question of His identity. " 'But what about you?' He asked. 'Who do you say I am?' " (Luke 9:20) He confirmed their conclusions at the Transfiguration (Luke 9:28-36).

He used daily life for object lessons at teachable moments. For example, the widow's offering in Mark 12 demonstrated true charity, and the illustration of physical birth helps shed light on the spiritual rebirth in John 3. He encouraged His followers to take risks and try out their faith, even when they stumbled and came up short as did Peter when he tried to walk on the water (Matt. 14:22-31).

Jesus taught with active example and with an enormous amount of flexibility, displaying sensitivity to the situation. He took advantage of teachable moments and expected those who followed Him to experience changed lives. He knew His audience intimately and drew on their individual life experiences as He brought them to change-points. He led His followers step-by-step, taking them to the next level when they evidenced readiness, quickly giving opportunities to practice the lessons He demonstrated. Though they would not have understood the principles of developmental task education, the disciples offer a realistic model of that modern andragogical concept.

OLD TESTAMENT ILLUSTRATIONS

Let's look at two examples of learning experiences described in the Old Testament. In both cases trusted associates led others through a lesson. In both cases newly gained insights led to immediate action.

Jethro and Moses

In Exodus 18 we read of an encounter between Moses and his father-in-law, Jethro. Moses had already brought the Israelites out of Egypt. He had acquired some significant leadership experience dealing with difficult followers as they battled fear, hunger, and thirst.

Jethro knew Moses well as a result of the 40 years Moses had spent in the desert as an exile from Egypt. Now Jethro caught up on all the news. "Moses told his father-in-law about everything the Lord had done to Pharaoh and the Egyptians for Israel's sake and about all the hardships they had met along the way and how the Lord had saved them" (v. 8). Jethro rejoiced with Moses over the Lord's deliverance and they worshiped together.

The next day, Jethro observed Moses in action as the judge of the people. He asked Moses to explain his motivation and methodology. Jethro responded after the explanation (rather bluntly it would seem) by saying, "What you are doing is not good. You and these people who come to you will only wear yourselves out. The work is too heavy for you; you cannot handle it alone" (v. 18).

With an exhortation for Moses to listen, Jethro detailed an organizational plan which would permit Moses to build more leaders, satisfy the need for a reputable method of conflict resolution, and keep himself from collapsing with exhaustion. Moses, apparently without hesitation, put his father-in-law's plan into immediate effect.

A brief analysis: Moses, still new to his leadership role, made some mistakes in the process. His experiences surfaced a need to learn more about administrative principles. Jethro, although he spoke bluntly, addressed Moses as the leader. He recognized Moses as such and appealed to that position as he revealed the solution. He, like Jesus, spoke the truth with an assurance that he knew not only the situation but the person. He affirmed in Moses what Moses knew to be true about himself, namely, he was the one in charge. Finally, Moses could and did try the idea immediately to test its effectiveness—a quick move from theory to practice.

Nathan and David

We may examine a different learning experience found in 2 Samuel 12. The first fourteen verses of this chapter detail an interchange between Nathan the prophet and David, king of Israel. David, first an adulterer and then the prime force behind a murder, appeared to be living comfortably with the results—his new wife Bathsheba and their newborn son.

Nathan tells a story of great injustice, skillfully drawing portraits of the two characters. "The rich man had a very large number of sheep and cattle, but the poor man had nothing except one little ewe lamb he had bought. He raised it, and it grew up with him and his children. It shared his food, drank from his cup, and even slept in his arms. It was like a daughter to him" (vv. 2-3). David, although rich at this time, was once a shepherd; he quickly identified with the poor man.

When Nathan proceeds to describe the rich man's evil deed (the slaughter of the poor man's lamb instead of one of his own for a traveler's meal), David, strongly empathizing with the poor man, burns with anger and orders fourfold restitution. Nathan then announced, "You are the man!" (v. 7) and laid out before David the evil of his own actions and the Lord's decision to move against him.

David immediately acknowledged his sin, repenting without defensiveness or explanation. From that experience he wrote Psalm 51, the powerful prayer of penitence.

What factors influenced such a profound learning experience? Notice that Nathan, having served as prophet in his court (2 Sam. 7:2), knew David and approached him both on the basis of David's position as king of Israel and his experience as a shepherd. As we have seen before, the learner's self-perception and past experiences serve as key factors. Nathan gave David the opportunity to recognize the gross injustice by an indirect approach, not an immediate outright accusation. David reached the necessary conclusion himself.

Finally, David was living in a state of great sin. Whether he consciously recognized it or not, he needed to be confronted with the truth of his actions and their results. Nathan, like Jethro and Jesus, decisively spoke the truth after laying the foundation for David to receive it. David suffered after the confrontation over the death of Bathsheba's newborn son, but he then resumed his life with the Lord's blessing.

APPLICABLE PRINCIPLES UNCOVERED

Many similar accounts abound in Scripture, but these suffice as a sampling. What principles of adult education can we draw from this brief survey of learning experiences seen in the Bible? Although none of them took place in a formal setting, that does not necessarily preclude the classroom as an appropriate place for adult education. It *does* mean that methods which enhance the adult learning process should be included in the classroom experience.

First, the teacher must know the students well in order to approach them on the basis of their self-perceptions. Armed with knowledge of backgrounds, the teacher may aim with more certainty at the heart of the individual, thus drawing closer to the goal of changed lives. These examples suggest that learning includes intensely personal experience between teacher and learner. Invariably, our Lord's teaching intentionally pulled the adult learner from dependence to self-directed learning. The disciples offer the most dramatic illustration.

Second, the learner must start on the basis of his or her own experience, whether drawing water at a well, living as a shepherd, or leading a huge number of people around the desert. The experiences provide a foundation of conscious knowledge on which to build, and they expose the need for further learning when present capabilities prove inadequate to cope with the situation.

Third, the learning experience is far more "do" than "know" oriented. The learner puts into practice as quickly as possible the lessons which have been explained or demonstrated. Intellectual assent or comprehension alone do not qualify. Practice then surfaces further needs so the learner desires more interaction with the learning facilitator. Jesus' methodology with His disciples makes this point particularly clear.

Fourth, the learning experiences consume time. It takes time to get to know people, to understand how they see themselves, to discern their experiences and their needs, to think of illustrations or stories which capture the imagination, and to design practical applications so learning moves beyond mere intellectual exercise to life change. True learning appears to demand a leisurely pace, as opposed to a hurried approach. And the immediacy of application (Moses, David, woman at the well) lays a foundation for our teaching today.

How do the Scriptures speak to the issue of adult education? Certainly not by displaying us neatly organized lists of steps, guaranteed to bring immediate results. Instead we read of people in a different culture and a different time, who grew from their learning experiences.

A BIBLICAL MODEL OF ADULT EDUCATION

Some years ago I pondered whether one could actually find a biblical and practical analysis of adult education in operation anywhere in the pages of Scripture. To be sure, we cannot read andragogical assumptions back into the Bible, but we have already seen their practice in various biblical accounts. Can we also find some indicators of educational content and process recommended for a local church in the first century? My search took me to the second chapter of Titus and Paul's guidelines for the congregation at Crete. Before reading any further, it would be wise to stop and review the entirety of Titus 2.

Adult Education Aims At Certain Target Groups

Nowhere else in Scripture do we have such a fascinating categorization of adults into five specific groups, and for each group an identification of the kinds of educational experiences they needed in the light of their age, status, role in the church, and cultural surroundings. Let's look at them one by one.

Older Men. The apostle writes to the young church leader, "Teach the older men to be temperate, worthy of respect, self-controlled, and sound in faith, in love and in endurance" (v. 2). He focuses not on the official elders of the congregation, but rather male senior citizens. Like the overseers and wives of the deacons (1 Tim. 3:2, 11), they are to be "sober" *(nēphalios);* "dignified" *(semnos);* "sound-minded" *(sōphron):* the NIV rendering of "self-controlled" is quite helpful since the word *(sōphron)* deals with the mastery of one's self, especially the curbing of desires and impulses leading to the sound and balanced judgment which should characterize the older men of the church.

In a strategic play on words in the first two verses, Paul urges Titus to "sound doctrine" and the older men of the church to be "sound in faith." In both cases he uses the adjective *hugiainontas* which might best be translated by the English word "healthy." Homer Kent talks about it this way:

> Healthy Christian lives are the result of healthful doctrine (v. 1). The three areas of Christian life where this health is to be clearly evident are faith, love, and patience. Each term has the definite article. Hence it is "the faith" (that is, Christian truth), "the love" (which is the Christian's duty, John 13:34), and "the patience" (which the Christian is to display on earth while waiting for his Lord, James 5:7-8).[6]

Older Women. Apparently the nurture needs of older women do not differ significantly from their male counterparts. The basic command focuses on reverence in life. To put it another way, they should possess inner character suitable to a sacred person, conveying the idea of a priestess carrying out the duties of her office. Of greatest significance in this second nurture group to whom Titus ministered is their responsibility to teach others. Paul introduces verse 4 by the common Greek word *hina,* indicating that Titus teaches the older women *(presbutidas)* so that they may train the younger women—adults teaching adults within the context of a historical local church.

Young Women. The verb rendered "train" *(sōphronizōsin)* offers a cognate of the adjective translated "self-control" in verse 5 and implies the idea of restoring one to her senses. What were the needs of young women in the first-century church? Considering the pagan context of Crete, God demanded a demonstration of godly family life in the midst of a barbarian culture. These young women were to be husband-lovers, children-lovers, and homeworkers. After all, writes Paul, "Even one of their own prophets has said, 'Cretans are always liars, evil brutes, lazy gluttons' " (Titus 1:12). So the adult education program of that first church on Crete focuses on developing godly homes by developing godly women. Hiebert writes:

> If Christian wives ignored these demands and flouted the role their culture demanded of good wives, the Gospel would be maligned, criticized, and discredited by non-Christians. Christianity would be judged especially by the impact that it had on the women. It, therefore, was the duty of the woman to protect God's revelation from profanation by living discreet and wholesome lives. For Christians, no lifestyle is justified that hinders "the Word of God," the message of God's salvation in Christ.[7]

Young Men. Since Titus himself was a young man, his modeling behavior could encourage other young men to be self-controlled or sound-minded *(sōphronein).* Apparently young men have not changed a great deal; they still tend to be somewhat unrestrained and impetuous, so the Spirit of God focuses on a specific need for adult education for this age-group in the church.

Slaves. One of the six paragraphs (two verses) describes the behavior of slaves. Doubtless early church slaves hoped for some kind of first-century theology of liberation, but found a different message throughout the New Testament. The adult education program for slaves, therefore, seems designed to meet the needs of subjection, serious efforts to please their masters, avoiding contradiction or argument, honesty, and the development of attractive godly lives. In a paragraph from the commentary by Spence, we gain the following insight:

> Indeed, the repeated warnings to this unfortunate and oppressed class (see Eph. 6:5; Col. 3:22; 1 Tim. 6:1) tell us that among the difficulties which Christianity had to surmount in its early years was the hard task of persuading "the slave" that the divine Master who promised him a home . . . among the many mansions of His father, meant not that the existing relations of society should be then changed, or its complex framework disturbed.[8]

When reading Paul's instructions to Titus regarding these five specific age-groups, one could wish that contemporary congregations had as clear-cut and specific an understanding of the needs of adults in the 1990s.

Adult Education Aims At Definitive Objectives

Tucked away amid the practical admonitions of Titus 2, we find an interesting paragraph on the foundations for godly living which offers both negative and positive instruction with respect to objectives for the adult education program at Crete. Of course, good educational objectives should be brief, clear, specific, and worded in terms of student achievement (see chap. 11). One would hardly expect the peerless educator Paul to offer us anything less.

The Student Shall Reject Ungodliness and Worldly Passions (v. 11). The incarnation of the Savior epitomized God's grace which itself becomes a teacher *(paideuō).* The objective is much more affective than cognitive since the training ministry of God's grace aims to bring the believer to sufficient maturity so that, as a distinctive act of the will, the Christian adult denounces the past with its ungodliness and worldliness.

The Student Shall Live a Self-controlled, Upright, and Godly Life (v. 12). This positive side emphasizes lifestyle as a long-term, comprehensive objective for adult education in the church. Three qualities of life, stated as adverbs, look inward, outward, and upward to reflect three distinct dimensions of Christian living "in the new age."

The Student Shall Actively Wait for Christ's Return (v. 13). The common Pauline use of the present tense here suggests expectation should mark the attitude of the mature believer who waits for Jesus to come back. Imagine the significant eschatological content which would be necessary to transform pagan Cretans into godly adults who actively desire the return of the Lord.

The Student Shall Eagerly Do That Which Is Good (v. 14). Paul tells Titus not to be satisfied with nominal Christians, but literally to make zealots for good works (the word "eager" is the Gk. noun *zēlotēs*).

Does Paul offer Titus brief, specific, clear, and behaviorally oriented objectives? Without question. They link creed and conduct, learning and life in a magnificent paragraph built around the model of the Lord Jesus Himself. What could be more relevant for the contemporary church?

Adult Education Operates on Various Levels of Human Experiences

Once one has identified congregational needs and spelled out objectives, the time has come to identify content for the learning process. Obviously Paul thought he had done this in the chapter since he ends with the words, "These, then, are the things you should teach" (v. 15). The "things" represent sound doctrine (healthy teaching) as verse 1 clearly identifies. Unlike the objectives, however, we cannot find the curriculum detailed in one or two verses adjacent to each other; it appears throughout the passage. Obviously everything taught to the different age-groups must be considered "core curriculum" as well as the content necessary to the fulfillment of the objectives described in verses 11-14.

Perhaps we can identify three areas of behavior toward which Paul directed the content of adult education at Crete.

Heavenly Relations. Words like "reverent," "pure," "upright," "godly," and the phrase "a people that are His very own" all indicate that biblical content aimed to produce personal holiness in the lives of adult believers.

Human Relations. Not only must adult Christians at Crete have proper behavior in relation to God, but also in relation to each other—hence words like self-control, love, temperance, subjection, integrity, and honesty. In the case of all five adult groups in Crete, we find some reference to the way they should relate to other Christians in that congregation.

Home Relations. One cannot overemphasize family life education as a part of adult education in the evangelical congregation (see chap. 17). The obvious biblical emphasis surfaces right here in our brief chapter with direct instruction to younger women, an emphasis on children, husbands, the extended family with respect to older men and older women—all these focus the spotlight of curriculum design on family relationships as a central concern in the first-century church.

Adult Education Requires a Discipling-Nurturing Leadership Style

Contemporary church leadership has evolved to meet needs down through the years. To be sure, certain biblical imperatives remain crucial, finding their center point in the teacher of adults. Consider a few suggestions.

The Pastor Is the Key. The Greek text of our chapter contains eleven words for instruction and the English text, thirteen. The difference lies in the assumed rendering of "teach" at the beginning of verses 2 and 3. Adult education in the church consists of talking, teaching, training, exhorting, instructing, and rebuking. Both the first and last verses of the chapter form bookends to describe the ministry of Titus: "You must teach" . . . "These, then, are the things you should teach." One catches on immediately that unless Titus carries out his role, the work of adult education will not get done at Crete.

Discipleship Patterns Predominate. This popular term does not actually appear in the passage, but Paul surely emphasizes the behavior of discipling as a teaching technique. Notice verse 7: "In everything set them an example by doing what is good. In your teaching show integrity, seriousness, and soundness of speech that cannot be condemned." Life precedes lecture and modeling replaces meddling in the life of the effective adult teacher genuinely concerned about biblical leadership (see chap. 22).

Opposition Should Be Expected. Paul warns Titus about "those who oppose you" (v. 8). Of whom does he speak? Judaizers? Gnostics? Apostates? I like the way Hiebert leaves the landscape wide open:

> Paul concluded his personal remarks to Titus with another purpose clause. The expression "those who oppose you" is apparently left intentionally vague to leave room for all types of critics. (The original is singular: "The opponent, one of the opposition.") When the objections are examined, the antici-

> pated result is that the critic "may be ashamed," either feeling personally ashamed of his own conduct or made to look foolish because he is shown to have no case.[9]

Adult Education Is Primarily Developmental

The treatment of educational approaches spreads throughout the chapter and can only be sorted out eclectically. But it does describe methodological considerations at Crete without getting into specific techniques. For example:

The Effective Adult Educator Thinks in Terms of Need. The identification of older and younger men and women in addition to the specific slave class suggests a clear understanding of group emphasis with specificity on individual development. Today we might target singles, single parents, elderly, divorced, and a host of other contemporary need groups. In the classic text *Wider Horizons in Christian Adult Education,* Malcolm Knowles gave us a value choice with respect to adult Christian education:

> If it chooses to define its mission as that of inculcating prescribed doctrines, I believe it must accept the consequences of being attractive primarily to dependent personalities. If it chooses to define its mission as being that of helping adults become increasingly able to inquire into matters of faith and morals—to grapple actively with deep theological issues—I believe the consequence will be a good deal of somewhat uncomfortable ferment, but a sense of vitality that would bring into active involvement many presently passive members and many more of the unchurched.[10]

The Effective Adult Educator Concentrates on Modeling. We have returned to this so frequently in Titus 2 that further discussion here would be redundant. The very essence of teaching by example requires constant attention to one's own learning as well as one's own spiritual consistency:

> The Minister of Education can function as a teacher who demonstrates and utilizes strategies for instructional experiences suited to the characteristics and needs of the learners. In his own teaching, he can become a model for the teaching practices of those involved in the church educational program.[11]

The Effective Adult Educator Concentrates on the Development of Seriousness. Words such as "sober," "sensible," and "seriousness" characterize our chapter. The latter word *(semnos)* becomes the second characteristic of Christian thinking identified in Philippians 4:8. Perhaps too much adult education in the late twentieth-century church offers food and fellowship without really preparing people for the serious spiritual battles of life or throwing the burden of productivity back on the learner.

In *The Seasons of a Man's Life,* Levinson emphasizes "the individual life structure" which describes a man's conscious efforts to shape his own destiny as well as the unconscious unfolding of psychological and biological capabilities.[12] If Levinson is correct, every man passes through a sequence of stable and transitional periods, usually lasting four to eight years each. During these transitions he builds, modifies, and rebuilds the very structures of his life. The implications of biblical nurture in such a process stand unchallenged.

What happens when a church carries out its adult education program correctly? According to Titus 2, three results accrue:

1. People will not malign the Word of God (v. 5). In context blasphemy seems possible because of the unruly behavior of young wives. Presumably unsaved husbands (of which there were probably as many in the first century as there are today) might blame the Gospel for causing it. The world judges any religion not so much by the truth of its doctrines as by the effect those doctrines have on the lives of its people. Certainly the New Testament gives us cause to understand this axiom of evaluation in the broader sense, namely, that godliness of believers turns away criticism of the Gospel.

2. Families will be strong (v. 4). Again, the close link between adult education and family life education need not be contrived. Long ago Larry Richards claimed that

> everything in home life—parents' attitudes, conversations, examples—is educative. It is dangerous to consider Christian nurture simply as moments set aside for family prayer or Bible study. The whole pattern of home life should reflect essential harmony with the faith we profess. . . . We must relate individual church ministries to parental ministry. . . . We must administer our church programs to help rather than hinder Christian training in the home.[13]

3. The Gospel will be attractive (v. 10). If the behavior of young wives can turn away criticism of God's Word, so the godly behavior of slaves as the product of the church's adult education program can make the teaching about God our Savior attractive. Presumably, modern-day employees inherit the slave passages of Scripture. If so, this teaching touches virtually every adult in the church. Imagine the impact on your community if every adult behaved on the job in ways that make the teaching about the Savior attractive. Like Titus, we must all become directors of lifelong learning with special focus on adult education.

Jesus, Jethro, Nathan, and Titus led the adults they touched into new depth of understanding. They communicated to the heart by addressing person's self-perception and life experiences. They concentrated on clarifying the real needs, not the superficial ones, creating a hunger in the learner for change. Felt needs moved learners to immediate application, further reinforcing the learning experience. The modern teacher shows immense wisdom by following such examples.

Notes

1. διδασκαλος or the vocative διδασκαλε, teacher. See Walter Bauer, *A Greek-English Lexicon of the New Testament and Other Early Christian Literature,* ed. William F. Arndt and F. Wilbur Gingrich, 2nd ed. by F. Wilbur Gingrich and Frederick W. Danker (Chicago: Univ. of Chicago Pr., 1979), 191. Hereinafter *BGD.*

2. Rengstorf notes: "The Gospels make it clear point by point that the relation between Jesus and the disciples corresponds to that of Rabbinic pupils to their masters and that the crowd treated Him with the respect accorded to teachers" (K.H. Rengstorf in Gerhard Kittel, ed., *Theological Dictionary of the New Testament,* trans. and ed. Geoffrey W. Bromiley [Grand Rapids: Eerdmans, 1965], 2:153–54. Hereinafter *TDNT*).

3. μαθητης, the cognative of μανθανω, learn, literally through instruction (BGD, 490).

4. Rengstorf (TDNT, 4:409) sees this as the most important verse describing the new learning of Jesus in opposition to the scribes, who claim that they alone can rightly expound Scripture. "From Him one can learn that the will of God and its fulfillment are not a burden and torment but bring rest and joy to all those who subject themselves to this will in fellowship with Jesus"

5. Ακολουθεω, *come after, accompany, go along with,* figuratively, *follow someone as a disciple* (BGD, 31). Kittel (TDNT, 1:213–14) demonstrates that this word in the New Testament is limited to those who follow after Christ and that it implies a self-commitment in a sense which breaks all other ties.

6. Homer A. Kent, Jr., *The Pastoral Epistles* (Chicago: Moody, 1958), 228.

7. D. Edmond Hiebert, *Titus*, vol. 11 of *The Expositor's Bible Commentary*, ed. Frank E. Gaebelein (Grand Rapids: Zondervan, 1978), 437.
8. H.D.M. Spence, *The Epistles to Timothy and Titus*, vol. 8 of *Ellicott's Commentary on the Whole Bible*, ed. Charles John Ellicott (Grand Rapids: Zondervan, n.d.), 257.
9. Hiebert, *Titus*, 438.
10. Malcolm S. Knowles, "A Theory of Christian Adult Education Methodology," in *Wider Horizons in Christian Adult Education*, ed. Lawrence C. Little (Pittsburgh: Univ. of Pittsburgh Pr., 1962), 87.
11. Allen Graves, "The Minister of Education as Educator," *Search* (Winter 1978): 48.
12. Daniel J. Levinson, *The Season of a Man's Life* (New York: Ballantine, 1978), 40–68.
13. Lawrence O. Richards, "Developing a Family-Centered Educational Program," in *Adult Education in the Church*, ed. Roy B. Zuck and Gene A. Getz (Chicago: Moody, 1970), 372.

For Further Reading

Anderson, Leith. *Dying for Change.* Minneapolis: Bethany House, 1990.

Barna, George. *The Frog in the Kettle.* Ventura, Calif.: Regal, 1990.

_____. *User Friendly Churches.* Ventura, Calif.: Regal, 1992.

Baynes, Richard and Richard McKinley. 77 *Dynamic Ideas for Teaching the Bible to Adults.* Cincinnati: Standard Pub., 1977.

Brookfield, Stephen D. *Understanding and Facilitating Adult Learning.* San Francisco: Jossey-Bass, 1988.

Cross, K. Patricia. *Adults as Learners.* San Francisco: Jossey-Bass, 1981.

DeBoy, James J., Jr. *Getting Started in Adult Religious Education.* New York: Paulist Press, 1970.

Knowles, Malcolm and Associates. *Andragogy in Action.* San Francisco: Jossey-Bass, 1984.

Knowles, Malcolm. *The Modern Practice of Adult Education: From Pedagogy to Andragogy.* New York: Association Press, 1970.

Levinson, Daniel J. *The Seasons of a Man's Life.* New York: Ballantine, 1978.

McKenzie, Leon. *The Religious Education of Adults.* Birmingham, Ala.: Religious Education Press, 1982.

Peters, John M. Peter Jarvis and Associates. *Adult Education: Evolution and Achievements in a Developing Field of Study.* San Francisco: Jossey-Bass, 1991.

Peterson, Gilbert A., ed., *The Christian Education of Adults.* Chicago: Moody, 1985.

Stafford, Tim. *As Our Years Increase.* Grand Rapids: Zondervan, 1989.

Stokes, Kenneth, ed., *Faith Development in the Adult Life Cycle.* New York: William H. Sadlier, 1982.

Wilbert, Warren N. *Teaching Chrisitan Adults.* Grand Rapids: Baker, 1980.

Zuck, Roy B. and Gene A. Getz, eds. *Adult Education in the Church.* Chicago: Moody, 1970.

TWO

THEOLOGICAL FOUNDATIONS FOR ADULT EDUCATION

Edward L. Hayes

The renewal of interest in adult education among evangelicals is one of the significant developments of our times. Undoubtedly, the rise of adult participation in church educational endeavors is a reflection of awakening community action in adult education. Increasing demands for skills brought about by an accelerating technology coupled with new opportunities spawned by expanding leisure time have provided the impetus for adults to go back to the classroom. Riding the crest of a revival in community and world culture, increasing numbers of adults are delving into subjects ranging from Plato to painting, music appreciation to mass communications. Community colleges, universities, high schools, religious and cultural groups offer a wide range of learning opportunities for the new wave of adult learners.

Within the sphere of local church education, a stirring is taking place among adults which indicates a growing restlessness and dissatisfaction with traditional approaches to adult education. Lay renewal, evidenced in many segments of Christendom, is forcing a new look at education programs and the power structure of church life. Recent developments in community life have brought an uneasiness among adults. Questions being raised about change, crisis, and conflict demand theological answers. As we approach the twenty-first century, evangelical church education may be facing its greatest crisis. The good will and relatively high level of participation among adults in Christian education, enjoyed since the evangelical resurgence of the '40s and '50s, may not prevail unless we make continuous attempts to upgrade adult education and to meet the basic issues of our times with authentic theological concern.

A PERSPECTIVE

Only a relatively few decades ago church attendance stood at an all-time low. The meteoric rise of the Sunday School burned itself out amid the apathy of the early years of the twentieth century. Born in eighteenth-century England to meet a social crisis among children subjected to unfair labor practices, the Sunday School became a useful instrument for evangelism on the American frontier. Late in the nineteenth century some Sunday Schools boasted large adult classes. According to observers of the scene, these adult groups possessed qualities of a formidable movement. The revivalist tradition held front and center position in American church life at the peak of the Sunday School's success.

Theological winds blowing late in the nineteenth century bore portents of a shift in American Christianity. An overly optimistic view of humankind and a concept of the church devoid of a mission were two prevailing foundation stones of a theology which crumbled in the decades of the dawning utopia of the twentieth century.

The roots of the religious education movement may be traced to the dual developments of liberal theology and educational pragmatism. Amid the awakening conscience of church leaders toward education lay a predisposition to follow the developments of the new education rather than adopt critically a theological base for religious education. The early years of the religious education movement were marked by a more careful attention to progressive education than an attempt to reconstruct an important theology. While on the one hand, assuming the stance of a liberal theology, religious education took its methodological cue from John Dewey.

In the decade of the '60s we saw a shift back to theological concern among liberal religious educators. The works of Miller, Munro, Smart, Little, the Cullys, and others served as partial correctives to a religious education suffering from theological malnutrition. To some extent that has played out in the recent decades although the interest has shifted to therapeutic concerns, value formation, and spirituality issues. Very little direct theologizing has been done by religious educators.

Within evangelical circles, theological concern has been slower in coming. Midpoint in the decade of the '60s an editorial appeared in *Christianity Today* which analyzed the liabilities of American Christianity. Carl F.H. Henry's critique was equally applicable to liberalism and conservatism when he wrote:

> The liabilities of American Christianity include . . . an absence of authentic theological concern and interest in churches, colleges, and even seminaries that has impoverished the sources of great preaching. In too many American churches and schools, theology has been displaced by psychology and sociology.[1]

In the mid-'50s church attendance reached a new high, and adult education, which suffered the long night of Sunday School decline during the early part of the twentieth century, again showed signs of virility. The emphasis on the total church program brought a return to family and adult participation in local church life. However, the resurgency of interest was mainly program-centered; theological concerns remained peripheral. Evangelism and missions, signs of virile and legitimate activism, were foremost in the renewal of evangelical church life. But theological concern became mired in budgets, buildings, and bus routes. Evangelical activism dominated theological thought.

Then came the '60s with its succession of crises. Growing fomentation among nearly all segments of society brought traditional evangelical church programming into question. Marked as "the Establishment," many churches were called into question by adults asking serious questions but not receiving theological answers. As never before in recent history, the church needed a theology for adult education and participation in the life of the congregation—a theology which stands the tests, equips for crisis, and faces the tough questions of the times.

Within evangelical circles, a full-blown theology of Christian education did not emerge until the appearance of Larry Richards' *A Theology of Christian Education* (1975) and Robert Pazmiño's *Foundational Issues in Christian Education* (1988). Other evangelical works included isolated chapters on biblical foundations and the like but little serious theological reflection on adult education. Although Pazmiño's treatment of the subject is somewhat abbreviated, it articulates four theological distinctives which set evangelicals apart: biblical authority, necessity of conversion, emphasis upon the redemptive work of Christ, and personal piety.[2]

In recent years the Sunday School has gone into decline within evangelicalism. New adult learning ventures reflect the rise of newer social groupings and the rise and effectiveness of independent Bible classes, often home-centered.

At the same time, we are witnessing the emergence of the

"superchurch" concept with large, self-contained, independent ministries, in some cases apart from mainline denominational influence or control. This phenomenon appears to reflect a wedding of American pragmatism and activistic individualism. They appear to be entrepreneurial experiments in religious experientialism somewhat detached from theological roots, relationally rather than doctrinally oriented.

THE RELEVANCY SYNDROME

Critics level the charge of irrelevancy against churches. According to the dissidents, churches have lost touch with the times, and an almost cultic appeal goes out to abandon the ship and join the action wherever it is. This action, we are told, may have little or no relationship to current church life. The irrelevancy charge has enough truth in it to give considerable credence to the pro-God but anti-church sentiment. Many churches have lost touch with their communities, and Christians end up speaking to themselves rather than serving Christ in the world. Many congregations do suffer from a "four walls" mentality and have concluded that the significant action lies not in the marketplace but in the church building. Much preaching and teaching does suffer from opaqueness and obscurity. The blunt, plain speech of the prophet touching the nerve center of life is indeed missing. In the process of rejecting the defective ministries of some local churches, some often conclude that theology is suspect and must change.

How relevant is Christian theology for today? Does orthodox Christian thought still retain its grip on society? The answers to these questions are not simple, but we must constantly differentiate between truth held in creed or formulated in doctrinal statements and truth espoused in action. However, the disparity between these two often leads to the critics' barbs. As for theology losing its grip on our thoughts, it may safely be asserted that Christianity has always been a minority faith even though the influence of its ethic has gone beyond its personal acceptance.

The term relevance suffers from lack of specific definition at any given point in time. An adequate theology will not be a "theology of reaction" or of consensus molded by the contradictory assessments of a particular period of history. We must therefore ask whether or not man and institutions shall stand in judgment before divine truth. Thus it seems more accurate to refer to "adequacy" of theology rather than "relevancy." Does the truth fit? Does it say anything to the painful, contemporary problems adults face in our culture?

The problems facing our society are complex. Rapid social change, loss of community, alienation between generations and between ethnic groups, religious pluralism, fermenting revolution, and the rise of democratization mark our times. Following the death of Robert Kennedy many asked, "Is there a sick society in the United States?" Senator William Fulbright ventured that the "great society has become a sick society." Internal problems unparalleled in our history called for solutions and remedies. The question of the sickness of any society calls for a theological answer. We now witness in the former Eastern European bloc nations a recovery of spiritual roots and a rising reaction to philosophical nihilism and religious atheism.

When rapid social change takes place, it becomes easy to ask if theology must change. Escalation of technology, violent social upheavals, and an advancing culture have led to "fadism" in theological circles. "We are on the way in a time of great concern with crucial problems," claims Gunther Bornkamm, New Testament scholar at Heidelberg. "But we do not have final answers, and I am unsure what is at the end of this theological road."[3] On the contemporary scene, theologians often outlive the influences of their own theologies. The realm of systematic theology suffers from confusion because it yet lacks a new binding concept. Barth's star has been sinking, and now Bultmann's follows it down. The death-of-God issue is "dead," its short-lived life spanning less than a decade. In the face of theological uncertainty, God calls us to the certitude of an adequate theology forged squarely from the Bible and relevant to daily life.

Evangelicals feel the tension between a theology that is basically countercultural or one that accommodates the culture. Preferring to emphasize what H. Richard Niebuhr articulated in his work, *Christ and Culture* (1956), evangelicals opt for "Christ the transformer of culture" model. In this way of thinking, culture reflects the fallen state. In Christ the redemption and renewal of both culture and the individual are viewed as possible.[4]

An adequate theology must stand the tests of rapid social change; it must equip adults for the crises of life, and it must face the tough questions of our human destiny. An openness in confronting modern problems will not dilute the Word of God. A certain liberating quality arises when we give the Word of God free course. Its timeless essence speaks to all generations and to basic problems. In short, it fits life.

THEOLOGICAL FOUNDATIONS

Several basic revelational postulates serve as underpinnings of a theory of adult education. Understandably, these are not unique to adult education, but a restatement of basic theological assumptions may provide a focus for continued study and action. It should be noted that this discussion addresses theological foundations for adult education; in *no* way should this be construed as a full-orbed theology of adult education—if indeed one is possible. Nor is the discussion designed as a theology for adult laypeople. Rather, certain imperatives emerge which may provide a normative statement useful in forging out new frontiers in adult learning.

The Centrality of the Bible in Adult Education

One does not have to look far to document the slippage of the Bible from the center of Christian educational concern. At best it has been relegated to the "resource" category in much of the curricula currently in use in mainline denominations, or to the role of a "special book" in the ongoing progress of revelation.

Without the authority of the Scriptures (*sola Scriptura* to the Protestant Reformers), Protestantism may soon become merely an echo of a decadent society. Conservative evangelical scholars assert that Christians do not pursue truth; rather, they possess it. The centrality of the Bible forms a major plank in the platform of evangelical education. The Scriptures are profitable "for teaching the faith and correcting error, for resetting the direction of a man's life and training him in good living" (2 Tim. 3:16, PH). All of this in order that the people of God may be perfectly fit and thoroughly equipped for every good work. Christian adult education conceived in this tradition is not speculative, tentative, or exploratory; it is rooted in the authority of God's Word. The church must hold the truth firmly to stabilize itself and hold it aloft so that all may see it.[5]

The Bible is the primary source of our theological and educational commitments in Scripture. Evangelicals must test all opinions on faith and practice by their adherence to the inspired writings. To what source can we go to find renewal of thought and action—"to what source but the Holy Scriptures?" asks Lois LeBar.[6]

Such a position of traditional conservatism has naturally given rise to objections. Does this not lead to a narrow, bigoted authoritarianism? Does this not lead to indoctrination of the highest order? Christian adult learning based on authoritative Scriptures, however, need not be a caricature of learning, a subtle brainwashing, a matter of running an intelligible cookie cutter which stamps out the same stereotype on plastic minds. Evangelicals believe they can commit to revelational dogma without closing the mind. Theodore Brameld, a leading educational philosopher, espouses a position of "defensible partiality" to help meet the dilemma created by the tension between dogma and relativism.

> What we learn is defensible simply insofar as the ends we support and the means we utilize are able to stand up against exposure to open, unrestricted criticism and comparison. What we learn is partial insofar as these ends and means still remain definite and positive to their majority advocates after the defense occurs.[7]

Brameld defends education based upon an authoritative stance. He rejects indoctrination which allows for no "open, unrestricted criticism and comparison." In this light he is not far from the Christian view of authority. While he rejects the existence of absolute truth, a position central to Christian thought, he does espouse a defensible position at the operational level of education. Christian adult education, while holding to a position of authoritative truth, rejects an authoritarian method. Looking at the issue in brief, it is useful to work out the dilemma created by the tension between dogma and relativism by holding to authoritative truth and rejecting unwarranted dogmatism.

Christian adult education dedicates itself to reflective commitment. Adults need not be subjected to one-way indoctrination. Rather, they should be encouraged to explore, to discover for themselves, and to subject their convictions to critical, scrupulous comparison with alternative doctrines. Truth is welcomed from any quarter, but the Scriptures stand normative. Profoundly convinced that all truth leads back to God, the Christian educator gratefully endorses the emphasis of John Calvin:

> If we believe that the spirit of God is the only foundation of truth, we shall neither reject nor despise the truth where ever it shall appear. . . . They are superstitious who dare not

borrow anything from profane writers. All truth is from God, and consequently, if wicked men have said anything that is true and just, we ought not to reject it; for it has come from God.[8]

Adult education can become a process through which the Holy Spirit guides learners to a free acceptance of truth—of biblical truth that liberates. A theology derived from Scripture is consistent with truth about God's world and highly adequate to the issues people face today.

A Christological Imperative

Truth is inherent in Jesus Christ because He provides the supreme revelation of God. He came "full of grace and truth" (John 1:14). Propositional truths in the Scriptures facilitate personal encounter and fellowship with Jesus Christ. Thus, the function of Scripture is instrumental—the means of bringing people face-to-face with Christ. God commands all people to repent and turn to Him from their sinful ways through faith in Jesus Christ.

Bible study for adults involves both an understanding of the truth and an application of it. Education that is Christian must be totally absorbed with Jesus Christ, as revealed in the Scriptures, and with leading us to spiritual maturity through Him. "Him we proclaim, warning everyone and teaching everyone in all wisdom, that we may present everyone mature in Christ" (Col. 1:28, NRSV).

The Human Factor

A Christian view of humanity is essential if we would discover how the revelation of Jesus Christ through the Scriptures impinges upon the affairs of humankind. The Scriptures function as an undistorted mirror by which we may see our own distortion. Christian theology posits humans as created in the image of God, possessing a responsible and responsive will, and capable of spiritual fellowship with the Creator. In the Genesis passage dealing with man's first failure, we possess the account of the original Fall—the entrance of sin into the world. This cataclysmic event marred the human scene, separating sinful humankind from the holy God. The reality of our sin does not lack empirical verification. But behavioral analysis alone fails to comprehend the depth of the biblical understanding of our sinfulness. The Apostle Paul, describing the human backdrop of the history of redemption, wrote, "You were spiritually dead through your sins and failures, all the time that you followed this world's ideas of living, and obeyed the evil ruler of the spiritual realm—who is indeed fully operative today in those who disobey God" (Eph. 2:1-2, PH). Humankind caught in the web of pride, spiritual rebellion, and separation from God can, nevertheless, respond by faith to divine love. Total depravity describes our incapacity to achieve wholeness and holiness apart from divine intervention. Grace is God's answer to our depravity.

Through Christ's death on the cross He provided a way whereby we could be reconciled to Himself. The Holy Spirit, in response to our faith in God's act of grace and mercy, makes us new creations in Jesus Christ. God commands all people everywhere to repent, turn from their wicked ways, and be converted.

The implications of a proper understanding of humanity to Christian adult education are many:

1. It means that education is concerned with relationships—the relationship between people and Jesus Christ and the relationship of people to their neighbors.
2. It means, furthermore, that Christian educators will be concerned with leading adult men and women to Christ for salvation from sin.
3. It also suggests that educators will seek to understand the spiritual nature of people, the meaning of the image of God in humans, and the learning capacities which God has given us.
4. In addition, it implies that Christian education will build on the human responses of belief and lead us to full maturity in Christ. Christian adult education will not confuse "child-like" faith with "easy-believism," but will rather seek to establish adults in the faith, grounded, settled, and not moved from the hope of the Gospel (Eph. 4:15; Col. 1:23; 1 Peter 5:10).
5. Above all, the Christian doctrine of humankind means that only in Jesus Christ can we realize our full potential. As the historic confession puts it, our "chief end is to glorify God and to enjoy Him forever."

The Corporate Mission and Ministry of the Church

One of the first tasks of theology is to expose confusion and uncertainty of the church concerning itself. This task requires that the church can adequately fulfill its mission. Every evangelical ought to be occupied with the renewal of church ministry. Of particular importance is a reaffirmation of the nature of the ministry itself and its relationship to lay mobilization.

By definition, the church of Jesus Christ consists of a called-out body of disciples devoted to fulfilling a ministry of the Word in the world. Transcending geographic locale, race, gender, and span of generations, the church is a corporate entity whose Head is the Lord Jesus Christ. Where the Spirit of God has worked in human lives, local expressions of the "body of Christ" have come into existence. Thus, the church may be referred to as both universal and visible, both translocal and local. The imagery depicting the church may be varied, but the ideal of a corporate unity is real. This radically new humanity touched by God's sovereign grace creates a group that has little in common but Christ. Our essential unity is bound up in the assertion of the Apostle Paul: "One Lord, one faith. . . . " (Eph. 4:5)

What the church of Jesus Christ is, determines what it does. The church carries out its role as a worshiping, edifying community of believers, proclaiming the Gospel of redemption, seeking to observe all things Jesus has commanded. A particular church seeking to embody the essential quality of the nature and mission of the larger corporate body should not be content to become ingrown and encased with useless custom and tradition. Rather, a church modeled after biblical guidelines will become a ministering body serving actively and meaningfully in a crisis-ridden world and bearing witness to the resurrected Christ. The only corrective to a lifeless institutionalized church is active obedience to the command of Christ to disciple all nations (Matt. 28:19-20).

Christian adult education in this context is designed to help people mature within the sphere of the church. Church education, rightly conceived and properly instituted, is education for Christian discipleship. The teaching focus of a church should be designed to assist every believer in becoming all that Jesus Christ intended for His church. Christian men and women who live and share in the context of a true community of faith seek to mutually edify one another and share their salvation in the world through evangelism, justice, works of mercy, and kindness to others.

Central to Christian ecclesiology is an adequate *understanding of the ministry.* More than a nurturing, edifying body, the church becomes a ministering body following Jesus Christ, whose example provides the norm for all Christian service. In the New Testament the ideal of "servantship" is ever present. Two words, *diakonos* and *doulos,* provide the focal point for a doctrine of ministry. Both are used by Jesus Christ. "Whosoever will be great among you, let him be your minister *[diakonos];* and whosoever will be chief among you, let him be your servant *[doulos]*" (Matt. 20:26-27, KJV).

The John 13 account of Christ washing the disciples' feet teaches us not to lust after power and position but after ministry. The New Testament uses *diakonos* both in a general way to indicate the nature of the service to be rendered by every Christian and in a technical way referring to an "order" of ministry—that of the deacons. The idea of lowly service (as implied in the term *doulos* as well) is fundamental in all Christian ministry. Philippians 2:7 speaks of Jesus as a slave or bondservant, wherein He set the pattern for us all.

A special order of servants seems to be implied in Acts 6. Neglected widows prompted the selection of special "ministers," in the proper use of the term, whose shared function with that of the apostles complemented the ministry of the Word. In no way is a hierarchy inferred by the differentiation of function. The ministry was the ministry of the whole church. Rather than being mere supporters of the ministry, these "deacons" became active ministry participants in the life of the church.

One of the partially misoriented understandings of the church is the *false division between clergy and laity.* Since the days of the sixteenth-century Reformation, theologians have addressed themselves to the function and status of the ministry, the ordained clergy. This subsidiary treatment, notes Kraemer, is an inexcusable lack.[9] As a result, the distinct role of the whole people of God has been eclipsed by a preoccupation with the "ministry" as a special class of individuals. No less an authority than Hans Küng, a spokesman for a new breed of post-Vatican II Catholic theologians, observes that a distinction between clergy and laity was unknown until the third century. In his monumental and important work, *The Church,* Küng set forth a position usually associated with Reformed theology, "The word *[laos]* in the New Testament, as also in the Old Testament, indicates no distinction within the community as between priests ('clerics') and people ('laity'). It indicates rather the fellowship of all in a single community."[10]

In the New Testament the church was never understood as being led by the clergy, with the laity as second-class members. The layperson in the church is only a layperson in the sense that he or she has neither the formal ordination to minister as an undershepherd of a congregation nor the special gift and training to fulfill that function. The only authentic difference lies in function and divine gift, providing for divisions of labor in the church. But this makes them no more ministers in terms of quality or kind than the so-called laypersons. The really essential element about the New Testament view of the ministry, according to Leon Morris, is the one basic ministry of Christ Himself. Our ministry is but a continuation of His.[11]

Another important dimension to a theology of the church which has direct bearing on adult education is the biblical teaching on *spiritual gifts.* The New Testament does not recognize any ministry carried out apart from God-given abilities. In 1 Corinthians 12:7 the manifestation of the Spirit is given to every believer. The Holy Spirit divides these grace gifts "to each one individually just as the Spirit chooses" (1 Cor. 12:11, NRSV). Some indication of the full scope of participation in church ministries appears in 1 Corinthians 14:26. And the Apostle Peter articulated similar teaching when he wrote, "As each one has received a gift, minister it to one another, as good stewards of the manifold grace of God" (1 Peter 4:10, NKJV).

The concept of gifts seems to refer to function rather than office, although special gifts were singled out. But the tremendous variety of exercised gifts indicates no predictable human pattern. Granted, God is a God of order, and the exhortation was given to do all things decently and in order, but the unique pattern of church ministry was the divine exercise of spiritual gifts "for the work of ministry" (Eph. 4:12, NKJV).

Adult education in the final decades of the twentieth century reflects this renewed interest in the *charismata,* exercise of gifts. A final facet of inquiry into a Christian ecclesiology with relevance to adult involvement is evidenced by the important New Testament teaching regarding the priesthood of all believers. We recall Martin Luther's famous dictum that all Christians are truly priests.[12]

The priesthood of believers means direct access to God (Rom. 5:2; Eph. 3:12; Heb. 10:22), the right and privilege to offer spiritual sacrifices (Rom. 12:1; Phil. 2:17; 4:18; 1 Peter 2:5), and the responsibility of witness in the world (1 Peter 2:9; 3:15). It is God who creates this priesthood.

Significant pronouncements which have come from the Second Vatican Council indicate a crack in the creedal position of conservative Catholicism: "the apostolate of the spoken word, which in certain situations is the required one, enable lay people to announce Christ, to explain his teaching, to spread it in a measure fitted to each one's ability and circumstance, and to profess it faithfully."[13] Küng carries this pronouncement further and denies the whole priestly order in the Roman Catholic Church.

The idea of the *priesthood of all believers* is foundational to a renewed church. Yet it must be more than a teaching to commend Protestantism. It must be a transforming, vital principle. More than a flag to march under, it must become a biblical idea that transforms.

Perhaps there is need for a new "article of faith" which asserts the role of laypersons in specific terms. Such a statement should acknowledge the interdependence and interexistence of all members of the body of Christ. A corrective to sterile inaction by congregations who are little more than passive audiences is the implementation of a theology of church which accounts for the total discipleship of the people of God. Only then will the church become what Eduard Schweizer describes as "a group to which Jesus' words and deeds have struck home."[14]

One disturbing factor remains. Laypersons do not generally conceive of themselves as ministers of the Gospel and as servants of Christ. Primarily they think of themselves as helpers of the pastors. A reversal of this general attitude is extremely important for two basic reasons.

First, the ground swell of reaction within congregations appears to be rooted in a dissatisfaction with this passive role. At least the guilt level is rising among increasing numbers. One layman expressed it bluntly when he said that "there must be more to my Christianity than going down to the church and laying linoleum in the church kitchen." The simple fact that laypersons are discovering significant ministries elsewhere than through organized churches indicates that church leaders may lack creative skills in mobilizing congregations for meaningful service. It may also mean that church leaders lack a theological understanding of the place and exercise of spiritual gifts by all church members.

Another reason laypersons need to see themselves as ministers, not merely pastoral helpers, is that the missionary and witnessing enterprise demands it. Years ago John R. Mott, writing of his commitment to discipleship, saw laywitness as an expression of the church and its calling and function in the world, "The most vital and fruitful periods in the history of the Christian Church have been those in which laymen have most vividly realized and most earnestly sought to discharge their responsibility to propagate the Christian faith."[15]

How can Christianity make its greatest impact on the world at the turn of the century? Only through total involvement by the people of God, the entire body of Christ—an involvement that is more than emotionalism prompted by guilt; an involvement rooted in Christian discipleship sharpened by knowledge of the Scriptures and Christian theology; an involvement that arises from more than a reaction to clericalism; an involvement that joins pastors and congregations into a formidable force for propagating the Gospel of Jesus Christ and acting justly in the world.

THE HOLY SPIRIT AND CHRISTIAN ADULT EDUCATION

Christian education is basically different from general education, writes Rachel Henderlite.[16] Discovering the difference can transform adult education from much of its current drabness and ineffectiveness to a revitalized education. In order that we might be able to make proper distinctions, certain aspects of the Holy Spirit are to be seen in relationship to the educative process.

As the divine Teacher in Christian education, the Holy Spirit instructs (John 14:26), reminds (John 14:26), guides (John 16:13), declares (John 16:13-15), and reveals (1 Cor. 2:9-10). The Holy Spirit is the Agent who illumines the mind and heart of humankind, enabling us to apprehend and appropriate the revealed truth of God.[17] The Holy Spirit is also the Energizer of the church. We live and learn in the age of the Spirit.

Yet the ministry of the Holy Spirit as Educator is linked closely to the Scriptures. Only by the Holy Spirit can eternal truth be correctly understood, interpreted, and personalized. He works on the written Word to internalize it in students' lives.

Such a work of the Spirit seems too restrictive to Nels Ferré. While he quite correctly views God as Educator in the broad sense of the term, he fails to link the work of the Spirit to Scripture. To Ferré the educative task of the Spirit looks not in shedding light on the inscripturated truth, but in creating new truth for a new age.[18] However, Ferré's theology contains no objective norms. Those who jettison the concept of a totally trustworthy and authoritative Scripture, revealed by the Holy Spirit, must exchange the rational notion of faith as walking in the light of God for what J.I. Packer calls "the irrational existential idea of faith as a leap in the dark."[19]

Discovering the relationship between the inner work of the

Spirit and the educative process is one of the great tasks of the Christian educator. A basic principle of evangelical Christian education is that the inner change and modification of behavior in the learner depends on the Spirit of God working through the Word of God. Jahsmann describes the relationship between the Holy Spirit and the learning process: "The understanding of this Word requires something more than verbal, intellectual definitions, explanations, and instructions. Though these are needed too, spiritual meanings of the Word must be *experienced* through the experience of the *Spirit* of the Word."[20]

The impingement of God's Word on human experience is carried out by the Spirit. Educational methods which call for discovery, insight, and thinking are best used in creating the proper climate for the Spirit to do His work. The Christian adult teacher who seeks to lead adults into the riches of God's truth will acknowledge the fact that the Holy Spirit is the Teacher of divine truth and, at best, the human teacher merely an associate. However, because human teachers assist the Holy Spirit in the education process, they "should seek to be under the full employment of the Spirit as clean and capable instruments. Effective Christian teaching takes place to the extent that teachers allow the Holy Spirit to speak through them and use them."[21]

THEOLOGY AND THE INNOVATIVE PROCESS

How can the church of Jesus Christ truly be the church? This question still calls for an answer, and each generation of believers will have to ask it again and again. It may appear rather odd that a discussion of theological foundations should take a turn toward innovation and reformation. Let it be clearly understood, however, that this does not imply tampering with God's revealed truth. The fixed norms of God's self-disclosure through the Bible still provide the compass for charting a course of change in our times. But change is essential for the life of the church. Truth never changes; methods do.

The rationale for change in the church is rooted to the nature of the Holy Spirit, the Spirit of liberty. It is inconceivable that there should be a fixed methodology in adult ministries of church education. In reality, the Bible gives us no fixed methodology, no once-for-all technique. The genius of the Christian advance in the world has been linked to freedom in the Spirit to innovate in communicating the Gospel and in creating educational settings for Christian nurture. Without irresponsible disorder in church programming, churches can nevertheless bring about change in the educative process. Without abandoning Christian truth to a "process theology," churches can exercise a certain methodological elasticity. Important issues confront adults in our generation, and these call for theological answers learned and discovered in church settings that maximize the latent power of Christians who live and learn in the Spirit.

Current attention given to "process theology" warrants a brief discussion. This theological movement emerged from the thought and writings of Alfred North Whitehead and Charles Hartshorne. Truth, by their definition, is not viewed as fixed or absolute. Holding that all things are in flux and accepting ancient Eastern thought, mainly Buddhist, that there are no static substances, process theology follows the Hegelian view of the dynamic nature of reality in history. Truth is a moving target, to be sought but never found. Truth is adaptive; not absolute. It bends easily to ecological and sociopolitical concerns. According to this view, God continues to speak to us, but such revelation is not limited to the Holy Scriptures. Intuition, praxis (truth at work), and other experientially defined ideas about God and His creation are elevated to prominence. As for sound hermeneutics or interpretation of the Bible, the basis of truth is found in ongoing history rather than the revealed Scriptures.[22]

Contemporary evangelical theology has amply answered the issues raised by process theology and other faddish theologies which deny the authority of Scripture. The work of Carl F.H. Henry, Francis Schaeffer, J.I. Packer, Gordon Lewis, Bruce Demarest, and others have provided contemporary theological substance to the current debate on the nature of God, truth, and reality. Reality is not in the process of becoming. It is fixed in the person of Jesus Christ and in the reliability of Scripture. This reality is binding as fully authoritative. Truth liberates.

Adult learning at the turn of the century needs to fix its bearing on eternal, unchanging truth. Methods will change. Strategies will come and go. But the timeless truth that God was in Jesus Christ reconciling the world to Himself provides an anchor in a restless era. Furthermore, the equally unchanging truth that every adult needs to be transformed by the power of God provides a working paradigm in a world that has bankrupted itself in its search for meaning.

CONCLUSION

The limitations of such a brief treatment seem obvious. I made no attempt to treat all the major doctrines. Some may question the basis for the selection of only a few themes—the Scriptures, Christ, humankind, the church, and the Holy Spirit. There was no particular reason for neglecting other areas except for the limitations of the chapter. If Christian educators and theologians feel provoked to explore the full sweep of Christian theology in the educational context, my purpose will, in part, have been fulfilled.

Albert Einstein once said that we live in an age of perfected means but confused ends. This may be true in the world of technology and of science. It may also be true in theological circles. Carl F.H. Henry has astutely observed that contemporary Christianity stands face-to-face with a major transition time in theology. This, he asserts, "affords evangelicals a providential moment for earnest engagement."[23] We are committed to bringing people to salvation, wholeness, and maturity in Jesus Christ, and to working justice in the world; but we may not be using the best means to accomplish these goals. At this point we all need the humility to admit that evangelical church education needs theological direction and freedom to explore ways to carry on creative adult education.

Notes

1. Carl F.H. Henry, "Perspective on American Christianity," *Christianity Today,* 23 April 1965, 29.
2. Robert W. Pazmiño, *Foundational Issues in Christian Education* (Grand Rapids: Baker, 1988), 49–59.
3. Quoted in Carl F.H. Henry, *Frontiers in Modern Theology* (Chicago: Moody, 1966), 83.
4. See David J. Hesselgrave, *Communicating Christ Cross-culturally* (Grand Rapids: Zondervan, 1979), 79–80. For a full discussion of prevailing theologies of culture and mission, see Arthur F. Glasser and Donald A. McGavran, eds., *Contemporary Theologies of Mission* (Grand Rapids: Baker, 1983). McGavran's chapter on "Contemporary Evangelical Theology of Mission" (chap. 6) is particularly helpful in developing an adult educational theology.
5. John Stott, *Christ the Controversialist* (Downers Grove, Ill.: InterVarsity, 1970), 26.
6. Lois E. LeBar, *Education That Is Christian* (Westwood, N.J.: Revell, 1958), 50.

7. Theodore Brameld, *Ends and Means in Education: A Midcentury Appraisal* (New York: Harper, 1952), 92–93.
8. John Calvin, *Commentaries on the Epistles to Timothy, Titus, and Philemon* (Grand Rapids: Eerdmans, 1959), 300–01. Calvin also discusses the nature of general truth in his *Institutes,* Book II, chap. 2, para. 15.
9. Hendrik Kraemer, *A Theology of the Laity* (Philadelphia: Westminster, 1958), 9.
10. Hans Küng, *The Church* (New York: Sheed & Ward, 1968), 125–26.
11. Leon Morris, *Ministers of God* (London: InterVarsity, 1964), 25.
12. Ewald M. Plass, comp., *What Luther Says* (St. Louis: Concordia, 1959), 3:1139.
13. *Teachings of the Second Vatican Council, Complete Texts of the Constitutions, Decrees, and Declarations* (Westminster, Md.: Newman, 1966), 328–29.
14. See Eduard Schweizer, *Church Order in the New Testament* (London: SCM, 1961) for a careful treatment of the entire subject of ministry in the New Testament.
15. John R. Mott, *Liberating the Lay Forces of Christianity* (New York: Macmillan, 1932), 1.
16. Rachel Henderlite, *The Holy Spirit in Christian Education* (Philadelphia: Westminster, 1964), 15.
17. Roy B. Zuck, *The Holy Spirit in Your Teaching* (Wheaton, Ill.: Victor Books, 1984), 35–46.
18. Nels F.S. Ferré, *A Theology for Christian Education* (Philadelphia: Westminster, 1967), 107.
19. James I. Packer, "The Necessity of the Revealed Word," in *The Bible: The Living Word of Revelation,* ed. Merrill C. Tenney (Grand Rapids: Zondervan, 1968), 49. See also J.I. Packer, *Keep in Step with the Spirit* (Old Tappan, N.J.: Revell, 1984).
20. Allan Hart Jahsmann, *Power Beyond Words* (St. Louis: Concordia, 1969), 113.
21. Zuck, *The Holy Spirit,* 76.
22. See John B. Cobb and D.R. Griffin, *Process Theology: An Introductory Exposition* (Philadelphia: Westminster, 1976); Alfred N. Whitehead, *Religion in the Making* (New York: Macmillan, 1926); and Charles Hartshorne, *The Divine Relativity: A Social Conception of God* (New Haven, Conn.: Yale University Press, 1948).
23. Henry, *Modern Theology, 142.*

For Further Reading

Carnell, E.J. *The Case for Biblical Christianity.* Grand Rapids: Eerdmans, 1969.

Clark, Gordon H. *A Christian Philosophy of Education.* Grand Rapids: Eerdmans, 1946.

Ferguson, Sinclair, and David Wright, eds. *New Dictionary of Theology.* Downers Grove, Ill.: InterVarsity, 1988.

Ferm, Deane. *Contemporary American Theologies: A Critical Survey.* New York: Seabury, 1981.

Ferré, Nels F.S. *A Theology for Christian Education.* Philadelphia: Westminster, 1967.

Fuller, Edmund, ed. *The Christian Idea of Education.* New Haven: Yale University Press, 1957.

Gaebelein, Frank. *Christian Education in a Democracy.* New York: Oxford University Press, 1951.

Henry, Carl F.H. *The Christian Mindset in a Secular Society.* Portland, Ore.: Multnomah, 1984.

———. *God, Revelation and Authority.* Waco, Texas: Word, 1976.

LeBar, Lois E. *Education That Is Christian.* Westwood, N.J.: Revell, 1958.

Lewis, Gordon and Bruce Demarest. *Integrative Theology.* 2 vols. Grand Rapids: Zondervan/Academie, 1987.

Little, Lawrence. *Foundations for a Philosophy of Christian Education.* Nashville: Abingdon, 1962.

Little, Sara. *The Role of the Bible in Contemporary Christian Education.* Richmond, Va.: John Knox, 1961.

Lynn, Robert W. *Protestant Strategies in Education.* New York: Association Press, 1964.

Packer, J.I. *Knowing God.* Downers Grove, Ill.: InterVarsity, 1973.

———. *A Quest for Godliness.* Wheaton, Ill.: Crossway, 1990.

Peterson, Gilbert A., ed. *The Christian Education of Adults.* Chicago: Moody, 1984.

Ramm, Bernard. *The Pattern of Religious Authority.* Grand Rapids: Eerdmans, 1959.

———. *After Fundamentalism: The Future of Evangelical Theology.* San Francisco: Harper and Row, 1983.

Richards, Larry. *A Theology of Christian Education.* Grand Rapids: Zondervan, 1975.

———. *Church Leadership.* Grand Rapids: Zondervan, 1988.

Schaeffer, Francis. *The God Who Is There.* Downers Grove, Ill.: InterVarsity, 1968.

Schreyer, George M. *Christian Education in Theological Focus.* Philadelphia: Christian Education Press, 1962.

Wilhoit, James. *Christian Education and the Search for Meaning.* Grand Rapids: Baker, 1986.

Woodbridge, J.D., et al. *The Gospel in America: Themes in the Story of America's Evangelicals.* Grand Rapids: Zondervan, 1979.

Wyckoff, D. Campbell. *The Gospel and Christian Education.* Philadelphia: Westminster, 1959.

Zuck, Roy B. *The Holy Spirit in Your Teaching.* rev. ed. Wheaton Ill.: Victor Books, 1984.

THREE
CHRISTIAN ADULTS AND SPIRITUAL FORMATION

James C. Wilhoit

The small group drew to a close. Some members linger to chat and finally the last ones leave, pausing at the door for a parting hug and a good-bye. As they leave they remember the sharing of the evening: the marital tension openly talked about, the wayward son lifted up in prayer, the plodding recovery of a workaholic husband, and that video—it spoke directly to where they live! As the last people leave, the host couple clasp their hands in front of the open door and smile in obvious satisfaction of being part of such a blessing—a caring small group. As they straighten up the furniture, they chat about the events of the evening and the people in their group whom they have come to love. In all their happy reflections they never consider asking, "But was it spiritual formation?" That question must be asked today about any adult educational program. We minister at a time when it is possible to attract people to need-oriented church programs which do not contribute to their spiritual formation.

FORMATION IN AN ALIEN CULTURE

The church finds itself today as nothing less than an outpost in an alien society. The church is called to form a people whose values differ from those of this alien society and yet she must remain in conversation with those in the larger society. A common approach to this twofold calling adopts a consumer-oriented strategy of providing attractive need-oriented programs. However, can these programs simultaneously carryout the twofold mandate of evangelism and nurture? That is an exceedingly difficult challenge, and we fear that our recent ministry responses to the larger consumer culture has led to an unprecedented rise in adult Christian miseducation.

Spiritual formation names that broad function of the church, begun at our redemption, which facilitates our transformation through the formation of a Christian mind, freeing ourselves from the allurements of the world's system and by opening ourselves to God's transforming grace. When the Christian life is set in contrast to this age's addiction to power, pleasure, and unbridled personal freedom, we can see why Hauerwas and Willimon declare that our spiritual formation requires "conversion, detoxification, and transformation."[2]

Through the centuries churches have fulfilled this calling and many are doing so today, but a consumer orientation and an overzealous following of the principles of andragogy may well undo the effectiveness of our adult education. Stephen Brookfield reminds teachers of adults of their proper prophetic role when he warns, "As educators . . . we cannot always accept adults' definition of needs as the operational criteria for our development of curriculum, design of programs, or evaluations of success."[3] Adult educators do their work on a ridge with steep cliffs on either side. On the one side is the allurement of certain traditional programs and styles which can result in cultural irrelevancy. On the other side dwells the consumer need-oriented approach which leads to accommodation of the Gospel through mere need-meeting and miseducation. Effective Christian education occurs on the ridge between these two extremes where the actual life experience of the learners confronts the Gospel. The easy answer of either chasm results in either irrelevancy on the one side or cultural accommodation on the other.

Spiritual formation is the delightful privilege of the church. No part of the church owns it; it rather comes as people open themselves to God's work through the symphony-like work of the church. The formation process includes establishing Christians in the church, nurturing the practices of piety, and teaching that fosters a renewed mind.

Adult education plays a role in all these areas. Caring classes can help to establish new Christians in the life of the church; but the primary focus of our teaching emphasizes: establishing habits of holiness and piety and fostering the development of a renewed mind. In seeking to do this we need to be aware of two characteristics of adults who are likely to be in our program. The first concern is the adult's ability to merely conform to the religious expectations of those in the church without experiencing deep transformation. The second is the presence of rampant individualism in our society.

TWO MARKS OF ADULT SPIRITUALITY

Spiritual Deformation

One key feature of adult spiritual life concerns the ability of adults to deceive themselves and others regarding their level of spirituality. The Christian educator concerned with spiritual formation must always be aware that adults are able to easily mimic desired religious behavior and vocabulary. Consequently, spiritual formation requires sensitively pushing people beyond "pat" answers and constantly reminding them that true spirituality and maturity result from a heart aflame in a Scripture-directed relationship with Jesus Christ.

At one level this concerns the tension between the immature and mature religion that Gordon Allport described forty years ago. He wrote, "Immature religion, whether in adult or child, is largely concerned with magical thinking, self-justification, and creature comfort. Thus it betrays its sustaining motives still to be the drives and desires of the body. By contrast, mature religion is less of a servant, and more of a master, in the economy of life."[4] A key attribute of mature religion for Allport was the control it exercised over the individual. In part this meant that it had ceased to be simply an extrinsic faith concerned with show, doing the right things, and with keeping rituals for personal benefit. Extrinsic religion can show up in all denominations and is often practiced unknowingly by persons who have deceived themselves into believing that their largely external religion flows from a true love for God. It must be an intrinsic faith which comes from a well-integrated set of values personally owned and held together by devotion to God. The mature faith "behaves no longer like an iron filing, twisting to follow the magnet of self-centered motives" because mature religion is "less of a servant, and more of a master."[5] It is sobering to realize that Jesus' most pointed criticism of the religious piety of His day concerned those preoccupied with the extrinsic. "And when you pray, do not be like the hypocrites, for they love to pray standing in the synagogues and on the street corners to be seen by men. I tell you the truth, they have received their reward in full" (Matt. 6:5).

The Christian competent educator needs to constantly put before people the necessity of faith that stems from the heart. It is very easy for people to find their faith fulfilled in simply being "a good Baptist" or a "church-going Lutheran"; but those charged with spiritual formation must push people past such false and foreign understandings of spirituality. Spiritual formation can only flourish in a church when it recognizes that a host of factors conspire to twist the Gospel and constantly push adults in the direction of believing that true religion consists of something other than loving Jesus and doing what He did. We must constantly point people to Jesus Christ and proclaim His Gospel of grace if we want to truly form Christians and overcome the deforming effects of the world.

Individualism

North American adults have fully entered the psychological age and have a sense that they are each "uniquely wired" and hence have a right to a certain outlook and way of patterning their lives. This stands in contrast to our view in which we expect all children to memorize, participate in certain games, or go to camp the same week. The reality of remarkable differences in adult temperament, personalities, and lifestyle choices proves to be an immense challenge for their spiritual formation. It means that many ready-made programs which assume that all adults pattern their religious life in the same way simply will not work across the church. Certain adults may find a particular structure or program very helpful, but it is doubtful that such patterns can be extended to an entire congregation.

A person's spiritual life cannot thrive if she doesn't carve out time to do business with God and use the means of grace offered through the church and the Word. Yet some adults claim that their personalities just do not allow them to sit still, or that they can only have intimate fellowship with God when their intuitions direct them. Spiritual direction takes on a whole new set of challenges in the face of such psychological awareness that has allowed people to perceive their comfort zones and personal quirks as sacrosanct. Spiritual change necessitates moving people in worship and prayer beyond where they feel comfortable and into areas where they can do their business with God even more fully.

FACTORS THAT ENHANCE ADULT SPIRITUAL RECEPTIVITY

Presence of Pain and Loss

Adolescents live in a world of self-perceived omnipotence and success. They may have experienced setbacks and disappointments, but most adolescents see life as filled with unlimited opportunities with momentary losses merely an aberration to what life generally deals out. They live with the expectation that if they make good choices, and don't do something "dumb," their lives will be marked by a pleasantness, and turmoil will fall upon someone else. One of the watershed differences between adolescents and adults lies in a recognition that the presence of pain and loss is part of life itself. Adults know this because their experiences show that life holds inherent disappointments and loss. A mature faith incorporates this aspect of reality deep within itself. The words of M. Scott Peck resonate with many adults when he says, "Life is difficult."[6] These difficulties take a myriad of forms, and our responses to them, as the aphorism tells us, make us either better or bitter.

Problems in relationships prove to be some of the most enduring sources of pain for adults. Estrangement from children and spouse brings incredible pain and is often accompanied by a sense of failure and with near debilitating guilt. At a less intense level, the moves which mark the lives of so many adults mean that friendships are disrupted and wonderful systems of support torn apart. Adults know the deep joy and satisfaction of long-term friendships, but they also know that relationships are tenuous and often a source of acute disappointment.

Job difficulties present another source of discouragement. Many adults have been led to believe that their identities can be found in their career or profession and find that corporate reorganizations or changes in business patterns and technology that leave them unemployed or underemployed prove devastating to their identity. In the late '70s and '80s, jobs were assigned a whole new value. As we enter the twenty-first century, many persons will be disappointed to find that work is neither deeply satisfying as they were led to believe nor humanely administered as management books advocate. Work outside the home plays a prominent role in the culture of North America, and the joys and disappointments of employment impact people whose lives we seek to form for Christ.

Many adults also experience the unwelcome limitations of chronic illness or disability. The constant pain and fatigue of chronic disease often requires adults to acknowledge a dependence on others that they find very difficult. Similarly, many adults discover addictions and problems of living that negatively affect their lives and require radical changes in how they order their lives. Finally, the tasks of adult life bring with them certain struggles and problems. Many adults find that they are simply unable to make ends meet financially. Particularly for single mothers, the constant struggle to balance roles of work and caregiving along with financial pressures exact a toll that can lead to debilitating lethargy and cynicism.

Vocation

Adults have the option of choosing their vocations, and vocation profoundly shapes the way adults understand their spiritual lives. By vocation we mean far more than what is done to earn a living. It describes the way adults perceive their roles in the world; in other words, what an adult believes is his or her purpose for being here. It is really an answer to the questions, "How will I make a difference?" and "How will I leave my mark?" For some, it is answered by investing themselves in their children. For others, by pouring themselves into a profession. For still others, by spending themselves on others.

Today the question of vocation is uniquely tied to the notion of individual giftedness and passion. People sense that they have an inherent right to exercise a vocation that flows out of their giftedness and passion—that this is how they will be most effective.

Another crucial question facing adults is the relationship of job and personal faith. Particularly for those who are socialized into a professional role and taught to only value certain questions and to dismiss others as outside their domain. They live their lives with a sense that job and faith are vital, but really exist in two different spheres. Faith may be expressed at work on occasion, such as when they witness to a distressed coworker; but otherwise, the two areas are seen as important but largely unrelated spheres of life. The Christian mind, though, requires that employment/professional life falls within the believer's overall sense of vocation as doing something important.

Awareness and Reality of Sin

Adults differ remarkably in their understanding of sin. Children have a sense of doing things wrong because parents and teachers remind them how they have erred. But adults whose lives are generally "under control" often believe they live relatively free from sin. Late twentieth-century Americans have largely set aside the notion of sin and have relegated it to a small segment of ethically irrelevant religious taboos. To the modern secular mind, sin has to do with what seems like antiquated rules of highly prescribed Sunday activities, not eating meat on Fridays, or avoiding certain forms of entertainment.

While at one level adults want to deny their firsthand involvement with sin, they know their inability to live as they truly wish to live. They know painfully well their inability to be the people they desire to be. For adults, sin shows itself most clearly in relationships. Our modern industrial world is tragically aware of the immense cost of fractured relationships and of people so devastated they are unable to commit themselves to anything other than relationships of convenience.

Adults are also aware of the presence of real evil in the world at large. The Holocaust and the vicious policies of Stalin, Mao Tse-tung, and Pol Pot are part of our collective consciousness. We know of terrorists who will stop at nothing to gain notoriety for their cause and of companies who have knowingly dumped toxic waste into water supplies. Children may see the news events which distress their parents as isolated phenomena, but modern adults see them as part of a pattern of widespread evil.

The adult mind has a keen sense of not measuring up in the various arenas in which we function. The standards are often undefined and affirmation often is missing, and at times modern culture seems to place a wholesale assault upon the individual's sense of self-worth and wholeness. Adults adopt strategies to deal with these assaults upon their esteem. Some are helpful, but many like workaholism or various forms of escape prove to be self-destructive and harmful to the relationships so critical to our well-being. Yet, adults have come to see the enduring presence of evil and desire spiritual strategies which openly confront this evil.

KEY ASSUMPTIONS IN ADULT SPIRITUAL FORMATION

Adults can embrace the spiritual life with a stability and wholehearted devotion which seldom comes in adolescence. Adults provide the formal leadership in churches, can influence others in their business and professional contacts, and are responsible for nurturing the faith of their families. Their spiritual formation is critical and cannot be assumed to be an automatic process. The reality that Christians live in an alien land requires that spiritual formation be guided by these principles.

- A commitment that being a Christian means living out of step with the dominant culture.

- A recognition that the spiritual life can be mimicked externally. The likelihood of people living a shallow extrinsic faith is heightened in churches which place an emphasis on narrow behavioral or ritual conformity.

- The need to provide both spiritual support and challenge.

- The importance of both finding patterns of devotion that fit people "where they are" and also introducing patterns that allow for deeper fellowship with God.

In the two sections which follow, we will address some negative factors which affect our spiritual life along with some concrete suggestions for spiritual formation. The process of formation consists of inviting people to participate in the life of the Spirit and seeking to remove the blocks to spiritual transformation.

BLOCKS TO SPIRITUAL GROWTH

Spiritual formation involves a twofold work of reducing the negative effects of common blocks or barriers to spiritual growth and fostering an opening of oneself to God. Both movements are absolutely necessary for spiritual growth to occur.

Busyness. Unless one is willing, by our standards, to waste time with God, there really won't be significant spiritual growth or change. The adage that if Satan is not able to bring your downfall through a public sin, then he'll do it simply by keeping you too busy contains a truth seen in the leaders of many churches. The spiritual life does not require radical retreat or disengagement from the world, but it requires a purposefulness of life and a willingness to allow priorities deep within us to establish how we order our days rather than turning our time over to the "tyranny of the urgent."

Time Orientation. Today different societies view time in very different ways. Certain aspects of how industrialized societies view time make the spiritual life less inviting. Ours is a future-oriented culture. We train our children to save and to delay gratification by going to college because we believe these will result, in the long run, in a happier and more productive life. We have a constant eye on the future as we set about our daily tasks, knowing that the labor we expend today could count for something even greater down the road. There is a cost to all this because we tend to downplay the delight of the present and question the relevance of the past. Family stories, traditional hymns, and traditions which build a sense of community are overlooked in the headlong rush into the future.

One will only spend time with God if he/she is willing to dwell in the present. We cannot enjoy God and contemplate the future benefits of our devotional time with Him any more than we can enjoy a meal with one eye on what the meal will do for us down the road. Food, music, and fellowship with God are among those activities that must be enjoyed in the present tense, and many time-harried moderns are incapable of leaving the future to delight in the present.

Laziness. At one level prayer requires no more than "to lie in the sunshine of God's grace"[7] and receiving the healing He freely offers. But some seem unwilling to expend the energy to sit in the sunshine of His grace. People spend time on what they believe is most important, and so at one level it is not wanton laziness that keeps them from spending time with Jesus in prayer and Bible study, but disordered principles. When people are challenged by the need to spend time with God, they often fail to make the necessary plans. When things are important to us we make plans to see that they get done, and so when the spiritual life is a high priority, people make plans to see that prayer, meditation, and Scripture study are part of their lives.

Pain. God is able and willing to meet us in our pain and to take us through it; but some find their pain too intense to stand in, and they flee from it in denial or self-destructive escapism. Some attribute their pain to God and therefore refuse to turn to the One who could heal them because they blame Him for their pain.

Guilt and fear of God. Too many people have subconsciously made God in their own image or in the image of a punitive parent figure. They know their own limitations—their spitefulness and self-protective behaviors. They know their inability to love, trust, and nurture others, so they find it inconceivable that God truly loves them. Some of them would claim to love God deeply, but by their actions they shrink from God's presence. This tragedy can hardly be fathomed because they see God being like them. They fail to see His outstretched arms waiting to embrace and heal them.

Identity confusion. Graduate professional programs do many things well and one of them is to create a strong professional identity. In our professionally oriented society many Christians fall into the spiritual trap of confusing their professional identity and success with their identity as a person. The latter looms so large it becomes the most important standard for judging life. The notion of cultivating a rich spiritual life almost seems unnecessary to those who succeed well as attorneys, accountants, or physicians. Many have allowed their professional identity to define who they are, and as long as they do well at the professionally described tasks of their occupation, they judge their lives to be well lived. This tragic entrapment is difficult to escape. The most effective words may come from successful professionals who can speak out of their own experience to the need for a self-understanding larger than how one earns a livelihood.

Performance justification. Spiritual life grows out of our justification. We have been declared righteous before God because Christ's work on the cross has been accepted through faith and not because of our own striving. When we see the spiritual life as a means of justification it becomes warped, twisted, and ugly. It is not by our performance that we are justified. It is by our trusting and abiding in Christ that we find everlasting rest. Performance justification is a heresy that has plagued the Christian church from its founding and knows no cultural or geographic barrier. However, the strong teaching of grace extended to those unwilling and unworthy compels us to draw near to God and be refreshed and renewed by Him.

FOSTERING SPIRITUAL FORMATION: OPENING THE WINDOWS

The first movement in spiritual formation removes the blocks to growth; the second parallel movement invites these adults to open themselves to God's transforming grace through spiritual disciplines. To a large measure, the responsibility of those charged with spiritual formation in the church requires them to establish a climate favorable to spiritual formation. The image of light and making light available provides a very helpful metaphor. Picture a once grand Victorian mansion with all the shades drawn and no signs of life about. You enter through the ornate front door and travel a creaking hallway, to find yourself in the front room. The stale smell, the dust, and general decay floods over you. You open the shades and the windows and within moments what had looked foreboding becomes a house of light and beauty.

The mansion with shades drawn depicts Christians trapped in activism, busyness, pain, or guilt. Spiritual formation means pulling up the shades, opening the windows, and letting the sunshine of God's grace stream in. Christ's grace comes in two contexts: (1) through the church by means of worship, wise counsel, fellowship, biblical preaching, and teaching; and (2) in our very private encounters with God as we pray, meditate, and read the Scriptures. Effective spiritual formation prepares Christians to be transformed through both of these dimensions of our spiritual life so that we "who with unveiled faces all reflect the Lord's glory, are being transformed into His likeness with ever-increasing glory, which comes from the Lord, who is the Spirit" (2 Cor. 3:18).

Notes

1. Stanley Hauerwas and William H. Willimon, *Resident Aliens: Life in the Christian Colony* (Nashville: Abingdon, 1989).
2. Ibid., 29.
3. Stephen Brookfield, *Understanding and Facilitating Adult Learning* (San Francisco: Jossey-Bass, 1986), 125–26.
4. Gordon Allport, *The Individual and His Religion: A Psychological Interpretation* (New York: Macmillan, 1953), 63.
5. Ibid., 63–64.
6. M. Scott Peck, *The Road Less Traveled: A New Psychology of Love, Traditional Values and Spiritual Growth* (New York: Simon & Schuster, 1978), 15.
7. Ole Hallesby, *Prayer*, trans. Clarence J. Carlsen (Minneapolis: Augsburg, 1975), 15.

For Further Reading

Baillie, John. *A Diary of Private Prayer.* New York: Scribners, 1949. A collection of thoughtful prayers for morning and evening which can easily be personalized.

Bloesch, Donald. *The Crisis of Piety: Essays Toward a Theology of the Chris-*

tian Life. 2nd ed. Colorado Springs: Helmers & Howard, 1988. A helpful collection of essays on aspects of the Christian life. Particularly relevant to those interested in the role of asceticism, liturgy, and mysticism. Reflects a strong concern for spiritual renewal leading to a prophetic witness.

______. *The Struggle of Prayer.* Colorado Springs: Helmers & Howard, 1988. An evangelical theology of prayer. The author addresses important issues related to both the practice and theology of prayer. He makes the case for viewing prayer as the heart of spirituality.

Foster, Richard. *Study Guide for Celebration of Discipline.* New York: Harper & Row, 1983. A useful companion to Foster's *Celebration of Discipline.* It includes helpful reading lists and practical suggestions for beginning the various disciplines.

Foster, Richard. *Celebration of Discipline.* rev. ed. San Francisco: Harper & Row, 1988. One of the few comprehensive treatments of the major spiritual disciplines in addition to being a very readable and practical guide.

Hallesby, Ole. *Prayer.* Translated by Clarence J. Carlsen. Minneapolis: Augsburg, 1975. A simple and attractive treatment of prayer that places emphasis on the character qualities, humility, and simplicity needed for effective prayer. Aimed at the maturing Christian who desires a more effective and meaningful prayer life.

Huggett, Joyce. *The Joy of Listening to God.* Downers Grove, Ill.: InterVarsity, 1986. Practical advice on using prayer to listen and contemplate. The book is based on the author's first hard experience of learning to wait upon God and enjoy His presence.

Hybels, Bill. *Too Busy Not to Pray.* Downers Grove, Ill.: InterVarsity, 1988. A practical guide to establishing a prayer life. It emphasizes the need for one's prayer life to include both intercession and listening.

Law, Philip, ed. *Praying with the New Testament.* London: SPCK, 1988. New Testament passages edited and arranged to serve as a guide to individual and corporate prayer. The passages are arranged into chapters which focus on major issues in our lives.

Lewis, C.S. *Letters to Malcolm: Chiefly on Prayer.* New York: Harcourt, Brace, 1962. A classic exploration of prayer. This is not a systematic treatment of prayer, but the reflections of a person of prayer on the difficulties, methods, joys, and problems of prayer. An easy-to-read source of insights into prayer.

Lovelace, Richard F. *Dynamics of Spiritual Life: An Evangelical Theology of Renewal.* Downers Grove, Ill.: InterVarsity, 1979.

Piper, John. *Desiring God: Meditations of a Christian Hedonist.* Portland, Ore.: Multnomah, 1987. A good book for anyone serious about maturing in faith. This book sketches out the purpose for Christian living and in doing so challenges many stereotypes about the spiritual or deeper life. It is a call to living a life built on the foundation of enjoying God.

Postema, Don. *Space for God.* Grand Rapids: Bible Way, 1983. "In this book Don Postema offers us a space to live gratefully in the presence of God. He gives us his personal spiritual journey, his experience in Christian ministry, his wide interest in art and literature, and most of all his own hospitable personality as the space in which we, who read this book, can listen fearlessly to God's own voice" (from the preface by Henri Nouwen).

Richards, Larry. *A Practical Theology of Spirituality.* Grand Rapids: Zondervan, 1987. A very readable and practical introduction into the whole area of developing a deeper spiritual life. Many suggestions on what to try.

Toon, Peter. *From Mind to Heart: Christian Meditation Today.* Grand Rapids: Baker, 1988. An introduction to meditation. The author does a good job of explaining the essence of Christian meditation. He wisely distinguishes meditation from other spiritual disciplines. Looks at meditation from biblical examples and different theological traditions.

White, John. *When the Spirit Comes in Power.* Downers Grove, Ill.: Inter-Varsity, 1988.

FOUR
CULTURAL FACTORS OF NORTH AMERICAN ADULTS

Gregory C. Carlson

The adult Christian educator faces a conundrum! Consider the following conflicting findings:

IN AMERICA . . .

Percent of people who consider "family" very important: 94.[1]
Percent of married Americans who have committed adultery: 31.[2]
Percent of recently married adults who lived with their new spouse before getting married: 60.[3]
Expectation of new marriages to end in divorce within 10 years: Over half.[4]

Percent of people who say religion is "very important" in their lives: 53.[5]
Percent of decline in Sunday School enrollment in twenty-two denominations between 1974–1984: 21.[6]
Number of closed churches in America: 66,000.[7]

Percentage of American Christians who own a VCR: 76.
Percentage who in the last year bought a videotape with Christian content: 1.[8]

What should we make of these paradoxical cultural trends? Can we define, delineate, and develop our sociological discernment in ways which will enhance effective adult ministry? Are andragogical perspectives of Christian education culturally driven?

CULTURAL FOUNDATIONS

Culture may be defined as "the common and usually shared behavior of the group."[9] This behavior includes the customs, norms, values, language, and expected ways of doing things. Sociology is "the analysis of human interaction."[10] Together culture and sociology provide a valuable basis for understanding education. Pazmiño states:

> In order to understand the process of Christian education, one must refer to culture and society. The very practice of Christian education assumes a cultural context. This is a given in our created world. God created persons with the capacity to create culture and to form societies. Without culture, Christianity would be an abstraction unrelated to human life.[11]

The Bible supports the view of cultural sensitivity in ministry (see chap. 19). Paul encapsuled this in 1 Corinthians 9:19-27 where he states, "I have become all things to all men." Jesus displayed the same attitude in telling John to "fulfill all righteousness" by baptizing Him (Matt. 3:15), and also when He told Peter to pay the temple tax (Matt. 17:27).

The early church developed a powerful cultural framework of its own. Pentecost resulted in a distinctive set of behaviors to which the believers "continually devoted themselves" (Acts 2:42). This framework made them distinctive. Acts 5:13 states, "But none of the rest dared to associate with them; however, the people held them in high esteem" (NASB).

The difficulty arises in understanding this biblical culture, and then making statements of truth relevant to our culture. According to Anderson, "We must pour the truth out of the container of first century Hebrew-Greek culture and into the container of twentieth-century American culture. When done properly, not a drop of truth is lost."[12]

CULTURAL FRAMEWORK FOR ANDRAGOGY

When interpreting culture, what structures does one use? Is there a grid of values which assist a Christian educator in understanding the culture of North American adults? The following categories can provide such a cultural framework.[13]

Person to Person Relationships

How does a society answer the question of decision-making within the group? Three orientations describe how people relate, or are governed. *Linealism* looks to a certain man or woman as the "leader," one who makes decisions for the entire group. Patriarchs, matriarchs, strong religious leaders, founders of churches, sometimes college administrators, and some pastors all exemplify linealism. *Collateralism* places power in the group. The commune, fraternity, gang, rotating leadership Bible study, and the board that seeks consensus demonstrate collateralism.

But *individualism* dominates North American values. Americans stress the right of the individual to be different, disagree, belong to a variety of groups, and compete against all others. Doing what one's parents might say (linealism) or yielding to peer pressure (collateralism) may be discouraged, making one's own choices, having things "my way" and individual achievement seem to be "in"! From the earliest years, we urge children to think and choose for themselves. Most Americans feel that individuals should be consulted about decisions which will affect them, since each person has a contribution which would be helpful to the outcome. Individualism is deeply ingrained in the fabric of our culture.

But what does the Bible say about person to person relationships? There is one Lord (Eph. 4:5), and surely there is a degree of loyalty, obedience, and deferment that all believers should give to Christ. Additionally, we have been placed within the context of a "body" (1 Cor. 12:12-14). And, as evangelicals, we may emphasize the "personal relationship" of each individual to Christ (John 1:12). The Scriptures urge Christians to be balanced in their view of the governance of the kingdom. Gaebelein states:

> What, then, are some principles of Christian action in a morally corrupt society? Short of the millennium, Scripture knows no such thing as a Christian world order; with utter realism it sees the church and the believer as in the world and therefore with responsibilities to it but at the same time as generically different from it.[14]

Activity Orientation

How do human beings within a culture express themselves in activity, and how do they approach the division of labor or work?

One of the three common modes we call *being orientation.* Being-oriented people can best be represented by those who simply exist; they enjoy life; theirs is a spontaneous expression of the human personality. They define life in terms of family, or perhaps some status or role. Being-in-becoming stresses growth, development, all aspects of the self receiving attention—a synthesis of intellect, emotions, and motives.

North Americans exhibit a *doing orientation* in their approach to work. They believe that if one follows a "course of action" or a plan, all problems will be solved. Americans have traditionally viewed life from a problem-solving, practical, progressive change perspective. "Within our own American culture, doing something in the area of work has long been highly valued."[15] However, this work ethic seems to be changing: "Workers around America frankly admit that they spend more than 20 percent (seven hours a week) of their time at work totally goofing off."[16]

The Scriptures seem to indicate that one attains a status of being when he or she becomes a believer. First Peter 2:9 states, "But you are a chosen race, a royal priesthood, a holy nation, a people for God's own possession" (NASB). Yet the Bible suggests that Christians are "in process." "Beloved, now we are children of God, and it has not appeared as yet what we shall be" (1 John 3:2, NASB). The Bible also says that we must obey or do the commands of the Lord Jesus Christ (John 14:21). The biblical perspective would therefore seem to be one of balance, with an emphasis upon showing the reality of God's work within (being) by a doing orientation without (Phil. 2:13; James 1:22, 25).

Time Orientation

People of the past tend to suspect the idea of progress. Asian countries often have a greater sense of history. Some churches have a strong sense of tradition; they look back to the glory days with a *past orientation. Present orientation* often exhibits itself in living for the "now." The youth subculture can often be characterized by life as if "there's no tomorrow."

But the dominant American time perspective focuses on the future. "For Americans, the orientation toward the future and the high value placed on work yield the principle that one can improve upon the present through hard work."[17] Saving money, waiting till retirement, marriage, a new job, a move, or "next time" all show how the future orientation is woven into the fabric of North American thought.

Scripture urges Christians to base their faith upon the realities of the past (1 Cor. 15:3-5) and to wage spiritual battle in the present (Eph. 6:10-14). However, *future orientation* seems the most dominant viewpoint of the Bible. Paul urges us not to be ignorant of "future things" (1 Thes. 4:13-18). John describes being ready to meet Jesus, and urges his readers "not [to] shrink away from Him in shame at His coming" (1 John 2:28, NASB). Believers in Christ are people "with eternity's values in view."

The Individual and Nature

Humanity lies at the mercy of nature; there is little one can do to prevent or change the obstacles placed before them in society. This demonstrates the *subjugation to nature* orientation. "What will be will be" can produce a feeling of hopelessness and helplessness. The *cooperation with nature* value structure teams up with the environment. The antipollution and save the earth movements may be described as an *integration with nature.* The environment shapes the subject or individual, and the individual merges with the natural world.

Dominant in the American mind-set is the idea that nature should be controlled to serve humanity. Control of nature is one of the most distinctive and salient features of the North American value structure. Naisbitt describes the shift from "institutional help to self-help." "Self-help has always been a part of American life."[18] Walsh and Middleton explain the secularism of America by saying, "Mankind—unlike nature—is thus neither limited by nor answerable to the law of God."[19] The ability to overcome disease, circumvent natural disaster (or at least minimize the impact), artificial insemination and other birth alternatives, organ transplants, using problems as a source of energy, and even "self-help education"[20] all exhibit the control of nature viewpoint.

Genesis records the giving of authority to "be fruitful and multiply, and fill the earth, and subdue it; and rule over the fish of the sea and over the birds of the sky, and over every living thing" (Gen. 1:28, NASB). This authority is repeated after the Fall (Gen. 3) and also after the Flood (Gen. 9:1ff). While one must be aware of the great gift of natural resources, it should be remembered that people have a responsibility over this world.

Human Nature Orientation

The rationality, mutability, and quality of human nature presents a challenge to Christian educators. Perhaps this cultural framework displays the greatest diversity in North American thought. How should we describe a child's nature at birth? Good, Evil, Neutral, or Evil-but-Perfectible are presented as alternatives. Americans seem to assume that humans are rational and changeable. "More than four out of five adults (83 percent) contend that people are basically good."[21] This fits nicely with the "control of nature" orientation above. How one answers the questions of discipline, work regulations, and perspective of self-image shows the basic value held in this area.

The Bible speaks clearly about the moral nature of people. Human beings exhibit depravity by nature and action (Rom. 3:23; Eph. 2:1-3). However, the Scriptures are equally lucid about the "new man" (2 Cor. 5:17; Rom. 6:4-10). The balance would seem to indicate an evil-but-perfectible orientation. This process takes place supernaturally "in Christ." But even unbelievers have a potential to learn. Where does this potential come from? Genesis 1:26 describes God making humankind "in His own image."

Possessions

The idea of a culture's possessions may be put on a continuum. Spiritualism reflects the belief that life does not consist of things. A concern for brotherhood, the sharing of wealth, supernatural phenomena, and even artistic expression may indicate a spiritual orientation to life. Thus, the counter-interest in the occult and the New Age movement by many in today's culture shows how strongly materialism is embedded within the cultural framework of mainstream North American adults.

The Christian adult educator faces a challenge because people continue to strive for success and accumulation of goods, yet few would claim materialism is the measure of a person.[22] Patterson and Kim state that "greed is impoverishing America."[23] It seems obvious that most people in the European community, North America, and other industrialized nations believe in a materialistic solution to life. Believers would be well-advised to heed Jesus' words in Luke 12:15 (life doesn't amount to possessions), and Matthew 6:21 (treasure heavenly possessions).

The dominant theme of the Bible supports the spiritual perspective: "Since, then, you have been raised with Christ, set your hearts on things above, where Christ is seated at the right hand of God. Set your minds on things above, not on earthly things" (Col. 3:1-2). Ephesians describes the believer as having "every spiritual blessing in the heavenly places in Christ" (Eph. 1:3, NASB).

What then is the dominant North American worldview? How can we understand what Patterson and Kim call "the outlook or image we have concerning the nature of the universe, the nature of humankind, the relationship between humanity and the universe, and other philosophical issues or orientations that help us define the cosmos and our place in it."[24]

According to Walsh and Middleton, the North American worldview sounds something like this:

> I am me, an individual, the free and independent master of my own destiny. I stand in a world full of natural potential, and my task is to utilize that potential to economic good. While I am hindered in this task by ignorance of nature and lack of tools for controlling it, nevertheless my hope rests in the good life of progress wherein nature yields its bounty for human benefit. Only then will all find happiness in a life of material affluence, with no needs and no dependence.[25]

CULTURAL FELLOWSHIP WITH ANDRAGOGY

The adult Christian educator finds that he or she is caught between andragogy and pedagogy.[26] A good deal of uncertainty swirls around the implementation of andragogical principles in adult education, stressing the need for philosophical review.[27] Is andragogy an appropriate paradigm for the Christian adult educator? How does andragogy relate to the climate of church education? What is the relationship of the dominant cultural mores and andragogy? "Cultural life . . . is not only rooted in the dominant world view, it also orients life in terms of that world view."[28]

The four basic assumptions of andragogy compare favorably with the cultural orientations of North American adults. This perhaps reveals the reason why andragogy "fits" Canadian and American education. The chart below summarizes the relationship.

CULTURE AND ANDRAGOGY: FAVORABLE COMPARISONS

ANDRAGOGICAL ASSUMPTIONS[29]	NORTH AMERICAN CULTURAL ORIENTATION
1. A self-concept which is self-directed.	a. The individual person-to-person relationship.

	b. Control of nature. c. Human nature is perfectible or basically good.
2. The rich and growing learner experience.	a. Doing activity orientation. b. Basically "good" human nature assessment which fits learner's view.
3. A readiness to learn which is oriented to social roles.	a. Control of nature fits social role enhancement. b. Materialism relates to problem-solving for roles.
4. Immediate application of learning.	a. Doing activity orientation. b. Future time orientation in that one must change NOW to be ready for the future.

Cultural Factors

What other cultural factors impact the education of adults in North America?

North Americans and Learning. Allen Tough from the University of Ontario discovered that "Almost everyone undertakes at least one or two major learning efforts a year, and some individuals undertake as many as 15 or 20. The median is eight learning projects a year, involving eight distinct areas of knowledge."[30]

Though that sounds encouraging, the unfortunate statistic concerning Americans reveals that formal education continues to diminish. While 26 percent of adults said they spend more time in school, 34 percent said they spend less.[31] We should be concerned about the division of the college population into the "haves" and "have nots." Dropouts and people who cannot read at the eighth-grade level (about 30 million),[32] should activate the church to action.

Barna projects higher costs and fewer graduates will mark education in the years ahead. Educational achievement will be a result of a person's socioeconomic situation. Second career students will become more common. Illiteracy will begin to pose problems for church ministry, especially the Sunday School.[33] Many of these factors represent opportunities; others seem discouraging hindrances.

North Americans and Secularism. While 90 percent of the

adults surveyed by Patterson and Kim say they believe in God, "for most people, religion plays virtually no role in shaping their opinions on a long list of important public questions."[34] Charles Colson warns of "barbarians in the classroom" by saying, "every area of education has been infected by this value-neutral philosophy."[35] Woodrow Kroll sounds a clarion call: "Because of this prevalent attitude of secular self-interest, many Christian colleges have adapted to meet the demand."[36] "But what does it mean when we say that the modern world is essentially secular? For most people it means that modern people have lost interest in religion."[37]

This worldview is sure to negatively impact religious education in a "post-Christian" society. On the contrary scene, many believe late twentieth-century North Americans are fascinated by the supernatural, particularly evidenced in cults and the New Age philosophy.

North Americans and Being Happy. We have lost our way. "While most of us do not have a philosophy of life to guide our decision-making, we do react to situations and opportunities in light of these objectives:" (1) We want to be loved. (2) We want to make a difference in this world. (3) We desire security. (4) We seek comfort.[38]

North Americans and Fragmentation. Nowhere is fragmentation more obvious than in the breakdown of the family. Statistics need not be stated since observation serves us well enough; the family is in trouble. But the durability and necessity of the family continues! Colson states, "No other structure can replace the family. Without it, our children have no moral foundation. Without it, they become moral illiterates whose only law is self."[39]

> It is likely today's much-noted self-centeredness is, in large part, a response to the stress of living in a society where inconstancy is the only constant and where the needed roots and abiding familiarities of life—private and public—are easily eradicated or never develop in the first place.[40]

North Americans and Spiritual Renewal. Walsh and Middleton write, "The brokenness of our present cultural situation calls for a healing response."[41] Does not our God desire for us to repent, know Him, and have our land healed? (2 Peter 3:9; 1 Chron. 7:14) As believers in Christ, it becomes imperative that we seek to be "salt and light" in our own society. Assessing and predicting a culture does not change it.

CHRISTIAN EDUCATIONAL IMPLICATIONS

Understanding the Culture

To penetrate a society, one must be culturally literate. Realizing that we change people, not cultures, it nonetheless becomes essential that we grip the dominant themes of our society. Anderson warns, "Suggesting that Christians 'learn the market' to be effective in their ministries sounds too secular for many . . . however, the concepts of learning and reaching the market are deeply rooted in the New Testament."[42] Acts 17, Romans 1:16, and 1 Corinthians 9:9-23 serve as examples of the Apostle Paul applying a "learn the market" mentality.

Training for Change

As Christians, we can assist ourselves and others in understanding the process, product, and procedures of change. Education which focuses on the necessary knowledge, attitudes, and skills for change will be education that transforms.

Affirming the Nonnegotiables

There are the basic tenets of the faith (1 Cor. 15:3-6). One must discern those areas in which diversity can be tolerated. Other areas will need strong convictions, firmly taught. Knowing the difference will require maturity, dependency, and wisdom.

Thinking Creatively

Finally, to be in the educational endeavor today, one must seek to say the same things in new ways, to address the familiar with fresh means. Only the Christian can stand and deliver a message of hope and help.

Notes

1. George Barna, *What Americans Believe* (Ventura, Calif.: Regal, 1991), 152.
2. James Patterson and Peter Kim, *The Day America Told the Truth* (New York: Prentice Hall, 1991), 94.
3. George Barna, *The Frog in the Kettle* (Ventura, Calif.: Regal, 1989), 67.
4. Ibid., 113.
5. Ibid., 187.
6. As reported in Kenneth O. Gangel, "Ten Steps to Sunday School Revival,"

Christian Education Journal 11 (Spring 1991): 31.

7. Earl Parvin, *Missions USA* (Chicago: Moody, 1985), 11.
8. Barna Research Group, "The Church Today: Insightful Statisics and Commentary," *Leadership* 12 (Summer 1991): 71.
9. Wilbur B. Brookover and David Gottlieb, *A Sociology of Education* (New York: American Book, 1964), 24.
10. Ibid., 11.
11. Robert W. Pazmiño, *Foundational Issues in Christian Education* (Grand Rapids: Baker, 1988), 153.
12. Leith Anderson, *Dying for Change* (Minneapolis: Bethany), 1990, 15.
13. Framework is developed from Keith W. Prichard and Thomas H. Buxton, *Concepts and Theories in Sociology of Education* (Lanham, Md.: University Press of America, 1988); Larry A. Samovar, Richard E. Porter, and Nemi C. Jain, *Understanding Intercultural Communication* (Belmont, Calif.: Wadsworth, 1981); and Edward C. Steward, *American Cultural Patterns* (Washington, D.C.: Society for Intercultural Education, Training, and Research, 1972).
14. Gaebelein, Frank E. *The Christian, the Arts, and Truth* (Portland, Ore.: Multnomah, 1985), 111.
15. Prichard and Buxton, *Sociology of Education,* 52.
16. Patterson and Kim, *The Day America*, 155.
17. Samovar, Porter, and Jain, *Intercultural Communication*, 72.
18. Naisbitt, John. *Megatrends* (New York: Warner, 1984), 145.
19. Brian J. Walsh and J. Richard Middleton, *The Transforming Vision* (Downers Grove, Ill.: InterVarsity, 1984), 119.
20. Naisbitt, *Megatrends*, 156–60.
21. Barna, *What Americans*, 89.
22. Ibid., 95.
23. Patterson and Kim, *The Day America*, 89.
24. Ibid., 90.
25. Walsh and Middleton, *Transforming Vision*, 227.
26. Christian, Randy. "Andragogical Assumptions and Christian Education," *Christian Education Journal* 9 (Spring 1989): 56.
27. Cross, K. Patricia. *Adults as Learners* (San Francisco: Jossey-Bass, 1984), 225–26.
28. Walsh and Middleton, *Transforming Vision*, 33.
29. Malcolm S. Knowles, *The Modern Practice of Adult Education* (New York: Cambridge, 1980), 43–54.
30. Allen Tough, *The Adult's Learning Projects,* 2nd ed. (San Diego: University Associates, 1979), 1.

31. Barna, 1991, *What Americans*, 61.
32. Barna, 1989, *The Frog*, 211.
33. Ibid., 210–20.
34. Patterson and Kim, *The Day America*, 199.
35. Charles Colson, *Against the Night* (Ann Arbor, Mich.: Servant, 1989), 82.
36. Woodrow Kroll, *The Vanishing Ministry* (Grand Rapids: Kregel, 1991), 41.
37. Walsh and Middleton, *Transforming Vision*, 117–18.
38. Barna, *The Frog*, 156–58.
39. Colson, *Against*, 77.
40. David Elkind, *The Hurried Child* (New York: Addison-Wesley, 1981), 26.
41. Walsh and Middleton, *Transforming Vision*, 149.
42. Anderson, *Dying*, 164.

For Further Reading

Anderson, Leith. *Dying for Change*. Minneapolis: Bethany, 1990.

Barna, George. *The Frog in the Kettle*. Ventura, Calif.: Regal, 1990.
_____. *User Friendly Churches*. Ventura, Calif.: Regal, 1991.

_____. *What Americans Believe*. Ventura, Calif.: Regal, 1991.

Barna Research Group. "The Church Today: Insightful Statistics and Commentary," *Leadership* 12 (Summer 1991).

Brookover, Wilbur B., and David Gottlieb. *A Sociology of Education*. New York: American Book, 1964.

Christian, Randy. "Andragogical Assumptions and Christian Education," *Christian Education Journal* 4 (Spring 1989).

Colson, Charles. *Against the Night*. Ann Arbor, Mich.: Servant, 1989.

Cross, K. Patricia, *Adults as Learners*. San Francisco: Jossey-Bass, 1984.

Elkind, David. *The Hurried Child*. New York: Addison-Wesley, 1981.

Gaebelein, Frank E. *The Christian, the Arts, and Truth*. Portland, Ore.: Multnomah, 1985.

Gangel, Kenneth O. "Ten Steps to Sunday School Revival." *Christian Education Journal* 6 (Spring 1991).

Knowles, Malcolm S. *The Modern Practice of Adult Education*. New York: Cambridge, 1980.

Kroll, Woodrow. *The Vanishing Ministry*. Grand Rapids: Kregel, 1991.

Naisbitt, John. *Megatrends*. New York: Warner, 1984.

Patterson, James, and Peter Kim. *The Day America Told the Truth*. New York: Prentice Hall, 1991.

Parvin, Earl. *Missions USA*. Chicago: Moody Press, 1985.

Pazmiño, Robert W. *Foundational Issues in Christian Education.* Grand Rapids: Baker, 1988.

Prichard, Keith W., and Thomas H. Buxton. *Concepts and Theories in Sociology of Education.* Lanham, Md.: University Press of America, 1988.

Samovar, Larry A., Richard E. Porter, and Nemi C. Jain. *Understanding Intercultural Communication.* Belmont, Calif.: Wadsworth, 1981.

Stewart, Edward C. *American Cultural Patterns.* Washington, D.C.: Society for Intercultural Education, Training, and Research, 1972.

Tough, Allen. *The Adult's Learning Projects,* 2nd ed. San Diego: University Associates, 1979.

Walsh, Brian J., and J. Richard Middleton. *The Transforming Vision.* Downers Grove, Ill.: InterVarsity, 1984.

FIVE
PSYCHOLOGY OF ADULTHOOD

John M. Dettoni

Adults are not fully mature—just more mature than children and adolescents. Adults can and should continue to develop and mature. The bumper sticker says it well: "Be patient. God's not done with me yet." Too frequently, adults (and even youth) assume that adulthood equals "arriving" at maturity. This is hardly the case. Adults, like younger human beings, continue to develop in a number of areas throughout their lives. Although less dramatic than that of infants or teenagers, the development of adults is crucial for their growth as whole persons. Without ongoing development, adults stagnate and become less rather than more mature. Stagnation is a rejection of God's will that we all grow, develop, and mature, "attaining to the whole measure of the fullness of Christ" (Eph. 4:13). Not to develop is to deny the very basics of Jesus' own experiences in which He "grew in wisdom and stature, and in favor with God and men" (Luke 2:52). There is no reason to limit this verse to only Jesus' infancy. He developed from less to more mature as a whole person throughout His lifetime until He was ready to take up the purpose of the Incarnation and to fulfill His role on earth. All adults can earn from Jesus' example of continued growth and development. We need to look to Him as our model for growth and maturity.

With Jesus' life as an example, this chapter examines adult psychology from a whole person developmental perspective. Whole person development occurs in six major domains: physical, cognitive, social, affective, moral, and faith/spiritual domains. These domains cover the whole of human personality. A brief look at each of these follows.

PHYSICAL DEVELOPMENT

The physical development of adults normally stops when a person is in the late twenties. Perhaps one of the final hallmarks of adulthood is achieved when the physical development curve stops its now-slowed ascent and begins its downward curve. Cuts and bruises, bumps and lumps that once healed in a few days now take a few weeks—a person realizes that physical development has ceased. Both males and females around the age of forty years face the battle of the bulge, a never-ceasing struggle for many to contain, let alone conquer. As adults enter their fifties and sixties, they become acutely aware of their physical bodies' decline. They get sick more easily than in late adolescence; they have less stamina than before; and they realize why God made them grandparents, not parents, at this age.

All of these physical changes have a profound effect on adults. They realize that what they observed in their aging parents, grandparents, and other older adults, is now occurring in them. For many adults, facing the beginning of the downward curve of physical development is a major trauma. This is often expressed by the morbid fortieth or fiftieth birthday parties presented by "friends." Somehow turning forty or fifty years old is a major milestone in understanding the changes in one's physical development and its meaning for the rest of life. Recognition of this feeds input into one's mind and heart: "I am getting older"; "I've got to make my mark on society now or never"; "I must get that promotion now or I'll never get it"; "I must strive to outshine those 'superkids' who are coming into the company lest they take over my job, too"; "I don't have the energy I used to have"; "What do all these physical changes mean to me? I feel like a junior higher who is beginning to develop, not knowing what sense to make of the changes in my body. Only now I am not developing, I'm deteriorating."

The shift from physical development to the beginning of physical decline has a profound psychological effect and plays a significant role in adults' self-perception. It affects their perception of how they believe they can think; how they feel they can function in social settings; the emotions they feel about themselves and toward others; their desire to make changes and to continue to develop in the areas of moral development and spiritual/faith development.

Adult physical development, however, is not all negative. Adults realize that they have achieved certain limits of physical development and attempt to come to terms with those limitations. Their physical comfort becomes a concern to them. How a room is set up, the comfort of seats, lighting, temperature—all aspects of the physical environment—become important now. They know, for example, that they need more light or become uncomfortable on hard chairs. Adults' awareness translates into educators being aware that the physical environment is of crucial importance when thinking about teaching adults.

The physical domain is certainly connected with the whole person. How one responds to the body's changes affects the total self. We are whole beings with interconnected systems of development which interact with each other and affect each other, often in dramatic ways.

COGNITIVE DEVELOPMENT

Cognitive development deals with the mental maturation process that allows one to handle more complex and more abstract thinking, ideas, and concepts. It is mental maturation. The noted psychologist Jean Piaget identified four stages of cognitive development, the first two being strictly related to childhood. Stage three, or concrete operations stage, usually begins in late childhood and may continue throughout adulthood. It is related to a person's ability to think only about real, concrete things, not abstract ideas and formal logic. Wadsworth has pointed out that one-half of the adults in the United States do not develop beyond concrete operations.[1]

Adults who fit into Piaget's concrete operations stage are able to do intellectual activities, including logical thought. Their thought, however, is limited to actuality, to concrete problems and issues, to the real, empirically perceived world. Possibility is limited to past concrete experiences or to present and future actualities. Adults who operate on the concrete operational stage cannot mentally apply logic to verbal or hypothetical problems. Abstract ideas, such as the Trinity and other theological formulae, cannot be fully appreciated by adults on the concrete stage. When the concept of God as a Trinity is taught in an abstract fashion to these adults, they either will not understand it; disregard it because it does not make sense to them (it is irrelevant); memorize it but will not be able to understand nor explain it; or try to make sense out of it in a mistaken manner. Concrete thinking adults will seek to make sense out of abstract theological ideas and can unknowingly make up heresy. For example, concrete thinking adults' understanding of the Trinity is usually either three Gods or one God who appears sometimes like the Father, sometimes like the Son, and sometimes like the Holy Spirit. Both of these ideas were declared heretical over 1,600 years ago by leaders at the Council of Nicaea.

Stage four, Piaget's formal operations, is the most mature stage of cognitive or mental development. Adults in this final stage of mental development are able to use logic to deal with all forms of problems. They can do verbal problems, think about hypothetical issues, deal realistically with the future, and think satisfactorily about abstract ideas and concepts. Past, present, and future contemplations are all available to adults on the formal operations stage. At that stage they can think about the possible, not just concrete things.

However, just because adults can function on formal operations does not mean that they necessarily always do so. Adults, like children and youth, function on the highest stage necessary to achieve what they need. They will function with abstract thinking if they find that concrete thinking will not satisfy their needs to adequately deal with an issue, concern, problem, or concept. For example, when adults are faced with an attempt to understand the concept of the Trinity, they must use formal or abstract thinking, and if they are capable of doing so, they will.[2] But much of mental operations for adults do not require formal thought. Therefore, adults use the cognitive development stage necessary to achieve what they need.

Educators need to be aware also that because adults can function in the marketplace with abstract thinking, does not mean they will do so within the church. They need to be encouraged to bring their whole mental development with them to their Bible studies, church experiences, devotional times, personal reflections—all of church life. It is not unusual to find a person who can think well on an abstract stage returning to a concrete way of thinking when it comes to spiritual matters. Such thinking is unfortunate since so much of Scripture is written on an abstract, not concrete level. For example, almost all the New Testament epistles are abstract, not concrete. Christians who either cannot or will not think abstractly miss a significant amount of the Bible's meaning for their lives.

DECISION-MAKING

William Perry[3] has identified nine positions of intellectual and ethical development, based upon his studies with college students. His nine positions are summarized in three major levels that more succinctly and simply provide access to adults' decision-making process (beginning actually with late adolescence). Crucial to Perry's contribution is his focus on the role of authorities in people's thought processes. Perry describes a person's interactions with those authorities and the many conflicting claims of truth by various authorities in their lives. For example, a person's pastor will teach one thing about the Great Tribulation and a respected radio Bible teacher will teach something quite different. To whom will people listen and how will they know which is correct?

Level One (which is composed of Perry's positions one through four) is characterized by people who think that certain authorities have absolute answers to life's issues and problems. People on this level simply need to find the correct authority and be told what to believe and how to act. Life for these people comes in black-and-white perspectives, and with absolutes that can be known absolutely because an authority tells them what is correct. They do not think for themselves but are told what to think. Their theme is "Tell me the answers"!

Eventually, people on Level One begin to realize that there are just too many authorities in life and that even the authorities disagree with each other. They soon tire of trying to determine which authority to heed and which to ignore. Before long they realize that the answers to life come in multiple forms and that authorities disagree among themselves. Whereas people begin this level with a dualistic approach to life, they end it with a realization that life's questions and issues have many different answers and they are not sure where truth resides. This leads them to Level Two.

Level Two consists of Perry's position five. This middle position is characterized by a view of life that is very relativistic. People realize that respected authorities disagree and that life is filled with questions with multiple answers from multiple authorities. People at this stage decide that no one has answers to life's questions and that life is helplessly relativistic. Their basic approach to life is "Don't bother me! I can believe anything I want; it doesn't matter what I believe or what you believe."

Level Two is a rather unstable place to be. People on this stage bounce from one decision to another without a firm grasp of reality. They eventually tire of not knowing who they are, where they are going, and what they should be or want to be in life. They recognize that authorities may disagree and there may be many answers to each of life's questions. They alone must determine one answer and commit themselves to it lest life's meaning be lost in a sea of uncertainty and relativism. This leads to Level Three.

Level Three is characterized by the recognition that commitments need to be made, even though the final answers may not be known and even though authorities may disagree. A person must commit to something or else be adrift in a directionless sea. People on this level make commitments to what they know of reality and what they know of themselves. They know that they "know in part" and "see through a glass darkly" (1 Cor. 13:12, KJV), yet they realize that they must commit themselves to what they know. In so doing, they receive new insight into themselves and others. The theme of people on this level is "Help me. Give me direction and input with which I can come to my own answers. Don't just tell me or ignore me; help me."

MORAL DEVELOPMENT

The key research in the area of moral development was done by Lawrence Kohlberg[4] who identified six stages of moral development. These stages are summarized in three levels. *Level One, Preconventional Moral Development,* consists of stages one and two. People on this level are concerned with the consequences of their actions on themselves. They decide that an act or decision is wrong if they might be (or actually are) punished, or if a certain decision or act does not help them. If, on the other hand, they are not punished or what happens is to their liking, then that is a good, moral decision and/or act. "If it feels good, it must be good" is their theme. People on this level respond to God's gracious invitation of salvation in order to escape hell and to get the "goodies" that God has promised to believers.

Level Two, Conventional Moral Development, comprises stages three and four. On this level people take the perspective of others and the laws of society to determine what is right or wrong, moral and immoral. God is viewed either as their Friend whom they would not want to disappoint or as the Lawgiver who knows best for humanity. They willingly obey Him because of their relationship with Him as Friend or as the just Lawgiver and Judge.

Level Three, Post-conventional Moral Development, consists of stages five and six. This third level goes beyond the egocentric "good feelings" of Level One and beyond the relational aspects of Level Two. It focuses on the meaning of justice: all are treated equally, and laws are created for human beings, not humans for the law. God is viewed by the Christian as the One who reveals His will to us, not so much in concrete particulars, as in principles based on divine justice and righteousness. In Level Three moral development, thinking and actions are embedded in the idea that all must be treated equally. Equality of treatment is justice. Not to do so, from Level Three's perspective, is to be unjust.

Level Four has been identified by this author. Kohlberg's suggestion of a possible seventh stage[5] has been identified as a Fourth Level, seventh stage called the Agape Stage that describes a level of moral development based on more than just legalistic-justice reasoning. This Level Four, stage seven thinking is grounded in God's love for the world and Christ's death for us that demonstrated both God's justice (Kohlberg's Level III) and even more importantly the Divine agape (Dettoni, Level IV, stage seven).[6] People who mature to Level Four of moral development follow Christ, who willingly and agapically gave Himself for all humanity without clinging to His rightful prerogatives of divinity (Phil. 2:6-11) and demonstrated God's complete justice, righteousness, and unlimited and unmerited agapic love.

FAITH DEVELOPMENT

James Fowler is well-known for his work in the area of faith development. He has identified six stages of faith development starting with childhood through mature adulthood.[7] Stages One and Two are primarily childhood stages in which children believe what their parents and other primary caregivers teach them about God. In Stage Three, children and many adults identify with a denomination or associate with a larger group of believers. Thus, many adult evangelicals identify with their denominations, a particular theological seminary's teachings, or a particular form of doctrine: Reformed or Calvinistic, Arminian, Wesleyan, Bible Church movement, Holiness, Vineyard, and so on. The teachings and lifestyle come from this larger pool of faith and practice.

It is not until *Stage Four* that older adolescents (seventeen years of age and older) and adults begin to investigate their faith for themselves. Stage Four begins the process of owning one's faith rather than simply accepting what has been taught to them. People begin to realize that they must have a faith that they have examined and not merely accepted from others. The people in this stage begin to take their faith very seriously. They now face the tensions that first surfaced in Stage Three faith and have now become personal issues. They develop their own theological boundaries. Their faith is now their own and they can defend it intelligently; they have examined it and have committed themselves to it in a new way.

For many adults, Stage Four is a terminal faith. They continue in their owned faith, facing the tensions of self versus community, of subjectivity versus objectivity, of seeking self-fulfillment versus service and ministry to others, and of the relative versus the absolute. But they never resolve these tensions.

Stage Five is definitely a middle-age adult stage. People on this stage are able to see that "all truth is God's truth" and that no denomination or church body has been able to garner all of God's being and truth into its theological formulae. Creeds and confessions are useful, but they point to a depth and height and breadth of God's total being that is beyond the creeds. As the hymn states, "My faith has found a resting place, not in device nor creed; I trust the Everliving One. . . ."

Stage Six is a relatively rare stage that few adults ever achieve. In this stage, older adults are able to see themselves in a deep and joyous communion with the Godhead. Ultimate truth and ultimate reality are known not just through the mediation of Scripture, but also through direct experiences with God. There is a sense of harmony with God and all of creation. Adults on this stage know the world through the people of the world and not just through their own eyes. Yet, while they are focusing on others, they are also able to focus inwardly, finding their values and meaning enriched by losing all to follow the radical claims of the kingdom of God.

PSYCHOSOCIAL DEVELOPMENT/AFFECTIVE DEVELOPMENT

Erik H. Erikson identified "eight ages of man" that all people must experience from infancy through adulthood.[8] The first five ages are identified with infancy, childhood, and adolescence. Erikson calls the Fifth Age *identity versus role confusion.* In this stage, an older adolescent or young adult must answer the deep questions of life: "Who am I? Whose am I? What will I be?" If people at this age do not satisfactorily answer these types of questions, they will not have a healthy self-identity and will be confused as to who they are and what they are to be.

The Sixth Age is entitled *intimacy versus isolation.* Young adults must be able to commit themselves to others in interpersonal relationships and to develop an ongoing ethical strengthening of those relationships. Adults in this age need to find that they can enter into warm, close, and supportive relationships that contribute mutually to one another's development as whole people. In this stage, an adult develops a deep, personal, trusting, and intimate commitment of love to a person of the opposite sex and continues to develop the self in relation to this other in their mutual vocations. Failure to achieve intimacy ends in isolation: to distance oneself from others, to view others as potentially dangerous challengers or interlopers, and to become socially dysfunctional.

The Seventh Age is called *generativity versus stagnation.* As Erikson says, "Generativity, then, is primarily the concern in establishing and guiding the next generation . . . [and includes] productivity and creativity."[9] This stage is the building block for values transmission to the next generation. Failure to achieve generativity will result in stagnation and a false intimacy along with "personal impoverishment." A person who fails at generativity, regardless of how financially successful he or she is, will not be successful in helping give the next generation a solid foundation on which to build their developing lives. The next generation is impoverished and the person in this Seventh Age becomes isolated, detached, and even to a degree reclusive. Such an individual cannot face helping the next generation take charge and mourns his or her own declining years.

Erikson's *Eighth Age* is called *ego integrity versus despair.* In this stage, older adults evaluate their lives and conclude that they have lived a life of integrity, that they have been who they should be, and that their relationships were the right ones. They can in one sense state that their lives have been "good" and that they are pleased with them, in spite of the negatives that have occurred along the way, and that they are willing to defend that life to others. The absence of ego integrity is despair. Death looms as a great fear: "time is now short, too short for the attempt to start another life and to try out alternate roads to integrity."[10]

PSYCHOLOGICAL-SPIRITUAL DEVELOPMENT

The above developmental thinkers and researchers have helped us to obtain a picture of continuous development throughout the human life span. Human beings enter this world and begin to learn, change, grow, and develop; and they continue to do so throughout their lifetimes. Not to do so is a special disease, a pathology, a sickness that causes stunting of growth.

One must *not* equate normal human psychological growth and development with spiritual growth and Christlike maturity in all things. We must recall that "Jesus grew in wisdom and stature, and in favor with God and men" (Luke 2:52). He continued to become mature as He grew. His was a holistic person's growth—growth and development in all aspects of His being. However, because people are growing older does not mean that they are becoming more mature. Nor is being able to handle complex ideas or discuss the Bible and theology more knowledgeably an indication of becoming more like Christ. Achieving higher stages of cognitive, moral, and faith development does not equate one-to-one with Christlikeness.

Higher stages of human development are necessary to understand more of God's Word, to know better where to apply it to the increasingly complex arenas of one's life, and to know how to relate more adequately to both God and others. People who are concrete thinkers will not be able to truly understand all that the Bible reveals about God's character because they are limited to God's concrete expressions. They will miss much of the riches of additional characteristics of God such as His holiness, sovereignty, and eternality.

Adults who think on the abstract stage in their vocation will not necessarily do so in the spiritual arena. Pastors and other teachers should encourage a more mature way of thinking not merely by providing answers to people's questions, but by helping people think for themselves and discover that we are all priests in the household of God (1 Peter 2:9). The role of teachers in the church is to encourage and facilitate development and understanding from less mature to more mature.

This is not to say, however, that people who have not matured to higher stages are less valuable. They are just not as mature and should be continually helped to "become mature, attaining to the whole measure of the fullness of Christ . . . [so that they] will in all things grow up into Him who is the Head" (Eph. 4:13, 15).

Spiritual development, or maturing more and more into Christ's likeness, is related to normal human development. Maturing in cognitive, moral, and faith development domains, one is able to understand more of the depths, heights, and breadths of the vastness of the Triune Godhead. Higher stages of adult psychological development allow for more adequate understanding and integration of divine revelation into one's being and behavior. We will never become fully mature until our ultimate transformation in glory. However, we continue to need to learn, grow, and develop. Our standard and goal is completeness and maturity as found in Christ.

IMPLICATIONS OF ADULT DEVELOPMENT

Even a cursory reading of the above material on human development gives a picture of an ever-active adult who pursues knowledge, wisdom, and growth. Adults continue to learn in all areas of their lives, especially in those areas in which they have interest. As Malcolm Knowles[11] has pointed out, adults in a learning environment are characterized by the following:

1. They are self-directed. They want and need to be in charge of their own lives, although they may have some dependency needs in various situations. Ultimately, however, they want to make their own decisions based on self-directedness.
2. Adults have a growing "reservoir of experience" which is the basis of their continued learning. They bring to learning environments a large inventory of relevant experiences. As a result, they learn more effectively through experiences than through traditional schooling, namely, lectures, tests, and recitations.
3. People learn best when they want to and they do this when what is to be learned is related to their current life situations. When adults sense a need to learn, they will do it!
4. Application to life is a crucial and critical factor in the learning experience. Adults, regardless of their stages of human development, tend to be concerned for the usefulness of what they are about to learn.

There is a fifth item—not directly mentioned by Knowles—that is a direct implication from our examination of adult psychological development. Adults can only learn what is on their level, or stages or ages of development. If an adult functions on the concrete cognitive development stage, is concerned with getting answers from authorities, makes moral decisions based on "what is good for me," and is indoctrinated by his or her church or denomination, then that person will not be able to make much sense out of more mature teaching and learning experiences. On the other hand, more mature adults will be able to make sense out of more complex learning experiences.

The teacher is responsible to provide learning experiences that are fit for the learners. Both 1 Corinthians 3:1-9 and Hebrews 5:11-14 suggest that some biblical teaching is "too mature" for some people and that the wise and effective teacher knows his or her learners sufficiently to give "milk" or "meat," depending on the psychological and spiritual development of the learners.

What is the end of all this? Teachers of adults need to know not only God's Word but also the ones with whom we study and whom we teach. The psychology of adult development helps us know learners' ways of making sense out of their experiences. With this knowledge, we who teach can construct meaningful learning experiences that engage adult learners on their levels of learning. We can involve them in the experiences of learning that enable them to continue to learn, grow, and develop more and more into the full maturity of Christ.

WHAT IS AN ADULT?

Adults are human beings who continue to grow, mature, and develop throughout their lifetimes. They may have completed their physical development, but this only indicates that they now know their physical abilities and limitations well. In all other areas, adults continue to develop. Not to develop is to have a special disease.

Adult learners may and should continue to develop in cognitive areas as they mature in their ability to think conceptually and not just concretely. They are able to make decisions based not just on some authority's say-so but upon their own developmental ability to commit themselves to what is best for them. They are able to mature from egocentric moral judgments and behaviors to heteronomic and eventually principled and even agapic reasoning. Their faith development matures from believing just what their local churches teach, to owning their own faith for themselves and continually integrating that faith in all areas of their lives. They have answered each of the major issues of life successfully and continue to integrate what they were into what they are becoming under the lordship of Jesus Christ and within God's sovereign will.

In summary, adults become increasingly more balanced, equilibrated persons who integrate more and more of their experiences, thinking, actions, and ways of being into a consistent whole that can be classified as an always maturing adult.

The task before church educators is to help, facilitate, encourage, and even urge adults to keep on developing in all the aspects of their lives. We who teach must be careful not to allow adult learners to become comfortable with easy answers, simple responses to complex issues, or to live an unexamined and unowned life. The commitment of adult educators needs to be the same as that of the Apostle Paul: "For you know that we dealt with each of you as a father deals with his own children, encouraging, comforting and urging you to live lives worthy of God, who calls you into His kingdom and glory" (1 Thes. 2:11).

Notes

1. Barry J. Wadsworth, *Piaget's Theory of Cognitive and Affective Development*, 4th ed. (New York: Longmans, 1989), 115.
2. For a more detailed description of Piaget's four stages, see Wadsworth, *Piaget's Theory.*
3. William C. Perry, Jr., *Forms of Intellectual and Ethical Development in the College Years* (New York: Holt, Rinehart, and Winston), 1970.
4. See Lawrence Kohlberg, *The Philosophy of Moral Development* (San Francisco: Harper and Row, 1981), vol. 1 and *The Psychology of Moral Development* (Harper and Row, 1984), vol. 2 of *Essays on Moral Development.*
5. Lawrence Kohlberg with Clark Power, "Moral Development, Religious Thinking, and the Question of a Seventh Stage," in Lawrence Kohlberg, *The Philosophy of Moral Development*, vol. 1 of *Essays On Moral Development* (San Francisco: Harper and Row, 1981), 311–72.
6. See Romans 3:21-26; 5:6-8. Also see John M. Dettoni, "Agape: Beyond Justice to Agape" (Unpublished paper in Syllabus for Ecology of Faith Development, San Clemente, Calif., 1990), 89–108.
7. James Fowler, *Stages of Faith* (San Francisco: Harper and Row, 1981).
8. Erik H. Erikson, *Childhood and Society*, 2nd ed. (New York: W.W. Norton, 1953), 247–74.
9. Ibid., 267.
10. Ibid., 269.
11. Malcolm S. Knowles, *The Modern Practice of Adult Education: From*

Pedagogy to Andragogy, rev. ed. (Chicago: Follett, 1980), 43–44, as well as throughout this book.

For Further Reading

Cross, K. Patricia. *Adults as Learners.* San Francisco: Jossey-Bass, 1981.

Dykstra, Craig and Sharon Parks, eds. *Faith Development and Fowler.* Birmingham, Ala.: Religious Education Press, 1986.

Fowler, James W. *Becoming Adult, Becoming Christian.* San Francisco: Harper and Row, 1984.

Gross, Ronald, ed. *Invitation to Lifelong Learning.* Chicago: Follett, 1982.

Kidd, J.R. *How Adults Learn,* rev. ed. Chicago: Follett, 1973.

Knowles, Malcolm. *Andragogy in Action.* San Francisco: Jossey-Bass, 1984.

Long, Huey B. *Adult Learning: Research and Practice.* New York: Cambridge, The Adult Education Company, 1983.

Sell, Charles M. *Transitions Through Adult Life.* Grand Rapids: Zondervan, 1991.

Wilhoit, Jim. *Christian Education and the Search for Meaning,* 2nd ed. Grand Rapids: Baker, 1991.

Wlodkowski, Raymond J. *Enhancing Adult Motivation to Learn.* San Francisco: Jossey-Bass, 1985.

SIX
CONTRIBUTIONS OF MALCOLM KNOWLES

Malcolm S. Knowles

I feel a need to open this chapter with a confession; I wish someone else had been asked to write it. He or she would be able to be more objective about my contributions to Christian adult education than I can be. But more importantly, she or he would be in a position to evaluate those contributions. Then I would be more interested. As it is, I can be only descriptive. Come to think of it, I am now interested in seeing if I can be descriptive without being dull. Here goes!

TRAINING AND EXPERIENCE

I didn't start out to be an adult educator. I prepared in my undergraduate studies at Harvard, and one semester of graduate studies at the Fletcher School of Law and Diplomacy at Tufts University, to be a diplomat. I passed my Foreign Service exam in 1935 and was notified by the State Department that they were filling only the most urgent vacancies at that time (the depth of the Great Depression) and only with people who had passed the exam in 1932—so there would be at least a three-year wait. Well, on August 20, 1935, I had acquired a wife, and needed a job.

NATIONAL YOUTH ADMINISTRATION

Happily, there appeared in the *Boston Globe* within a few days an article announcing the establishment by the Works Progress Administration of a new program for unemployed youth, the National Youth Administration. The program consisted of half-time work to provide some income and half-time study to improve the employability of the youth. I quickly called the Massachusetts State Director for an appointment and, because of some experience I had gained as a volunteer at Harvard leading a youth group in a settlement house in South Boston, I got the job of Training Director in the state office of the NYA.

Although I thought of it as a "holding job," I soon fell in love with the work—doing a needs survey to find out what skills employers looked for in new workers; organizing a schedule of classes; hiring instructors; getting out promotional materials; and managing the program. Fortunately, my supervisor in the national office was Eduard C. Lindeman, one of the pioneer adult educators in the country. And so I soon learned that my work was adult education. When the State Department notified me in 1938 of vacancies open in the Foreign Service, I wired right back that I no longer had interest; I had changed career plans—I was now an adult educator.

In 1926, Lindeman had written *The Meaning of Adult Education* and he gave me a copy of that book to read. This was the first book about adult education I had seen and it really excited me; in fact, I reread it about every year or two now as a source of inspiration. It is really quite remarkable that in 1926 one could be writing things about adult learners and adult learning that we only now discover are true. And he did it just from intuition and experience.

During the five years I held that job I began to sense that the young adults in our classes were a different breed from the students I had known in high school and college. Before registering in a class, they wanted to know how it would help them get a job and succeed in it. I noticed that the classes in which the instructors lectured hours on end had a high dropout rate, whereas those in which the instructors engaged the students in participatory activities were flooded with registrations. In retrospect, I now realize that the groundwork being laid at that time would later blossom into my andragogical model of adult learning.

BOSTON YMCA

In 1940 the Boston YMCA invited me to come over and develop its adult education program. During my four years there (and later in the YMCAs of Detroit and Chicago) I was challenged to adapt my notions about adult learning to the setting of Christian adult education. It wasn't until I went to the Chicago YMCA in 1946 and enrolled in the graduate adult education program at the University of Chicago (with Cyril Houle as my mentor) that I began formal study of adult education as a professional field.

During my time with the YMCA, I ran into the same kind of experience that I had with the NYA—hiring instructors who proved to be effective and others who didn't. I observed that the effective teachers tended to be less formal. I started making notes and collecting material about what they did; the techniques they used; the relationships they established. My first book, published in 1950, was titled *Informal Adult Education.* It describes the informal relationship I thought to be critical at that point. Later I began to grasp what it really means for individuals to take responsibility for their own learning. At that point I began formalizing my concepts of andragogy.

GEORGE WILLIAMS COLLEGE

Then came "the day I changed from teacher to facilitator." That day, and I can nail it down to a particular day, resulted from a part-time teaching experience at George Williams College in Boston. The first time they asked me to teach the class, I taught as I had been taught—lecture notes, quizzes, examinations. I was really quite pleased with how well I controlled the students. They behaved well; they did their homework; they wrote their quizzes and term papers; I really felt I must be a good teacher.

Then the following semester I had my first course with Carl Rogers. He was totally low-key and non-directive. I have never done so much reading for a course in my life as I did the week after that first class. I went to the library and checked out all the books and articles Rogers had written because I wanted to find out all about him. That caused me to think. When I am "turned on" to something, when my curiosity is aroused, when I am given responsibility for my own learning, then I put much more energy into learning than when I simply do what other people tell me.

George Williams asked me to teach the course a second time. On the opening day I decided to apply the principles Carl Rogers used and give the responsibility to learners. On the opening day, I had them organize teams and develop learning plans, identifying what each person wanted to learn, how she would learn it, and how he would demonstrate that he learned it. The students got so excited and energetic that they spent a lot more time working in that course than the previous year. That day I changed from teacher to facilitator.

After I received my Ph.D. in 1960, I went to Boston University as a professor of adult education, and then to North Carolina State University in 1974, from which I retired in 1979. I strongly believe that the nature of my contribution to the field has been greatly influenced by over ten years experience on the job before starting my formal training. My perspective in all my writing, teaching, and workshops has been that of a practitioner.

UNDERSTANDING LEARNING THEORY

Behavioristic Model

From the point of view of learning theory I see three models of man from which learning theories have been derived. The earliest saw man as machine—the mechanistic or ***behaviorist*** model which assumed that humans function the way machines do. In other words, one injects an input of fuel or stimulus, controls the way it is processed, and then predetermines the output. The earliest theorists—Pavlov, Thorndike, and Skinner—all operated from this model, assuming that learning consisted of a programmer determining what behavior should be. For the behaviorist, appropriate educational strategies include teaching machines, programmed instruction, and behavioral modification.

Cognitive Model

The next model (in terms of time of development) is what I call the *cognitive* model. It operates from a perception of man as brain, based upon the notion that the one thing that differentiates humans from other animals is a brain capable of critical thinking and problem-solving. Therefore, education purposes to develop that brain to think critically and instruction becomes the appropriate educational strategy.

Organismic Model

The third model I think of as *organismic.* Each individual has her own built-in GNA, unique potential, and no two human beings are the same. Therefore, the purpose of education is to develop each individual to his unique potential and the most effective strategy for doing this becomes self-directed learning or inquiry. I believe each of these models describes part of our reality. In some circumstances we, indeed, do behave like machines. When I learned to type using the touch system, I really just extended myself into the machine. It seemed appropriate that behaviorist or mechanistic strategies be used to teach my fingers to hit the right keys. Much of life is concerned with solving problems and thinking critically so the cognitive theorists help us with that reality. But most learning, and certainly most significant learning, seems far more complex than either of those models takes into account. Therefore, I think most learning is appropriately self-directed.

Nature of the Learner

One more thought. Christian educators give a good bit of attention to the moral/spiritual nature of the learner. As an educator and psychologist, I agree with Carl Rogers and Abraham Maslow that every individual strives to become what he is capable of becoming. Maslow calls it self-actualization; Rogers calls it self-fulfillment. Human beings make choices which move them in the direction of these ends.

THE ANDRAGOGICAL MODEL AND CHRISTIAN ADULT EDUCATION

The articles annotated in Appendix B suggest that the andragogical model of adult learning provides guidelines for gearing Christian adult education toward the development of "mature Christian persons" in contrast to "dependent Christian persons." I presented this theme succinctly in Lawrence Little's *Wider Horizons in Christian Adult Education:*

Possible Directions of Christian Maturation

From (The Pedagogical Model)	*Toward* (The Andragogical Model)
Dependence on others for religious ideas	Ability to identify and think about religious issues for one's self

Ignorance of the traditions and literature of the Christian church	Informed understanding of the traditions and literature of the Christian church
Passive conformity to prevailing patterns of behavior of church members	Creative questing for continuously more effective ways to to translate Christian ideals into behavior
Narrow interest in religious matters	Constantly expanding interest in religion
Selfish concern for personal problems	Altrusic concern for the welfare of others
Vague definition of personal value system	Clear and integrated perception of personal value system
Self-righteousness about state of personal religious development	Humility about state of perssonal religious development
Fragmentary application of Christian ideals to life	Total application of Christian ideals to life

My major contribution to both general adult education and Christian adult education is no doubt my andragogical model of adult learning, summarized in the chart on page 97.

The body of theory and practice on which teacher-directed learning is based often acquires the label "pedagogy," from the Greek work *paid* (meaning child) and *agogus* (meaning guide or leader)—thus being defined as the art and science of teaching children.

The body of theory and practice on which we base self-directed learning has been labeled "andragogy," from the Greek word *aner* (meaning adult)—thus being defined as the art and science of helping adults (maturing human beings) learn.

These two models do not represent bad/good or child/adult dichotomies, but rather a continuum of assumptions to be checked out in terms of their rightness for particular learners in particular situations. If a pedagogical assumption seems realistic

ASSUMPTIONS		
About	Pedagogical	Andragogical
Concept of the learner	Dependent personality	Increasingly self-directing
Role of learner's experience	To be built on more than used as a resource	A rich resource for learning by self and others
Readiness to learn	Uniform by age-level & curriculum	Develops from life tasks & problems
Orientation to learning	Subject-centered	Task- or problem-centered
Motivation	By external rewards and punishment	By internal incentives, curiosity

PROCESS ELEMENTS		
Elements	Pedagogical	Andragogical
Climate	Tense, low trust, formal, cold, aloof, authority-oriented, competitive, judgmental	Relaxed, trusting, Mutually respectful, informal, warm, collaborative, supportive
Planning	Primarily by teacher	Mutually by learners and facilitator
Diagnosis of needs	Primarily by teacher	By mutual assessment
Setting of objectives	Primarily by teacher	By mutual negotiation
Designing learning plans	Teachers' content plans Course syllabus Logical sequence	Learning contracts Learning projects Sequenced by readiness
Learning activities	Transmittal techniques Assigned readings	Inquiry projects Independent study Experiential techniques
Evaluation	By teacher Norm-referenced (on a curve) With grades	By learner-collected evidence validated by peers, facilitators, experts Criterion-referenced

Figure 6.1

for a particular situation, then pedagogical strategies are appropriate. For example, if a learner enters a totally strange content area, he or she will be dependent on a teacher until enough content has been acquired to enable self-directed inquiry to begin.

GROWTH AND CHANGE IN ANDRAGOGICAL PROCESS

When I first started prescribing the andragogical model in 1968, I saw them as two opposite models. Between 1970 and 1980 when I revised *The Modern Practice of Adult Education,* more and more teachers in elementary and secondary schools had discovered the andragogical model and started experimenting with it. They reported to me that in many situations learning was much more effective when they used the andragogical model. Also, some teachers of adults reported circumstances in which adults needed pedagogical structure, at least to start off with.

PARALLEL ASSUMPTIONS

The subtitle of my 1970 edition of *Modern Practice* was "Pedagogy versus Andragogy." In the 1980 revision the subtitle became "From Pedagogy to Andragogy." Now I see two parallel sets of assumptions to be checked out regarding a given learner in a given situation. One problem I have run into is the tendency on the part of some "disciples" to see the andragogical model as absolute and to assume that they have to be loyal to it and can't deviate from it. That same problem seems to plague those who champion the pedagogical model. In fact, our academic system tends to penalize people who aren't faithful to the pedagogical model. But I see the andragogical model to be a system of ideas that incorporates the assumptions of pedagogy rather than ideology that one must practice purely.

SELF-DIRECTED LEARNING

Some consider all this progression; I see it as situational. The reason I don't see it as progressive is that we all start out as self-directed learners. We learn to find the nipple, to crawl, and to walk. And we learn to talk on our own. Nobody taught any of us how to talk our first language. And we learn how to use our leisure time. Even in preschool and kindergarten the mode is self-directed learning.

But then we go into first grade and all of a sudden get into a lock-step, predetermined, progressive curriculum. As our studies progress in difficulty, we become dependent personalities. The teachers tell us what to do, how to do it, when to do it, and if we have done it. Yet good evidence exists that even first-graders can take a lot more responsibility for their own learning than traditional pedagogical models have shown. In fact, I believe that the primary learning in the early school years should be learning how to learn, to develop the skills of inquiry. The content/knowledge can be more appropriately gained as one acquires skills in self-directed learning.

CRITICAL VARIABLES IN MODEL CHOICE

The critical factor in choice of model is *the degree of familiarity and previous experience with the content to be learned.* If I enrolled tomorrow in a course in the mathematics of nuclear physics, I would need a didactic instructor to teach me what the content was all about, what language that particular specialty used, and where I could find resources. I would need such instruction, however, only until I had become familiar enough with the content territory to start taking some initiative on my own.

I think also if I wanted to learn to operate a totally new machine, one that I had never seen before, I would need to have someone show me all about it. But, once I had mastered the skill, I would be increasingly able to start taking the initiative on my own, using the machine in ways I had not been taught, and exploring areas for which I no longer needed a teacher.

Perhaps the most critical variable in andragogy is the level of the learner's skill in taking responsibility for his or her own learning. For this reason I urge people who want to experiment with the andragogical model to build into their program design a "front end." They must first expose the learner to the concept or notion of self-directed learning as contrasted with dependent didactic learning, and to practice some of the skills involved—self-diagnosis, how to identify resources, how to plan a learning project.

I cannot think of any situation in which a large lecture hall group is any longer appropriate. Before Gutenberg that was probably needed, but today we can get everything in other ways (e.g., reading, multimedia presentations) more efficiently than we can get them in a lecture. I also think that learning is a social activity; we learn better when we interact with other people. Therefore, the small group format or caring tutorial kind of relationship offers the ideal.

I perceive that motivation of learners is my responsibility, not theirs. I discount the idea of a genetically low-motivated learner. Motivation to learn comes from arousing in the learner a perception of the benefits from learning something, or the negative consequences of not learning it. This is where the teacher shoulders a heavy responsibility to make a good case for why certain content will be beneficial and to provide some actual hands-on experiences that will bring this home to people.

APPENDIX A

Annotated Bibliography—Books

Informal Adult Education. New York: Association Press, 1950. My first book (a revision of my master's thesis) in which I describe what I perceived to be the most innovative and successful practices in organizing and managing programs and teaching adults in a variety of nonacademic settings.

Teaching Adults in Informal Courses. New York: Association Press, 1954. A small paperback book focusing on innovative teaching methods.

How to Develop Better Leaders, Hulda Knowles, coauthor. New York: Association Press, 1955. A paperback focusing on leadership training.

Introduction to Group Dynamics, Hulda Knowles, coauthor. New York: Association Press, 1959; rev. ed., New York: Cambridge, 1972. A layperson's guide to the research literature on group dynamics.

Handbook of Adult Education in the United States, ed. Chicago: Adult Education Association of the U.S.A., 1960. A collection of essays giving an overview of the thinking about the types of programs in adult education at that time.

The Adult Education Movement in the United States. New York: Holt, Rinehart, and Winston, 1962; rev. ed., Huntington, N.Y.: Krieger, 1977. An extension of my doctoral dissertation, giving a historical perspective on the development of adult education in this country.

Higher Adult Education in the United States. Washington: American Council of Education, 1969. A descriptive analysis of adult and continuing education programs in colleges and universities.

The Modern Practice of Adult Education. New York: Cambridge, 1970; rev. ed., 1980. My first full presentation of the andragogical model of adult learning and its implications for practice.

The Adult Learner: A Neglected Species. Houston: Gulf, 1973; 2nd ed., 1978; 3rd ed., 1984; 4th ed., 1990. An overview of research findings regarding adult learning and their implications for practice.

Self-Directed Learning: A Guide for Learners and Teachers. New York: Cambridge, 1975. Suggested techniques for adults on how to be self-directed learners and for teachers on how to facilitate self-directed adult learning.

Andragogy in Action. San Francisco: Jossey-Bass, 1984. A collection of essays describing how the andragogical model of adult learning is being applied in educational institutions, business and industry, religious institutions, government agencies, and voluntary organizations.

Using Learning Contracts. San Francisco: Jossey-Bass, 1986. A collection of essays describing how contract learning is being implemented in a variety of settings.

The Making of An Adult Educator. San Francisco: Jossey-Bass, 1989. My "autobiographical journey" through a career in adult education greatly expands the brief overview of this chapter.

APPENDIX B

Selected Articles By Malcolm Knowles

"Adults Are Learning." *Crossroads* (Presbyterian), October-December 1950.

"Techniques of Constructive Controversy." *Christian Register* (Universalist-Unitarian), March 1951.

"Psychology, Religion, and Life." *St. Louis Unitarian*, January 1952.

"Role Playing at Home." *Presbyterian Survey*, May 1954.

"Keep Your Discussion on the Track." *Methodist Adult Teacher*, August 1956.

"The Coming of Age of Adult Education in America." *National Catholic Education Association Bulletin*, August 1957.

"Participation—A Golden Key to Learning." *Westminster Adult Leader* (Methodist), January–March 1958.

"Methods for Helping Adults Learn," *International Journal of Religious Education*, May 1959.

"Use Effective Methods with Adults," *Presbyterian Action*, August 1959.

"The Church Can Help Adults Learn," *The Church School* (Methodist), October 1959.

"The Effects of Community Influences on Adult Life." In *The Future Course of Christian Adult Education*, edited by Lawrence C. Little. Pittsburgh: University of Pittsburgh Press, 1959.

"Leisure." In *Westminster Dictionary of Christian Education*. Philadelphia: Westminster Press, 1962.

"A Hard Look at Christian Adult Education," review of the book by John Fry. *Adult Leadership,* March 1962.

"A Theory of Christian Adult Education Methodology." In *Wider Horizons in Christian Adult Education,* edited by Lawrence C. Little, Pittsburgh: University of Pittsburgh Press, 1962.

"Andragogy, Not Pedagogy," *The Methodist Woman,* October 1968.

"Assumptions of Adult Learning: Andragogy Not Pedagogy," *The Southern Baptist Educator,* June 1973.

"The Growth of Adult Secular Education and Its Thirty-Five Year Development," interview with Wayne Lindecker. *The Church School* (Methodist), October 1976.

"Adult Learning Processes: Pedagogy and Andragogy," *Religious Education,* March/April 1977.

"An Adult Educator's Reflections on Faith Development in the Adult Life Cycle." In *Faith Development in the Adult Life Cycle,* edited by Kenneth Stokes. New York: William H. Sadlier, 1982.

"A Theory of Christian Adult Education Methodology." In *Christian Adulthood: Catechetical Resources*. Washington, D.C.: United States Catholic Conference, 1982.

SEVEN

LEARNING FROM GENDER DIFFERENCES

Catherine M. Stonehouse

The label on my favorite sweatshirt reads, "ONE SIZE." The designers believed one size would fit everyone. Much adult Christian education seems to presume one size, or one form, will fit all. Such assumptions cause us to go blithely on our way, not noticing differences, special needs, or better ways of doing things.

Carol Gilligan, author of *In a Different Voice,* believes we have ignored the differences between men and women far too long. She observes that we are accustomed to seeing life through men's eyes. In research, when women responded differently from men, their perspective was often ignored and the standards of wholeness or maturity based on the male responses.[1]

But in the past fifteen years women's development has been a major focus of research and of advances in developmental understandings. The research done with women seems to be opening new insights into the development of both genders.

These new understandings, I believe, are important for adult Christian education. As leaders in the church, we desire to understand our people as fully as possible so that we can most effectively lead them toward faith and maturity. Developmentalists study God's creation and human beings, directly and in depth. In their work we can find insights into the Creator's design for learning and growth. These insights do not stand alone for the Christian educator. We bring them under the evaluation of biblical perspectives and combine them with theological understandings to guide us in ministry.

This chapter will present a summary of findings from the work of Carol Gilligan on moral development, Mary Field Belenky et al.

on women's ways of knowing, and Robert Kegan on the development of self. Then we will look at what is essential if the church is to be a healthy place for the growth and becoming of both women and men.

THE VOICES OF WOMEN

Working on moral development research as a colleague with Lawrence Kohlberg, Carol Gilligan began to hear certain themes in the responses of girls and women as they wrestled with moral dilemmas. They seemed to focus on issues which men and boys did not consider. Intrigued by these differences, she set out to study their moral reasoning.

Two significant differences wove through the responses Gilligan heard. First, women described themselves developing in the context of relationships. Men, however, talked about increasing separation and autonomy. Secondly, women's understanding of morality seemed rooted in a sense of responsibility to care for persons and through that caring to maintain relationships.[2] The men in Kohlberg's research had focused on a morality of fairness and justice expressed in concerns about rights and rules.

Although important differences exist in the development of men and women, the differences are not total. Their paths of moral development also share many similarities. They both begin with a self-centered perspective and move on to a perspective which values goodness, a goodness that is defined by others. The third perspective values truth, a truth known within the person, not simply laid on from without.[3] But the significant differences found along those developmental paths need to be better understood. We turn now to examine in more detail Gilligan's findings on how women understand the self and morality.

Perspective I

How would you describe yourself to yourself? Gilligan and her colleagues asked this question in interviews they conducted. Young girls or women stunted in development have difficulty answering the question. Their perspective on the self is undefined. They have not thought or talked about who they are.

Even though they cannot reflect on themselves, the focus of their caring is on self with little if any sense of responsibility for others. The transition to Perspective II occurs as the maturing child begins to see her approach to life as selfish and desires to take responsibility for others. Women understand the movement from childhood to adulthood as a move from selfishness to responsibility.[4]

Perspective II

Society's view of what one ought to be strongly influences the Perspective II understanding of self. As girls become aware of the consequences of behaviors, they realize others are often hurt by actions which consider only the self. They don't want to be selfish, hurtful people. They want to be good women. And society gives them the definition of goodness, a woman who cares unselfishly for others.

Women accept the expectation that they should be giving themselves on behalf of others. Belenky and her colleagues found that "women typically approach adulthood with the understanding that the care and empowerment of others is central to their life's work."[5] Taking care of others so that they are protected from being hurt is the morally right thing for a woman to do.

When women see themselves as persons who care, their self-worth is enhanced. As they care for others they are doing the right thing. They are being good women and they value goodness. But their sense of worth rests on the approval of the outside voices who have defined goodness.[6] If they are unable to please those they care for or are unable to meet society's standards for caring, their sense of worth is devastated.

In this phase of their development, women feel comfortable caring for their own interests only if doing so also contributes to the well-being of others.[7] If personal needs cannot be met while meeting the needs of family or friends, the "good" woman will sacrifice her needs. Self-sacrifice is virtuous.

But women become increasingly aware of an inner voice, the voice of a self with unmet needs—needs that differ from those she serves. They recognize a self who has a perspective worth listening to, which ought to be considered when making decisions. They realize all is not well. Feeling forced into self-sacrifice, resentment builds.[8] Women find themselves in a terrible bind. Choosing to do the "selfish" thing at the expense of caring for others generates a great sense of guilt resulting often in anger with the self. But the resentment that builds through forced self-sacrifice explodes in anger, damaging the persons one cares for and valued relationships. If the anger does not explode, it turns inward on the self.

Inward focused anger which is not dealt with becomes depression. This too is hurtful to others as well as the self.

Women must discover their right to consider themselves when making responsible choices. With this discovery they begin to view life and morality from Perspective III.

Perspective III

The woman now knows herself, not just in terms of how others see her, but through reflection on the inner self. She is aware of her own needs, judgments, and beliefs. Through attention to inner and outer voices in Perspective III, women become aware that the self and others are interdependent.[9] One cannot truly care for others without caring for the self and vice versa. Now caring is not motivated by a desire to please others but a commitment to help a growing number of persons, including the self, become what they were meant to be.[10] The responsibility is no longer an "ought" laid on her by society but a self-chosen ethic of care.[11]

Resolving moral conflict calls for an honest assessment of the needs of all involved. If I am to act responsibly, I must be honest about my inner feelings and motives. I need to know the real feelings, needs, and motives of others. Honesty is highly valued in Perspective III.[12]

The knowing necessary for making right decisions comes through open honest communication. For the girls studied by Gilligan and her colleagues, fairness and listening were bound together. Listening was "a profoundly moral phenomenon."[13] I am morally bound to listen to your point of view before making a decision. And if you are fair, you will listen to my side of the story before making a decision that impacts me. Taking time to really listen and communicate is a must in the morality of care.

Voices in Harmony

Gilligan describes the music of morality as a fugue with two themes, justice and care. At times the fugue played by a person may sound only one theme, either justice or care. At other times both themes can be heard but one is predominant. Research indicates that in the moral music of men the theme of justice tends to be the singular or at least the predominant theme.

Women tend to play the theme of care as their predominant melody. Moral maturity for women and men is marked by the harmonious orchestration of both justice and care.[14] The life of the community will be served best when men and women sing in harmony the moral songs they know best.

WOMEN'S WAYS OF KNOWING

What are the best sources of knowledge? How should information be processed to come to the most satisfactory understandings? Answers to these questions change as one develops, and then may differ for men and women. Insights into these changes and differences are presented in Women's Ways of Knowing. Belenky and her colleagues identified five kinds of knowers in the women they studied: silent women, knowers of received knowledge, subjective knowledge, procedural knowledge, and constructive knowledge.

Silent Women

Severely abused or deprived women are often silent. Words were used on them as weapons, expressions of anger, to diminish them. These women learned that when they tried to use words they incurred wrath and punishment.[15] In their eyes women are powerless and unable to think for themselves. They must depend on authorities for guidance, authorities who never explain why, but simply order and expect obedience.[16] These women do not learn by listening to words. They plead, "show me."[17]

Received Knowledge

Received knowers listen to the voices of others. All knowledge, even knowledge about the self, is received from others. Authorities are the source of truth. Learning is understood as receiving information from authorities and is best done through listening.[18]

Women reflecting this way of knowing believe they are capable of receiving knowledge from authorities and even passing it on to others. But they do not perceive they have anything of their own to offer. Friendships are often critical for breaking women out of this way of thinking. As they support and care for one another and share from their experiences, they discover an inner wisdom that is helpful.[19] This discovery launches a major transition in the woman's way of knowing.

Subjective Knowledge

Subjective knowers listen to the inner voice. They become their own authority. Truth and knowledge are perceived as personal and private, subjectively known through intuition. Only from the inner voice can one know for sure what is right. Each person can therefore know what is right only for him or herself. If this is true, all opinions are of equal value. The subjective knower has one evaluative tool for judging between opinions. These women believe that firsthand experience is the only reliable source of knowledge. They question opinions not backed by firsthand experience.[20]

Subjective knowers learn best through observing themselves and others in the school of experience and relationships. Subjective knowers become skilled in learning from paying attention to their own voice, the details of everyday life situations, and the experiences of those with whom they have connections.[21]

Sooner or later the subjective way of knowing comes into question. Respected authorities may question its adequacy. Or, the woman herself may sense the need for better procedures in evaluating opinions.

Procedural Knowledge

Procedural knowledge is listening to reason. The knower learns and applies objective procedures for obtaining and communicating knowledge.

When listening to the reasoning of women, researchers heard responses that matched the reasoning described by William Perry from his research with Harvard students, mainly men. But many women used a different form of reasoning. Gilligan, Belenky, and their colleagues refer to these two ways of thinking as separate and connected knowing. Research indicates that the way of knowing is not gender specific but it may be gender related. More men seem to be separate knowers and more women connected knowers. Although persons are not limited to one mode of thinking, they do prefer one over the other.[22]

Separate knowers value impersonal, analytical, objective procedures for establishing what is true. They diligently strive to keep personal feelings out of the process. Doubting is the game of the separate knower. Everything is doubted until its truth can be proven. They look for what is wrong in an argument rather than for what is right.[23]

Connected knowers build on their belief that experience yields the most trustworthy knowledge. They realize, however, that knowledge from limited personal experience is not sufficient. They seek for procedures enabling them to learn from the experience of others. Empathy is a highly valued quality. Believing is the game connected knowers play. The purpose of listening is more for understanding than critique. They assume something is true until it is proven false and listen for ideas they can accept, pushing aside what does not ring true.[24]

Many women, especially educated professionals, learn to use the procedures of separate knowing very well. For some it is their preferred mode. But there is a tendency among women to become discontent with separate knowing. Even those who highly value the objective see that the subjective, connected perspective must also be considered.[25]

Constructive Knowledge

Constructive knowing integrates the inner and the outer voices, the objective and the personal. Each person's knowledge is constructed by integrating the voices. The knower is an important part of what is known and cannot be separated from the knowing.

Constructive knowing will also endeavor to integrate abstract truth and experiential knowledge. The experiential context does make a difference in the way abstract truth should be applied. And personal, experiential learning must stand the critique of objective principles.[26]

A preferred way of constructivist learning is through "really talking." Participants in the process create an environment which encourages mutual sharing of even embryonic ideas and enhances their growth. No one tries to dominate or force personal ideas. Careful listening and questioning for the purpose of understanding are important learning skills.[27] Ideally, integrated knowing would engage both men and women in "really talking."

THE EVOLVING SELF

Robert Kegan, in *The Evolving Self: Problem and Process in Human Development,* sees in human beings two fundamental yet paradoxical yearnings. We long for autonomy or independence but also for inclusion. The tension between these equally valid yearnings draws us on in the process of development.

As one's understanding of self develops, it moves through stages which Kegan calls evolutionary truces. Each truce represents a new understanding of self which is temporarily satisfying. One truce will resolve the tension between the basic yearnings in favor of inclusion, the next in favor of autonomy and so on, back and forth.[28] Kegan identifies five evolutionary truces, the Impulsive, Imperial, Interpersonal, Institutional, and Interindividual. We will briefly look at the last three.

The Interpersonal Self

In the interpersonal truce, self is defined in terms of relationships and not differentiated from them. The person is his or her relationships rather than having relationships. The expectations of others determine what one ought to be and have major control over the behavior of the self. Relationships and fulfilling the expectations of others give meaning to life. The person highly values inclusion.[29]

If asked, "Who are you?" the interpersonal self answers, "I am so and so's husband—or wife—and so and so's son—or daughter." The person who has no identity beyond relationships is profoundly threatened if the other party in the relationship desires more space. If the relationship ends in death or separation, a major part of the self is gone.

The Institutional Self

As persons differentiate the self from relationships they move into the institutional truce. They value autonomy and control. We might say they are their ability to be independent and keep everything under control. They know what they want and organize the world around them to meet the needs of the self. In relationships they control what they give and receive. The institutional self fears the loss of control and being absorbed in relationship.[30]

Many people establish their institutional self in the workplace. They describe themselves in terms of what they do and what they control. "I am a teacher, a nurse, or an accountant. I am responsible for a class of thirty children, the coronary care unit, or accounts payable." Doing well and being a success in one's vocation is important for self-worth. The institutional self may invest great amounts of time and energy in the job with little left for relationships.

The Interindividual Self

During the institutional truce one comes to understand the needs and wants of the autonomous self. That more clearly established self is brought back into relationship in the interindividual truce. True intimacy is now possible. There is a known self to give in relationships with other valued individuals. In the new interdependent relationship there is mutual commitment to maintaining the distinctness of each person while creating an environment for growth not possible in autonomous isolation. Relationships are co-regulated. Opportunities for both inclusion and independence are protected and there is mutual commitment to the enhancement of each person's growth.[31] Independence and relatedness or inclusion are held together in creative tension.

Support for Development

Kegan believes that for each evolutionary truce persons need a setting in which they come to know the self in a developmentally appropriate way. He refers to this setting as the culture of embeddedness. Healthy development calls for being held and supported at the appropriate time and then released to grow. Development can be stifled if the support system holds on too long or if the support system for the next evolutionary truce is not provided.[32]

THE CHURCH ENHANCING DEVELOPMENT

What do these developmental findings have to say to us about adult Christian education and life in the church? Let me highlight selected insights which I believe are critical to our effectiveness and suggest ways in which they might impact our ministries.

Valuing the Process

Gilligan, Belenky et al., and Kegan describe a process of development which takes place through experience, over time. It is a process which includes major transitions that are often disruptive and painful. At each level between transitions important learning is going on. Although the perspectives of various levels are incomplete and viewed as inadequate by those farther along the developmental path, what is being learned at each level is important. The new learnings are essential building blocks for the more comprehensive perspective of the next level.

Understanding the process of development is important to Christian educators because persons relate to God with their developing selves. Where I am along the developmental path will influence my experiencing of God and understanding of the Christian faith. If the path of healthy development is the design of the Creator, which I believe to be true, the church will want to enhance the development of all with whom it ministers.

Christian educators are most effective when they understand the process of development and what agendas are being worked on at each level. An introduction to developmental perspectives will enhance a teacher's self-understanding while equipping for more effective ministry.

Developmentalists tell us to value what is being learned in each phase of development. But we are often fearful of the incomplete views of self and morality described by researchers along the developmental path. We want to move people to the end of the road now. Listening only to the inner voice seems so relativistic, the institutional self so self-centered. But in each of these phases important understandings are being fashioned, understandings needed for a mature, integrated grasp of what it means to love God with all my being and my neighbor as myself.

Condemning persons for seeing life as they do will not move them forward. We will be most effective if we meet people where they are, celebrate the good things they are learning, support them as they realize the limitations of their present approaches, and walk with them into new discoveries.

We serve our people well when we communicate that life is a process of becoming in which transition and change are expected and healthy. Because the development of men and women is not identical, they need help in understanding one another. Some of the turmoil in marriages is rooted in developmental changes taking place or needed in the life of husband or wife. If these developmental transitions are understood, couples can deal with them and both partners grow through the experience. When what is happening within the persons is not understood, growth is often thwarted or the marriage unnecessarily blows apart.

If we believe development is a lifelong process, we will be concerned about lifelong learning. The eighteen-year-old cannot be prepared for the developmental transitions of the early thirties, fifties, or seventies. Persons need the insight and support of the faith community as they go through the transitions of life.

Valuing the Knowledge of Experience

To women, knowledge gained through experience is important. Women value abstract principles when they help make sense of experience.[33] They question "truth" that has not been tested in the real world or for which they see no application to life. Effective Christian education for women will not begin and end with consideration of abstract doctrinal principles. It will value experiential knowledge as a means of discovering the need for the principles. Sharing of relevant life experiences will aid in understanding biblical principles and doctrines. It will explore ways of living biblical truth so that the experiences of life are changed.

Is this emphasis on experience appropriate for Christian education? How does God view the importance of experiential knowledge? God's ultimate self-revelation was experiential. In the person of Jesus, God came to live among human beings and be experienced (John 1:14). The first seventeen books of the Old Testament recount the experiences of the people of God. The first five books of the New Testament tell the story of events in the life of Jesus and the early church. Abstract statements of doctrinal principles proclaimed by the prophets or the apostles responded to real life events and offered directives for living. This biblical pattern suggests that knowledge gained from and applied in experience should be important to men as well as women. Adult learning theory[34] and learning style theory[35] also highlight the importance of experience in adult learning.

Studies of Scripture and doctrine should begin with a look at the real lives of the learners. What have they experienced which would cause them to see the need for or the reality of the truth to be learned? If there is no such experience, they may not be ready to learn that truth. If reflection on events in their lives reminds them of unanswered questions and a desire for better understanding, adults will enter into the study of the Bible with excitement in search of the needed insight. That excitement builds if from week to week group members identify practical applications for principles discovered. As they support one another in doing what they have learned to do, God, at work through them, changes their world.

Going Beyond the Conventional

Culture-bound traditional views of women and men describe persons below the developmental potential seen in the research we have looked at. Conventional views of male and female roles exert pressure to put the lid on development. Our society expects women to function as interpersonal selves which many psychologists consider appropriate for adolescents. The institutional truce is seen as the end of the road for men and some forms of feminism also call women to this level, which is less than they can be.

Thwarting development has been devastating particularly for

women. Research studies report that for every man who suffers depression there are from two to six times as many women sufferers.[36] Varied factors may play into women's vulnerability to depression. However, I believe a major cause is the restriction of their development. The inward-focused anger from enforced self-sacrifice and guilt over not being as selfless as society expects becomes depression.

God calls the church to live beyond the norms of a culture tainted by the Fall, to provide a community where each person can become all God intends for him or her to be. Through redemption we can again live out the design of Creation, male and female together reflecting the image of God and doing God's work following their mutual commission given in Genesis 1:28.

But in many cases the church has not lived above the norms of society. Some interpretations of what the Bible teaches about the role of women would keep women as received knowers dependent on male authorities and demand self-sacrificing submission. When women living under these teachings begin to hear the inner voice, which is a natural process of development, and begin to question the rightness of their lot, they are in trouble. Society tells them their questions and thoughts are selfish, and the church tells them they are sinful. Under the load of that guilt, development stops for many Christian women. Not only are they deprived of the joy of becoming all God intended them to be, but what they have to offer for doing God's work in the world is limited.

Many evangelical Christians have honest questions about the Bible's teachings on women. Those questions have sent evangelical scholars to in-depth study of the issues in Scripture and many excellent books have been published on the topic in recent years.[37] We need to provide opportunities for women and men in church to study some of these resources and to reassess their understanding of the Bible's teaching on women. A Sunday School class, small group, or even one or two persons could engage in this exploration.

Providing Support

Healthy development is enhanced by what Kegan calls a culture of embeddedness, a setting where persons are affirmed and supported in being who they are ready to be. The church through its Christian education ministries can provide communities of support. They might be a young mother's Bible study, breakfast prayer and share groups for men, small accountability groups, Sunday

School classes, and the list could go on. We need to be sure there are places where people can master the learnings of conventional levels of development. But there must also be places where they find support and affirmation as they follow God's call beyond the cultural norms toward maturity.

In these groups persons will walk with one another through the times of transition. The group is a safe place where the inner voice can be expressed without the threat of rejection. A place where questions, struggles, and doubts are understood. Friends listen, support, and encourage one another, not in maintaining the status quo, but in becoming.

There is need for reconnecting the generations in the church. Middle-aged and older men and women who understand the processes of development and are walking with God into maturity have much to offer younger men and women. In our mobile society where people are separated from their extended family and in cases where mothers or fathers were unable to give their children what they needed, young people long for spiritual mothers and fathers, aunts and uncles. In small groups or one-on-one, older adults can walk with the young through their transitions, sharing their relationship with God, mentoring them toward wholeness and maturity. But this will not happen on a large scale unless Christian education leaders take the initiative to make connections.

Belenky and her colleagues found that confirmation and community are essential for women's development.[38] In the Christian education groups of our churches women need to be affirmed as persons capable of knowing God profoundly and capable of learning from Scripture what God has to say.

Women enjoy a class or group in which knowledge flows two ways, from students to teacher as well as from teacher to students.[39] Most women who prefer to sit quietly and listen to the teacher talk are convinced they have no knowledge worth contributing and are not capable of discerning what the Scriptures mean. Such women need teachers who will draw out their thoughts and affirm the worth of their contributions.[40]

Women learn best in a community where it is safe to raise troubling questions and try out ideas as understandings begin to form.[41] They need to know their questions will not be treated as dumb or unimportant. They need to be confident that the teacher and other group members will listen to understand what they are trying to express and will help them stretch their thinking and expand the understanding just being born.

The teacher greatly influences the character of the learning environment. If my class is to become a community, I must first believe that all members of the group do have significant contributions to make. I will view myself as a fellow learner with responsibility to facilitate learning, not as the authority with answers to be handed down. When students watch a teacher value what others have to say, a sense of safety builds. Group members also influence the learning climate. Discuss with them the goal of becoming a safe, nurturing community and how to do that.

Hearing All the Voices

Gilligan calls for orchestrating the themes of care and justice, the harmonious interplay of the moral song known best by women and that known best by men. Belenky and her colleagues present a maturity of knowing where both connected knowing preferred by women and separate knowing preferred by men enhance one another. Kegan's interindividual truce seems to be an integration of the yearning for inclusion, most strongly felt by women, and the yearning for independence, most strongly felt by men. A comprehensive, holistic view of morality, knowledge, and relationships comes through the integration of the perspectives of women and men.

When an expert in the law asked Jesus, "Which is the greatest commandment?" He responded by cogently condensing the law into the principles from which it flows. "Love the Lord your God with all your heart and with all your soul and with all your mind. . . . And . . . love your neighbor as yourself" (Matt. 22:37, 39). The principles are stated in terms of love. Jesus Christ brings into a harmonious whole moral principles and relationships of care. Men find here the principles they need to determine what is just, women find in them their deep concern for caring articulated.

We will most clearly see how to live out God's greatest commandments in the home, the church, and the world when we listen carefully to the voices of both men and women. If the voices of women are to be heard, women must be respected as persons worth listening to. Teachers and class members, both men and women, must be committed to "real talking." That involves listening and questioning to understand, draw out, and formulate ideas before exploring for weaknesses or countering with an alternative perspective.

SUMMARY

In adult Christian education, does one "size" fit all? Not when the particular differences of either men or women are ignored. Adult education in the church will contribute most to the life and ministry of God's people when it understands the strengths, concerns, and needs of both women and men. Out of those understandings will come some gender-focused specialized ministries. But much of Christian education will continue to involve men and women learning together from one another. Life and ministry is enriched when all perspectives and concerns are respected and the insights of both women and men are utilized in building God's kingdom.

Notes

1. Carol Gilligan, *In a Different Voice: Psychological Theory and Women's Development* (Cambridge, Mass.: Harvard Univ. Pr., 1982), 6–7.
2. Ibid., 17–19.
3. Carol Gilligan, Annie Rogers, and Lyn Mikel Brown, "Epilogue: Soundings into Development," in *Making Connections: The Relational Worlds of Adolescent Girls at Emma Willard School*, ed. Carol Gilligan, Nona P. Lyons, and Trudy J. Hanmer (Cambridge, Mass.: Harvard Univ. Pr., 1990), 317.
4. Gilligan, *Different Voice*, 74, 76.
5. Mary Field Belenky et al., *Women's Ways of Knowing: The Development of Self, Voice, and Mind* (New York: Basic Books, 1986), 48.
6. Gilligan, *Different Voice*, 78–79.
7. Belenky, *Women's Ways*, 47.
8. Gilligan, *Different Voice,* 81.
9. Ibid., 74.
10. Ibid., 171.
11. Ibid., 90.
12. Ibid., 83.
13. Elizabeth Bernstein and Carol Gilligan, "Unfairness and Not Listening: Converging Themes in Emma Willard Girl's Development," in *Making Connections*, 147.
14. Gilligan, Rogers, and Brown, "Epilogue," in *Making Connections*, 314–15, 320–22.
15. Belenky, *Women's Ways*, 24.
16. Ibid., 28–30.
17. Ibid., 24.

18. Ibid., 36–39.
19. Ibid.
20. Ibid., 54, 93.
21. Ibid., 85.
22. Ibid., 102–3.
23. Ibid., 104, 109.
24. Ibid., 112–14.
25. Ibid., 124–25.
26. Ibid., 137–39.
27. Ibid., 144–45, 149
28. Robert Kegan, *The Evolving Self: Problem and Process in Human Development* (Cambridge, Mass.: Harvard Univ. Pr., 1982).
29. Ibid., 96–100, 204–6.
30. Ibid., 100–103, 222–23.
31. Ibid., 103–6, 253–54.
32. Ibid., 210–12.
33. Belenky, *Women's Ways*, 200–201.
34. Kenneth O. Gangel, "Teaching Adults in the Church," in *The Christian Educator's Handbook on Teaching*, ed. Kenneth O. Gangel and Howard G. Hendricks (Wheaton, Ill.: Victor, 1988),150–51.
35. David Kolb, *Experiential Learning: Experience as the Source of Learning and Development* (Englewood Cliffs, N.J.: Prentice Hall, 1983).
36. Maggie Scarf, *Unfinished Business: Pressure Points in the Lives of Women* (New York: Ballantine, 1980), 3.
37. E.g., see Mary Evans, *Woman in the Bible* (Downers Grove, Ill.: InterVarsity, 1983); Gretchen Gaebelein Hull, *Equal to Serve* (Old Tappan, N.J.: Revell, 1987); and Kari Torjesen Malcolm, *Women at the Crossroads* (Downers Grove, Ill.: InterVarsity, 1982).
38. Belenky, *Women's Ways*, 193–94.
39. Ibid., 217.
40. Ibid., 218.
41. Ibid., 221.

For Further Reading

Belenky, Mary Field, Blythe McVicker Clinchy, Nancy Rule Goldberger, and Jill Mattuck Tarule. *Women's Ways of Knowing: The Development of Self, Voice, and Mind.* New York: Basic Books, 1986.

Bernstein, Elizabeth, and Carol Gilligan. "Unfairness and Not Listening: Converging Themes in Emma Willard Girl's Development." In *Making Connec-*

tions: The Relational Worlds of Adolescent Girls at Emma Willard School, edited by Carol Gilligan, Nona P. Lyons, and Trudy J. Hanmer. Cambridge, Mass.: Harvard Univ. Pr., 1990.

Cook, Kaye, and Lance Lee. *Man and Woman, Alone and Together*. Wheaton, Ill.: BridgePoint/Victor Books, 1992.

Evans, Mary. *Woman in the Bible.* Downers Grove, Ill.: InterVarsity, 1983.

Gangel, Kenneth O. "Teaching Adults in the Church." In *The Christian Educator's Handbook on Teaching,* edited by Kenneth O. Gangel and Howard G. Hendricks. Wheaton, Ill.: Victor Books, 1988.

Gilligan, Carol. *In a Different Voice: Psychological Theory and Women's Development.* Cambridge, Mass.: Harvard Univ. Pr., 1982.

Gilligan, Carol, Annie Rogers, and Lyn Mikel Brown. "Epilogue: Soundings into Development." In *Making Connections: The Relational Worlds of Adolescent Girls at Emma Willard School,* edited by Carol Gilligan, Nona P. Lyons, and Trudy J. Hanmer. Cambridge, Mass.: Harvard Univ. Pr., 1990.

Hull, Gretchen Gaebelein. *Equal to Serve.* Old Tappan, N.J.: Revell, 1987.

Kegan, Robert. *The Evolving Self: Problem and Process in Human Development.* Cambridge, Mass.: Harvard Univ. Pr., 1982.

Kolb, David. *Experiential Learning: Experience as the Source of Learning and Development.* Englewood Cliffs, N.J.: Prentice Hall, 1983.

Malcolm, Kari Torjesen. *Women at the Crossroads.* Downers Grove, Ill.: InterVarsity, 1982.

Perry, W.G. *Forms of Intellectual and Ethical Development in the College Years.* New York: Holt, Rinehart, and Winston, 1970.

Scarf, Maggie. *Unfinished Business: Pressure Points in the Lives of Women.* New York: Ballantine, 1980.

EIGHT
HOW ADULTS LEARN
Richard Patterson

Christian educators tend to "boil down" theory to more manageable, simple guidelines. It is the nature of human beings to do so. We've done it with Bible doctrine and theological issues for many centuries. We argue that it is just too complicated to maintain all these theories with cohesion and yet minister in a simple, yet effective, methodological approach. Most of us do not naturally seek complexity. Yet, complexity weaves the fabric of how adults learn.

PERSPECTIVE COMPLEXITY

The story is told of the building of the great St. Paul's Cathedral in London. Someone asked three workmen about their jobs. One answered that he was "Trimmin' and layin' bricks." The second answered that he was "earn'n wages to feed me fam'ly." While the third workman replied, "I'm helpin' Sir Christopher Wren build a majestic monument to the glory of God." It was the same job, but three very different perspectives were offered by the laborers. Out of this type of perspective complexity we understand how adults learn.

Draves argues that adults come to the learning setting with great perspective complexity when he tells us that:

> When twelve people walk into your class for the first time, each one will come already equipped with various experiences, attitudes, perceptions, and ideas. Each person will or-

> ganize his or her thoughts differently, and each will be able to absorb new knowledge and ideas in his or her own way.
>
> The adult's mental learning state is not a blank chalkboard on which you, the teacher, can write as you wish. Neither is the adult learner's head an empty pail for you to fill with your knowledge and ideas. The adult learner's chalkboard already has many messages on it, and his mental pail is almost full already. Your job as teacher is not to fill a *tabula rasa,* but to help your participants reorganize their own thoughts and skills. A prerequisite to helping adults learn is to understand how they learn.[1]

However, learning variety coupled with personal learner discovery has not characterized Christian education in the church. We have incorrectly assumed that providing more information will inevitably produce greater learning. Thus, the church has tended to overwhelm the adult learner with great amounts of data in the vain assumption that such an educational approach will surely generate fresh, meaningful adult learning. Unfortunately, it does not. It produces informational glut which, in turn, spawns adult disinterest and high dropout rates. Today's adults are very directional with their time and energy, and activities which show little promise of being personally meaningful have little or no priority to them. Individual perspective complexity demands an educational philosophy that reflects this diversity.

Our goal in this chapter is not to examine in great detail all the learning theories or educational psychologies in vogue today. Rather, we want to gain insight into the mechanics of adult learning in such a way as to create a sound platform on which the Christian educator can build a teaching methodology. We cannot explain in detail what actually happens in the adult mind which causes learning, nor can we define the mechanical features that constitute the internal workings of adult learning. We just do not know these details in the same manner as we know that one gear meshing with another produces certain torque and directional power.

All our learning theory is just that, theory. However, several observable elements, characteristics, and components seem identifiable when adults learn, and we can isolate and use them as guidelines for the forming of a viable teaching methodology. In this milieu we offer what is currently understood about how adults learn.

SURVEYING THE THEORIES

Theoretical Scope

J.R. Kidd identifies a controversy in learning theory by citing three groups into which he places all adult learning theorists.[2] He sees these three groups as behaviorists, represented by people like Thorndike and Skinner; cognitists, represented by Bruner, Ausubel, and Hunt; and humanists, as seen in Rogers, Maslow, and Perls. Of course, there are many other learning theorists (such as Erikson and Piaget) who have contributed significantly to this growing field of adult learning theory as well.

But just as theory without effective practice is empty, practice not based upon sound theory is blind. As necessary as these learning theorists are to us, we must be careful to not accept what any one of them has postulated as the total descriptor of adult learning. For it does appear that laboratory observations of adults produce different data than some of the theorists. Some laboratory data are supported by synthesis of some of these theorists, but the experiential data are not totally supportive of any single one. As Christian educators, we must assess what these learning theorists suggest but also synthesize their thinking with what the Bible tells us about humans and what we observe as learning phenomena.

Biblical Essentials

Since we have committed ourselves to the Word of God as our sole authority for thought, faith, and practice, we must begin with theology. We need to know what God says about the human condition and potential. Furthermore, we need to know just how God intends to realize His potential for humankind. Only when we wed sound learning theory to biblical theology can we expect to find efficacious teaching/learning methodology. The Word of God serves as our beginning point in this quest of how adults learn. Only through this biblical grid can we construct a truly Christian understanding of how adults learn. It is assumed, consequently, that every learning theory, concept, principle, or element cited in this chapter must be conditioned and measured by this foundational biblical matrix.

The Bible teaches that though the human condition is sinful and beyond human repair (Rom. 3:10, 23), we are also capable of perfection, for Jesus exhorted us to, "Be perfect, therefore, as your Heavenly Father is perfect" (Matt. 5:48). To understand such biblical perfection, we must allow the Bible to interpret perfection for us. We must be careful to not read into "perfection" something that the Bible does not teach. Scripture tells us that one of the aspects is *positional* perfection: "Because by one sacrifice he has made perfect forever those who are being made holy" (Heb. 10:14). Of course, this is personal salvation through the shed blood of Christ. Another aspect of this biblical perfection is *prophetic* perfection, which declares that one day we will be perfect, similar to the Son of God when He has taken us, through death, to be with Him (1 John 3:2). A third aspect is *progressive* perfection. A reference for this type of perfection is found in 2 Corinthians 7:1: "Since we have these promises, dear friends, let us purify ourselves from everything that contaminates body and spirit, perfecting holiness out of reverence for God."

This biblical definition of perfection, then, is the goal our Lord has declared for us as adults. He has given us His Word, the Bible, as the *message* to foster such perfection,"All Scripture is God-breathed and is useful for teaching, rebuking, correcting, and training in righteousness, so that the man of God may be thoroughly equipped ['perfect' in the KJV] for every good work" (2 Tim. 3:16-17).

God has also given not only the message, but the *means* to such perfection through the church. "It was He who gave some to be apostles, some to be prophets, some to be evangelists, and some to be pastors and teachers, to prepare God's people ['perfecting' in the KJV] for works of service, so that the body of Christ may be built up until we all reach unity in the faith and in the knowledge of the Son of God and become mature, attaining to the whole measure of the fullness of Christ" (Eph. 4:11-13).

God has also given us the *method* to accomplish this biblical perfection, as Paul argues, when he says, "We proclaim Him, admonishing and teaching everyone with all wisdom, so that we may present everyone perfect in Christ" (Col. 1:28). As an aside, note that Paul suggests that we, the workers for Christ, will present those we have won, discipled, and equipped to the Lord as "perfect" in Christ. There is an eternal role for the church worker and one of the facets of that role seems to be the heavenly and public presenting of those persons we have influenced in becoming perfect, as the Bible describes such perfection. Thus, we have a divine mandate that not only declares our goal for all people but also provides the reward of such ministry endeavor for the church worker and supplies the message, means, and method to accomplish that goal through the Holy Spirit.

In addition to the learning theories cited, then, we have a declaration from God that He has a divine goal for each man or woman and that he has provided a message, a means, and a method that will attain that goal for the Christian educator. As Christian educators we must synthesize what learning theorists present, but we must also adjust that synthesis to what God says about humans. This learning theory synthesis must also be confronted with the observable phenomena that we find when we teach adults. So we have a threefold-tension-learning theory synthesis; biblical information about adults; and adult learning phenomena—that will gorge the best learning theory for the Christian educator.

EXAMINING THE APPROACHES

Pedagogy Versus Andragogy

Though the term andragogy has been with us since the 1800s, Malcolm Knowles first popularized the concept.[3] Andragogy was Knowles' effort to counter a nearly total dependence upon pedagogy as a teaching/learning approach for adults. In a pedagogical classroom model the teacher is the expert in the content area and presents information to the learner who passively absorbs whatever is required. Since what many adult educators had postulated and observed about adults strongly argued that pedagogy was not an adult-effective learning approach, andragogy became the educational cry of the reformer. Andragogy, they argued, was a preferable teaching/learning concept since it was based upon the observable learning phenomena that adults learned what they considered important to them, and that adults needed to be highly participative in the learning process.

Andragogy Versus Synergogy

Abuses of the pedagogical model were matched by abuses of the andragogical model. Some andragogical devotees allowed their belief regarding how adults learn to degenerate into the "blind leading the blind," by fostering extensive sharing sessions with no authoritative source for truth. From this abuse syndrome rose yet another adult teaching/learning approach termed *synergogy*.[4] Synergogy attempts to avoid the abuses of some applied andragogy by positioning a truth source in the adult learning experience. It is creative and intriguing and offers considerable promise to the Christian educator.

It became clear, however, that whether due to the various learning theories, or the observable learning phenomena of adults, pedagogy provided a poor model of teaching/learning for adults. Adults just did not learn in the same ways as children. Thus, how adults did learn became the conditioning factor in how adults were taught. Unfortunately, however, little of this dialectic influenced the church. Without an understanding of how adults learn, the church continued to champion pedagogy and content-driven curriculum as opposed to andragogy, or synergogy, and needs-driven curriculum.

ANALYZING THE PSYCHOLOGY

Developmental Tasks

Coupled with the learning theorists, an entire spectrum of educational psychologists also bring valuable insights into how adults learn. Robert J. Havighurst gave us extremely important insight when he observed that all human beings have, what he termed, developmental tasks that they need to complete in life.[5] He described these tasks which arise at a certain time of life, successful achievement of which leads to happiness and success with later tasks, while failure leads to unhappiness in the individual, disapproval by the society, and difficulty with later tasks. Havighurst carefully identified these tasks for all age-groups, including three separate age groupings in adulthood.

Further, Havighurst observed what he called the "teachable moment" when certain tasks come with great urgency to a person during a relatively short period of time. At this time one has intense motive to learn and effective education results. It should be quite obvious that such insight into those true motivators of adult life interest will provide the Christian educator with valuable structure for a valid philosophy of how adults learn.

A Need Hierarchy

Similarly, Abraham Maslow provides another component in our understanding of how adults learn when he observes that all people seek self-actualization but only when lower needs have been first met.[6] He observes that upon fulfillment of the physical needs, people seek their safety needs. And upon satisfaction of that safety need, they seek belongingness, then self-esteem, and finally self-actualization. Maslow calls this the need hierarchy.

If Christian educators intend to bring adults to this step of self-actualization (actually our biblical "perfection" concept cited earlier), we must be careful to assure that these lower needs are met first. For example, Barna observes that the belonging need, the need to be unconditionally accepted regardless of performance, is not commonly found in many churches.[7] According to Maslow, bringing those adults to self-actualization (biblical "perfection") is impossible until this belonging need is met.

Motivational Elements

There is another motivational insight we need to see in order to properly form our understanding of how adults learn. We find it in the work of Wlodkowski.[8] Through his clinical observations, he finds six motivators common and necessary to adult learning: (1) Attitude (the learner must have a satisfying experience in the learning setting); (2) Needs (the learning experience must focus upon what the adult perceives to be his or her needs); (3) Stimulation (the learner must feel challenged that this experience will be personally productive); (4) Affect (there needs to be a "feel" that the learner is, in fact, achieving, progressing, and conquering); (5) Competence (the learner actually experiences genuine and meaningful accomplishment of need satisfaction); and (6) Reinforcement (there is positive feedback as to personal accomplishment).

These three psychological insights of Havighurst, Maslow, and Wlodkowski are critical in determining how adults learn. Educators must know that there are predictable tasks, a need hierarchy, and identifiable motivators for adults to fulfill. Those elements must then form the content matrix of our curriculum. When we focus the "message," the Word of God, upon these identifiable developmental tasks, the need hierarchy and these cited motivators, we focus God's therapy upon those needs which, when satisfied, will produce the "progressive perfection" cited earlier.

When we apply Maslow's need hierarchy to learning theory, it becomes clear that the learner must have a biblical sense of community (or unconditional belongingness) in order for us to accomplish our divine mandate. When we consider how the educational motivators of Wlodkowski impact learning theory, we begin to see how essential it is for us to provide high learner participation and personal fulfillment in every educational learning setting.

Notice that we are building a composite view of how adults learn. It will include the synthesis input of the learning theorists, the divine biblical mandate, and the motivational insights as to why adults learn. However, we need to discover another element of this formula—those learning approaches most productive with adults.

DISCOVERING A WORKABLE PRINCIPLE

The Perceptual Approach

This new element of our formula regarding how adults learn is what Verduin and Clark term the perceptual approach.[9] This concept states that all behavior arises from perceptions existing for individuals at the moment they exhibit the behavior. Since the basic task of Christian educators aims at changing adult behavior to satisfy the divine mandate, we surely need to know whatever will impact that behavior.

Verduin and Clark argue for three assumptions necessary to this approach: (1) that all behavior is a function of perceptions; (2) that adults will self-start toward anything that promises self-meaning; and (3) that adults desire to enhance themselves and achieve self-actualization. If changing an adult's behavior is a consequence of perception, and we see our educational task as changing learner behaviors, then as Christian educators, we must assist learners in changing their perceptions. Adopting new behavior reflective of the divine mandate can only be accomplished by adults modifying the way in which they perceive their "universe."

Perception and Behavior

Every adult constructs his or her own world through the perceptions each have made regarding that world. Out of this percepted world they behave. Obviously as we guide them into a differing perception of that same world they will also behave differently.[10] The identifiable determinants of these perceptions include one's beliefs, values, needs, attitudes, and self-experience.

Remember, the adult's perception of each of these determinants seems to be truth to the individual. Adults will always behave as though their belief, value, need, attitude, self-experience is true and accurate, for their perception of each of these, to them, matches truth. To the individual, perception equals truth.

Behavior and Interpretation

What is the educational significance of this concept? Each adult brings this perceptual "package" into the learning experience we have structured. This perceptual "package" differs for each learner. It includes both the past experiences of the learner and the learner's *interpretation* of these past experiences.[11] Thus, though past experiences cannot change, the adult's interpretation of them can.

With adults, however, we are not very successful in changing these interpretations through pedagogical techniques. To attempt to do so, is to impose threat to the learning setting. And threat will most certainly restrict perceptual change. Interpretational change will only occur when adults feel free to reexamine their beliefs, values, needs, attitudes, and self-experience.

Simply adding new information to the adult may or may not change behavior. One's perceptions are least likely to be modified through the introduction of new information, regardless of how charismatic the presentation may be. But when the adult learner personally discovers new perceptions, of old information as well as of new, then comes the internal motivation to change behavior to coincide with the new perception.[12] To facilitate such personal discovery of fresh perceptions, teaching methodology that stresses group work, problem-solving, personal investigation, and task-oriented educational activities is essential.

Interpretation and the Educational Domains

One further thought regarding this workable principle (that behavior change results from perception change) is that its scope covers all three educational domains (Bloom, Knox, Krathwohl, Masia, and Simpson). All three domains—cognitive, affective, and psychomotor (or conative)—are hierarchical in nature. That is, each domain has a taxonomy whereby the lower category is included in each successive higher category.

The cognitive domain sees cognitive growth beginning with knowledge and moving upward in maturity to comprehension, application, analysis, synthesis, and finally, evaluation. The affective domain sees such emotional growth beginning with receiving the new experience, then responding to it, valuing it, organizing or placing it into one's personal system, and finally, becoming characterized by that emotional growth. The psychomotor, or conative domain, dealing with the skills a person develops, begins with perception, moving to a "set" of mental, physical, or emotional readiness, to a guided response of trial and error, to a habitual usage of the new experience, to a further complexity of that experience, to adapting it to other applications, and finally, origination, where the learner applies the newly acquired skill to a personal modification or use of the skill.

Remember our principle of perceptions? Since it produces behavior, it applies to each of these domains. The adult's perception of truth in each of the domains will always be the progenitor of the adult's behavior in each of the domains. Because we want to guide adults into new behavior patterns, to meet their developmental needs in ways that move them to fulfillment of God's goals of positional, progressive, and prophetic perfection, our task as teachers will be to introduce, nurture, and sustain those perceptions that produce such behavior.

Behavior produced through fear or threat does not become internalized. Behavior generated through peer pressure or intimidation is only public in practice. Only behavior that flows from a discovery of truth, personally perceived as God sees it through His Word, can produce behavior that truly becomes habitual and God-honoring.

SENSING ADULT LEARNING RHYTHMS

Brookfield has coined an interesting word to describe the observable patterns of adult learning. He calls these patterns "rhythms."[13] Through the study of these rhythms, or repetitious measurable patterns, the curtain of confusion is pulled back and we are able to understand better how adults learn. Brookfield has done extensive research of his own, as well as gleaned from the studies of others, regarding the learning experiences of thousands of adult students. From these observations emerges a set of data which may not construct a fully comprehensible theory of learning, but do provide us with much more concrete information about how adults learn than many of the textbooks which seem to prescribe some personal dictum of learning.

Seven elements of the learning experience appear to have the greatest replicability across the thousands of students Brookfield and others studied. These seven are, in his terms, the imposter syndrome, emotionality, challenge, reflection, incremental fluctuation, unexpectedness, and a learning community. Let's describe each one in some detail.

The Impostor Syndrome

An element of the learning experience, this syndrome argues that rather than the adult being a confident, self-directed person entering the learning environment, he or she feels that all other learners are brighter, have better experiences and hold greater promise. Such adults feel they are "impostors" in this educational setting. Certainly such a feeling can generate enormous power and will negatively affect the learning setting. Coming to the learning setting with this type of "baggage" does not tell us how adults learn, but it does tell us that they have a basic relational need that must be satisfied early in the learning setting. This negative self-image surrounding the learning setting is a strong inhibitor of adult learning. The adult educator must develop creative strategies for coping with it.

Emotionality. Rarely, if ever, do learners describe the positive effects of their learning in intellectual terms. They tell of their exciting learning discoveries in very emotional terms. Yet, as educators we tend to neglect the emotional side of learning in favor of the cognitive. If the emotional side carries the most important retention of the learner, it would seem that we, as educators, need to place this truth at a higher priority in our learning theory as to how adults learn.

Challenge. Here we see the third element. The learners that Brookfield and others studied cited that those times of most significant learning occurred when they also faced the greatest personal challenge in the educational experience. They felt uncomfortable and at risk either with an informational dilemma or educational problem which offered no clear solution. When students felt they had grappled successfully with this challenge, they experienced a feeling of exhilaration that carried strong discovery and retention.

Reflection. Learners universally felt they did not have sufficient time for reflection upon the information presented. They received masses of information and were expected to "master" those data by rote memorization but not afforded the time necessary to interpret the information, assimilate it into their past experiences, or build the necessary connections for fresh perspective. Adult learners commonly cry that information overload robs them of the richness of the experience.

Incremental Fluctuation. Incremental fluctuation is Brookfield's term for the vacillation learners experience when attempting to assimilate new information. Learners respond with initial enthusiasm to new data, but then feel anxiety about assimilating this new information into past experience. Thus, they retreat to the comfortable territory of home (past experiences and their perceptions). However, learners find they are now no longer comfortable in that past perception. Things just aren't the same anymore. So, eventually adults gather enough courage to venture forth again into the "new" information area. This movement back and forth from the new and back to familiar security is a dialectical tension which forms an incumbent part of adult learning.

Unexpectedness. Learners frequently express that the most important experiences in their learning happened very unexpectedly, almost by surprise. Much of this is seen as the learner discovers that he or she is no longer teacher-dependent, but self-directed. This usually happens in the Leroy Ford expression of the "Aha moment."[14] Again, however, this is not necessarily an intellectual experience; it is much more affective.

Learning Community. Finally, the importance of the learning community provides an element in the studies of learners' experiences that surfaced with high repetition. Learners recall with great vividness how critical a supportive community was to them in their positive learning experience. This community was not necessarily the entire class; it more frequently was a smaller group upon whom they could depend for emotional support throughout the course.

Since these seven elements describe the way learners experience learning, we can assume that they are also a very important component of how adults learn.

SUMMARY

We've looked briefly at the learning theorists, the approaches that adult learning proponents champion, and the educational psychology behind the adult learner. A workable principle argues that adults learn as they adjust their perceptions of past experiences and form new perceptions in response to new information and/or experiences. These perceptual determinants include their beliefs, values, needs, attitudes, and self-experience. As these perceptual determinants change, the adult learns within three domains—the cognitive, the affective, and the psychomotor (or conative).

We've also seen that God has given a divine mandate for each adult: biblical perfection (or true maturity). God gave us His message as divine therapy for these adult needs; He gave us the means in the form of the church to facilitate this message; and He gave us the method, the "with all wisdom" of Colossians 1:28 (which we suggest as an andragogical teaching methodology), that is focused upon those needs. In the learner's eyes, the adult learning experience occurs in the context of the seven elements reviewed in the chapter.

Notes

1. William Draves, *How to Teach Adults* (Manhattan, Kan.: LERN, 1984), 7.
2. J.R. Kidd, *How Adults Learn* (New York: Association Press, 1973), 25.
3. Malcolm Knowles, *The Adult Learner: A Neglected Species* (Houston: Gulf, 1973), 1–3.
4. Jane Sygley Mouton and Robert R. Blake, *Synergogy* (San Francisco: Jossey-Bass, 1987), 6.
5. Robert J. Havighurst, *Developmental Tasks and Education* (New York: Longman, Greens and Co., 1948), 33.
6. Abraham Maslow, *Toward a Psychology of Being* (Princeton, N.J.: Nostrand, 1962), 18.
7. George Barna, *User Friendly Churches* (Ventura, Calif.: Regal, 1991), 59–67, 177–78.
8. Raymond J. Wlodkowski, *Enhancing Adult Motivation to Learn* (San Francisco: Jossey-Bass, 1988), 45–71.
9. John R. Verduin and Thomas A. Clark, *Distance Education: The Foundations of Effective Practice* (San Francisco: Jossey-Bass, 1991), 140–65.
10. Lawrence J. Crabb, *Understanding People* (Grand Rapids: Zondervan, 1987), 122–41.
11. Ibid., 158–59.
12. Stephen D. Brookfield, *Understanding and Facilitating Adult Learning* (San Francisco: Jossey-Bass, 1986), 40–59.
13. Stephen Brookfield, *The Skillful Teacher* (San Francisco: Jossey-Bass, 1990), 43–56.
14. Leroy Ford, *Design for Teaching and Learning* (Nashville, Tenn.: Broadman, 1978), 360.

For Further Reading

Barna, George. *User Friendly Churches.* Ventura, Calif.: Regal, 1991.

Brookfield, Stephen. *The Skillful Teacher.* San Francisco: Jossey-Bass, 1990.

_____. *Understanding and Facilitating Adult Learning.* San Francisco: Jossey-Bass, 1986.

Crabb, Lawrence J. *Understanding People.* Grand Rapids: Zondervan, 1987.

Draves, William. *How To Teach Adults.* Manhattan, Kan.: LERN, 1984.

Ford, Leroy. *Design for Teaching and Learning.* Nashville: Broadman, 1978.

Kidd, J.R. *How Adults Learn.* New York: Association Press, 1973.

Knowles, Malcolm. *The Adult Learner: A Neglected Species.* Houston: Gulf, 1973.

Maslow, Abraham. *Toward a Psychology of Being.* Princeton, N.J.: Nostrand, 1962.

Moulton, Jane Sygley and Robert R. Blake. *Synergogy.* San Francisco: Jossey-Bass, 1987.

Verduin, John R. and Thomas A. Clark. *Distance Education: The Foundation of Effective Practice.* San Francisco: Jossey-Bass, 1991.

NINE
INDUCTIVE TEACHING: STRATEGY FOR THE ADULT EDUCATOR

Duane H. Elmer

What images come to mind when you hear the word "teaching"? Someone up-front talking? School? People sitting in rows listening? It is not surprising if these images first come to mind. Most teaching occurs this way. Sure, we get creative occasionally and try some discussion, but it is only a temporary measure to grab students' attention so we can get back to the real way to learn—telling them. Telling has its place in learning, but probably not nearly as prominent as most of us make it. Reliance on one method of teaching severely limits effectiveness.

JESUS THE INDUCTIVE TEACHER

Any casual reader of the Gospels can easily count a dozen or more strategies Jesus used as a teacher to educate His disciples, only one of which was telling. Since Jesus had an absolute grasp on truth and since He could hold crowds spellbound with His lecturing, why did He resort to frequent excursions into the domain of inductive teaching strategies? Perhaps an even more startling question is why we do it so infrequently.

Jesus, by His own teaching style, seemed firmly convinced that the best kind of learning environment finds telling strategically dispersed in measured ways throughout inductive kinds of learning activities. So confident was He of the inductive approach that He felt no particular compulsion to be with His disciples all the time to "guide and insure" their learning. He would send them out (or away) and not see them until they returned, at which time

He asked them to talk about their experience. The simple point here is that Jesus frequently taught inductively. In the context of designed inductive experiences, His telling became much more powerful.

THE GOOD NEWS AND THE GOOD NEWS

Inductive teaching transfers much of the responsibility for learning to the learner, and this brings with it some risks. Reducing "telling" and using strategies of learner engagement generally enhances learning. Yet, such strategies can be quite time-consuming and often make it appear that less actual content has been taught. Also when lessons are less structured, there can be more uncertainty for the teacher. A successful inductive teacher must be comfortable with these realities.

If inductive teaching represents uncharted waters for you and the learners, early attempts will bring some anxiety for everyone; but keep at it. You will almost certainly be delighted with the results. The rewards for this kind of teaching are many. They include heightened interest in learning, a greater sense of community, increased respect for one another, greater likelihood of applying truth, and a realization that the Holy Spirit is doing some very significant work in each life. Inductive teaching requires that the teacher develop new skills, but the rewards are ample.

ASSUMPTIONS

Inductive teaching is based on three assumptions. First, learning can happen, and may most effectively happen, when the teacher avoids doing all the talking. The major disadvantage of a class in which the teacher talks constantly is that primarily the teacher has been stimulated to think about and act upon the information. Learners generally remain passive both in thought and application.

Second, a deliberate kind of sharing with learners is necessary—sharing talk time, sharing thoughts, and sharing vulnerabilities. Learning becomes a joint venture. Teacher and students enter into it as proactive parties. Neither is intended to dominate all that happens. But if both bring their respective resources, the outcomes can be desirable for both. The teacher takes responsibility for the overall design and direction of the class, but will conduct it in such a way as to engage the students' minds proactively.

A third assumption reminds us that learning occurs in an atmosphere of trust. One accomplishes little in the classroom without basic trust between students and teacher. Where suspicion or uncertainty prevails, learners will reveal little of what lies deep in their minds or hearts. One shares meaningfully only with someone who has earned trust.

A DIFFERENT KIND OF TEACHER

Inductive teaching calls for quite different skills not always resident in a teacher but not hard to learn. In addition to organizing and delivering information, the inductive teacher needs to:

- structure learning experiences that bring the learners into some kind of cognitive and/or physical interaction with the lesson content;
- believe learning can happen when you are not talking;
- ask probing, even provoking questions;
- guide conversation and discussion without closing it down;
- listen for understanding rather than evaluation;
- engage in open dialogue;
- handle spontaneous issues and questions;
- be vulnerable, communicate that you are a trustworthy and safe person;
- tolerate ambiguity;
- be comfortable with silence;
- interact while also communicating acceptance;
- be willing to take some risks.

Educators sometimes call these "process skills" because the teacher now becomes the facilitator of a process whereby learners are more proactive in learning. Inductive teaching is not for the faint of heart but neither does it take extraordinary courage. Mostly it takes an open mind and some willingness. Move slowly, but expect to be addicted to the power of this dynamic approach.

CASE STUDY OF A RISK TAKER

While the number of my success stories in teaching are not as many as I had hoped at the beginning, I rehearse one which represents an early venture into inductive teaching. Having just finished a graduate class in creative teaching methods (instructional simulations, to be specific), my Sunday School class seemed the perfect target for my new knowledge.

We would get into stimulating, even captivating, discussions, I reasoned. They would be spellbound by the electricity of creative learning activities. Weekly, lives would be radically changed by God as He used the genius of my inductive teaching strategies. On rare occasions I fantasized the spontaneous standing ovation for which I would be prepared to offer a humble bow. Such were the dreams and imaginations of a young teacher.

The first six weeks brought astounding failure. My questions provoked the occasional "pat" answer, but usually stimulated little more than numbing silence with eyes focused on the floor. The bewildering looks and minimal compliance provided no evidence to suggest that I was even getting close to my prized outcomes. The creeping sense of failure began to shake my confidence. Perhaps the others were right; maybe the straight lecture is the only way.

Discovering the history of this class began to explain some things. They had never been expected to enter into discussion, or do anything other than sit, listen, and spout the safe answer. The height of creativity was a film. Most had entered this kind of experience every week of their Sunday School memory. Could they change? Would it be fair to ask them? Would the outcomes be better and worth the effort? My graduate creativity class suggested it was worth keeping on.

After six weeks of putting up with silence and often answering my own questions, something began to happen. The bolder ones began to express their real thoughts and feelings. "Pat" answers still came, but I and others in the class would not allow them to go unclarified. I worked hard to show acceptance of any effort to contribute to the discussion. I frequently affirmed participants for contributing. Enthusiasm, openness, honesty, and vulnerability grew. Learners shared their doubts without reprisal. We began to view each other as real people, not Sunday morning mannequins.

Signals that my hoped-for outcomes were happening came in curious ways. A larger percentage of the class members were attending and vocally participating. One Sunday brought an incredible victory. A class member raised her hand to speak (raising hands was not mandatory). I did not catch the significance of the hush that fell over the class nor the stares that accompanied it. As Lynn stuttered her comments, I understood her past reluctance to speak and why the hush had descended. Upon leaving class that day, one young man said to me, "You don't know it, but you made history today."

"How's that?" I asked.

"I have been in public school and Sunday School classes with Lynn from kindergarten until now, and this is the first time I have ever heard her speak in public."

Lynn's severe stuttering made it easier to understand her silence. She took a big risk whenever she opened her mouth. Vulnerability is never easy. Yet the class atmosphere had so excited her that she had to take the risk of speaking. Now everyone understood why Lynn sat there every Sunday polite and proper but always silent.

I was both gratified and confused. Gratification came in realizing that the learners were positive about honestly interacting with the Scriptures and life. The confusion came because I realized that in most classes I had done less than half the talking and in many cases, probably less than twenty percent. Yet, by my reckoning, the results were profound. How could they learn so much with so little talking from me? I had begun to discover the power of inductive teaching. From a hindsight of twenty-five years of teaching, I remain awestruck at what God can do if I allow others to join me in the teaching-learning process.

SOME INDUCTIVE METHODS

Simulations

> A simulation is like a kiss, interesting to read about but much more interesting to participate in. And those that do, tend to repeat it.
>
> R. Stadsklev

Simulations, related to the field of experiential learning, are structured experiences that seek to imitate some piece of reality. For example, before the astronauts walked on the moon, they practiced "moon walking" right here on earth in a near weightless environment and on a surface believed to be like that of the lunar surface. It was not quite the real thing but the astronauts experienced real emotions, made real decisions, and tried to solve "real" problems. Monopoly™ provides one of the world's most famous simulations. Some researchers have found that people play Monopoly™ about the same way they run their businesses.

The early use of simulations was restricted mostly to technical training. For example, most airline pilots spend many hours in a simulator before their first flight. In the simulator they respond to all the routine items and also to every known emergency. Their responses are carefully monitored, and when the training ends they are judged competent or incompetent—all because of a simulation. Simpler simulations of "flying" (or "race car driving," "fighting aliens," or whatever) are available by the hundreds for the home computer or in video parlors. Just watch the players sometime: perspiration, tense muscles, elevated heart beat, frustration or elation, and fierce concentration provide ample evidence of the "reality" of simulations.

Why Use Simulations? Several reasons exist for using simulations over real-life experiences. First, often *reality is not available or not desirable.* For example, one might want to learn about death without experiencing it. But learning about it only by telling may not have the desired effect. One can learn about death by simulating various aspects of it—sitting in total silence and isolation for an hour, writing a will, naming whom you will miss most, describing what you would do if you had one more day of life, writing a letter to your parents from your "grave," and similar activities.

Reality is often too expensive. I would love to take the students in my intercultural class to a foreign country for an extended dose of cross-cultural reality. Since it is too expensive, I can use several simulations to help them get a sense of reality and thus develop more realistic expectations when they actually enter another culture.

Simulations become necessary when *reality is too dangerous.* The use of simulators to train military and commercial pilots has saved countless lives. But more to our adult education context, some of the dangerous parts of reality that might be taught through simulations are drug addiction, premarital or extramarital sex, disobedience to God, selfishness, gossip, lust, pride, broken relationships—virtually all the sins and difficulties we face. A simulation teaches the negative consequences in such a way that the learners are better equipped to resist engaging in the reality.

Often, *reality takes too much time.* A cross-cultural trip to a foreign country or even a field trip into the inner city (which we do) consumes a great deal of time. And frequently not all the learning components emerge. But in a simulation, time is truncated into an hour, more or less, and designed to highlight the major components to be experienced and learned.

Benefits of Simulation Experiences. Learners are involved physically, emotionally, intellectually and, with the ministry of the Spirit, spiritually. Any engagement with reality or "reality" (i.e., simulated reality) calls for the involvement of the whole being.

Values are brought to one's awareness and *exposed.* This allows for self-reflection and examination, an environment conducive to the convicting work of God.

Structured experiences often *generate disequilibrium.* Students discover discrepancies between what they believed and what God says, or between what they are doing and what God says they ought to be doing. Disequilibrium is the moment of pause, the moment of truth, the moment of choice.

Simulations tend to be an *enjoyable* way to learn. As we mingle learning and experience, the fun collaborates with the serious. Time goes faster. A less threatening environment creates a greater freedom to learn.

Learning tends to be *more permanent.* Generally, we retain up to 10 percent of the factual material presented in a lecture. Most is forgotten. But a simulation, being a concrete experience, is not soon forgotten. Students of mine from fifteen to twenty years back recount not only the simulation itself, but how various people behaved in it. The same people quickly note how they remember the lessons from that experience.

Class members feel an increased sense of ownership. Not only is this *my* class, but what I am learning is mine because I am involved in the process.

Simulations *stimulate intrinsic motivation.* The use of rewards, punishments, or other extrinsic forms of motivation incrementally decline as internal motivation increases. The dynamic of participation is its own internal motivator.

Learners make "real" choices and experience "real" consequences. Learners exercise their decision-making skills which reveal their underlying values. With values awareness they can determine what they would like to change.

Keep in mind that simulations and other inductive forms of teaching are not a snake oil that magically makes everything right. Other components of good teaching must be present. Inductive teaching, considered by most to be harder than lecturing, requires creative energies for preparation and presence of mind during class that is exhausting—but worth it.

A simulation, then, is an activity designed to place the learner in a situation that approximates reality and in which the learner is free to participate. The purpose is to create a better learning—a learning that engages the whole person and which, ultimately, brings likeness to Christ.

Asking Questions

> We take a telling posture and then wonder why their behavior never changes.
>
> Unknown

Asking mind-stimulating questions represents another inductive strategy useful in adult learning. One of the most powerful learning tools for both teacher and learner, questions help the teacher discover the world of the learner. Questions help the learner evaluate and formulate beliefs. Questions help teacher and learner engage in learning and appropriating God's truth—solving the problems of life. Yet, few teachers have mastered the art of posing the kinds of questions that promote learning and, hopefully, behavioral change. Apart from the fact that it is hard work to pose good questions, what else may account for the paucity of questioning as part of an adult education strategy?

Barriers to Building Good Questions. "Illusion of omniscience" describes a major problem facing those who teach others. The teacher who dwells in monologue carries the assumption that he or she is the only one who has anything important to say and that the others will be served best by listening. In such a situation the teacher is perceived as the expert with all the answers and the learner as the "open receptacle," eagerly awaiting the answers to life's issues.

"Illusion of ignorance" is the flip side of the above. Why spend time creating good questions if the learners know little or nothing? Why should we waste time sharing ignorance? Don't students simply need to be taught the answers? Isn't it the role of the teacher to give answers? The teacher has studied, often had specialized training, is experienced and, therefore, equipped to tell the learners.

"Illusion of change" suggests that telling people changes people. By the time most learners enter junior and junior-high levels of Sunday School, they have already heard the answers eight to ten times. Will telling them once more make the difference? Or, will it make a difference if we approach God's truth differently by assuming they need to wrestle with the answers they already know?

"Illusion of disinterest" refers to the reluctance of learners to interact. "When I ask questions, they just silently look down while a cloud of awkwardness creeps across everyone." Or, "Only a few ever respond, and it seems the discussion never goes anywhere." This common complaint can be misused by a teacher as license to continue in the telling mode.

Overcoming the Barriers/Illusions. The above four illusions, all false, lodge too comfortably in most of us in varying degrees. Recognizing them as barriers and working hard to overcome them will produce superior learning in people of all ages. Following are a few thoughts toward that end.

1. If your class members only see or hear you on Sunday morning (or whatever your teaching time may be) they will be less likely to respond openly since they do not know you well. Answering questions honestly requires vulnerability. People must be confident that you will not hurt or embarrass them before they will expose their real thoughts. Being with them in other situations will help overcome this barrier. If learners are comfortable with and trust the teacher, the discussion should flourish.

2. If you inherited a class from someone who specialized in monologue and was happy with "pat" answers to the infrequent and poorly designed question, it will take time for the learners to adjust to your style and expectations. My experience suggests that they are eager to discuss, but only in an environment of safety and trust.

3. The most successful way to eliminate good response to your questions is to have criticized, belittled, or embarrassed someone's response in the past. This will be true of most age-groups, but especially teenagers and more timid adults. No one will open his mouth if it means risking humiliation. Most teachers do not intend to do these things, but if the class even gets the hint that you reject something they say, they put on a cloak of silence. We rationalize by believing that we can reject their words or acts without conveying rejection of them. Such reasoning never seemed to work well for me. Most people make no distinction between rejecting their words and rejecting them.

So what does one do? Let them wallow in error? Several summary responses come to mind.

1. Explore and probe their thinking rather than moving into a quick evaluative and judgmental posture. Why did they say that? What is the history of that statement?

2. Sometimes other members of the group will challenge an idea. They may challenge poorly (at which point you may need to defend the one criticized or judged) or they may challenge sensitively, thus giving you a bridge into good discussion.

3. Use "I" messages. "You" messages tend to create defensiveness and feelings of rejection. For example, "I hear you saying. . . . Am I accurate?" Or, "I have not thought that way myself, tell me more about your reasoning." These three techniques are especially necessary when relationships are relatively new and fragile.

4. People change their attitudes and behaviors but not usually because they have been told. Typically, something has caused them to think about their ways and to reconsider the direction they had been taking. People change when they think. In monologue only the teacher thinks. Questions bring dialogue. In dialogue learners think for themselves, which becomes the context for most significant change.

5. When I get to know my students as people with a history of experiences, the last word I would use to characterize them is "ignorant." Most of us do not consciously believe that our students are ignorant. But, when lecture is virtually all they get, that assumption is operating whether we like it or not. When dialogue is a short commodity in the classroom experience, learners assume they have nothing to offer.

6. Most of us, looking back on our best learning experiences, do not recall a lecture or sermon. Probably it was a person who dialogued with us; a group that we met with where the discussion was stimulating; an experience shared with others that challenged our old way of thinking; a private conversation where two people shared freely about matters rarely discussed and found a refuge in each other. Assuming our own most valued learning experiences were not in a "monologue" context, why should we rely on that so heavily, if not exclusively, in creating learning environments for others, especially adults. Information transmission by itself rarely provides a significant learning experience.

7. Faith is not doctrine, memorizing Bible verses, or some private experience. Faith is a relationship with Jesus Christ that reveals its vitality in loving Him and one another. Doctrine, Bible verses, and experiences are components but the essence of faith is

relationship. Is the same true for learning? A critical factor in learning is the nature of the relationship between the teacher and the learners. Knowledge quickly fades after the test or a sermon. But the fragrance of a beautiful relationship lingers throughout one's life, immortalizing God's truth. Jesus seems to be suggesting this when He says, "I know My sheep, and My sheep know Me" (John 10:14). But He did not stop there. Based on the relationship of the Shepherd and His sheep, a most significant phrase occurs: "and His sheep follow Him" (John 10:4). Both knowledge and obedience, faith and works, naturally flow from a healthy relationship.

Additional Inductive Teaching Strategies

Jesus used many inductive forms to help His followers grasp both the content and the experience of a relationship with Himself. Simulations and questions were examined in depth but the remaining, while worthy of examination, will only be briefly noted and illustrated. The ones I have used came to me in the normal course of reading, listening to a speaker, or attending a conference. Having a category of "inductive teaching ideas" will alert you to the things that come your way naturally.

Parables. Jesus seemed to enjoy stories. Parables are intended to communicate a truth in an indirect way. But it requires that others think about it, at which point the lesson should be obvious. Consider this parable:

The Guru's Cat

> When the guru sat down to worship each evening the ashram cat would get in the way and distract the worshipers. So he ordered the cat be tied during the evening worship. Long after the guru died, the cat continued to be tied during evening worship. And when the cat eventually died, another cat was brought to the ashram so that it could be duly tied during the evening worship. Centuries later learned treatises were written by the guru's disciples on the essential role of a cat in all properly conducted worship.
>
> Author unknown

Ask the learners what this means. Continue with discussion about the "cats" in our worship. What parts of worship are tradition and what parts are mandated by Scripture? Are there any "cats" they would like to throw out? Why or why not? Are there some they might like to add that would make worship more meaningful for them? How would others feel about such an addition?

Problem-Solving. Of course, there are many forms problem-solving can take. You can find moral and ethical dilemmas, case studies, riddles, and hard choice situations. Suppose you wanted to talk about the Father and the Son and their absolute uniqueness. I like the following quotation as a starter. I give a copy to each learner and sometimes let them work in small groups trying to solve it.

> Two artists met one time within a little wood.
> Each brought his finest painting stroked by his complete uniqueness.
> When each revealed his canvas to the other—they were identical.
> So once in every solar system there are two fingerprints alike.
> But only once.[1]

Self-awareness/Self-discovery. These inductive activities can be fun but need to be spaced. Sometimes they get overused and lose their punch. Usually some artifacts are required: 3 x 5 cards; paper to write or draw on; a thin, flexible wire to shape; a checklist; a personality test; and others.

To start my Human Development and Ministry class, I give everyone a twelve to fifteen inch wire, thin yet strong so it can be twisted yet straightened out again easily. I tell them to shape the wire in a form that represents a significant growth experience for them. Since conflict and hardship often produce growth, much of that comes out. People create the oddest shapes with their wires but the most serious revelations accompany them—parent's divorce, an abusive home, broken friendships, cancer, untimely death, and vocational shifts. The little wires represent a piece of their personal stories.

Use of objects in getting at self-awareness is helpful. It makes things easier. In quiet they draw or shape or whatever. When it comes time to explain, they talk about the object they hold up. It becomes easier to talk about the object and what it represents than to capture in words the ill-formed thoughts in the mind or the emotions of the heart. People are more at ease when they look at an object rather than the person who is sharing.

Games. The Ungame (available from the Ungame® Co.), one of the better ones to foster discussion and openness among players, can be used as a self-awareness/other-awareness activity among adults or as a way to bridge generations in dialogue: youth with older people, even those of the grandparent generation, parents with children, church leaders with parishioners, young converts with veteran Christians, or whatever combinations of people you might wish to connect.

Prepare some good debriefing questions so that you can get the most benefit from this inductive strategy.

CONCLUSION

Inductive teaching can be a very powerful means by which God is able to change our thinking and our living. Its power for the adult educator lies in a three-way synergism: the teacher who engages the learner in the learning process; the learner who proactively assumes some of the responsibility for learning; and the Holy Spirit who is able to take these efforts and bring the desired changes in both teacher and learner. It is then that we will share in John's joy of "children walking in the truth" (2 John 4).

Notes

1. Calvin Miller, *The Singer* (Downers Grove, Ill.: InterVarsity, 1978), 15.

For Further Reading

Blank, Marion, and Sheila J. White. "Questions: A Powerful but Misused Form of Classroom Exchange." *Topics in Language Disorders* 6 (1986): 1–12.

Gibbs, G. Ian. *Dictionary of Gaming, Modeling, and Simulation.* Beverly Hills, Calif.: Sage, 1978.

Lunetta, Vincent N., and Harold J. Peters. "Simulations in Education: Sharpening an Old Tool." *Curriculum Review* (March–April 1985): 24, 30–32, 34.

Payne, Stanley. *The Art of Asking Questions.* Princeton, N.J.: Princeton Univ. Pr., 1980.

Reuben, Brent, and Richard Budd. *Human Communication Handbook: Simulations and Games,* vols. 1, 2. Rochelle Park, N.J.: Hayden, 1978.

Stanford, Gene, and Barbara Dodds Stanford. *Learning Discussion Skills Through Games.* New York: Citation Press, 1969.

Taylor, John L. *Learning and the Simulation Game.* Beverly Hills, Calif.: Sage, 1978.

TEN
SMALL GROUPS IN ADULT EDUCATION
Samuel L. Canine

As Tom drove home from the deacons' meeting, his mind wandered back over the last two-and-a-half hours. He could have predicted some comments and decisions made this evening, but he was pleasantly surprised how supportive the men had been.

> "Mom" died two weeks ago. I actually sensed these men at the meeting tonight cared deeply about the loss my family has suffered. It amazes me when God's people come alongside and willingly share the pain and confusion that fill my life. Their ability to anticipate my hurt and help me by praying and sharing the burden means more than I can express. The sincerity of their tears as we prayed spoke to my own suffering. I am so thankful for the opportunity to minister with these dedicated servants of the Lord.

Tom has experienced the help and caring a small group provides when it functions as God intends.

This chapter is concerned with using small groups in adult Christian education. It is organized around seven important questions related to small groups.

WHAT IS A GROUP?

Each of the following definitions of a "group" provides insight concerning the essence of a group:

> A Christian group can be defined as a gathering of believers

> with mutual interests working toward a common goal.[1]

In this first definition Gangel presents three foundational elements. First, "mutual interests" help to bond the group together. It is the rationale that forms and keeps the group formed regardless of purpose or duration. Something serves as glue to keep the group together. Second, the believers forming a group are characterized as "working." Some energy must be expended. This does not label all groups as task-oriented. "Work" could be understood as building relationships with other believers. Third, these believers are moving toward a "common goal." Bonding, energy, and objective surface from this definition.

Joseph Luft also helps us understand how to define a group:

> A group is a living system, self-regulating through shared perception and interaction, sensing and feedback, and through interchange with its environment.[2]

Luft's definition presents a group as a separate, identifiable entity, calling it a "living system." This opens consideration for topics like the "personality" or "life-cycle" of a group. He further adds the dimension of control with the words "self-governing." Communication and conflict emerge as an integral part of this second definition. The words, "interchange with its environment" admit that no group functions without reference to a larger audience. Implicit and, at times, explicit communication occur between a group and those surrounding the group.

Gerald Phillips, in *Communication and the Small Group,* presents the following definition of a group:

> A number of people adhering to a similar set of ideas or principles, or advocating a common goal, though perhaps disagreeing about methods of achieving the goal, or sharing a common method of carrying on business, resolving conflict, or demonstrating awareness of each other.[3]

The third definition not only suggests conflict but assumes it will occur. The give and take concerning interaction within a group appears from Phillips' definition.

When all three definitions are considered, a group may be defined as a number of people who demonstrate community, energy, purpose, life, control, and conflict while communicating to and with a watching world.

WHAT ARE THE COMPONENTS IMPORTANT TO GROUPS?

Groups form and function on the basis of need. A person must place higher value on being within the group than being outside of it. The extent to which we sense belonging to a group determines how committed we are to it. It is not enough to be on the inside of a group; we must be aware of our position and role within the group.

A clear and positive role within a group helps a person build significance. Flexibility should usually characterize most group functions. Even when the group has a designated leader, it is often appropriate for the leadership function to be shared. For example, if the meeting requires a detailed discussion of money matters, the treasurer of a group may exercise leadership by taking a more prominent role. In nearly every group some will withdraw from any role of leadership. In many instances we have perpetrated this hesitancy by faulty notions of leadership and how it functions. Once group members accept the freedom of shared roles it becomes easier for them to identify and embrace their own contributions to group success.

A group member constantly measures personal status or identity. We each have an idea of who we are to the group and what we bring to the group's process. But often this changes from the feedback we receive from other group members. Many factors contribute to status or identity. If we have not listened well or supported someone else when he or she presented a report or project, we are less likely to be accepted by that individual. Position, age, past performance, positive/negative attitude, resources, power, communication skills—all these bear on the standing the group bestows on each member. If we fail to weigh what the group considers our roles to be, we can be assured of some rude surprises.

Affection develops slowly within a group, but it is a necessary element to produce satisfaction and optimal efficiency.[4] The routine activity of standing boards and committees within a church may cause the members to treat affection with lesser value. But even in the most task-oriented group, affection must be present or the group will fail to function as it should. Group members bring a different need for the attachment and support from fellow group members. The best expectation allows each member to determine a personal comfort zone for affection given and received. Time can become a wonderful ally as group members work at building affectionate relationships.

Cohesiveness results from group affection. To be "cohesive" a group must exhibit the feeling of closeness or tightness. We find high cohesiveness where members share a great number of values and behaviors. When cohesiveness characterizes a group, it weathers conflict without disintegration. Strong allegiance to group commitment reigns. Frequently, cohesiveness comes from group members getting to know one another outside of a formal meeting. Two or three group members may golf, play tennis, or shop regularly together. This helps to glue relationships so that greater honesty and sincerity can be expressed.

When a group develops cohesiveness, the members consider each other as more than fellow-board or fellow-committee members. They count each other as friends. This changes the atmosphere in which work will be conducted. A strong sense of family permits the group to accomplish much more than would otherwise be possible.

Social climate usually reveals itself as positive or negative. "Does it feel good to be a part of this group?" or "Am I just enduring my role in this group?" Previous experience with group members tends to push us toward a predisposition about social climate. We expect a positive climate when we sense we are contributing to the group process. Where battles have been waged the likelihood for negative social climate increases greatly. No doubt you have experienced a group meeting when everyone was "in good spirits." It amazes us as to how much can be decided when the entire group finds itself agreeable as a meeting begins.

The final component for group effectiveness focuses on sensitivity to group process. Groups, by nature, require give-and-take activities to occur with greater frequency than interpersonal or mass communication. Speaking and listening skills are unveiled with greater regularity in the group setting. A group member finds oneself more responsible to accurately and regularly pick up communication signals. Unfortunately, few boards or committees insist on speaking and listening abilities as prerequisites! Therefore, an individual can enter group work in a church with little knowledge of group communication skills. Perhaps some ongoing groups would profit from investing time to learn the dynamics of how a small group operates.[5]

WHAT LEADERSHIP FUNCTIONS SHOULD BE PRESENT IN GROUPS?

In many small groups we designate who will be the leader. We desire to hold someone accountable for accomplishing this group's mission. But realistically, the leadership function becomes shared by most people in the group. The group may have a "chairperson," but this in no way guarantees all leadership will emerge from this individual. At times, different leadership functions may be needed by the group. Consider the following:

1. The Liaison. This person has connections with the world outside the group. She usually serves as a channel of communication between the group and the rest of the Sunday School class or church. People like this possess expert communication skills and know how to define different roles within the organization. Special information may also be at their disposal. For example, in our imagination let's establish a committee to design, develop, and implement plans for a Valentine's Day banquet. We will make the wife of the treasurer one of the committee members. If the committee has money questions or problems adhering to the budget, she will probably find herself in a liaison role.

2. The Problem-solver. This function surfaces from the group members who are uncanny in knowing where the group is, where it ought to be, and why it is not moving in the direction of the target. The ability to influence discussion toward a mutually agreed goal distinguishes the person with this leadership gift. The net result allows for the group to rapidly move through an agenda and sense accomplishment with the task finished.

3. The Humorist. Every group at some point needs a person who can bring relief to the group process. This leadership skill functions to keep spirits from sagging. Group members demonstrating this ability help to relax other group members so that greater catharsis can be achieved. Feelings can often be more easily expressed when the door opens on its humor hinge. This presupposes a legitimate use of humor. Occasionally, a group becomes victimized by a clown who never sees anything as serious. The timing of wit and humor can help any group better fulfill the group's goals. But clownish activity must be removed from group experience.

4. The Doubter. This leader appears skeptical by nature. Tough questions are raised to stimulate group thinking. Each group desperately needs a good doubter. They keep the group from forming consensus too early. "But what about. . . ?" frequently falls from this person's lips. Some in the group may find this individual frustrating. The doubter drags his feet, does not move quickly to second motions, and responds differently than most in the group. The group may be tempted to wish he would be absent from more meetings since he keeps the group from rapid progress. This person sees things differently. Often he will contribute the off-the-wall suggestions. Sometimes the group's basic assumptions can be challenged by this person. But the doubter may also spare the group some grief later, since he usually thoroughly examines a matter from every conceivable angle. This person safeguards the group from falling into groupthink and overreliance on the tried and true.

5. *The Record Keeper*. This may or may not be a secretary or treasurer. Such a person functions as the resident historian of the group. Often he or she brings more experience, age, or longevity to the group dynamics. When a person functions too regularly as a record keeper, innovation and creativity may suffer. This historian can glorify the past to the extent it robs the present and future of proper consideration. Usually the group does benefit from the stability this leadership perspective provides.

6. *The Builder*. To be around this group member is to be encouraged. Builders make everyone feel important. It takes mature social skills for this leadership function to occur. The group atmosphere becomes positively charged by the verbal and non-verbal communication of this person. Builders always seem to sense when constructive comments are needed to smooth ruffled feathers and bruised egos. Diverse, yet well-developed interpersonal skills are part of the contribution they make to the overall effectiveness of the group.

7. *The Pleasant Person*. It appears that nothing bothers this group member. He demonstrates obedience without question. Rebellion would be the last thing on his mind. He is predisposed to agreement. He will not initiate anything, but allegiance and responsibility rate high with this individual. He may have difficulty understanding why two group members disagree or have trouble accepting each other's opinion. He accepts everyone easily without reservation. He probably will not exhibit much conviction on any given issue. In times of group warfare the pleasant person can be valuable to the whole group. He will be at the forefront of peaceful settlement of problems.

8. *The Concept Person*. This person provides the pioneer func-

tion of a group. She has truckloads of creativity and a vivid imagination. The concept person brainstorms well and sees multiple viable options in any discussion. Risk comes easy to the idea individual. Sometimes, she may move faster than the group finds comfortable, and can become discouraged if the group drags along more slowly than her work tempo dictates. When the idea person functions well, the group prospers with rich potential outcomes.

The previous eight leadership functions assume a sharing of roles within the group. One person may display two or more of the leadership types discussed. The circumstances, history, and subject, will help to determine what each member considers as appropriate leadership function at any given time.

WHAT PROCESS DOES A PROBLEM SOLVING GROUP NORMALLY DEMONSTRATE?

If the group follows a normal sequence, five steps will describe the process.[6] To the extent a group deviates from these steps, problem solving by a group will become more difficult.

1. Definition and analysis of the problem. Freedom for all members of the group must be guaranteed. This first phase presents a danger in that a group may be lured to move too quickly to the second phase of problem solving. The problem should be probed in detail. The group should ask questions like, "Are we examining the root problem?" "Have we considered all the facts, details, or perspectives which bear on this discussion?" "Is one person in the group conspicuously quiet?" "Why?" "Should we allow some time to pass before agreeing on a definition of the problem?"

2. Establish the criteria or standards for the solution. Groups too frequently pass over this phase. But the question still looms as important, "How will we know if we have succeeded?" This examines the presuppositions of the group. It explores values, beliefs, and attitudes.

3. Discovery of possible solutions. Creative ideation will greatly assist the ultimate product of the group. Predictability always leaves us with some uncertainty. But what are the probable outcomes if we follow this course of action? Usually, the more possible solutions the group can generate, the higher caliber the decision-making.

4. Evaluation of each solution. Both strengths and weaknesses should be addressed. Emotional attachment by any group member must be discouraged. If a group operates as a team, the recognition will be shared by everyone in the group. The group must seek to be as objective as possible.

5. Implementation of the solution. The group should develop a timetable with a group member's name linked to a time when given action will have occurred. If personalization does not take place, much time can be wasted and group activity stymied.

WHAT ARE A LEADER'S OBLIGATIONS?

Four essential duties can be expected of any designated leader.[7] First, the group can assume the leader will adhere to an agenda. Second, you can anticipate a designated leader will aid in structuring procedures or in adhering to procedures that facilitate the group's orderly function. Third, the group can assume the leader will attempt to create or develop a positive group atmosphere by discouraging attacks on personalities, polarization, and hostility. It is reasonable to expect the leader will encourage mutual respect, openness, and attraction among the group members. Fourth, the group can assume the leader will monitor the progress and problems the group demonstrates.

WHAT IS REASONABLE TO EXPECT FROM ALL GROUP MEMBERS?

Em Griffin suggests the following eight areas of commitment to the group process.[8] The group will only be as strong as the weakest link in this chain of eight duties.

1. Attendance. A sense of interdependency must be present if interpersonal relationships within the group are to grow.

2. Affirmation. Nothing can detour my genuine love for a fellow member of this group. Each member needs to communicate this in actions and words.

3. Confidentiality. What we say in this place stays in this place. A mutual trustworthiness must characterize interpersonal relationships within the group.

4. Openness. Each member will risk the joys as well as the hurts within the group context.

5. Honesty. Speaking the truth in love will be practiced. This means the good and the bad in a relationship. Integrity demands we crusade against cover-up.

6. *Sensitivity.* A strong effort will be made to see every discussion through the eyes of the other group members. When silence is desired it will be granted.

7. *Accountability.* Each of us will assume responsibility for our words and actions. We will avoid blaming others in a group for our personal feelings.

8. *Prayer.* We will regularly bring each other before the Lord in prayer. This means we will have a mutual ministry sharing areas of our lives where prayer is needed.

CONCLUSION

We have assumed the necessity of small group ministry for the effective advancement of adult education. We cannot be asked, "Will we have them?" But the question must be asked, "Will our small group ministry be effective?" This chapter introduced six critical questions concerning groups. The answers to these questions should assist us on the path toward more effective adult education.

Through the centuries small groups have played a crucial role in adult spiritual formation. Small groups provide the Christian educator with a marvelous tool for fostering transformation. By their very nature small groups provide affinity and support. However, they are not inevitably educative. At times groups offer support, but no challenge or accountability, to their members. Their proper use requires a delicate balance between relying on the natural and spontaneous side of small groups and forming them into intentional learning and caring communities.

Notes

1. Kenneth O. Gangel, *Feeding and Leading* (Wheaton, Ill.: Victor, 1989), 229.
2. Joseph Luft, *Group Processes: An Introduction to Group Dynamics*, 3rd ed. (Mountain View, Calif.: Mayfield, 1984), 2.
3. Gerald M. Phillips, *Communication and the Small Group*, 2nd ed. (New York: Bobbs-Merrill, 1973), 16.
4. For fuller treatment the reader should consult B. Schultz, "Characteristics of Emergent Leaders of Continuing Problem-solving Groups," *Journal of*

Psychology 88 (1974): 167–73.

5. A practical book to consider, written in layperson terminology, would be Em Griffin, *Getting Together* (Downers Grove, Ill.: InterVarsity, 1982).

6. For a detailed treatment of group decision-making, the reader should consider, Bobb Biehl and Ted W. Engstrom, *Increasing Your Boardroom Confidence* (Phoenix: Questar, 1988).

7. The appendix of Biehl and Engstrom's *Increasing Your Boardroom Confidence* presents some excellent checklists.

8. Griffin, *Getting Together*, 35–36.

For Further Reading

Griffin, Em. *Getting Together.* Downers Grove, Ill.: InterVarsity, 1982.

Hestenes, Roberta. *Using the Bible in Groups.* Philadelphia: Westminster, 1985.

Luft, Joseph. *Group Processes: An Introduction to Group Dynamics*, 3rd ed. Mountain View, Calif.: Mayfield, 1984.

Plueddemann, Jim and Carol Plueddemann. *Pilgrims in Progress: Growing Through Groups.* Wheaton, Ill.: Harold Shaw, 1990.

ELEVEN

SETTING AND ACHIEVING OBJECTIVES FOR ADULT LEARNING

Warren S. Benson

THE CASE OF LARRY AND LAURA

Larry and Laura had just enrolled in their first class at seminary. Their instructor was long noted for his academic stature in biblical and theological studies. Larry and Laura were both excited about being enrolled in his class, expectant of the volumes of wisdom they would glean under his instruction.

At each class session, the teacher stood in front of the room, opened the period with a moment of prayer and then filled the remainder with eloquent lecture and didactric instruction. At first these fresh eager students felt comfortable with this instructional approach. Like sponges, their notes absorbed every word their teacher uttered.

After a while, however, Larry and Laura grew increasingly frustrated with the course taught solely in the didactic mode. The professor never allowed time for questions. When someone did suggest a line of inquiry concerning the subject matter, he would give quick answers himself, rather than allowing the class to discuss an issue.

And so it continued—Larry and Laura passively absorbing knowledge, occasionally reproducing verbatim on an exam what they had been taught. When they graduated, the institution commended both for their high academic marks, all the while patting itself on the back for another success story in preparing men and women for ministry.

In their first church experience, Larry and Laura faced a divisive doctrinal dispute. Unfortunately, the issue under dispute had never been addressed in their theological training. Skilled in academics, these young servants could only reproduce answers to didactically presented information. Their training had not equipped them with the tools necessary to produce new information in the face of new problems. In short, they had no educational referent upon which to respond in the face of the doctrinal dispute. Unable to resolve its docrinal problem, the church split, and Larry and Laura resigned their ministry.

Who failed? To some extent, Larry and Laura, for they were unable to handle the problem they faced in their ministry. But they are not unique; casual observation of seminary graduates indicates a high failure rate for first ministry experiences. Unacceptably high. Why?[1]

THE CASE OF ANNE AND ALLAN

Anne and Allan have been members of a Bible teaching church and adult Sunday School class for years. They have a profound respect for Scripture and engage in private Bible reading and prayer. Over the years they have sat in the worship services and Sunday School classes, but increasingly have failed to apply the truth of the Bible.

As they broadened their knowledge of biblical content, they gradually lost contact with those who need to know the Gospel of Jesus Christ. They reveled in their friendships at the church, but slowly became defensive regarding the urgency of touching the lives of non-Christians. Their correct theology has been divorced from the realities of their community.

Matthew's party, at which Jesus ate with Matthew's friends and other sinners (Matt. 9:9-13; Luke 5:27-32), is of only literary interest to Allan's and Anne's thought processes, let alone their experience. Evangelism seems a splendid topic for Bible study, yet they consider it someone else's responsibility, although they give generously to overseas missions, camping ministries, and Christian schools.

Facing their community directly has become threatening. They seldom open their home to non-Christians; they have failed to identify the needs of neighbors; and they no longer possess a heart of mercy. Anne and Allan have tuned out this dimension of Christian responsibility though they retain a growing conviction that the Good News they clutch so closely is indeed worthy of sharing.

Who failed? Yes, to some extent Anne and Allan have, but why this cavalier indifference? Why this disregard for the clear teaching of the Bible?

BRIEF ANALYSIS

Churches and Christian schools alike often suffer a common weakness with their immediate constituencies: a minimal amount of information taught gets transferred into the lives of learners. The content so often appreciated does not actualize in experience; truth never integrates into the realities of life.

Accountability becomes a concept glibly preached and taught, yet seldom practiced. This tragic oversight and prostitution of the pedagogical process often results in a bittersweet encounter at the judgment seat of Christ. What is the responsibility of those who teach the Allans and Annes, the Larrys and Lauras? James 3:1 says that we who teach will be judged more strictly.

This seemingly benign subject, setting and achieving learning objectives, is of far greater cruciality than one may think at first. After all, what happens to people as a result of our teaching affords an issue of monumental consequence!

Foundational Concepts

Theologically and biblically, the power of the Holy Spirit working through the Scriptures (Heb. 4:12) and the godly life of the teacher (1 Thes. 1:4-10; 2:7-12) is fundamental to the teaching-learning process and mission (see chaps. 1 and 2). Spirit and Word are not up for reconsideration for refutation. A student's alertness in Bible teaching is tightly tied to the authority of Scripture, the centrality of Jesus Christ as Savior and Lord, and the ministry of the Holy Spirit who guides people to recognize, understand, and appropriate truth. As that happens, the supreme Bible teaching goal of bringing people to faith and then to spiritual maturity will be actualized (Eph. 4:11-16).[2]

The Teacher's Person

It is not sufficient for the teacher of biblical content to be a Christian, a person in good standing in the church and community, or to be an unusually fine communicator. These are of importance, particularly being a committed follower of Jesus Christ, but do not represent the total. Possessing the spiritual gift of teaching is an indispensable factor for success in teaching. Stanley R. Allaby has defined it as follows:

> The spiritual gift of teaching is the Spirit-endowed ability to acquire truth, to model it in one's life, to communicate it systematically and clearly, and to apply it in a manner that increasingly transforms the student into the image of Christ.[3]

While each element of this definition has value, the most difficult and most perplexing part is how to apply the Book so that our students become like Jesus Christ. Even when one teaches in a theological academic setting, it is not enough to present content under the delusion that somehow Isaiah 55:11 will cover a multitude of pedagogical gaffes: "so is My word that goes out from My mouth. It will not return to Me empty, but will accomplish what I desire and achieve the purpose for which I sent it."

That verse remains true, but we must not use it as a crutch or safety net. Our Lord calls us to excellence in handling Scripture, not to mediocrity. Achieving that high standard should demand that we utilize the best insights available.

In summary, to teach for the greatest amount of transformation toward Christlikeness in our students, there should be godliness in our lives and superior methodology in our teaching.

GETTING THE BIG PICTURE

Where do we begin? The process initiates in the larger context of the institution. Every church and school should establish a directional instrument—a mission statement. However, some keep moving the target to where the arrow went! They find it easier to shoot without taking proper aim. A cartoon character once boasted, "I don't know where I'm going, but I'm making great time!" A mission statement brings clarity to our purposes, goals, and objectives.

Mission Statements/Institutional Purposes

Most churches and schools have purposes and mission statements. However, they dare not exist only in the minds of the leaders; they must be in writing. Further, these directional compasses should be followed as benchmarks for the ministry of that school or church. Not infrequently we treat these statements as if they are inconse-

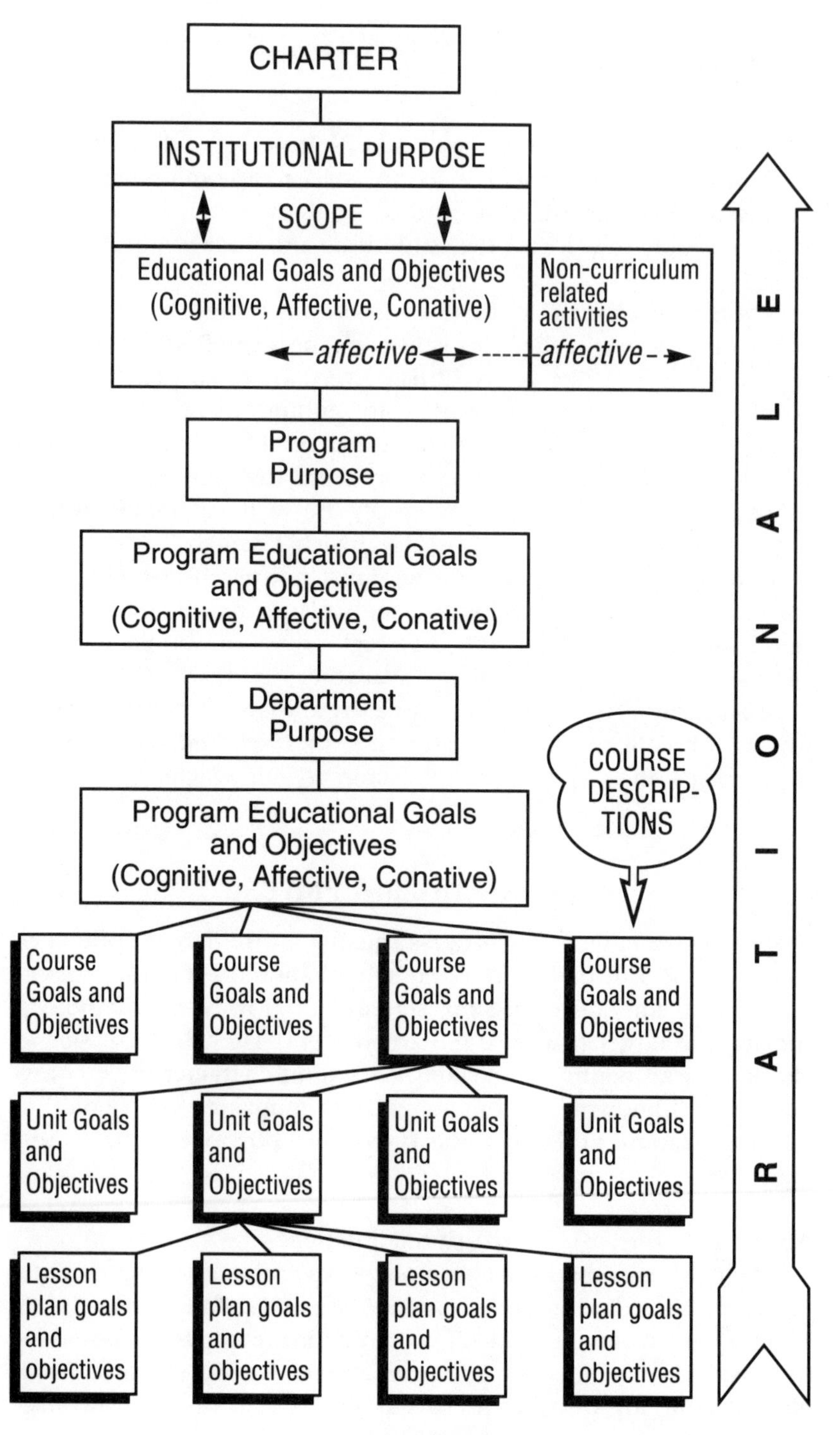
CHARTER
INSTITUTIONAL PURPOSE
SCOPE
Educational Goals and Objectives (Cognitive, Affective, Conative)
affective
Non-curriculum related activities
affective
Program Purpose
Program Educational Goals and Objectives (Cognitive, Affective, Conative)
Department Purpose
Program Educational Goals and Objectives (Cognitive, Affective, Conative)
COURSE DESCRIP-TIONS
Course Goals and Objectives
Course Goals and Objectives
Course Goals and Objectives
Course Goals and Objectives
Unit Goals and Objectives
Unit Goals and Objectives
Unit Goals and Objectives
Unit Goals and Objectives
Lesson plan goals and objectives
Lesson plan goals and objectives
Lesson plan goals and objectives
Lesson plan goals and objectives
RATIONALE

Figure 11.1

quential. This tends to happen when new leadership comes on the scene (whether pastor and laity or presidents/administrators and instructors) or when a block of time has elapsed since the writing of the purpose commitments. We should evaluate these valuable tools annually. And all teachers should reflect on whether they can work within those ground rules.

Program Purposes

But where does the adult study group or Sunday School class fit? As Figure 11.1[4] on page 162 indicates, there should be a hierarchy of purposes, goals, and objectives. The chart can be intimidating and even confusing unless several basic definitions are understood.

The term *purpose* "describes who? does what? for whom?" That is the big picture. A goal is a broad statement of learning intent which (1) identifies the kind of learning desired and (2) expresses the subject in a chewable bite. Educational objectives are the cognitive, affective, and conative/psychomotor behavioral indicators of goal achievement. They express the outcomes or competencies which indicate goal achievement.[5] Many educators substitute the term "conative" for psychomotor which focuses on "skills based on performance abilities."[6] We will use conative in this chapter.

For the school, these goals and objectives furnish the material from which administrators and faculties develop programs, departments, and courses of study. For the church, goal setting provides indicators to show where the congregation wants to be.

The adult study group should accept the church's goals as its guideline in a planned sequence of time. Goal setting is then based on the local church's mission statement and its assessment of context and potential for reaching those goals. "Goals, therefore, are *means* to move the congregation in the direction it wants to go. They are not *ends* in themselves, but means to help the congregation accomplish the end results; its mission."[7] And the study group should reflect and embody those goals.

Shawchuck and Perry suggest that a good goal should meet the following tests: it is to be mission-directed, desirable, conceivable, assignable, believable, achievable, measurable, and controllable.[8]

Thus far I have attempted to give you, the Bible teacher, an overview of the tapestry of educational purposes and goals. An additional word is needed before we get into the fabric of teaching the Bible to a group of people—the objectives in the class setting.

The term "program" in the chart may remain an enigma to you.

In the context of the academic community, a program would be the grouping of disciplines that have the most in common; for example, sociology and psychology are two of the social sciences whereas history and Engish literature belong to the humanities. In the church, programs emerge from an agency such as the Sunday School, such as small group Bible studies or cell groups that may have their genesis in adult Sunday School classes. In some churches the youth ministry (middle school/junior high and high school) is often called the "youth program" and in that definition reflects the academic use of the term.

SETTING OBJECTIVES

Scripture provides the primary material, the content of the teaching-learning process. Understanding people's needs gives direction for when, how, and even what we teach. As you have noticed, this volume devotes considerable space to describing the process of adult spiritual formation (chap. 3), the cultural factors of North American adults (chap. 4), why and how adults think, respond, and learn (chaps. 5 and 8), the significant reasons for using inductive approaches to Bible study (chap. 9), and finally, the explosive power of small groups and the inherent factor of accountability (chap. 10). In the remaining chapters you will find helpful discussions about the people who make up the adult grouping (chaps. 13–19).

This present chapter is surrounded by important data that will equip you to sense and grasp the personal, sociological, psychological, and spiritual needs of your people, and what and how you, despite your own limitations, can address those needs. With that newfound awareness you can seek wisdom from God in comprehending the biblical passage to be taught and guidance in understanding the perspectives, biases, and potential of people so that a wedding of people and Bible will cause them to follow and obey God's answers.

First Class Session

At the first meeting of the class you should solicit the students' insights regarding their expectations of the class. In a Sunday School or evening small group context you have probably chosen the topic or biblical book to be studied *together* (on occasion they are assigned).

You should give them an opportunity to express verbally what they particularly want you to emphasize. For example, in the Book of 1 Peter, it might be peace in the midst of turbulence, handling trials and suffering, insights for wives and husbands, and developing a godly lifestyle. You then begin to have a "feel" for their particular needs. You may use a questionnaire and give them ten minutes of silence to write their reflections before they share their ideas verbally. Understanding Anne and Allan, Larry and Laura, gives you direction and sensitivity.

In the academic setting, classes/courses will be assigned by the academic dean or the department chairperson. Certain freedoms for revising the syllabus, after meeting with students in the first class session, are not only acceptable but desirable with some limitations. Unfortunately, too many academicians dismiss that possibility and teach a given class as they always have in the past. However, all course content should be reviewed by the instructor with prayer and precision in light of the students' needs, but more importantly, through the leadership of the Holy Spirit.

As the class/group/course proceeds, the teacher should be ready to make adjustments without losing the essence of why this course was put into the curriculum. As a teacher, I relish these changes which bring freshness and dynamic to the content. I am currently making sweeping changes in a course that I have taught for fifteen years. And after the class begins, I will further fine tune it in light of the needs of these particular students, in terms of the course's overall goals, and the objectives of each class session.

Hook your teaching to good goals and objectives. In view of what one wants to accomplish, establish accurate goals and objectives. First though, note the simple but significant distinction between a goal and an objective.

An instructional objective is an intended outcome that can be identified with greater objectivity and precision than a goal. Goals, usually three to seven in number, are set for a class/group/course to achieve. Objectives are the aims and foci for our daily or weekly class session. If you develop a printed syllabus, the goals are usually listed immediately after the paragraph denoted "Course Description." Students quickly forget the goals because they live in the existential present and can only remember yesterday and today's session. Continually we must deftly relate the big picture, the goals, to the objectives of the daily or weekly meetings.

The goals provide overall direction while the objectives determine where the class is headed in each session. Now the hierarchy of purposes (mission statement), goals, and objectives have become crystal clear. Unfortunately, a few writers of Sunday School curricula use goals and objectives interchangeably which complicate matters and make muddy what should be unmistakably evident.

The Short-term Perspective

The Bible book or topic has been chosen for study. The curriculum has been laid out in weekly "chewable bites." The general and specific needs of the group have been ascertained; for example, young marrieds are attempting to establish strong relationships with their spouses, but children are coming along and the weekends which formerly were free for trips and activities are now restricted as they build a family.

As you study the passage or topic to be taught, pray for discernment. Prayer cannot be underplayed. It is determinative. You are responsible for helping your students make connection with the concepts and experiences emerging from the content. The Holy Spirit waits to give them insight and understanding. It must not be taught in a vacuum, as if this material fails to have relevance to the pulls and tugs of their lives.

Three Foci in Choosing Objectives

To relate to those pulls and tugs we must connect the Bible to life by determining whether our major emphasis in any given session should be the cognitive (knowing and understanding), the affective (attitudes and feelings), or the conative/psychomotor/behavioral (activity, skill). Put very simply, if lives are to be changed, the students must come to know and understand, be challenged to change their attitudes and feelings, and as a result be willing to rearrange their actions and intentions.

Teach for one primary outcome in a session. To teach holistically all three should be involved, but one is to be selected to receive the major emphasis. Christian educator LeRoy Ford suggests that in developing a goal/objective oriented learning process, we remember that:

1. Learning goals lead to primary learning outcomes.
2. Primary learning outcomes lead to principles of learning.
3. Principles of learning lead to appropriate learning activities.
4. Learning activities lead to reaching the learning goals.[9]

THE QUALITIES OF AN OBJECTIVE

Remember, an instructional objective can be observed and recognized as successful or unsuccessful. That behavioral thrust bears the signature of Robert Mager's *Preparing Instructional Objectives,* published in 1962 and revised in 1975.[10] For ten years that slim volume seemed to have an electrifying effect on the educational establishment. It and other Mager writings contributed to that which became known as the behavioral objectives movement.[11]

Educational conferences and worshops were and still are replete with his and other similar thinkers' ideas. Teachers tried to develop objectives that could be quantified and demonstrated. However, some efforts were unsatisfactory because many constructs and concepts are difficult to identify in behavioral terms. This is of significance to Christian theology and Bible teaching because many decisions to follow biblical teaching are not immediately observable (though in time those decisions should become discernible).

In 1972, D. Cecil Clark's *Using Instructional Objectives in Teaching* brought additional balance to this one-sided perspective. Clark argued that covert behavior, that which "cannot be directly seen or heard" on the part of the teacher, was just as legitimate an objective as overt behavior—that which "can be directly seen or heard by the teacher."[12] Through teachers' persistent desire to affect change in the life of the learner, the concept of instructional objectives became distorted for a brief period.

To summarize, an objective should possess the following qualities:

1. A statement about the learner, not the teacher;
2. The learner's behavior;
3. The topic at which the learner's behavior is directed;
4. The consequences of the learning experience, not the experience itself.[13]

This concept of an objective relating to what the student will learn is essential. It must not be treated superficially. The instructor must design the context and climate for learning with as much precision as is possible. We gratefully acknowledge that the Holy Spirit goes beyond our abilities to perceive people's needs. The Spirit knows with unerring wisdom what areas of a person's life need purifying or which decisions will lead to action.

The Holy Spirit's presence and work, however, should not diminish our drive for excellence in setting on-target objectives. Robert Mager challenges teachers to think carefully when writing objectives so that they are meaningful.

> A meaningfully stated objective, then, is one that succeeds in communicating your *intent;* the best statement is the one that excludes the greatest number of possible meanings other than your intent.
>
> Unfortunately, many slippery words open themselves to a wide range of interpretation. . . . If you use only such broad terms (or fuzzies) when trying to communicate a specific instructional intent, you leave yourself open to misinterpretation.[14]

Consider the following phrases in this light:

Words Open to Many Interpretations	**Words Open to Fewer Interpretations**
to know	to write
to understand	to recite
to *really* understand	to identify
to appreciate	to sort
to *fully* appreciate	to solve
to grasp the significance of	to construct
to enjoy	to build
to believe	to compare
to have faith in	to contrast
to internalize	to smile[15]

Christians have a tendency to use the words in the left-hand column in designing and writing objectives, but that list is less measurable. While we may readily be negative toward Mager's ideas because of what we might think is an effort in downplaying faith and belief, such a conclusion is erroneous. Objectives should be specific and exact. If a theme does not lend itself to specific outcomes, it is too broad and universal. The more vigorous our thinking regarding outcomes, the more likely we will see them accomplished and achieved in the experience of our students.

Some educators such as Elliot Eisner suggest that "strict adherence to behavioral objectives restricts the development of curriculum, discourages the occurrence of other important learning outcomes, and fails to recognize that among the most important outcomes of instruction are those that relate to attitudes."[16] Eisner calls for expressive objectives as well as behavioral objectives which "involve a conscious recognition by the teacher that the visible and measurable outcomes of a learning experience are not the only outcomes of that experience and, in many cases, not necessarily the most important."[17]

While D. Cecil Clark provided clarification regarding overt and covert aspects of behavioral objectives, Krathwohl, Eisner, and others gave the affective domain proper significance with the cognitive and the conative. David Y.N. Wu convincingly demonstrates that Jesus Christ emphasized affective content in His teaching.[18]

THE COGNITIVE DOMAIN

LeRoy Ford claims that there are two primary learning outcomes in the cognitive domain—knowledge and understanding. Mark Simpson suggests that Scripture calls for a third—wisdom—and he may be correct.[19] However, no discussion of this domain should fail to consider the ideas of Benjamin Bloom and his associates.

Bloom, Krathwohl, and a contingent of educators developed taxonomies of educational goals and objectives in the cognitive and affective domains.[20] Their work created a stir because it produced many fresh insights. First, though, we must look at an important definition. "Cognitive learning is concerned primarily with the acquisition of information, the development of strategies for processing information, with decision-making processes, and with logical processes."[21]

Mark E. Simpson[22] has summarized the six levels of cognitive learning in this manner:

PRIMARY LEARNING OUTCOME: KNOWLEDGE

Only one of the six levels of Bloom's taxonomy in the cognitive domain focuses on the primary learning outcome of knowledge (Ford 1978). This first and lowest level of cognitive learning is *knowledge* (Bloom 1956).

At the knowledge level, learning emphasizes the remembering of concrete and abstract facts. Three subclasses of knowledge level learning include: (1) the knowledge of specifics, such as terminology, and knowledge of facts; (2) the knowledge of ways and means, such as conventions, trends and sequences, and classifications and categories; and (3) the knowledge of universals and abstractions, including principles and generalizations, and theories and structures (Bloom 1956). Most educational systems focus on this level of learning (Stice 1987).[23]

PRIMARY LEARNING OUTCOME: UNDERSTANDING

The remaining five levels of Bloom's taxonomy in the cognitive domain focus on the primary learning outcome of understanding (Ford 1978). These five levels of cognitive learning are *comprehension, application, analysis, synthesis,* and *evaluation* (Bloom 1956).

Comprehension. This focuses on learning the correct use of abstractions when solutions are specified. Three subclasses of comprehension level learning include: (1) translation; (2) interpretation; and (3) extrapolation (Bloom 1956).

Application. At the application level of learning, the emphasis of learning aims at the correct use of abstractions when *no* solutions are specified (Bloom 1956). This third level of learning, according to Bloom, tends to be the highest learning focus of some educational institutions, especially when lecture or didactic based, even though it is still a lower level of learning (Stice 1987). The application level of cognitive learning does not have any subclassifications.

Analysis. This is the fourth level of learning and the first of the higher levels of cognition. At the analysis level, learning focuses on the breaking down of concrete facts and abstractions into constituent parts in order to detect relationships and organizational patterns. Three subclasses of analysis level learning include: (1) the analysis of elements; (2) the analysis of relationships; and (3) the analysis of organizational principles (Bloom 1956).

Synthesis. The fifth level of learning is the putting together of constituent elements into a new whole. Synthesis has three subclasses of learning: (1) the production of unique communications; (2) the production of a plan or set of operations; and (3) the derivation of a set of abstractions or relationships (Bloom 1956).

Evaluation. The sixth and highest level of Bloom's taxonomy makes judgments about the value of a concrete fact or abstractions for some purpose, such as ideas, works, solutions, methods, materials, and so forth. Two subclasses of evaluation learning include (1) judgment by internal evidence, and (2) judgment by external criteria (Bloom 1956).

LEVELS OF LEARNING AND LEARNING OUTCOMES

One of the purposes underlying the creation of the cognitive taxonomy was to assist researchers in the investigation of the relationship of testing and educational practice (Bloom 1956). Research studies utilizing Bloom's taxonomy have included discoveries such as:

1. the significant relationship between the cognitive level of questions asked and the cognitive level of the subsequent answers (Wilen and Clegg 1986); [24]

2. lecturing as a passive mode of instruction does not engage students in the higher cognitive levels—active student involvement is necessary to operate at the analysis, synthesis, and evaluation levels (Stice 1987);

3. convergent questions focus on the lower levels of knowledge, comprehension, and application learning while divergent questions focus on the high cognitive levels (Wilen and Clegg 1986);

4. a summary of studies indicates that over half of classroom instruction is at the lower levels of learning, and that much of classroom instruction is at the lower levels of learning, and that much of classroom interaction is at these lower levels (Hough 1983);[25]

5. accumulation of knowledge level learning is not sufficient to engage in the higher levels—the development of processing skills is thus necessary for analysis, synthesis, and evaluation level learning to occur (Yinger 1980).[26]

These data suggest that Bible teachers and professors should write objectives for a class by following certain key ideas:

1. Incorporate inquiry and discovery methodology to augment the lecture and encourage students to think at higher levels. Give thought and prayer to where these methods may lead the interaction.
2. Use interviews, small groups, debate, role-playing, forums, field trips, and other techniques that promote discussion of the biblical passage or topic.
3. Use divergent questions (those that differ and deviate from each other), rather than convergent questions (those that connect and come together) to produce a rich variety of possible solutions to a problem.
4. Use the questions of the students to lift the discussion to a higher level of thinking. Do not respond to their questions with answers at the same level at which they are asked.
5. Teach them how to think. Use tutorials with small groups as a more formal approach or informally at a restaurant over coffee.
6. Teachers who enjoy words and presenting material should guard against dominating the class. The more student involvement, the greater the tendency toward superior learning. Balance between lecture and discussion should be our goal.
7. Remember: the development of good objectives will help free us up as instructors to be vehicles and instruments for greater learning—both for ourselves and our students.

JUSTIFICATION FOR THE USE OF INSTRUCTIONAL OBJECTIVES

D. Cecil Clark aptly recounts how the teacher may get rid of the "fuzzy and unsure feeling that instructional objectives are designed to reduce and often eliminate." If one uses them with discretion and wisdom:

1. The teacher will have a method by which to measure, at least partially, important objectives not measured in the past. At times, we have omitted crucial and difficult-to-define objectives in favor of the unimportant.

2. Both teacher and student will have greater visible evidence that the objectives have been achieved.

3. The student will experience considerably more freedom in achieving an objective. Based on personal abilities and background, the teacher should construct a unique set of objectives tailored to the student's needs.

4. The student will feel a greater focus and direction on what is important, on what to study for, and on what he will be evaluated.

5. In the long run, both teacher and student will save time and energy. Benefits for the teacher come in (1) selecting instructional materials; (2) planning learning activities; and (3) evaluating student learning. The student gains a clearer picture of the content to be studied and understands the implications for his lifestyle in that content.

6. The students will participate more in their own instruction if we encourage them to help determine how their behavior patterns will be affected as they relate to the content.

7. The teacher will feel greater security with this more direct evidence of teaching effectiveness. Yet instructional objectives are statements of measurable student conative activities which include desire and volition as well as actual physical or performance actions.[27]

In much of our Bible teaching, there is too much vagueness and imprecision. We tend to walk into a class and, in effect, back up the truck, dump our biblical load, and pull away from our people. We must study our people as well as our Bibles, determine their needs, relate the Bible to those needs, and write down what the Holy Spirit directs us to say to them. It takes time and effort. There are no shortcuts! But it is eminently worthwhile and satisfying.

If we would be catalysts for educational change, we must function in more exact ways and leave less to chance. Be aware of both process and outcomes. Do not be consumed with content. Keep these in proper balance. Measurable objectives reflect a concern for students and *their* growth and accomplishments. I have found that the clearer my objectives, the more free I am to have the Holy Spirit change and nuance what I teach, what emphases I make, and adjust my prepared material to the time allotted. The Holy Spirit nudges me to sense what people need and how the Bible can speak to their situational contexts. This does not minimize the absolute necessity for thorough study and well-honed objectives.

Assist the Lauras and Larrys, the Annes and Allans to absorb information actively and gain understanding through guiding their inquiry and discovery learning. Help them to practice the skill of problem-solving in light of scriptural principles. Unloading the truck is not sufficient. Meaningful interaction in which vulnerability, accountability, and integrity are readily apparent can enable Larry and Laura to handle divisive doctrinal disputes and Allan and Anne to achieve confidence and responsibility in touching their neighbor's lives. Then Proverbs 2:1-5 becomes a reality.

> My son, if you accept my words and
> store up my commands within you,
> turning your ear to wisdom
> and applying your heart to understanding,
> and if you call out for insight
> and cry aloud for understanding,
> and if you look for it as for silver
> and search for it as for hidden treasure,
> then you will understand the fear of the Lord
> and find the knowledge of God.

Notes

1. Mark E. Simpson, "Old Wine in New Wineskins: Inquiry and Problem Solving Skill Development for the Transference of Learning in Theological Education" (Ed.D. paper, Trinity Evangelical Divinity School, June 1991), 1–2.
2. On transformational Christian education, see my chapter, "Education and Nurture," in *A Living Legacy—Essays on the Evangelical Free Church Movement—Past, Present and Future* (Minneapolis: Free Church Publications, 1990), 211–40, and the chapter by Jim Wilhoit, "Transformational Christian Education: The Teacher As Guide," in *Christian Education and the Search for Meaning,* 2nd ed. (Grand Rapids: Baker, 1991), 105–14.
3. Stanley R. Allaby, "How to Discover and Test Whether You Have the Teaching Gift," *Journal of Pastoral Practice* 2, (1978): 178.
4. LeRoy Ford, *A Curriculum Design Manual for Theological Education: A Learning Outcomes Focus* (Nashville: Broadman, 1991), 80. Adapted by author, used by permission.
5. Ibid., 23.
6. Kenneth O. Gangel, "Teaching Adults in the Church," in *The Christian Educator's Handbook on Teaching,* ed. Kenneth O. Gangel and Howard G. Hendricks (Wheaton, Ill.: Victor, 1988), 152. See also Thomas H. Groome, *Sharing Faith: A Comprehensive Approach to Religious Education and Pastoral Ministry* (San Francisco: Harper, 1991).
7. Norman Shawchuck and Lloyd L. Perry, *Revitalizing the Twentieth-Century Church* (Chicago: Moody, 1982), 32.
8. Ibid., 34.

9. LeRoy Ford, *Design for Teaching and Training* (Nashville: Broadman, 1978), 76.

10. Robert F. Mager, *Preparing Instructional Objectives*, 2nd ed. (Palo Alto, Calif.: Fearon, 1975).

11. Without question, the writings of Ralph W. Tyler, especially his durable *Basic Principles of Currriculum and Instruction* (Chicago: University of Chicago Press, 1950), and the Bloom and Krathwohl taxonomies, set the stage for the colorful and pragmatic books by Mager.

12. D. Cecil Clark, *Using Instructional Objectives in Teaching* (Glenview, Ill.: Scott, Foresman 1972), 4.

13. Ibid., 118.

14. Robert F. Mager, *Measuring Instructional Content* (Belmont, Calif.: Fearon, 1973); *Analyzing Performance Problems* (Belmont, Calif.: Fearon, 1970); and *Developing Attitude Toward Learning* (Palo Alto, Calif.: Fearon, 1968).

15. Mager, *Instructional Objectives,* 20.

16. E.W. Eisner, "Educational Objectives: Help or Hindrance?" *School Review* 75 (1967): 250–60.

17. Guy R. Lefrancois, *Psychology for Teaching*, 4th ed. (Belmont, Calif.: Wadsworth, 1982), 133.

18. David Y.N. Wu, "Affective Teaching in Jesus' Teaching: A Closer Look at the Footwashing in John 13:1-20," *Christian Education Journal* 11 (Winter 1991): 79–83.

19. Simpson, "Old Wine in New Wineskins," 1–2.

20. B.S. Bloom, et al., *Taxonomy of Educational Objectives, Handbook I: Cognitive Domain* (New York: David McKay, 1956); and D.R. Krathwohl, B.S. Bloom, and B.B. Masia, *Taxonomy of Educational Objectives, Handbook II: Affective Domain* (New York: David McKay, 1964).

21. Lefrancois, *Psychology*, 372.

22. Mark E. Simpson, "Does Scripture Suggest a Seventh Level of Learning? Knowledge, Understanding, and Wisdom in the Context of Scripture and in Contrast with Bloom's Taxonomy" (Ed.D. paper, Trinity Evangelical Divinity School, June 1991). Adapted by author.

23. James E. Stice, "Farther Reflections, Useful Resources," in *Developing Critical Thinking and Problem-Solving Abilities,* ed. James E. Stice (San Francisco: Jossey-Bass, 1987), 101–10.

24. William W. Wilen and Ambrose A. Clegg, Jr., "Effective Questions and Questioning: A Research Review," *Theory and Research in Social Education* 14 (1986): 153–61.

25. Robert Stephen Hough, "A Taxonomic Analysis of Reflection—Eliciting Techniques in Experiential Learning" (Ph.D. diss., Michigan State University, 1983).

26. Robert J. Yinger, "Can We Really Teach Them to Think?" in *Fostering Critical Thinking,* ed. R.E. Young (San Francisco: Jossey-Bass, 1980),

11–52.

27. Clark, *Instructional Objectives,* 27–35.

For Further Reading

Apps, Jerold W. *The Adult Learner on Campus.* Chicago: Follett, 1981.

Bateman, Walter L. *Open to Questions: The Art of Teaching and Learning by Inquiry.* San Francisco: Jossey-Bass, 1990.

Biehler, Robert F., and Jack Snowman. *Psychology Applied to Teaching.* 4th ed. Boston: Houghton Mifflin, 1982.

Bowman, Jr. Locke. *Teaching for Christian Hearts, Souls, and Minds.* New York: Harper and Row, 1990.

Brookfield, Stephen D. *The Skillful Teacher.* San Francisco: Jossey-Bass, 1990.

———. *Understanding and Facilitating Adult Learning.* San Francisco: Jossey-Bass, 1986.

Coleman, Lyman, and Marty Scales. *Serendipity Training Manual for Groups.* Littleton, Colo.: Serendipity, 1989.

Cross, K. Patricia. *Adults As Learners.* San Francisco: Jossey-Bass, 1981.

Ericksen, Stanford C. *The Essence of Good Teaching.* San Francisco: Jossey-Bass, 1985.

Fagerstrom, Douglas L. *Singles Ministry Handbook.* Wheaton, Ill.: Victor, 1988.

Fiske, Marjorie, and David A. Chiriboga. *Change and Continuity in Adult Life.* San Francisco: Jossey-Bass, 1990.

Friedeman, Matt. *The Master Plan of Teaching.* Wheaton, Ill.: Victor, 1990.

Gorman, Julie A. *A Training Manual for Small Group Leaders.* Wheaton, Ill.: Victor, 1991. See all ten volumes in Groupbuilder Resource series she has edited.

Grippin, Pauline, and Sean Peters. *Learning Theory and Learning Outcomes.* Lanham, Md.: University Press of America, 1984.

Gullette, Margaret Morganrotte, ed. *The Art and Craft of Teaching.* Cambridge, Mass.: Harvard-Danforth Center for Teaching and Learning, 1982.

Hestenes, Roberta. *Using the Bible in Groups.* Philadelphia: Westminster Press, 1985.

Hicks, Robert. *Uneasy Manhood.* Nashville: Oliver Nelson, 1991.

Holmes, Arthur F. *Shaping Character: Moral Education in the Christian College.* Grand Rapids: Eerdmans, 1991.

Hudson, Frederic M. *The Adult Years: Mastering the Art of Self-Renewal.* San Francisco: Jossey-Bass, 1991.

Johnson, Kent L. *Paul the Teacher.* Minneapolis: Augsburg, 1986.

Knowles, Malcolm S. *The Making of an Adult Educator.* San Francisco: Jossey-Bass, 1989.

Knox, Alan B. *Helping Adults Learn.* San Francisco: Jossey-Bass, 1986.

Koons, Carolyn A., and Michael J. Anthony. *Single Adult Passages.* Grand Rapids: Baker, 1991.

Kuhlman, Edward. *Master Teacher.* Old Tappan, N.J.: Revell, 1986.

LeBar, Lois E., and James E. Plueddemann. *Education That Is Christian.* Wheaton, Ill.: Victor, 1989.

Lockerbie, D. Bruce. *Thinking and Acting Like a Christian.* Portland, Ore.: Multnomah, 1989.

Lowman, Joseph. *Mastering the Techniques of Teaching.* San Francisco: Jossey-Bass, 1984.

Mezirow, Jack, and Associates. *Fostering Critical Reflection in Adulthood.* San Francisco: Jossey-Bass, 1990.

Moore, Mary Elizabeth Mullino. *Teaching from the Heart: Theology and Educational Method.* Minneapolis: Fortress, 1991.

Morgan, Norah, and Juliana Saxton. *Teaching, Questioning, and Learning.* London and New York: Routledge, 1991.

Murray, Dick. *Teaching the Bible to Youth and Adults.* Nashville: Abingdon, 1987.

Osmer, Richard Robert. *A Teachable Spirit: Recovering the Teaching Office in the Church.* Louisville: Westminster/John Knox Press, 1990.

Peace, Richard. *Small Group Evangelism.* Downers Grove, Ill.: InterVarsity, 1985.

Seldin, Peter, and Associates. *How Administrators Can Improve Teaching.* San Francisco: Jossey-Bass, 1990.

Sell, Charles M. *Transitions Through Adult Life.* Grand Rapids: Zondervan, 1991.

Smith, Robert M., and Associates. *Learning to Learn Across the Life Span.* San Francisco: Jossey-Bass, 1990.

Stafford, Tim. *As Our Years Increase.* Grand Rapids: Zondervan, 1989.

Stubblefield, Jerry M., ed. *A Church Ministering to Adults.* Nashville: Broadman, 1986.

Trueblood, D. Elton, *The Teacher.* Nashville: Broadman, 1980.

Wilhoit, Jim, and Leland Ryken. *Effective Bible Teaching.* Grand Rapids: Baker, 1988.

TWELVE

CURRICULUM FOR ADULT EDUCATION

James C. Galvin and David R. Veerman

The word "curriculum" may evoke thoughts of selecting the right text or writing specific materials. But the selection and writing of materials form only part of the process. First the educator must *plan.* So "curriculum for adult education" is, in essence, the process of planning educational experiences for adults.

Planning, by definition, is a systematic and rational approach, not haphazard and impulsive. Without careful planning, the educational design becomes sloppy and disoriented. That's what happens when a teacher does what he feels like doing or uses what she had in seminary or college. Programs thrown together in that manner will be ineffective, or hit and miss at best. Instead, a responsible and effective approach to designing educational programs for adults is rational, logical, as well as thought through. Educators must consider where they want to go and the best way to get there.

The next question follows naturally. Is there a *best way* to go about planning programs for adult education? Answering that question is the thrust of this chapter.

MISTAKES

Unfortunately, teachers often design educational programs for adults by copying the wrong educational models. This can be a fatal mistake for adult education. These teachers may organize and run the program:

- like educational programs for children (pedagogical model),
- like an extension of a seminary (academic model),
- like a place where knowledge is deposited in the heads of the learners (banking model),
- like a debate or like a trial (adversarial model).

These improper models don't fit the "consumers"—the students. Each of these educational approaches may be very effective with a specific audience. But just because an approach works well in one classroom is no guarantee that it will work with adults generally. Effective curriculum design must begin with a careful analysis of the prospective students.

AN IMPORTANT DISTINCTION

Malcolm Knowles found a remarkable consensus among adult educators in the formal steps of successful program design when he made a distinction between credit (degree-oriented) and noncredit programs.[1] The degree programs tended to follow traditional academic patterns. Students had paid for the course and were working toward a specific degree. Those two facts alone insured a certain level of motivation to learn and succeed in class. But noncredit programs had to be much more in tune with the students whose motivational patterns were not so easily defined. Successful noncredit programs used a different process, and this process is more suited to adult education.

Here are the five steps that Knowles discovered in those successful noncredit programs:

1. Determine the needs of the constituents;
2. Enlist their participation in planning;
3. Formulate clear objectives,
4. Design a program plan;
5. Plan and carry out a system of evaluation.

We will consider each of these steps and make the application to curriculum for Christian education of adults.

DETERMINE THE NEEDS OF THE CONSTITUENTS

Educational programs for adults must be based on the needs and interests of adults. These men and women take the courses voluntarily; they do not have to "go to school." And in most churches, they don't pay a fee to take the course; they have no financial investment in the class. It is vitally important, therefore, that program planners know what will motivate their potential learners to learn. Do these men and women want to learn facts and information? Do they want to find answers to specific questions? Do they want to learn skills? Do they want to meet felt needs? Do they want to grow and mature in certain areas of their lives? In short, what do they really want out of the class?

Here are several ways to find the answers to that final crucial question.

- You can watch, observe, and ask around to find out what potential students say they are interested in. The interests of new parents, for example, will center around child rearing, home, and family. Others may be interested in how to bring their faith into the workplace. Many needs will be obvious if you open your eyes and ears.

- You can read market research or other descriptions of people like your target audience. If you want to reach "Baby Boomers," read about their needs. If your community has an influx of transferees each summer, look for articles that discuss their concerns. Take advantage of the research others have done.

- You can organize a formal or informal focus group. Pull together a small group of adults from your target population, and ask for their advice on structuring the program. Most Christian adults will quite willingly come to a brief meeting which purposes to design a program to help them.

- You can design a formal or informal survey of interests and felt needs. Again, if the survey is well thought through and easy to answer, most adults will be willing to take a few minutes to fill it out. Usually they will be happy and grateful to be part of the planning process.

- You can meet with all the potential participants to discuss their needs, especially if the group is not too large.

Remember that adults are motivated to learn, but they attend a class or group for their own reasons. Houle[2] identified three main categories of adult learners:

1. The *goal-oriented adult* who wants to attain one or more specific objectives of his or her own choosing. For example, a woman might want to receive an Evangelical Training Association certificate so that she can be a better Sunday School teacher. Someone else may want to learn how to witness more effectively. The student's goal may or may not parallel the teacher's goal.

2. The *learning-oriented adult* is motivated by the desire to gain knowledge. For example, some Christians express interest in studying the Bible because they want to understand it better—they want Bible knowledge. Others want to grow in grace or become better men or women of God. These are the regulars, the faithful attenders.

3. The *activity-oriented adult* is attracted by the nature of the event. He or she wants to meet people, socialize, get out of the house. These people come for the fellowship. They may want to be together with other singles, young mothers, newlyweds. One of the highlights for them in any adult Sunday School class is the coffee break.

When planning the curriculum, keep in mind that all three categories of learners show up in most classes. Students will have a range of motivations for attending. Plan accordingly and don't assume that people attend just because they enjoy sitting under your teaching.

ENLIST THEIR PARTICIPATION IN PLANNING

Knowles observes that student participation in the planning process leads to other good things.

- They feel a greater sense of responsibility to the program because they helped in its creation—they buy in. The class becomes "theirs." It's not just *your* class anymore.

- They recognize some needs in their lives not felt before. In other words, *real needs become felt needs through a process of self-assessment.*

- They learn almost as much through planning as through the instruction itself.

FORMULATE CLEAR OBJECTIVES

The planning should result in determining the objectives of the program. All educational programs, whether designed by the participants or designed by the teacher, should have specific objectives so that learning has direction and focus. In addition, clear and complete objectives define the content and shape of the selected learning activities; and specific objectives are invaluable aids in evaluation—we know whether or not the class has been effective by how well we meet our objectives.

One helpful technique in determining objectives is to finish this sentence: "As a result of this session (or program or class), the participants will ______________________________."

The blank can be filled in with the desired life change or with content to be learned. This helpful formula helps the planner to focus on life change in the adult learner. It helps focus on end results and the activity of the student, rather than the teacher. This formula is useful both for general goals as well as specific objectives. For a series on Christian parenting, this general goal could be stated: "As a result of this series, parents will know how to foster Christian values in their homes." A more specific objective for a single class session could read, "As a result of this session, the participants will rearrange their schedules so that they can have at least one meal together as a family every day."

For a class on Reformed theology, the overall goal could read, "As a result of this course, students will understand the basics of Reformed theology." An objective for one class could be: "As a result of this session, students will be able to explain the doctrine of election to another believer." Setting objectives is covered more thoroughly in chapter 11.

The point here is that the needs of the prospective students should inform your content and the direction of your goals and objectives.

In this process, however, remember that the teacher may have goals for teaching, but students have their reasons for learning. These two have to be brought together. Either (1) the teacher plows ahead and the learners buy in or withdraw; (2) the learners and teacher decide the educational goals together; or (3) the teacher designs the course and then the teacher and learners merge their goals by a process of negotiation.

It is much more effective to enlist student participation in planning the program and determining objectives than if the teacher makes all the curriculum decisions alone. This way, the planning process itself can have educational value.

DESIGN A PROGRAM PLAN

After determining general goals and specific objectives, we outline the content and teaching methods to be employed. Here you will find it helpful to think in terms of learning activities or experiences.

Learning takes place through what the learner experiences, not what the teacher does. These learning experiences embody both the content and methods of instruction to be used. Ralph Tyler[3] has outlined five general principles for selecting learning activities:

1. Students must have experiences that give them an opportunity to practice the kind of behavior implied by the objective. So the practice portion of a lesson is just as vital as the input portion.

2. The student obtains satisfaction from carrying out the behavior implied by the objective. If the experiences selected are distasteful or unsatisfying, learning is much less likely to occur. This means that the teacher must be in touch with the interests and needs of the students.

3. The experiences must be appropriate for the learners—neither too difficult nor too easy. The teacher must begin where the learners are, not where he or she thinks they should be. Students cannot be forced to go way over their heads or stretch beyond their capabilities. The teacher must judge student readiness for the tasks to be performed.

4. Many particular experiences can be used to attain the same educational objective. This means that the teacher will have a wide range of creative possibilities for selecting learning activities. We can capitalize on his interests, draw on areas of her own expertise, use resources in new ways, and overcome constraints such as lack of equipment or inadequate classroom space.

5. The same learning experience will usually bring about several outcomes. The positive side is that one learning experience can work toward attaining two or three of the specific objectives. This leads to more efficient use of resources. But the teacher also has to keep on the lookout for *undesirable* results that accompany the intended learning goal. While the students may be able to parse key Greek words, they may also learn to hate Greek. They may be able to explain difficult passages in Revelation, but decide never to

read the book again when the course finishes.

Selecting learning experiences is not a cold, mechanical process. Instead, it is a living, dynamic, and creative process as the teacher considers objectives, reflects on potential learning experiences, and expands the possibilities of what might be done in class. Then the experiences can be checked with a set of questions appropriate for the situation. For example, does this learning experience lead toward attaining the objective? Will it be fun? Satisfying? Rewarding for the learners? Are the learners ready for this? Does it meet several of the learning objectives or important organizational values?

Then the learning experiences can be revised or refined to make them more effective. Learning experiences for adults can include role-plays, case studies, field trips, dramas, work sheets, simulation games, projects, quizzes, presentations, small group work, stories, interviews, physical challenges, and skits. The list is almost endless. This process of creating and selecting learning experiences requires both artistry and careful evaluation. This is the heart of the process of designing educational programs.

After the learning experiences have been selected, they need to be sequenced and organized into individual lessons. We recommend using the HOPE format developed by Robert Carkhuff.[4]

H = Hook
O = Overview
P = Presentation
E = Exercise

The "Hook" is a creative opener that surfaces a felt need, or simply demonstrates where the learners are currently in the development of a skill. It can also simply be an exercise in which the students review the material covered in the previous session.

In the "Overview" we introduce the content and show why it is important. We also share practical uses of the material.

"Presentation" describes the content transmission whether through lecture, audio, video, or other medium.

During the "Exercise," learners have the chance to reflect on the content, practice skills, plan applications, and so forth.

PLAN AND CARRY OUT A SYSTEM OF EVALUATION

Most educators will say that evaluation is an important step in planning and implementing learning programs. Yet few people actually evaluate in a systematic way. Many reasons are given: "It takes too much time"; "It takes too much effort"; "I don't know how to do it"; or "It might mean that I have to change my program."

One principle to keep in mind is that evaluation always takes place in one way or another. Both teacher and students are mentally judging the merit and worth of their experiences as the course progresses. They have feelings and opinions on the value of the teaching and learning. So if evaluation will happen anyway, it might as well be a rational and systematic process of gathering information to improve the program.

Carkhuff[5] identifies five levels of evaluation for a thorough evaluation of learner outcomes in any educational program:

1. *Involvement:* learners pay attention and participate in the course and exercises.
2. *Exploration:* learners think about key issues and can share their thoughts and feelings about these issues.
3. *Understanding:* learners can discuss how key issues relate to them and to their jobs and can identify the skills required.
4. *Action:* learners can perform the skills adequately in the class and apply the skills in their life situations immediately after the course.
5. *Sustained Change:* learners are able to apply the skills under a variety of conditions and to transfer the skills to a variety of situations.

These five levels of learner outcomes help us determine the effectiveness of any educational program for adults. Failure at any of the levels shows the planner where additional refinement is needed in the course.

- If adults do not become involved, more attention needs to be given to their needs, interests, and concerns at the beginning of the course.
- If the learners do not explore the content, more attention needs to be given to the appropriateness of the content and how it is delivered.
- If learners fail to understand, then more time to discuss and think about the information is needed.
- If they fail to perform the skills adequately in class, then more practice time is required.
- If use of the skills deteriorates after a short time, then more

attention to transfer to learning and overcoming barriers is needed in the class.

• The primary purpose of evaluative information is to improve the class by making midcourse corrections along the way, or for improving the course for the next time it is taught. This feedback can also be useful in the continued development of the teacher and the students. Evaluation of the course itself can also be used as a summary learning exercise in some settings.

IMPLICATIONS FOR PROGRAM PLANNERS

Here is a summary of some important principles for adult learning and the implications for those who are developing curriculum for them. Donald Brundage[6] found thirty-six key principles of adult learning that have implications for planning programs for adult learners. Of these, four have particular significance for us:

• Adults are highly motivated to learn in areas relevant to their current life situations, developmental tasks, social roles, and life crises or transitions. Thus, learning is facilitated when content of skills can be immediately applied to real-life experiences. This means that we should plan programs around actual and current needs of the learners.

• Learners value their own motives, felt needs, and personal goals for learning. This means that our programs should allow opportunities for people to assess their own needs and establish their own objectives. If this is not possible, the teacher should give full information about the course objectives already selected so the learners may adjust their own expectations and goals, or withdraw from the course.

• Adults tend to experience stress at the start of educational programs. Learning increases uncertainty and change. This means that we should reduce the threat level at the start, by giving opportunities to talk through anxieties, creating a safe climate, and providing ample time to complete assignments.

• Most groups of adults represent a variety of learning styles, perspectives, and proficiencies. *There is no one best teaching style to use with adults.* Each style or method will work with some learners, situations, and content. So emergent teaching plans work best; they tend to be the most responsive to felt needs of the learners.

This means that our plans should be flexible. We should make them, then be ready to refine and adapt them to the particular adult learners in the group.

NUGGETS

Here are some additional ideas we have discovered by experience in teaching adults:

- Don't tightly pack sessions with content. Allow time to discuss, reflect, integrate with other aspects of life.
- The past experience of adults is a valid source of learning for everyone. Allow time for sharing and show high regard for past personal experiences of group members.
- Get input from key members of the class before preparing the materials. Have the class discuss and approve any study guide you use.
- Work to reduce the threat level during the first session. Adults need time to "enter" the learning situation that you have set up.
- Plan a long break if your sessions are longer than ninety minutes. Adults need time to stand up, stretch, go to the bathroom, and socialize.
- Use no more than 50 percent lecture in any session. Balance lecture with discussion and other participatory exercises or participants will say that you talk too much.
- Respect your adult learners as people. Demonstrate this by using good responding skills. A teacher skilled interpersonally who uses these skills in discussions will see classes that normally don't want to discuss come alive.
- Avoid yes/no questions. Almost all of them can be restated in a way that causes students to think. (For example, instead of asking, "Does God expect Christians to be perfect?" you could ask, "Why do some Christians think that God expects them to be perfect?") Think through your discussion questions carefully.
- Ask a question and then be quiet. It might take a few moments before anyone ventures an opinion in some groups, but discussion will come if you have the discipline to be quiet.
- Allow the class to take the discussion off track from time to time. This is similar to preaching the sermon that God gives you in the pulpit rather than insisting on presenting the one that is written in your notes.
- Relate all teaching material to everyday life. And whatever you do, make it practical.

Notes

1. Malcolm S. Knowles, ed. *Handbook of Adult Education in the United States.* Washington, D.C.: Adult Education Association of the U.S.A., 1960.
2. Cyril O. Houle. *The Inquiring Mind.* Madison, Wis.: Univ. of Wisconsin Pr., 1961.
3. Ralph W. Tyler. *Basic Principles of Curriculum and Instruction.* Chicago, Ill.: Univ. of Chicago Pr., 1950.
4. Robert R. Carkhuff and Sharon G. Fisher. *Instructional Systems Design, Volume 1.* Amherst, Mass.: Human Resource Development Pr., 1984.
5. Robert R. Carkhuff. *Training Delivery Skills: Making the Training Delivery.* Amherst, Mass.: Human Resource Development Pr., 1984.
6. Donald H. Brundage and Dorothy Mackeracher. *Adult Learning Principles and Their Application to Program Planning.* Toronto, Ont.: Ontario Institute for Studies in Education, 1980.

For Further Reading

Boone, Edgar J. *Developing Programs in Adult Education.* Englewood Cliffs, N.J.: Prentice-Hall, 1985.

Brundage, Donald H., and Dorothy Mackeracher. *Adult Learning Principles and Their Application to Program Planning.* Toronto, Ont.: Ontario Institute for Studies in Education, 1980.

Brunner, des Edmund, David S. Wilder, Corinne Kirchner, and John S. Newberry, Jr. *An Overview of Adult Education Research.* Washington, D.C.: Adult Education Association of the U.S.A., 1970.

Carkhuff, Robert R. *Training Delivery Skills: Making the Training Delivery.* Amherst, Mass.: Human Resource Development Pr., 1984.

Carkhuff, Robert R., and Sharon G. Fisher. *Instructional Systems Design,* Vol. 1. Amherst, Mass.: Human Resource Development Pr., 1984.

Davis, Larry Nolan. *Planning, Conducting, Evaluating Workshops.* Austin, Texas: Learning Concepts, 1974.

Dickinson, Gary. *Teaching Adults: A Handbook for Instructors.* Toronto, Ont.: New Pr., 1973.

Houle, Cyril O. *The Inquiring Mind.* Madison, Wis.: Univ. of Wisconsin Pr., 1961.

Ingram, James B. *Curriculum Integration and Lifelong Education.* Elmsford, N.Y.: Pergamon Pr., 1979.

Knowles, Malcolm S., ed. *Handbook of Adult Education in the United States.* Washington, D.C.: Adult Education Association of the U.S.A., 1960.

Merriam, Sharan B., and Rosemary S. Caffarella. *Learning in Adulthood: A Comprehensive Guide.* San Francisco: Jossey-Bass, 1991.

Smith, Robert M., George F. Aker, and J.R. Kidd, eds. *Handbook of Adult Education.* New York: Macmillan, 1970.

Tyler, Ralph W. *Basic Principles of Curriculum and Instruction.* Chicago:

Univ. of Chicago Pr., 1950.

Verduin, John R. *Curriculum Building for Adult Learning.* Carbondale, Ill.: Southern Illinois Univ. Pr., 1980.

THIRTEEN

TEACHING YOUNG ADULTS

Fred R. Wilson

You look over some of the people in your class. George is in his first year of college almost 2,000 miles from home. He's taking courses in business, theology, and government to help select a career direction while gaining experience in several different part-time jobs.

Toni, who dropped out of high school, recently signed up for a hitch in the U.S. Army to get some job training since she has no plans for marriage.

John met Mary at college. They both dropped out to get married and earn some money to continue their college studies. While John sings in the church music program, Mary helps teach a toddler Sunday School class and has plans to teach in a Christian elementary school.

Sam and Lonie have been married seven years and have a four-year-old son Jimmy. Grandmother watches Jimmy while both parents work—Lonie as a manager in a computer services business while Sam works as a high school P.E. teacher.

Linda is the mother of an eight-year-old girl. Her first husband divorced her after nine years for another woman. She now lives with her folks and is searching for a job while attending college two evenings a week.

While each of these individuals is unique, they are all going through similar but diverse experiences related to autonomy, career, education, personal goals, marriage, and adjustment to new experiences. They have one common characteristic: each is called a "young adult" in our society because they fall into the eighteen to thirty-five-year age range.

This chapter starts by examining the issues and tasks of chronological periods in the young adult life cycle, with special emphasis on the years from eighteen to thirty-five. Next, a description of identity, intimacy, moral, and faith development in early adulthood are presented to provide a visual sense of the inner changes that may be occurring. The chapter concludes with an overview of specific adult education strategies that may assist those ministering to young adults.

WHAT IS AN ADULT?

Children were studied in the seventeenth century, adolescents in the early twentieth century, and the aged a few decades later.[1] However, it was not until the 1940s that gerontology was recognized as a new field of academic study, and only in the early 1950s that social scientists saw old age as significant for study.[2] In fact, it was not until the 1970s that the first real interest was shown in the early adult years. The following table summarizes the major definitions of adulthood.

Figure 13.1: Definitions of Adult/Adulthood

View	Definition
Social Science	Everything that happens after a certain age[4]
Traits	Gain a status, title, achieve certain characteristics[5]
Legal	Chronological age of majority; responsible for actions[6]
Social-Cultural	Social perception, assuming a specific role[7]
Developmental	Interaction of past and future, the whole person, and events

Psychologists most strongly favor the life-span developmental approach to understanding adulthood.[8] Each phase of adulthood is viewed in terms of both what has gone before and what is yet to come. In this approach adulthood is perceived as a life-long process with specific life stages including antecedents and consequences. The developmental approach is concerned with the interaction of psychological, biological, and social-cultural influences on adulthood. This perspective takes seriously the events and experiences affecting the whole person as we seek to teach and educate young adults.

BASIC CONCEPTS OF LIFE-CYCLE STAGES

It is helpful in ministering to young adults to assume that adulthood is not a stable and monolithic state, but rather a number of successive life periods. Each period ushers in its own variety of learning tasks. Young adult lives are patterned in a somewhat predictable sequence. There are certain key issues and tasks associated with being a young adult whether single, married, separated, divorced, or remarried.

Life Structure

Young adults face certain issues and adaptive tasks. These serve as marker events and tend to imply characteristic decisions and actions people adopt in relation to life events. As young adults move through this period, changes will occur in their "life structures."[9] Life structure describes the way a person is externally related to society by social roles in both work, church, and intimate relationships. It also relates to the internal meanings that these roles take on, including an internal clock that marks the passage of time in terms of changed perceptions of a person's place in the life cycle. Gould explored changes in adults' attitudes about various aspects of their lives in relation to time.[10] He writes, "While children mark the passing of years by their changing bodies, adults change their minds. Passing years and passing events slowly accumulate like a viscous wave, eventually releasing their energy and assuming new forms in altered relationships with both time and people."[11]

Developmental Tasks and Events

Many researchers have identified developmental tasks and events for young adults that are remarkably similar to each other. Developmental tasks are the physiological, psychological, and social-cultural demands a person must satisfy in order to be judged by self and others to be a reasonable and successful person. Some tasks appear to be external in nature, such as learning the skills to make a living, organizing a household. However, there are also internal components even with these tasks. A person's values, aspirations, and inner thought life also influence these tasks according to Havinghurst.[12] These tasks provide teachable moments when students are especially sensitive and unusually ready to learn.

Adaptation, Growth, and Transformation

Much of life-cycle research has focused on how adults adapt to these various tasks as well as planned and unplanned life events. A more recent emphasis has turned to the concept of growth. Growth comes by using life transition tasks and events to forge greater personal integrity, character, and effectiveness in the world.[13] Teachers of young adults need to view these life-cycle tasks and events as opportunities to introduce and support spiritual transformation rather than as mere difficulties to which a young adult must adapt.

Transitions

Understanding the nature of particular young adult transitions and the processes by which individuals tend to cope with these changes is essential. Generally, transitions take place in three ways: a person moves from one life-span period to another; the changing of roles; and through events that mark life—entering the work force, marriage. Transitions from one period to another can be due to biological changes (childbearing years for women), social-cultural events (roles in career and family), and the inner meaning of events to the person (psychological mid-life crisis). Some events are evident (balding, childbearing) or they may be unnoticed, although still dramatic (losing a job). They may be sudden, or more likely cumulative in nature.[14] Coping with transitions provides a major influence on their motivation to learn and change. Curriculum choices by the teacher and young adult cannot afford to ignore these concerns.

DEVELOPMENTAL PERIODS OF EARLY ADULTHOOD

By 1981 at least four major books and studies had been published along with a modest number of articles examining areas of young adult development. The following chart presents the periods of early adulthood based on the work of Vaillant[15], Sheehy[16], and Levinson and Gould, mentioned above.

Figure 13.2:
Young Adult Stages

	Levinson	Gould	Sheehy	Vaillant
17–22	Early Adult Transition	16–22 Leaving Our Parents' World	Pulling Up Roots	18–40 Intimacy & Career

22–28	Entering the Adult World	22–28 I'm Nobody's Baby Now	The Trying Twenties	Consolidation
28–33	Age 30 Transition	28–34 Opening Up to What's Inside	Passages to the Thirties	
33–40	Settling Down			

Early Adult Transition: Seventeen to Twenty-Two

All societies make clear distinctions between the status of children and adults. Most simple societies have a basic formula for inducting their youth into adulthood. Youth undergo certain rituals or rites of passage which vary in amount of stress produced after which, magically, they are adults. This status is more clearly defined for primitive societies than for more civilized young people. Kilpatrick believes that modern youth experience a prolonged period of crisis which helps develop character, creativity, and autonomy that leads to higher cultural levels.[17]

Levinson (whose research dealt only with men) calls this the "Early Adult Transition," a movement between adolescent life centered in the family of origin and entry into the adult world. It starts between sixteen and eighteen and ends between twenty and twenty-four. It usually lasts about five years. Transitional periods are like bridges between two periods of relative stability and building. One's old life is gradually left behind, but the new life that will replace it has not yet emerged. The following list of characteristics helps define a transitional period and how it affects a person.

1. It is a *boundary zone* between two or more or less defined or structured periods or stages of life. It is a period of struggle to find out who one is. For some the feelings are intense; for others, they are mild enough to seem almost nonexistent.

2. One tends to *terminate* or *modify* one's relationships with important people and institutions. Feelings of denial, anger, depression, bargaining, and acceptance are common.

3. It is a period during which one *questions* the world and one's place in it. Questions cover the full range from values to how one does things, to how one relates to authority, religion, and country.

4. The questioning leads naturally to *experimenting* with new or different ways of doing things. It includes such things as one's

relationship to the opposite sex, friends to associate with, and career choices and changes. This is when the neglected parts of the self seek expression.

5. Through questioning and experimenting one begins to *initiate new patterns* that lead to commitment in such areas as love, marriage, and career. These are revised life structures one is willing to test in a period of stability.

6. Transition periods *come to an end* when questioning and exploring lose their urgency and begin to make commitments in the critical areas of life. Some people refuse to move out of transitional periods.

The task of "leaving the pre-adult world" involves separating from one's parents and becoming more independent financially and psychologically. Levinson notes that only 18 percent of his respondents maintained a close personal relationship with parents while 20 percent experienced a serious conflict with their parents. The majority moved away, geographically or socially, without a major conflict, or to avoid one.

Entering the Adult World: Twenty-Two to Twenty-Eight

Levinson states this relatively tranquil period is repeated each decade after a period of transition. A man tests the life structure or Dream he has formed during the early adult transition by exploring and making tentative commitments that he believes can always be changed. It is also the time to make choices and carry them out, to "grow up" in terms of establishing an occupation or marriage, and to define goals. Seventy-five per cent of his sample men had married by this stage, and each man had made an initial, but serious, occupational choice. The essence of this period is the tension between these two demands, to explore and to commit. There are even doubts for those who had made firm earlier commitments in marriage and career.

Levinson notes two unique relationships are especially important during this phase: the "mentor" and the "special woman." A mentor is usually older than the protégé—too old to be a peer and too young to be seen as a parent. The mentor is experienced and kind of a "guru" who is both responsible and successful with respect to one or more areas of life. They provide challenge and support for the mentee in several ways: (1) they act as models or exemplars; (2) they engage in teacher/trainer functions, helping one to develop expertise; (3) they often act as sponsors, helping the mentored one to enter the system or to find advancement in it; (4) they act as hosts or guides when entering a new occupation. Mentors initiate others to the values, customs, norms, standards, and rules of the social system. The relationship tends to be transitional and may occur more than once in early adulthood.

The second unique relationship for men is the "special woman." She not only brings out the affectionate, romantic, and sexual feelings related to adjusting to the opposite sex, but also provides support for his Dream in ways similar to a mentor. She can encourage his sense of self and serves as a critic, guide, and sponsor as he works toward a goal. She influences his Dream and supports his growth from dependency on his birth family toward autonomous interdependence. Other research suggests that a special man can also assist a woman in similar ways. A crucial factor of this period is the extent to which each is committed to nourish and support the other's Dream.

Sheehy pays particular attention to the complexities of marriage during this period. She believes these years are ruled largely by external forces since few couples are aware of their own or their mate's inner life. She sees the goal of the twenties as trying to stabilize the marriage relationship.

Vaillant characterizes this phase as the time for "career consolidation of adolescent idealism" exchanged for "making the grade." Instead of dwelling on a choice of mate or career, the Harvard graduates in his study were mainly concerned about competition with other men in their field. Those who were charming at nineteen were now engulfed in the world of "gray flannel suits."

Gould describes this phase as "I'm Nobody's Baby Now." Men and women learn that trying is not enough, that working hard does not always bring success, and that you can't expect someone else to provide one's own fulfillment.

Ministry Implications

During this period, a teacher has the opportunity to help young adults perceive their careers and dreams as they examine their ideas and expectations of competition, achievement, power, wealth, and success. They need to be challenged to find Christian mentors who have worked through a sense of how Christ relates to their vocations and families.

Those who are married need special assistance in developing the intricacies of intimacy that move past the idealism of romance into the commitment, compromise, and sacrifice needed for an enduring relationship in the midst of handling conflict. Singles need to be supported in building healthy concepts of sexuality, friendship, and loneliness grounded on a positive identity. Other issues emerging include moving from friendship to dating, the difference between engagement and marriage, the decision to have children, the changes brought by pregnancy and living with the first baby, and child discipline at home and in school.

Age Thirty Transition: Twenty-Eight to Thirty-Three

Levinson found a transition period between ages twenty-eight and thirty-three during which young adults could choose to rework parts of the life structure that were tentatively constructed earlier. For some this is a relatively peaceful change. For others there is a "crisis" or painful transition with fears of a chaotic disruption, or an inability to achieve a satisfactory life structure. Sixty-two percent of the men in his study experienced moderate to severe crisis at this time. There is a growing sense that change must be made soon or one will be locked into or out of certain commitments that will become more difficult to change.

Sheehy points out that many people are terrified by all the choices they make in their twenties, but that they seldom realize that change is inevitable during this period. A person examines career and position, evaluates family and marriage, and struggles to gain order and stability. Commitments to occupation, marriage partners, and values are requestioned. She points out that part of the restlessness comes from feeling too restricted and narrow. Men have outgrown their previous choices for a career and other areas of their lives. Inner aspects that were set aside in the twenties due to the passing of time, meeting of other people's goals, and inner conflicts now resurface. Several responses to this time of restructuring include: (1) striking out on a new or adapted Dream that is more realistic; (2) pushing for a new marriage partner or reshaping one's expectations for it; (3) expanding one's personal life as part of one's concerns.

Gould identifies a new central misconception to be faced. "Life is simple and controllable. There are no significant coexisting contradictory forces within me." He calls this the period of "Opening Up to What's Inside," since it involves discovering (or rediscovering) aspects, feelings, goals, interests, and talents ignored or hidden during an earlier period. Sometimes these were pushed aside because they interfered with the beliefs or goals of the earlier period. Sometimes they caused conflict and were suppressed. Or they required time that was not available because so much effort was involved in establishing independence and securing position for one's self in the social and career world.

Gould reports that this transition, when resolved, is followed by a deeper sense of acceptance of self or the development of a personal philosophy of life. It may also lead to a more realistic understanding of one's strengths and abilities. One also has begun to recognize the contradictory and competing forces within with those in the social-cultural world.

Ministry Implications

The teacher of young adults at this stage has the exciting challenge of assisting them to reflect on where they are in their careers, marriages, parenting, and Christian life. Opportunities must be made available to identify alternative choices and appropriate avenues for change. Their inner lives must be renewed as they review goals, inner conflicts, and the changes of time as they affect their Dream, partnership, career decisions, and personal misconceptions about life and faith.

Settling Down: Thirty-Three to Forty

Following the young adult second transition, Levinson has identified a second period of relative stability where the second stable life structure is applied. Sheehy calls this the "Rooting and Extending" period. Her interviewees tended to focus on buying a home and climbing the career ladder. Often child-rearing begins a decline in social contacts outside the home. She also notes that this is a period of low morale in marital satisfaction as the romantic ideas of the twenties lose their glamour.

Levinson also reports that his respondents settled down emotionally from the times of earlier turbulence. In doing so, they settled for a few of their major goals and began building a life structure around those central choices. This is a time of getting serious and deciding what is really important in life. It is a stage when one has outgrown the need of a mentor relationship and takes one's place as a full adult, or as Levinson calls it, "Becoming One's Own Man." Neither Gould nor Vaillant found this settling down phase in their studies.

Ministry Implications

While the adults of this period face many of the same issues found in the earlier parts of young adulthood, the teacher of young adults must also consider the needs of those whose marriages have come to separation or ended in divorce. Almost two-thirds of first divorces for women occur by age thirty. This suggests a need for support of their inner healing, role models of single parenting, and help in raising children and handling financial problems. Remarriage and blended families present other challenging areas of ministry.

YOUNG ADULT MATURATION

In contrast to the tasks and life issues that come out of a chronological look at young adulthood, there are also major personal changes taking place in the young adult's identity, intimacy, morality, and faith perspectives. While examining these areas, specific suggestions on how the teacher may influence each area are provided.

Identity Development

Identity is commonly described as having a fairly stable sense of who you are that seems to be supported by significant others in your life. Erickson referred to identity as a psychosocial concept containing both an inner psychological aspect (fairly stable sense of who one is) and an external or social aspect (seems to be supported by significant others in ones life).[18] Newman and Newman defined identity as "the environmental commitment to a personal integration of values, goals, and abilities."[19] During young adulthood the individual tends to move away from a self-centered perspective of morals, purposes, and values that are strongly influenced by the peer group to a place where personal commitments are made in light of the available options. These choices are tested, affirmed, and revised as part of their worldview.

During the early adult transition Marcia has identified how four different groups handle the development of their identity.[20] The *moratorium* group invests little in themselves or others. Their values are vague and they delay commitment, while at the same time striving to find the right way. It is a time of stepping out.

The *identity-foreclosed group* appears sure of what they want. They make commitments without a crisis or a strenuous search. Often they have passively accepted the identity their parents or other significant others have set for them. They are "locked in" people.

The *identity-diffused group* shrinks from the task of defining what they want or how they feel. Others expect more from them, but they are unable to question enough to rebel against parents or authority figures, or to struggle toward resolution. They perform acceptably in school and in social roles, but feel like misfits through the failures of earlier attempts that have immobilized their feelings of inferiority and alienation. They are the "do nothing about it" people.

The *identity-achieved group* has been in a crisis and come through it. They have developed a sustained personal stance with regard to their sense of purpose and view of the world.

Parks argues that identity is not fully accomplished by the end of adolescence. Rather, the young adult has become both self-conscious and aware that the self "has power over the becoming of the self."[21] Thus, the teacher of young adults is likely to find them at various points along a continuum—from an immature to a mature identity. The teacher's challenge is to provide opportunities so that reflection on and testing of one's identity can be verified as well as stimulated to personal commitment.

Intimacy Development

Intimacy is more than learning the art of love with the opposite sex. It includes the development of commitment to a person, with the capacity for open and honest exposure of one's inner self to that person. This can take place physically, emotionally, intellectually, socially, and spiritually—across the life spectrum. The alternative is loneliness and isolation. Isolation includes such feelings as separation, exclusion, coldness, fear, and insecurity.

Erickson[22] argues that a strong sense of identity is necessary to achieve a sense of intimacy with another person. During young adulthood, as the identity becomes more secure, intimacy is more likely to develop. Love between a male and female moves from being highly emotional and self-centered to an acceptance of, trust in, self-disclosure to, and understanding of another person. Intimacy involves companionship and healthy communication.

Intimacy is influenced by an integration of many earlier experiences. Such areas as infant-caregiver relations, quality of care, sibling relations, extended family relations, and childhood/peer friendships need to be explored. Stereotypes about the opposite sex may also interfere in developing healthy intimacy. Since cohabitation has become much more acceptable the past twenty years as a means of testing a relationship, and divorce seems to be one way of finding a more fulfilling relationship, the teacher of young adults must create an environment in which biblical intimacy can be developed and supported.

Moral Development

Lawrence Kohlberg has proposed that people's moral thinking progresses through different stages into adulthood.[23] The young adult leaving the adolescent scene is generally at a stage three level of morality. Stage three morality finds the person obeying parents, peers, and institutions out of social conformity. This person tends to act according to what he or she believes the expectations of significant others are.

As a person moves out of stage three, one's perspective broadens to include the expectations of society and a desire to keep the laws and rules of society. This is made possible as the young adult's ability to think abstractly progresses. Here the young adult disciplines oneself to keep the norms of the society. It is hard to step back and criticize or choose a separate set of values or laws. This begins at stage five.

Movement to stage five is a major shift away from significant others and one's country as the basis of one's values. At stage five the individual becomes one's own person, separate from the group or society in which he or she claims membership. This change is encouraged through increasing contact with others who are different. Rules, culture, customs, and experiences are seen as relative. In response to this new awareness, the individual either absolutizes the group's rules or chooses rules based on higher principles such as justice.

While there are many problems with Kohlberg's system, it does help to point out the fact that young adults are changing in how they view morality. Stage four individuals tend to lack empathy. They are also unwilling to accept that there is no rule for every situation and that their church or nation does not always have the right answer in every situation. To facilitate change is difficult. Kohlberg's major contribution is the use of moral dilemmas during which people are encouraged to integrate their beliefs to formulate a solution. Exposure to conflicting views and values is essential for growth. The individual must be encouraged to find reasons for what he or she believes.

Faith Development

James Fowler's research on human faith development has sparked renewed interest in Christian spiritual growth.[24] Fowler identified six stages of faith based on intensive interviews with adults at various stages of life. He identifies structures in *how* a person believes as opposed to the content of *what* a person believes. Faith is not the content but the trust and commitment a person makes to a central power (God, church, state) or value (justice, love, mercy). He believes there is a natural sequence that a person goes through over life. Although this may be perceived as contradicting a Christian faith based on God's revelation of specific doctrinal truth, Fowler's findings may be helpful in understanding the human side of how a person puts faith in something as the basic organizing purpose for life—from childhood through adulthood. Assuming the difference is not in God's supernatural working, Fowler examines the rational, emotional, social, and other areas of human development that relate to human faith.

At stage three, Fowler believes people conform to the expectations and values of significant people in their lives. This Synthetic-Conventional faith has not yet been criticized by the young adult because his identity has not been affirmed and owned. Movement into stage four faith requires a confident grasp of one's identity and sense of personal autonomy. Such people are ready to step out of what they hold as true and begin to reflect on or examine the adequacy of that faith.

At stage four, the young adult has moved from a conforming faith to an Individualtive-Reflective faith. A stage four faith takes personal responsibility for commitment, attitudes, beliefs, and way of life. While stage three faith finds its source of authority in other people or external influences, stage four faith questions the opinion of the majority and places authority in one's own self.

The move from stage three to stage four faith involves a recognition that there are a number of competing sources of authority and values. The person moves through a process identified by William Perry.[25] This process proceeds from the perspective that there is only one answer based on absolutes and authority to a period of relativism where every perspective and view is an equal or possible way to look at life.

The final step of commitment comes when the young adult chooses the option or position he or she will take. The commitment is influenced by one's personal experiences, awareness of various sources of authority, and the nature of a pluralistic world. Thus, people make a commitment in the midst of a relative, pluralistic world. The decision tends to be based on personal relevance rather than the discovery of "absolute truth." Thus, a person accepts responsibility for his or her basis of faith.

Although evangelicals hold to absolute truth, it does not mean that they cannot move from a stage three to a stage four faith. While some may hold to their faith based on external factors such as parents, friends, or denomination, many adults come to a time at which they must wrestle with their pre-adult formulations of faith. The base of authority moves from the group to God's Word. Young adult faith moves from blind acceptance of Scripture and allegiance to a group to a position of personal allegiance to allowing one's understanding of Scripture to influence his or her conclusions.

By not moving on to stage four faith, young adults are forced into dependency upon the group and an external authority. This may cause despair when they try to relate their faith to their own conflicts and react to the disappointing lives of other faith authorities. They may become prime candidates for cultic groups who demand blind allegiance and conformity. These groups stress group loyalty while denying the person's own individual identity in Christ. It is only as young adults surrender their own egos to Christ that change begins to take place. They may also find it difficult to make decisions for themselves. They may so foreclose their identity that they have mental or emotional difficulties. Thus, the Christian community must encourage young adults to make their own decisions, assisting them to become more like Christ. They need to participate in developing the reasons for what they believe and what they do.

SPECIFIC YOUNG ADULT TEACHING IMPLICATIONS

Many excellent suggestions on running a young adult ministry are summarized in Figure 13.3 on page 204. These helpful suggestions have their origin in biblical and ministry reflection and are not strongly tied to young adult developmental tasks.

Figure 13.3: Suggestions for Developing Young Adult Ministry Strategies[26]

Stubblefield	Merriam & Ferro	Hershey
Bible teaching program for each young adult	Develop a clear statement of mission/ purpose/goals/	Give away responsibility (active participation)
Special discipleship training, mission education, & music programs	Organization Models: Kerygma: proclamation Koinonia: fellowship Diakonia: service Didache: teaching Martyria: witness	Focus on a faith that matters (relevant) Opportunities for belonging (intimacy)
Special classes for the divorced & always single	Don't isolate as an age-group	Reach out to the local community
Marriage Effectiveness Classes: Spouse & Parenting	Don't equate single & young adult	Sensitivity to newcomers Give them ownership of the program
Sensitivity to blended families & needs	Respect them as adults	Affirm their diversity
Attractive church facilities for children	Promote terminal/ focused classes, workshops & retreats	Survey needs

Some specific areas to consider in becoming a more effective teacher of young adults include: clarifying your role as the instructor, assessing needs, choosing and implementing learning activities, building a supportive and active learning environment, providing challenging teaching-learning interactions, and helping adults apply what they learn.[27] As a teacher of young adults, you must become a master teacher who understands and balances the challenge to grow and positive support for change. This requires that you master the biblical content. This will help you focus on important aspects and avoid trivial areas. Mastery allows you to select and use the best methods for approaching the biblical content, as well as giving you the freedom to be flexible and responsive to adult learner needs and development.

But what kind of teaching topics should you implement as a teacher? The following chart adapted from McCoy[28] provides an overview of young adult developmental periods, the tasks young adults face, specific program responses that may be taken, and a statement of the outcomes sought. Your goal as a teacher must be to help enhance young adult learning in light of their developmental tasks from a Christian perspective.

Figure 13.4:
Young Adult Development and Program Response

Developmental Periods	Developmental Tasks	Program Response	Outcomes Sought
Leaving Adolescence 18–22	1. Separating from one's parents	1. Personal assertiveness seminars	1. Biblically based autonomy
	2. Selecting initial career	2. Career & occupational workshops	2. Christian vocational call
	3. Gaining work experience	3. Work & school preparation	3. Acquire work & education experience
	4. Relating with peers	4. Relational skills & small groups workshops	4. Growing social confidence
	5. Managing home alone	5. Housekeeping & buying skills workshops	5. Informed purchasing & living
	6. Managing work & leisure time	6. Time management training	6. Wise use of God's time
	7. Adjusting to independence	7. Loneliness & independence workshops	7. Acceptance of singleness
	8. Solving problems	8. Creative problem-solving seminars	8. Positive alternative solutions
	9. Handling stress from change	9. Stress management workshops	9. Peaceful change & growth
Joining the Adult World 23–28	1. Selecting a spouse	1. Marriage workshops	1. Satisfying Christian marriage
	2. Climbing the career ladder	2. Work advancement skill training	2. Career growth & fulfillment
	3. Becoming a parent	3. Parenting seminars	3. Healthy child & parent relations
	4. Involvement in community	4. Gifts, civic, & volunteer workshops	4. Active in community & church
	5. Consuming wisely	5. Financial management seminars	5. Wise consumer investment
	6. Buying a home	6. Purchase/maintain a home workshop	6. Healthy home environment
	7. Building social friendships	7. Human relations training	7. Social skills
	8. Achieving autonomy	8. Healthy identity/esteem seminars	8. Healthy sense of autonomy
	9. Solving problems	9. Creative problem-solving seminar	9. Positive decision-making
	10. Handling stress from change	10. Stress management workshops	10. Peaceful change & growth
	1. Evaluating personal values	1. Clarifying values seminars	1. Commitment to owned values
	2. Appraising personal relations	2. Communication workshops	2. Satisfying personal relations
	3. Reviewing career	3. Job evaluation &	3. Job satisfaction &

	progress	adjustment workshops	achievement
Evaluating Initial Adult Choices 29–32	4. Adjusting to growing children	4. Parent-child relations seminars	4. Positive parent-child relations
	5. Managing a home	5. Personal finances & home workshops	5. Healthy home life & finances
	6. Reviewing community activity	6. Gifts, civic, & volunteer workshops	6. Active in community & church
	7. Reexamining marriage	7. Marriage workshops and socials	7. Satisfying Christian marriage
	8. Solving problems	8. Creative problem-solving seminars	8. Creative problem solving
	9. Handling stress from change	9. Stress management workshops	9. Peaceful change & growth
Settling Down 33–35	1. Climbing the career ladder	1. Work advancement skill training	1. Career growth & fulfillment
	2. Involvement in community	2. Gifts, civic, & volunteer workshops	2. Active in community & church
	3. Deepening marriage relations	3. Marriage workshops and socials	3. Satisfying Christian marriage
	4. Adjusting to growing children	4. Raising teenagers seminars	4. Positive parent-teen relations
	5. Managing a home	5. Personal finances & home workshops	5. Healthy home life & finances
	6. Solving problems	6. Creative problem-solving seminars	6. Positive decision-making
	7. Handling stress from change	7. Stress management workshops	7. Peaceful change & growth

Another primary task for you as a teacher is to encourage the young adult participants to make useful decisions about their learning activities.[29] Your teaching style must take into account the young adults' learning styles.[30] This calls for you to respect each student as unique, provide reasons for participation related to their needs, provide options for young adults that match their learning preference, and understand the learner's level of proficiency.

Specific principles you, as a teacher of young adults, are urged to keep in mind include the following:

1. Develop materials that relate to their developmental tasks as young adults. Relate Bible teaching to the issues and tasks they face as young adults. The goal is to move past a total focus on learning content so that there is a relationship established between the content and the needs of each person at this stage of development. Thus, George needs to see how God's will relates to career decision-making and daily choices, while Linda has a different agenda.

2. Provide a balance between content presentation and active learner involvement and feedback. Young adults have personal experience and unique training that can be tapped to benefit the other members of the group. Linda undoubtedly has some excel-

lent insight on selecting a mate, while Sam and Lonie can assist John and Mary in their adjustments to mixing marriage and dual careers.

3. Plan for a variety of learning activities such as discussion, practice, and problem-solving.[31] Use questions posed to the whole group as well as small groups related to their developmental issues to create interest in the learning activity. Synergy is essential for growth.

4. Assist learners in their personal search for meaning in the topic being studied. Encourage them to apply the principles from Scripture to their specific concerns. Provide times for active dialogue as well as reflective times of self-examination, questioning, and setting of goals. Toni needs more than an opportunity to discuss facing the temptations in the service.

5. Vary the methods used in the learning situation. Don't fall into a predictable rut. This requires mastering each methodology while being willing to add new tools to your teaching arsenal. Mary is used to working with children with short attention spans and expects the same variety they need.

6. Pay attention to the interpersonal relationships between you and your students as well as among the students themselves.[32] A positive learning environment is essential for removing masks, risking intimacy, and challenging one's values and faith assumptions. If Sam and Lonie are angry at each other, it's bound to influence the whole learning situation unless sensitively considered in how the class functions.

7. Provide models and examples that participants can acquire and investigate. Expose them to a variety of resources and situations where they can test and begin to own the models they have heard about in class. Linda's relating to her parents and George's learning to live on his own provide excellent teachable moments as well as moral dilemmas.

8. Support young adults in becoming self-directive.[33] Provide options and resources and invite participation in decision-making so that they are influencing the teaching-learning being developed. They want to be involved.

CONCLUSION

As a teacher of young adults you have many exciting challenges ahead! A knowledge of who young adults are and how one might approach them is only the beginning of potential, significant change in their lives. Your teaching must continue to focus on Jesus Christ and the use of God's Word under the direction of the Holy Spirit for radical transformation to take place.

Notes

1. W.D. Jordan, "Searching for Adulthood in America," *Daedalus* 105 (April 1976): 1–11, points out that even in 1968 there was no article on adulthood in the *International Encyclopedia of the Social Sciences.*
2. S.R. Graubard, Preface to the issue "Adulthood," *Daedalus* 105 (February 1976): v–viii, feels that we are entering the century of the adult, at least in America.
3. D. Rogers, *The Adult Years* (Englewood Cliffs, N.Y.: Prentice-Hall, 1979) identified several reasons why interest has developed in the study of the adult life cycle. These might be summarized as follows: 1. Adulthood was the only uncharted stage before closure could take place. 2. Younger childhood samples had grown up and still had valuable data to be collected. 3. Curiosity. 4. Affluence. 5. Societal support for stakng out adult claims to "personhood" outside of child rearing (p. 5).
4. Graubard, "Adulthood," v.
5. See W.J. Boausma, "Christian Adulthood," *Daedalus* 105 (February 1976): 77–92; Erik H. Erikson, "Reflection on Dr. Barg's Life Cycle," *Daedalus* 105 (February 1976): 1–28; and W. Stegner, "The Writer and the Concept of Adulthood," *Daedalus* 105 (April 1976): 39–48.
6. J. Goldstein, "On Being Adult and Being Adult in Secular Law," *Daedalus* 105 (April 1976): 69–87.
7. W. Stegner, *The Writer,* A.S. Dibner, "The Psychology of Normal Aging," in *Understanding Aging: A Multidisciplinary Approach,* ed. M. Spencer and C. Dovi (New York: Appleton-Century-Crofts, 1975).
8. G.H. Elder, Jr. and R.C. Rockwell, "Marital Timing in Women's Life Patterns," *Journal of Family History* 1 (1975): 34–53.
9. Daniel Levinson, *The Seasons of a Man's Life* (New York: Knopf, 1978).
10. R.L. Gould, *Transformations: Growth and Change in Adult Life* (New York: Simon & Schuster, 1978).
11. R.L. Gould, "Adult Life Stages: Growth Towards Self-Tolerance," *Psychology Today*, (February 1975), 78.
12. Robert J. Havighurst, *Developmental Tasks and Education* (New York: McKay, 1972).
13. R.G. Kuhlen, "Developmental Changes in Motivation During the Adult Years," in *Relations of Development and Aging,* ed. J.E. Birron (Springfield, Ill.: Charles C. Thomas Pr., 1975) proposed that the growth-expansion motives such as achievement, power, creativity, and self-actualization dominate an individual's behavior during the first half of life as an adult; however, these motives may change during a person's life because

he or she has been relatively satisfied and because the person moves into new social positions. He also suggests that with advancing age there is a shift from active direct gratification of needs to gratifications obtained in more indirect and vicarious fashion.

14. Gerard Egan and M.A. Cowan, *Moving into Adulthood* (Monterey, Calif.: Brooks-Cole, 1980). See also Bernice L. Neugarten, *Middle Age and Aging* (Chicago: Univ. of Chicago Pr., 1968). For gender differences in handling stage changes see M.F. Lowenthal, M. Thurnher, and D. Chiriboga, *Four Stages of Life* (San Francisco: Jossey-Bass, 1974).

15. G.C. Vaillant, *Adaptation to Life* (Boston: Little, Brown, 1977).

16. Gail Sheehy, *Passages: Predictable Crises of Adult Life* (New York: Dutton, 1976).

17. W. Kilpatrick, "Identity, Youth and the Dissolution of Culture," *Adolescence* 9 (1974):407–12.

18. Erik H. Erickson, *Identity and the Life Cycle* (New York: Norton, 1980).

19. B. Newman and P. Newman, *Development Through Life* (Homewood, Ill.: Dorsey Pr., 1975), 219.

20. J.E. Marcia, "Development and Validation of Ego-identity Status," *Journal of Personality and Social Psychology* 3 (1966):551–59.

21. Sharon Parks, *The Critical Years: The Young Adult Search for a Faith to Live By* (New York: Harper and Row, 1986), 76.

22. Erik H. Erickson, *Identity: Youth and Crisis* (New York: Norton, 1963). See also A.W. Chickering, *Education and Identity* (San Francisco: Jossey-Bass, 1981) and Charles Sell, *Transition Through Adult Life* (Grand Rapids: Zondervan, 1991).

23. Lawrence Kohlberg, "Stages of Moral Development as a Basis for Moral Education," in *Moral Development, Moral Education and Kohlberg,* ed. Brenda Munsey (Birmingham, Ala.: Religious Education Pr., 1980).

24. James Fowler, *Stages of Faith* (San Francisco: Harper and Row, 1981).

25. William Perry, *Forms of Intellectual and Ethical Development in the College Years* (New York: Holt, Rinehart and Winston, 1979).

26. See Jerry Stubblefield, *A Church Ministering to Adults* (Nashville: Broadman, 1986); Sharon Merriam and Trenton Ferro, "Working with Young Adults," in *Handbook of Adult Religious Education*, ed. Nancy Foltz (Birmingham, Ala.: Religious Education Press, 1986); and Terry Hershey, *Young Adult Ministry* (Loveland, Colo.: Group Books, 1986).

27. Alan Knox, *Helping Adults Learn* (San Francisco: Jossey-Bass, 1986).

28. V.R. McCoy, "Adult Life-Cycle Change," *Lifelong Learning: The Adult Years* 26 (October 1977):14–18.

29. See Warren N. Wilbert, *Teaching Christian Adults* (Grand Rapids: Baker, 1980); and Warren N. Wilbert, *Strategies for Teaching Christian Adults* (Grand Rapids: Baker, 1984). In addition, see Joseph Lowman, *Mastering the Techniques of Teaching* (San Francisco: Jossey-Bass, 1984); and Stan-

ford C. Ericksen, *The Essence of Good Teaching* (San Francisco: Jossey-Bass, 1984) are very helpful in this area.

30. See D.A. Kolb, *Experiential Learning: Experience as the Source of Learning and Development* (New Jersey: Prentice-Hall, 1984); L.A. Bonham "Learning Style Use: In Need of Perspective," *Lifelong Learning: An Omnibus of Practice and Research* 11 (1988):14–17, 19; and G.J. Conti and R.B. Welborn, "The Interaction of Teaching Style and Learning Style on Traditional and Non-traditional Learners," in *Proceedings of the 28th Annual Adult Education Research Conference* (University of Wyoming, Conferences and Institutes, Laramie, n.d.) 49–54.

31. See Jack Mezirow and Associates, *Fostering Critical Reflection in Adulthood: A Guide to Transformative and Emancipatory Learning* (San Francisco: Jossey-Bass, 1990); and Peter Elbow, *Embracing Contraries: Explorations in Learning and Teaching* (New York: Oxford Univ. Pr., 1986).

32. See Stephen R. Covey, *The Seven Habits of Highly Effective People: Powerful Lessons in Personal Change* (New York: Simon and Schuster, 1989); and S. Miller, D. Wackman, E. Nunnally, and P. Miller, *Connecting with Self and Others* (Littleton, Colo.: Interpersonal Communications, 1988).

33. See Malcolm Knowles, *Self-Directed Learning: A Guide for Learners and Teachers* (Chicago: Association Pr. 1975); Malcolm S. Knowles and Associates, *Andragogy in Action: Applying Modern Principles of Adult Learning* (San Francisco: Jossey-Bass, 1984); and R. Hiemstra and B. Sisco, *Individualizing Instruction: Making Learning Personal, Empowering, and Successful* (San Francisco: Jossey-Bass, 1990).

For Further Reading

Brookfield, Stephen D. *Understanding and Facilitating Adult Learning.* San Francisco: Jossey-Bass, 1986.

Cross, K. Patricia. *Adults As Learners.* San Francisco: Jossey-Bass, 1981.

Daloz, Laurent A. *Effective Teaching and Mentoring.* San Francisco: Jossey-Bass, 1986.

Foltz, Nancy. *Handbook of Adult Religious Education.* Birmingham, Ala.: Religious Education Press, 1986.

Hershey, Terry. *Young Adult Ministry.* Loveland, Colo.: Group Books, 1986.

Parks, Sharon. *The Critical Years: The Young Adult Search for a Faith to Live By.* New York: Harper and Row, 1986.

Peterson, Gilbert A., ed. *The Christian Education of Adults.* Chicago: Moody, 1985.

Sell, Charles. *Transitions Through Adult Life.* Grand Rapids: Zondervan, 1991.

Smith, Robert M. *Learning to Learn Across the Life Span.* San Francisco: Jossey-Bass, 1990.

Wlodkowski, Raymond J. *Enhancing Adult Motivation to Learn.* San Francisco: Jossey-Bass, 1985.

FOURTEEN

TEACHING MIDDLE ADULTS

Wesley R. Willis

One initial task in considering educational ministries for middle adults is determining just who belongs in the category. What is the extent of the middle stage of the adult period of life—just when does middle age begin and end?

If we were to ask senior adults, they might decribe a middle adult as "anyone younger than us." On the other hand, ask teenagers to define middle age and they might place it as early as the twenties. And to the person actually living in the middle years, it often is "just a little bit older than I am right now."

Part of the difficulty comes in determining the basis for decision. Is middle age the middle third of life? If so, then we could decide to include any between the ages of twenty-five and fifty. However, this would place many still in graduate school at the beginning of middle age. Or is it more realistic to define it as the middle third of productive adult life? In which case we might settle on ages thirty-five to fifty. But this would mean that those from fifty on would be considered senior adults.

Most would agree that the range of years included in middle age is older than it was a few years ago, and not merely because so many of us would like to delay the inevitable. With an aging population, and extended productivity, many have concluded that earlier definitions of middle adulthood began and ended too soon. Robert Havighurst, well known as a leader in human development, in 1953[1] and later in 1970[2] listed middle adults as those between the ages of thirty and fifty-five.

Bernice Neugarten suggested that "middle-aged people look to their positions within different life contexts—body, career, family—rather than to chronological age for their primary clues in clocking themselves."[3] While positions in life contexts may provide a good guide for adult self-insight, personal and individual experiences vary too greatly to rely on them for suggesting the scope of middle adult education.

Perhaps it would suffice to suggest that we consider middle adults as those who are in the middle third of adulthood (which is the time between the teen years and death). The middle third, then, would extend from somewhere in the late thirties to the late fifties. By this criterion the middle adult phase of life would *follow* the establishment of family and career and *precede* final preparations and entrance into retirement.

It should be obvious that a stage of life which extends twenty or more years actually includes multiple shorter stages. Gilbert Peterson suggested that "the middle-aged group can be divided into two groups: The younger middle-aged from thirty-five to forty-nine, and the older middle-aged from fifty to sixty-four."[4] And, in fact, educators subdivide these two groupings into any number of shorter stages reflective of growth and development, corresponding to significant events which may occur during the middle years.

MIDDLE AGE: A TIME OF TRANSITIONS

Perhaps educators gain better understanding of middle adulthood by recognizing that adults must work through numerous transitions during these years. Some major transitions include a significant level of trauma, while other relatively minor changes require little overt attention.

However, major or minor, all of these transitions (changes) generate stress in an individual's life.

> Adults experience a number of physiological, social, and psychological changes after they reach the "midpoint" in life. The combination of these changes creates stress and the need to learn new strategies for coping with life.[5]

Sometimes the stress level rises dramatically to the point at which a person will act in apparently illogical or counterproductive ways in an attempt to relieve that stress, or at least to make it more bearable. Often we describe such an adult as undergoing a midlife crisis, perhaps escalating to the crisis stage because the adult has not learned appropriate coping skills.

One objective of adult Christian education aims to help adults understand the normal events in the middle years, and then to choose appropriate behaviors based on God's revealed will. All adults need to learn how to cope with changes they will encounter.

> Men experience a decrease in strength and the ability to learn and perform large psychomotor skills. Women lose the ability to have children at some stage during middle life. All of these changes can create stress for the learner as the effect creates an awareness of change and of the aging process which will lead to death.[6]

Most of the time persons experiencing stress accompanying these transitions manage quite well, ordinarily not even realizing that they are handling stress. But even minor transitions require energy to cope. And this energy drain depletes physical and emotional reserves. Adults manage multiple transitions more easily when they understand what makes them feel the way they do. If adults understand themselves and have learned appropriate behavior, they will more likely choose wise responses so that they not only survive transitions but even thrive in the midst of change.

Consider some of the transitions normal adults may encounter as they move through their middle years.

Middle Adult Transitions

Child-rearing – Empty Nest
Physical Strength – Growing Weakness
Unlimited Anticipation – Perceived Limitation
Health – Infirmity
Anticipating Marriage – Accepting Celibacy
Provision for Others – Provision for Self
Unbounded Energy – Growing Weariness
Meaningful Employment – Un (or under) employed
Satisfying Marriage – Loss of Spouse
Large Social Group – Fewer Close Friends
Active Lifestyle – Passive Lifestyle

It would seem apparent that such transitions produce considerable uneasiness for those moving through them. As the level of uneasiness rises, the accompanying stress level rises also. And if the tension is not resolved, the cumulative impact of such changes can present a formidable barrier to health and productivity.

And yet, while an adult strives to handle the stress resulting from the unsought (and often undesirable) changes, these middle years can be times of growth and development—times of spiritual maturing.

> In the midst of these changes, many adults at the midpoint in life must come to terms with mortality. It is not possible to delay indefinitely the tasks which are to be accomplished. Mid-life is an appropriate time to examine the meaning of life and the values and priorities which we have held to this time. The psychological stress of confronting mortality which results in the rethinking of meaning, values, activities, and relationships can be lessened through learning.[7]

One excellent source of meaningful, well-conceived, well-presented Christian education should be the local church. Later in this chapter we will consider specific approaches to such a meaningful educational program.

TWO CATEGORIES OF MIDDLE ADULTS

Ministering to middle adults in the last decade of the twentieth century and the first decade of the twenty-first century presents a unique challenge to Christian educators. The challenge derives directly from the differences between the adults who are part of the "Baby Boom" generation and those who preceded them. Baby Boomers are those adults born between 1946 and 1964. The first of the Boomers entered middle adult years in the decade of the 1980s and the last members will leave middle adulthood early in the next century. In the meantime, educators must design and implement middle adult educational ministries targeted increasingly to the Baby Boomers.

While all adults ultimately confront the tasks and transitions of the middle years, Baby Boomers offer additional challenges due to their unique value system. Since the oldest Boomers have already entered their middle years, and since they will dominate the middle adult population, educators would be well advised to tailor programs to meet those Boomers' needs.

Leith Anderson described ministry to Baby Boomers in an article published in the *Christian Education Journal*.[8] Anderson discussed six key characteristics of this generation.

1. Low Institutional Loyalty. While the immediately preceding generation was fiercely loyal to their institutions, Boomers tend to be significantly more flexible. "They readily surrender loyalty to institutions for interests of self."[9]

2. Stopovers. Flexibility in loyalty, and a desire to have personal needs met, encourages an attitude of "shopping around." And this is seen nowhere more than in church attendance. Various churches at various stages in life, and even a variety of churches at any given time, are normal for the Boomers.

3. High Expectations. These adults want the best, and they feel that they deserve it. Making do temporarily with low quality personal possessions, or inadequate church programs and facilities, is not acceptable. As confirmed consumers, they want the best and are willing to pay for it.

4. Short-Term Commitments. Many have observed that Boomers have a renewed interest in and commitment to family. And yet this commitment, like many others, is valid only as long as the individual feels that the relationship meets his or her own needs. When Baby Boomers perceive that their needs remain unsatisfied, commitment may well evaporate.

5. Pluralism. Anderson defines this as a desire for—even a passion for—variety, choices, and options. But although Boomers are demanding and selective, they also fiercely grant the same privilege to others. And this value logically leads into the sixth trait.

6. Tolerance of Contradiction. Baby Boomers hold values and beliefs that seem mutually exclusive. They claim to believe the Bible, and yet they don't practice it consistently. They remain in the church, but reject its teaching.

Ministry to the younger segment of middle adults (the Boomers) is complicated by the value system they hold. George Barna helps us understand Boomers.

> A massive realignment of thinking is taking place in which people are transferring many elements formerly deemed "necessary" into the realm of the "optional." And, of course, the optional then becomes a personal matter, which people may choose to define as desirable, but inconsequential. Church attendance, Bible reading, prayer, worship, involvement in a local church body—all of these appear to be in

transition, shifting from the necessary to the optional.[10]

According to Barna's research, adult church attendance in the United States (which had been fluctuating in the low to mid 40 percent range during the 1980s) increased to almost 50 percent of the total adult population by 1991.[11] And yet there seems to be little true spiritual growth, either in knowledge or practice. This is true not only of nominal Christians, but of those who describe themselves as born again.

> A plurality of adults believe that the notion that "God helps those who help themselves" is drawn directly from the Bible. In fact, a larger proportion of born again Christians than non-Christians strongly affirmed the Bible as the source of this statement. It is, of course, neither from the Bible (Benjamin Franklin originally penned the statement) nor consistent with the teaching of the Bible.[12]

EDUCATIONAL MINISTRIES TO MIDDLE ADULTS

Given the nature and needs of middle adults near the turn of the century, how should we approach the design and implementation of educational programs? Since Baby Boomers comprise the younger part of these middle years, we must recognize that we are not dealing with a homogeneous group. But if we do target our approach to younger adults in the group, we probably also will minister to older persons appropriately.

In fact, changing our approach seems long overdue. Many educators question the viability of current church educational programming. This is due, in part, to minimal emphasis by many churches on progamming for adults. Chuck Nichols maintains that "Christian educators cannot be satisfied with the overemphasis on ministry to children and youth. This concept is reinforced by Scripture where we notice that in both the Old and New Testaments the emphasis seems to be on adults."[13]

And even where churches have placed some emphasis on adult education, frequently it has been minimally effective. Leon McKenzie asserts that "adult religious education, as it is practiced in most churches and parishes, is largely ineffective."[14] He maintains that the reason for such a state is the lack of relevance in how we teach adults. "The message is clear: Religion is something to do in church on Sundays; religion has little to do with the way we experience our being-in-the-world on weekdays as we pursue mundane endeavors.''[15]

But it doesn't have to be that way. We can plan and execute effective adult educational ministries. Adults can and will learn if we approach them wisely and appropriately. Consider the following suggestions.

Teach the Bible

The abundance of bad Bible teaching provides no reason for churches to neglect their mandate to teach God's Word. George Barna concluded that Baby Boomers desperately need solid, accurate Bible instruction.[16] And Perry Downs agrees as he considers the sense of despair among adults today.

> The underlying problem which has led to this despair is the loss of any notion of Truth. Today's society is characterized by relativism in virtually all realms of thinking. There are no absolutes, and Truth has been replaced by opinion and feeling. One person's opinion is as valid as the next, and corresponding to reality is no longer considered.[17]

Clear, authoritative Bible teaching constitutes the best antidote for error. And even if traditionally we have taught the Bible poorly to adults, we need not continue the practice. Indeed, excellent Bible instruction would be welcomed by those who have endured so much of the other kind. And authoritative teaching is not incompatible with effective education, especially if the following guidelines also are followed.

Speak to Real Needs

As we maintain our commitment to teach God's Word, we also must reevaluate our philosophy of teaching. Educators should seek to demonstrate the relevance of instruction, even though the ''system'' that we have come to know often neglects the practical implications of biblical truth.

> The ''system'' exalts the transmission of theological concepts and neglects to stress the necessity of effective sensitivity to the life situations of adults. What is implied by this ''system'' is a fixation on subject matter and a turning away from the adult work-a-day world. As a result, the question ''Who is the

twentieth century adult?" is never asked.[18]

All the needs that we considered at the beginning of this chapter (e.g., stress due to physiological changes, social changes, job, and family pressures) are topics to address. And speaking to such issues is totally compatible with authoritative Bible teaching. Charles Sell has concluded that we can teach God's Word and still speak to an adult's need. "The key is to discover his direction and offer related learning opportunities that will also focus on the theological and biblical information he needs."[19] Perhaps our failure to speak to real life needs of adults has contributed to the church's perceived irrelevancy.

> The local churches of America face a tenuous future, given the deteriorating images they possess. While half of the population strongly believe that the Christian faith remains relevant to the way we live today, only half as many believe that the local Christian churches possess such relevance.[20]

Listen to What Adults Say They Want

Unfortunately, educators often plan programs "for" others, but neglect to consult them in the process. And while we may think we know what middle adults need, it is easy to miss the mark.

Adults, and especially Baby Boomers, have opinions and are anxious to articulate them, given the chance. It is amazing how many adults who are competent leaders in other areas of life, seem to shift into neutral when they enter a church building. We need to break through such cultivated passivity and create effective, relevant educational ministries. Do you want to know what adults want and need? Get radical; ask them!

Permit Freedom of Choice

Adults, and especially today's middle adults made up of Baby Boomers and older middle adults, want to be given choices. Rather than arbitrary groupings of middle adults, allow a measure of self-selection. Many church leaders who have tried to group adults by superficial categories have found that adults have not complained or rebelled. They have done worse; they have stopped attending completely.

Malcolm Knowles has pleaded for a unique approach to adult instruction. And a significant part of this approach includes permitting learners freedom of choice. Building on the work of

Knowles, Christian has observed, "As a person matures, his self-concept moves from one of being a dependent personality toward one of being a self-directed human being."[21] If we capitalize on traits such as independence and self-direction, we will be able to offer effective educational programs for middle adults.

One logical way to permit such choice is to structure courses in such a way that the objectives are communicated clearly (and then pursued effectively, of course) for every program and individual course that we offer. Then permit adults the freedom (and responsibility) to make intelligent choices. Some of these choices may include overtly topical studies that directly speak to middle adult needs. Others could be Bible book studies with benefits to the participant clearly explained in advance. However we approach programming, it is wise to incorporate flexibility and freedom of choice for those whom we teach. Based on multiple studies of adult learners, R.E.Y. Wickett, writing in the *Handbook of Adult Religious Education,* explained:

> Educators of middle-aged adults need to understand that self-directed learning is a fact. Middle-aged adults want to be involved in decisions about their learning. They will take what they wish from activities which are planned by others and, when necessary, they will plan the learning which they desire.[22]

Select Appropriate Methods

Some have assumed that the ability to learn declines as adults reach the middle years. But in reality, adults seem less willing to put up with boring, irrelevant instruction. In a way it's like the question directed to a spouse by the partner who repeatedly served the same leftover meal. "What do you mean you don't like this meal? You liked it on Sunday; you liked it on Monday; you liked it on Tuesday. Now all of a sudden on Wednesday you say that you don't like it!" Perhaps the repetition of ineffective instructional methods finally exasperates middle adults.

Effective instruction will permit freedom and flexibility in classroom management. "If we are to treat our adults as adult learners, there must be much greater freedom to learn and openness in our educational process to allow them to direct their own educational inquiries."[23]

The instructional process must be cooperative and interactive. Lecture alone is out. Rather, a combination of providing valuable information with genuine discussion is imperative. Knowles explained the importance of both the teacher's attitude and the teacher's methods.

> Teachers convey in many ways whether their attitude is one of interest in and respect for the students or whether they see the students essentially as receiving sets for transmissions of wisdom . . . but probably the behavior that most explicitly demonstrates that a teacher really cares about students and respects their contribution is the act of really listening to what the students say.[24]

Conduct Educational Programs with Excellence

Like no preceding generation, Baby Boomers expect and demand excellence. Unquestionably, middle adults have pressing needs. And many of these adults understand their needs very well. But if educators offer inappropriate or shoddy programs, adults may well reject those programs even if they address legitimate needs. On the other hand, adults ordinarily value well-planned and well-executed educational programs.

And the promotion and publicity need to be of an appropriate quality too. Today's consumers are accustomed to well crafted and effectively delivered messages. We must "sell" middle adult programs, not merely offer them. More than one program director has done everything correctly right up to the time of communicating that program to the proposed constituents, and people have stayed away in great numbers. The problem may not have been with any part of the program itself, but merely poor promotion and publicity.

Middle adults have great and growing needs. They need to cope with change and the stress that accompanies such change. And middle adults want help in all of their tasks. Repeated studies have proven that they do want, and will respond to, effective educational ministries. "Properly interpreted, these findings should shatter any image of the adult as a stubborn, passive, unmotivated, reluctant Sunday churchgoer who must be forced, cajoled, and dragged into adult department sessions."[25]

But middle adults must arrive at the conclusion that specific programs will meet their needs. And not all will participate for the same reasons.

> Some of the important reasons for participating in an educa-

> tional activity are related to the benefits an individual receives for participating, such as interest in the subject matter or enjoyment of the method of learning, the setting, or the interaction with other people. Other reasons for participation relate to the benefits derived as one applies the outcome of the learning activity to achieve other purposes.[26]

Adults in the middle decades of their lives have great needs; and we educators have great opportunities to meet those needs. But merely conducting programs without carefully assessing needs with a view of designing appropriate curriculum will prove ineffective. When Christian educators implement effective learning experiences, everyone benefits. Middle adults can achieve their potential and, in turn, they can help others grow and develop too.

Notes

1. Robert J. Havighurst, *Human Development and Education* (New York: Longmans, Green, 1953), 268.
2. Robert J. Havighurst, *Development Tasks and Education*, 2nd ed. (New York: David McKay, 1970), 5.
3. Bernice L. Neugarten, *Middle Age and Aging* (Chicago: Univ. of Chicago Pr., 1968), 64.
4. Gilbert A. Peterson, ed., *The Christian Education of Adults* (Chicago: Moody, 1984), 51.
5. Nancy T. Foltz, ed., *Handbook of Adult Religious Education* (Birmingham, Ala.: Religious Education Pr., 1986), 85.
6. Ibid., 85.
7. Ibid., 86.
8. Leith C. Anderson, "A Senior Pastor's Perspective on Baby Boomers," *Christian Education Journal* 11 (Autumn 1990): 69ff.
9. Ibid., 70.
10. George Barna, *What Americans Believe* (Ventura, Calif.: Regal, 1991), 28.
11. Ibid., 237.
12. Ibid., 175.
13. Charles H. Nichols, "Building the Philosophical Foundation," *Christian Education Journal* 11 (Spring 1991): 24.
14. Leon McKenzie, *The Religious Education of Adults* (Birmingham, Ala.: Religious Education Pr., 1982), 1.
15. Ibid., 9.
16. Barna, *What Americans*, 28.

17. Perry G. Downs, "Baby Boomers' Ministry Needs," *Christian Education Journal* 11 (Autumn 1990): 25.
18. McKenzie, *Religious Education*, 79.
19. Charles M. Sell, "The Emerging Shape of Adult Christian Education," *Christian Education Journal* 4 (Autumn 1983): 68.
20. Barna, *What Americans*, 30.
21. Randy Christian, "Andragogical Assumptions and Christian Education," *Christian Education Journal* 9 (Spring 1989): 52.
22. Foltz, *Adult Religious*, 93.
23. Downs, "Baby Boomers," 77.
24. Malcolm S. Knowles, *The Modern Practice of Adult Education* (Chicago: Association Press, 1980), 47.
25. Sell, "Emerging Shape," 68.
26. Alan B. Knox, *Developing, Administrating, and Evaluating Adult Education* (San Francisco: Jossey-Bass, 1980), 129–30.

For Further Reading

Barna, George. *What Americans Believe.* Ventura, Calif.: Regal, 1991.

Fagerstrom, Douglas L., ed., *Singles Ministry Handbook.* Wheaton, Ill.: Victor, 1988.

Foltz, Nancy T., ed., *Handbook of Adult Religious Education.* Birmingham, Ala.: Religious Education Pr., 1986.

Knowles, Malcolm S., *The Modern Practice of Adult Education: From Pedagogy to Andragogy.* Chicago: Association Pr., 1980.

McKenzie, Leon, *The Religious Education of Adults.* Birmingham, Ala., Religious Education Pr., 1982.

Peterson, Gilbert A., ed., *The Christian Education of Adults.* Chicago: Moody, 1984.

FIFTEEN
TEACHING OLDER ADULTS

Robert E. Fillinger

As the guest speaker in a local church, a student of mine accepted the task of teaching a class of older adults. At one point during the lesson he announced, "Let's form small groups and examine this issue together." To his surprise and embarrassment one of the class members stood and said (with emphasis), "Young man, we do *not* do groups in this class."

Such an incident tends to reinforce some of the stereotypes we embrace about older persons and their ability to learn and adopt new approaches to the teaching-learning process. We even have colloquialisms that confirm our mythology about the elderly. Although there is abundant research evidence to the contrary, we say things like, "You can't teach an old dog new tricks." Older adults themselves buy into the idea that they can't learn. "Well," they sometimes say, "my memory isn't what it used to be."

It must be clear to everyone who works with older adults, or wants to, that our ministry with them must not be distorted by stereotypical portraits of the elderly. Can we be more precise in our portrayal of older adults? And what do we need to know to work effectively with them?

IDENTIFYING THE OLDER ADULT

The American Association of Retired Persons speaks of the aging of the world's population as a "social phenomenon without historical precedent."[1] The statistics which substantiate this "phenomenon" are quite dramatic, but for us who work with the elderly, these numbers also form part of the mandate not to ignore or underestimate this significant segment of our society. For example, the median age in the United States has soared past thirty-two and persons over sixty-five now outnumber teenagers.

Ken Dychtwald points out in his book that "two-thirds of all the men and women who have lived beyond the age of 65 in the entire history of the world are alive today."[2] The author speaks of three demographic phenomena: the senior boom; the birth dearth; and the aging of the Baby Boom, which by 2050 will produce a population of 67.4 million persons over sixty-five (21.8 percent of the population).[3] That approximately doubles the current population of sixty-five-plus persons. But statistics alone do not tell us all we need to know about older adults.

Until quite recently, we have been accustomed to speak of "adults," as though that term embraced a neat, homogeneous category of persons, all possessing similar qualities, characteristics, and needs. Adult educators, together with educational and developmental psychologists, have laid that idea to rest as we discover the amazing diversity that exists among adults. Through the entire developmental period known as adulthood, we have identified different needs, social roles, and developmental tasks. In an effort to distinguish the unique needs and characteristics among senior adults, gerontologists commonly speak not simply of older adults but of the "young-old," the "middle-old," and "the old-old."

The diversity of adulthood does not diminish as one grows older. Perhaps it is enhanced or emphasized. We now characterize older persons by an accumulation of the habits, idiosyncrasies, experiences, skills, and knowledge of a lifetime. All this, of course, creates a person distinct from any other. The teacher of adults can hardly afford to ignore these differences depicting the older person as an adult who has merely lived longer than other adults. Older adults, while similar in many respects to other adults, have *age-related* needs and characteristics which make them unique. When we respond to these differences and interact with them, more effective teaching of senior adults often results.

Other factors affect our ministry with older adults. Persons over sixty-five in our society are healthier, have more formal education, are more active (many of them prefer not to retire), and will live longer than the elderly of earlier generations. Other things might be noted. For example, older persons are more political and issue-oriented than ever before. Teachers of older persons must recognize that all these factors impinge (directly or indirectly) on the teaching-learning experience. Knowledge of these matters increases our ability to work effectively with older persons in the community of faith. They are, so to speak, prerequisites for the teacher of senior adults.

THE BIBLE AND AGING

In the epilogue of his book on aging, *As Our Years Increase,* Tim Stafford writes to his father-in-law, "The lesson is that old age is not a problem to be solved. It is a part of life to be experienced, for the elder and for his family."[4] This perspective seems to reflect the biblical approach to aging. The Bible does not address aging as a topic to be defined or interpreted. Nor does it develop a discreet theology of aging (though the Puritan divines dealt at length with this), but it does speak directly and significantly about age and aged persons.

The Bible treats aging realistically. It recognizes that limitations accompany old age (e.g., weakened eyesight, diminished sexual activity, reduced effectiveness of the senses). But even with these limitations, the aged person has achieved a desirable state. The elderly often (but not always) acquire wisdom and understanding. According to biblical writers, older persons deserve our love and respect.

Furthermore, the Bible challenges the elderly to remain active in ministry. Anna, who served the Lord in the temple until well past eighty, provides a good example. Spiritual maturity and a responsible Christian life should be diligently sought. The Scriptures never suggest that age provides an excuse to relax our efforts to grow in our relationship to God. The spiritual pilgrimage never ends. The Apostle Paul admonishes a young Titus to, "Teach the older men to be temperate, worthy of respect, self-controlled, and sound in faith, in love, and in endurance. Likewise, teach the older women to be reverent in the way they live, not to be slanderers or addicted to much wine, but to teach that which is good" (Titus 2:2-3).

It can be asserted, therefore, that while the Bible is abundantly clear about the responsibility of the church to teach, it does not establish specific guidelines regulating the educational task with older adults. We must love, honor, and respect them. We must challenge them to live circumspectly, to set a good example, and to grow in the grace and knowledge of the Lord.

THE OLDER ADULT LEARNER

This chapter is not intended to be a gerontological primer. Rather, it addresses the general question of what we need to understand in order to work effectively with older adults in teaching-learning situations.[5] One of the questions most important to us asks, "Can older adults learn?" That is, do the losses which occur during the aging process impair cognitive functions to the extent that ability to participate in teaching-learning experiences is seriously diminished?

The Adult Learner and Research

Perhaps the watershed in considering this issue came out of the work of E.L. Thorndike, who contended that the power to learn declines only slightly during the process of aging.[6] Later, his student Irving Lorge concluded that the rate (or speed) at which one learns may decline as one ages without affecting the ability or power to learn.

Lorge pointed out that Thorndike's work had been based on cross-sectional studies. A different perspective emerged when conclusions were based on longitudinal studies. Commenting on this point, Arenberg and Robertson state: "Under conditions of fast pacing, whether the presentation rate or the response rate is increased, the older learner is usually handicapped; his [or her] performance is especially benefitted by *self-pacing*."[7]

Consider the implications of self-pacing for creating appropriate teaching-learning climates. Of course, a great deal of research has been done since then and we have developed and refined our knowledge about such things as short- and long-term memory, primary and secondary memory, the effects of aging on the human brain, and the limitations that result from physical decline during aging. So, the assertion that older adults have the ability to learn through the entire life span is not disputed in most circles, although it is recognized that cognitive functions may be interrupted or hindered by cardiovascular, psychological, or physical malfunction.

Such information is more than theoretical. It helps us to understand that the senior adults in our classes are not sinking into an unchartered fog of senility and disorientation. They are vital human beings with gifts and abilities, still growing in their understanding of life and its responsibilities.

Frequently, our stereotypes make it difficult for us to think of senior adulthood as a period of growth. Nevertheless, a voluminous and growing literature indicates that old age can be a period of growth. Furthermore, the experience of a significant number of older persons confirms the conclusions of these studies. We hear of second, third, and fourth careers being launched; of new talents being discovered; and of the fulfillment of lifelong goals. In psychological and educational literature, the names of Havighurst, Knowles, Levinson, Erikson, Gould, Stokes, Fowler, Sell, McClusky, and many others come to mind along with terms like "marker events," "crises," "transitions," "stages," and "developmental tasks," terms which have become entrenched in our educational terminology.

Developmental Stages and Needs in the Adult Life Cycle

The concept of developmental stages or cycles, now quite common, and at times, perhaps, even pushed to extremes, proves extremely helpful in our work with older persons. Over forty years ago, Robert Havighurst of the University of Chicago developed his idea of social roles and developmental tasks.[8]

When one considers social roles, for example, it is not difficult to perceive of them as a kind of curriculum guide. He elaborates such roles as husband, wife, parent, worker, member of the community, church member.

Developmentalists speak not only of social roles, but also developmental tasks. The tasks define specifically what it means to fulfill the responsibilities of social roles. For our purposes, it is important to note that developmental tasks change over time. For example, in old age one does not cease being a parent, but the tasks of an older parent who occupies an "empty nest" are different than those of young adults parenting school-age children.

If, as we have hinted above, these roles and tasks can serve as a kind of curriculum guide, does the Scripture have anything to say about them? And what about the changes that take place in these roles as one ages? Even though the Bible may not speak systematically or at length about these matters, it is not silent.

In the Old Testament, for example, reproduction and old age are related. When the angel of the Lord spoke to both Abraham and Sarah, announcing that they would have a child, they both laughed (Gen. 17–18). After all, could a woman over ninety enjoy these pleasures? And in the beautiful story of Naomi and Ruth, bereft of her husband and sons, Naomi says to Ruth, "Am I going to have more sons? . . . I am too old to have another husband"

(Ruth 1:11ff). Still another fascinating description of old age involves David's encounter with Barzillai. When the king invites him to return to Jerusalem, he talks about the losses he has suffered . . . his hearing, his eyesight, his sense of taste. He speaks poignantly of his desire to die "in my own town near the tomb of my father" (2 Sam. 19:31-38). The issue of adult children and aging parents is dramatically illustrated in the experience of Eli and his sons (1 Sam. 2:27-36; 4:11-22).

The New Testament speaks of similar matters. Children are responsible to obey parents, and parents nurture children to obey the Lord. Paul writes to Timothy about older men and women and admonishes children and grandchildren to put "their religion into practice by caring for their own family and so repaying their parents and grandparents, for this is pleasing to God" (1 Tim. 5:1-10). Of course, we are also familiar with the passages which describe husband-wife and father-child relationships. Furthermore, the elderly may also be included in such categories as weak, poor, oppressed, and sick, and the Scripture leaves no doubt about our obligation to such persons.[9]

Perhaps these illustrations are enough to demonstrate that we can find scriptural foundation for these roles of human experience. The Bible does not always apply its teaching within specific age parameters, but it is quite clear that the Bible speaks frequently about these areas of everyday life. An awareness of these roles and transitions in life helps to make us more sensitive to the needs of the senior adult learner.

The developmental tasks of "later maturity," as Havighurst calls them, are also helpful guidelines in understanding the older adult learner:

1. Adjusting to decreasing physical strength and health;
2. Adjustment to retirement and reduced income;
3. Adjusting to the death of a spouse;
4. Meeting social and civic obligations; and
5. Establishing satisfactory physical living arrangements.[10]

These various concerns commonly confront everyone who works with older adults. Again, does the church have interest or influence in these areas of life? Does the Bible have anything to say about such matters? In a sense, the questions are rhetorical, but being aware of these matters reminds us that if we want to minister to the needs of whole persons, we need to be equipped to discern the nature of those needs.

We must be careful, however, not to apply these ideas as if they were precise formulas. We are unique in our personalities. So what may be problematic for one person presents no difficulties at all for another. Linda Jane Vogel warns us that it is "important to remember that they are descriptive of a large number of persons in our culture but that they [developmental tasks] should not be viewed as prescriptive for any particular individual"[11]

Howard Y. McClusky suggests another helpful approach to understanding the adult learner. He writes specifically of the needs of persons in the later years and identifies five need categories: *coping* needs (How do we cope with the loss of job, friends, spouse, money, influence?); *expressive* needs (How do we help people share themselves, their gifts and resources, with others?); *contributive* needs (How do we help individuals give and feel needed?); *influence* needs (Everyone needs to feel that she or he is making some impact on society.); need for *transcendence* (How do we help persons find meaning in life and death?).[12] When we view the older person in light of this analysis of later adulthood, an almost limitless number of ideas come to mind for working effectively with them.

Assumptions about the Older Adult Learner

One additional perspective will be helpful to us as we look at the older learner. Malcolm S. Knowles has suggested that we can make certain assumptions about the adult learner.[13] Even though these assumptions apply to the adult learner in general, they may be equally valid for the older adult. It must also be remembered that Knowles' assumptions are set in an andragogical context. (See chap. 6.)

According to Knowles, it is important to notice that these assumptions are not simply theoretical formulations. If one accepts the assumptions as valid, they imply what he calls "process elements."[14] That is, these assumptions ought to directly influence what we do in any teaching-learning context.

Perhaps a slight word of caution is appropriate here. As evangelical teachers, we are responsible to communicate an objective body of truth. We cannot sacrifice that responsibility in the interest of process. But the two are not mutually exclusive. We can be true to our call as teachers of God's Word and still employ practices that effectively communicate truth. To put it another way, we can fulfill our mandate as teachers while we employ practices that assist learners to internalize God's truth.

THE OLDER PERSON AND THE TEACHING-LEARNING EXPERIENCE

While we must not diminish the importance of understanding the older adult learner, "where the rubber meets the road" is the actual teaching-learning situation, whatever the nature of that situation. Teacher and learner come together here. Serious effort to bring about some kind of change characterizes the learning experience.

Unfortunately, we often approach our work with older adults believing that, at worst, they cannot change and, at best, they are always reluctant to do so. We must keep in mind that the later years subject most adults to a torrent of serious life-altering changes. A spouse dies; the family home must be sold; one must move to another neighborhood or state; income diminishes; little by little independence disappears; support groups diminish; and societal pressures increase. The amazing fact is that most older adults *do* adjust to these significant alterations. We who teach seniors do them an injustice when we perceive our task as maintaining the status quo, a kind of "let's-keep-them-happy" mentality. When we immerse older learners in the teaching-learning process, we engage them in a significant and, ideally, a life-altering task. The elderly will respond to the innovation that creative teaching can bring. If we cannot believe that, one wonders why we engage in the task in the first place.

The concluding part of this chapter will not be a "how-to" manual of teaching activities, but it can suggest some guidelines for our conduct in the teaching situation. The first guideline reminds us that we must not underestimate the importance of the statements we have already made about the older person as a learner. We often refer to such things as "only theory," but theory is foundational. For example, older adults can learn; they are engaged in the development of social roles; they are performing age-related tasks; and they have identifiable needs. These ideas, when we become aware of their reality, can give us clear guidance in the performance of our teaching responsibilities. We also ought to bear in mind that senior adults often prove reluctant to "buy into" new methodologies. We often characterize them as "set in their ways," or "not open to change." Rather than cast them in this stereotypical manner, we must understand that the "old dog" may not resist "new tricks" simply because they are new, but because he or she remains unconvinced that the new way provides something better than the old. Older persons pass new things through the filter of a whole lifetime of experience, habits, and learning. When we develop an awareness of this process, the reluctance we have mentioned becomes part of a natural process and not merely an age-related intolerance of change.

The elderly also come into the teaching-learning situation with various anxieties or a lack of self-confidence. These feelings can come from a number of sources—lack of formal education, failing eyesight, or hearing. Understanding these matters should encourage the teacher to create a relaxed, trusting, and informal climate. If we see older adults as a rich resource, we should create an atmosphere in which they have the opportunity to participate in the teaching process. Involve them in diagnosing their own needs and in choosing materials that will be used.

We have mentioned "self-pacing" in this chapter. Our primary goal should not be to "finish the lesson" but to deal adequately with the learner's needs. This will involve some judgment calls by the teacher, but it is better to spend too much time on a topic than too little.

Probably most teachers are concerned about what should happen in the teaching-learning session. That is, "What methods or activities should I use?" The following suggestions can be helpful for the teacher deciding what to do:

1. Introduce new methods slowly. The personality of your group should guide you in this matter.
2. Choose methods appropriate for the group, the lesson, and the location.
3. Choose methods that tap the experience and gifts of the group.
4. Choose methods that help fulfill goals. Never select an activity because it "fills time."

With regard to specific methods and activities, the teacher of older adults should be guided by whether or not learners will be involved in the process. We do a disservice by permitting them to sit and merely listen to someone talk. The lecture is certainly an appropriate method; however, it is often overused.

In her book on older adults, Vogel gives a helpful list of methods we may use. In addition to the lecture, she includes discussion, media presentations (films, filmstrips, audio and video tapes), storytelling, demonstrations, hands-on experiences, small group work, and role play.[15] The imagination of the teacher is probably the major limitation to the variety of methods and activities available for our work with senior adults.

Finally, we ought to bear in mind that learning and growth toward spiritual wholeness does not take place exclusively in classrooms. Field trips, luncheons, seminars, ministry activities (in the church building and in the community), and social occasions all provide opportunities to be involved in life and to make progress toward the high calling that we all—old and young—have in Jesus Christ.

Teachers of senior adults should see their work not as a ministry of "maintenance" for persons in their "declining years" but as an exciting outreach to more than 30 million people. "Effective teachers of older adults should be clear about their own self-concept and their own values. They should be knowledgeable about what they teach and possess the skills of an enabler. They should be aware of and sensitive to the needs and potentials of those they seek to teach."[16]

Notes

1. "The Aging of the World Population," in *Working Age,* May/June 1991. AARP newsletter.
2. Ken Dychtwald and Joe Flower, *Age Wage* (Los Angeles: Jeremy P. Tarcher, 1989), 6.
3. Ibid., 4–9.
4. Tim Stafford, *As Our Years Increase* (Grand Rapids: Zondervan, 1989).
5. The psychology of adulthood, how adults learn, and other related topics have been considered elsewhere in this volume. The discussion here will be brief and related specifically to older persons.
6. E.L. Thorndike, *Adult Learning* (New York: Macmillan, 1928).
7. David L. Arenberg and Elizabeth A. Robertson, "The Older Individual As a Learner," in *Learning for Aging*, ed. Stanley Grabowski and W. Dean Mason (Washington, D.C.: Adult Education Association of the U.S.A., 1976), 30 (italics mine).
8. Robert J. Havighurst, *Developmental Tasks and Education* (New York: David McKay, 1952), 92–98. For an expanded and more contemporary list of developmental tasks in adulthood, see Malcolm S. Knowles, *The Modern Practice of Adult Education*, rev. (Chicago: Association Press-Follet, 1980), 263–64.
9. Frank Stagg, *The Bible Speaks on Aging* (Nashville: Broadman, 1981). This is a very helpful book that gives a clear view of what the Bible says

about aging without very much interpretation.

10. Havighurst, *Developmental Tasks,* 92–98.

11. Linda Jane Vogel, *The Religious Education of Older Adults* (Birmingham, Ala.: Religious Education Pr., 1984), 12.

12. Howard Y. McClusky, "Education for Aging: The Scope of the Field and Perspective for the Future," in *Learning for Aging*, ed. Stanley Grabowski and W. Dean Mason (Washington, D.C.: Adult Education Association of the U.S.A., 1976), 330–38.

13. The work of Knowles is discussed in another section of this book. Therefore, this treatment is intentionally brief.

14. Knowles, *The Modern Practice,* 390.

15. Vogel, *Older Adults*, 124–29.

16. Ibid., 115.

For Further Reading

Dychtwald, Ken, and Joe Flower. *Age Wave.* Los Angeles: Jeremy P. Tarcher, 1989.

Freeman, Carroll B. *The Senior Years.* Nashville: Broadman, 1979.

Havighurst, Robert J. *Developmental Tasks and Education.* 2nd ed. New York: David McKay, 1952.

Knowles, Malcolm S. *The Adult Learner: A Neglected Species.* Houston: Gulf, 1973.

_____. *Self-directed Learning.* New York: Association Press, 1975.

_____. *The Modern Practice of Adult Education.* rev. Chicago: Association Press-Follett, 1980.

McKenzie, Leon. *Adult Religious Education.* Mystic, Conn.: Twenty-Third Pubns., 1975.

_____. *The Religious Education of Adults.* Birmingham, Ala.: Religious Education Pr., 1982.

Minor, Harold D., ed. *Creative Procedures for Adult Groups.* Nashville: Abingdon, 1966.

Sell, Charles M. *Transition Through Adult Life.* Grand Rapids: Zondervan, 1991.

Stafford, Tim. *As Our Years Increase.* Grand Rapids: Pyranee/Zondervan, 1989.

Stagg, Frank. *The Bible Speaks on Aging.* Nashville: Broadman, 1981.

Vogel, Linda Jane. *The Religious Education of Older Adults.* Birmingham, Ala.: Religious Education Pr., 1984.

SIXTEEN
SINGLE ADULTS AND SINGLE PARENTS

Patricia A. Chapman

An advertising supplement fell out of the local Sunday paper. The top coupon ad promoted Microwave Singles, a single serving cake. Now it is possible to have dessert for just one person. Apparently the advertising world has learned the wisdom of focusing on the large singles population.

By the year 2000, over 50 percent of the population of the United States will be single. Some 40-50 million single adults live in the U.S. today (1988 U.S. Census report) and represent an eclectic segment of the population.

"Singles" are composed of four distinct groups: (1) never married, (2) divorced, (3) widowed, and (4) separated. Each of these groups contains single parents. Each group has its own distinct characteristics, concerns, and developmental tasks; each harbors a number of subgroups within it.

This chapter looks at single adults and single parents within the developmental framework of early, middle, and later adulthood. Within these categories I find it helpful to consider single adult development as it relates to individual, family, career, and spiritual development. Singles face the tough personal challenge of balancing life in these four vital areas. Each section will conclude with suggestions for appropriate ministry.

IMPORTANCE OF A SINGLES MINISTRY

Singleness is a growing trend in the U.S. today. Five factors contribute to this trend: (1) 50 percent of marriages ending in divorce; (2) adults marrying later in life; (3) an increased tendency to cohabit rather than marry; (4) incarceration of a spouse; and (5) older adults remaining single after becoming widowed or divorced.

The needs of singles are generally similar with loneliness the most common problem. Singles can connect for jobs and careers, but often have difficulty making the kinds of social connections they need to keep them from becoming lonely. Related to this is depression, a major reason people enter hospitals. This leads to another need—relationships. All three are closely related. It seems that singles constantly look for ways to fill a void in their lives, the void created from lack of intimate relationships, or not being significant in the life of another.

Today's church has a rare opportunity for dynamic ministry among singles. Many large congregations across the U.S. now include a pastor to singles on their paid staffs. If the church wishes to meet the needs of unchurched singles and single parents, it must take off the blinders and really understand them. A place to belong, people that care, wholesome activities, and positive Christlike role models all make the church which promotes them more attractive to lonely singles.

SOME APPROACHES TO SINGLE ADULT MINISTRY

Singles ministry approaches vary from church to church. One approach lets the singles blend into the congregation so their identity is virtually hidden. If asked, many pastors could not even estimate how many of their parishioners are single. Also, many pastors seem at a loss to know how and where to begin such a ministry.

One often finds a different approach in smaller churches. When asked, "Do you have a singles ministry in your church?" church leaders respond, "We sure do. The class meets over in the pastor's study at nine on Sunday morning." This could be called a one-class-fits-all mentality. But how much does a forty-five-year-old single-again man with children have in common with a never-married twenty-seven-year-old career-oriented woman? Or a sixty-seven-year-old widow with a twenty-three-year-old college graduate taking on the world for the first time? One class doesn't fit all. Church leaders must develop sensitivity to the varying needs of each age-group.

A third approach ignores the "problem" completely. Convinced that classes for singles only become matchmaking groups, and believing that remarriage for the divorced is out of the question, some pastors ignore the "problem" completely. Yet all the time they wonder why other churches in the area attract such large and growing singles groups.

A fourth approach is to hire a full-time pastor to singles. Often, such a staff member is married, allowing the couple to minister to both men and women. Singles ministries must be tailored to the needs and abilities of each individual church.

YOUNG SINGLE ADULTS

Young adults (eighteen to twenty-one) now experience "adult" activities (sex, drugs, alcohol, travel, political and social activism) at younger ages. In spite of this, however, they take longer to mature and assume adult responsibilities.[1] One moment the late adolescent (eighteen- to nineteen-year-old) can appear to function as a child and the next as an adult. "Reason and emotion, rationality and irrationality, are constantly juxtaposed" states Okun.[2] They continue their education into their twenties while still living at home and still dependent on their parents. Marriage and the establishment of separate living quarters waits until later.

For the single young adult, the transition between adolescence and young adulthood holds complex problems. Society harbors certain expectations of one who has observed a twenty-first birthday, such as being able to support oneself, acting "like an adult," and selecting a mate.[3] Single young adults often experience conflicts with these expectations as they search for ways to express their own adulthood. Emphasizing career development at this stage while delaying marriage may raise questions from family and peers.

Tasks

Young adults face two major developmental tasks: (1) the formation of an integrated adult identity that allows for career, family, and other interpersonal role commitments; and (2) the formation and maintenance of intimate relationships. The "second task is hard to accomplish if the first has not been successfully resolved."[4] If during the young adult period one chooses to remain single while establishing a career, to take advantage of travel opportunities, to become involved in risky business ventures, thereby neglecting the development of intimate relationships, one is not fulfilling the "expectations about behavior that people carry in their heads and use to regulate their own behavior [as well as to] respond to others' behavior."[5]

The choice to delay the establishment of the intimate relationship of marriage in the early adult period is considered an event that happens outside the normal sequence of life events, what Neugarten calls an example of a "paranormative" event.[6] Young Christian single adults struggle with their sexuality, often repressing their true feelings and causing guilt.

Around the "age of thirty-five, one begins to reassess and reevaluate the choices and decisions made in the thirties," claims Okun.[7] This will include choice of a mate, "commitments to a career, children, relationships, time management, energy, and other resources." Levinson suggests that this is a time to reassess "the dream," to develop relationships with mentors, select a career, and choose a mate.[8] Vaillant claims that it is a period of guilt, a time in which the young adult defends and represses reactions more often.[9] Young adults, still single at thirty-five, have more to defend and repress. The process of reassessment and reevaluation will require the adult to face the reality of a lifetime of singleness. Dreams of having a family have all but evaporated.

Life Issues Young Adults Face:

- *Autonomy* signifies a mature type of independence—living without constant reassurance, approval, and affection.
- *Values and morals* relate to autonomy. Young adults must resolve the conflicts and competing influences between the family and themselves.
- *Career choice*—It may be difficult for the young adult to make that initial job and/or career choice which can either open or limit doors to future options.
- *Time management* requires balancing the demands of work, family, and personal desires and interests. Sometimes there may be more demands on single people, under the false assumption that they have more time to give to causes.
- *Relationships*—Interpersonal relationships expand one's social network through joining a church singles' group there and meeting new people.
- *Spiritual growth*—If one becomes an adult while an unbeliever, and then trusts Christ, he or she faces a whole new dimension of life. If, on the other hand, one has been a Christian for many years,

spiritual growth may take on renewed interest.[10]

Ministry Opportunities

For the searching young adult, the church should provide ministry guidelines through small group home Bible studies and fellowship. Topics can include a Bible character study, surviving singleness, learning how to develop intimacy, and personal finance. Topics will not be a problem for creative leaders.

Effective churches can meet other needs of singles through a variety of ways such as:

- plan retreats just for singles;
- take trips, such as skiing, boating, mountain climbing, hiking, traveling abroad, going on a cruise, or just taking in local sights;
- plan a picnic or day in the park;
- design activities for those with children;
- arrange a theater party or musical event.

Creative leadership will spark singles to participate in the meeting of their own needs.

MIDDLE ADULTHOOD

"Pushing forty is exercise enough" claimed the T-shirt worn by Paul. They sell them with the "Over-the-Hill" party supplies. And then there's *Lear's: the Magazine for the Woman Who Wasn't Born Yesterday.* Does "Life begin at Forty" as advertised? With all this good-hearted teasing, is it any wonder that singles over forty feel they are on the downside of life? Gould says that at midlife, adults begin to seriously take a look at where they have been and wonder how many years they have left.[11] What will the future hold? At forty, single adults often cope with the reality of singleness, and that can be traumatic. Suddenly, middle age has arrived. One's body changes may herald that fateful birthday. Oftentimes, it may be as simple as the party that family or friends hold to commemorate that milestone.

While married people cope with their adolescent children and aging parents, it appears to them that their single friends seem only concerned about where to vacation and with whom. They seem lucky to be able to do what they want. But the appearance of more time and money may be only an illusion. Also, friends may not realize that loneliness is a companion for singles. They have no one to come home to, no one to take trips with, no one to be there when the going gets tough.

Midlife reassessment and reevaluation may hit singles a bit harder as they face the future alone. Let's briefly review the tasks and issues of midlife single adults along with some suggestions for ministry opportunities.

Tasks

Interiority refers to an examination of inner experiences, fantasies, values, beliefs, conflicts, and attitudes.[12] Middle adults reformulate their life-styles. Activities in which one formerly engaged are perhaps not physically as easy or possible as before. Occasionally a middle-ager may seem like an adolescent having a fling before it's too late. Values and beliefs previously held may be discarded.

In a 1991 study Charles Wachler reported that "Overall, middle-aged bachelors appeared reluctant to get involved, make demands, or assert their needs in relationships. Isolation was evident in their lives. This defensive process did permit interaction, but it cut off and repressed their emotions." He concluded that "only 5 percent of bachelors after age forty will ever marry. These bachelors often make very good companions but, if women push them too far or ask for more than they are capable of giving, these bachelors will frequently push them away or end the relationship."[13]

Interpersonal relationships at this stage are reassessed and restructured, sometimes resulting in divorce. Many midlife adults may decide to find a more interesting partner or perhaps simply change partners. Divorce can devastate a couple emotionally, financially, and even physically. Suddenly they may find themselves at the bottom of the socioeconomic heap.

"*Climacteric*" describes a time when "both men and women undergo endocrine changes that affect their moods as well as their sexual behavior."[14] In women it is signaled by menopause; men experience a substantial but gradual drop in hormone level.

Issues

At midlife singles experience significant changes in their perspective of issues. The never-married may find these issues of no concern. Those who become single again through divorce, separation, or widowhood, perceive them as major concerns—*job security and boredom, preparation for retirement, the future develop-*

ment and launching of the children, awareness of the *shortness of life,* and facing various *losses,* such as missed opportunities, spouses, launched children, and jobs.

• *Self-assessment and reassessing* of primary relationships causes the ranks of singles to swell as more adults become single-again at midlife. Also, self-assessment may lead to the belief that one lacks worth, because of rejection from a divorce, loneliness from widowhood, or continued never-married status. It may validate a low self-image. As a result, suicide is not uncommon.

• *Physical changes* become more apparent. The infamous "middle-age spread" that plagues many midlife men signals aging to others. A noticeable slowing down in stamina manifests the beginning of health deterioration. Skin changes appearance and texture; hair changes color or disappears. The seasons of one's life have passed late summer.

• *Health* becomes a greater concern as chronic diseases and fatal illnesses become a reality at midlife. Some are life-style related (alcohol or tobacco use). Neugarten calls for new attention to "body-monitoring."[15] The adult realizes he or she is not invincible. Health concerns center around five leading causes of death:

1. Heart disease
2. Cancer
3. Blood vessel diseases (other than heart)
4. Accidents
5. Cirrhosis (liver disease related to alcohol)[16]

Singles are not exempt from these issues, though they may handle them in a different way. However, there is very little research on middle-age never-married singles.[17]

Ministry Opportunities

The never-married single may find this period less stressful since some of the more identity-related issues have been handled earlier. Some singles don't mind being included in groups consisting mostly of married couples. Others, however, may feel uncomfortable in such groups and prefer to be with other single adults.

Nevertheless, churches should make every effort to provide a network of support through growth groups, small group Bible studies, retreats, seminars, social activities, and all-church family activities. Middle-age singles, especially those searching to fill the void in their lives, look for help in "finding and linking the real me," centered on building a relationship with Christ. Other helpful seminars might aim at specific topics such as: "Renegotiating MidLife," "The Single Adult and Finances," or "How to Have a Meaningful Single Life."

OLDER ADULTHOOD

We find more singles in this age-group (fifty-five and over) than married, because widowed or divorced people often don't remarry at this stage of life. It is an age of both losses and gains. Some older adults find freedom from former responsibilities, both familial and career, and go on to enjoy the "golden years." For many others, there is no gold—just a great deal of loneliness and isolation. According to Birren "there are two faces of aging in our society: optimistic and pessimistic."[18] The optimist enjoys a high quality of life, always looking for something new—opportunities, products, services, and personal growth—while the pessimist faces poverty, poor health, and no caring network.

Older singles face problems similar to those faced by married or formerly married individuals. However, the older never-married face the prospect of living their last years alone or with minimal familial support. An older single with children may live alone, but is often cared for by adult children.

The aging process embodies *biological, psychological,* and *sociological* processes. Each of these processes contains changes that increase our susceptibility to illness and then death.[19] A brief look at these three processes may be helpful in alerting the church to ministry opportunities.

The *biological* process of aging includes physiological changes such as diminished hearing (particularly in the higher registers) and diminished sight, which includes decreasing ability to adjust focus and adapt to light and darkness. Also there is a diminished ability to smell and to recognize the taste of food. Okun lists a total of nineteen biological changes that happen to people in the aging process.[20]

One can hardly separate the *psychological* changes from their physiological, social, and environmental contexts. Neugarten observes that psychological differences increase with age. Many variables must be held responsible for these changes: life experiences, health, financial, and longevity.[21] Older adults need a significant relationship-support network. It may be intrafamilial, depending on communication and surviving kin.

Sociological theories of aging tend to focus on the status of the aged. In our particular culture, the elderly have largely been held in low esteem. By contrast, many cultures around the world hold their elders in high regard, seeking their wisdom and looking to them as transmitters of cultural mores. Our culture views senior citizens as excess baggage even as their life expectancy increases. *Prevention's Giant Book of Health Facts* (1991) predicts that by the year 2050, 22 percent of the U.S. population will be over sixty-five.[22] Today many consider euthanasia a humane means of solving the problem of warehousing infirm elders, many of whom no longer live "meaningful" lives.

One federal study reveals that suicide rates for Americans sixty-five and older jumped 21 percent between 1980 and 1986. Reasons for this trend seem unclear, and the increase is larger than expected.

Ministry Opportunities

Church staffs must become more sensitive to the changes brought about by the aging of their congregations. Older adults need opportunities to build support networks. Small home Bible studies and planned recreation appropriate for active seniors constitute but two of many options.

Often healthy seniors with retirement incomes want meaningful responsibility in the church. Retired executives often provide enormous assistance to church administration, usually at no cost. Consider also the pool of retired secretaries who can assist in the church office. All of these people are a godsend to the overworked staff. A word of caution: the church needs to be careful to use but not abuse them.

SINGLE PARENTS

Hagar provides an example of a single mother. Single mothers referred to in Scripture include the widow of Nain, the widow of Zarephath, and most likely, Tamar. Neither Hagar nor Tamar could be considered widows, however. Hagar may have been raped. Tamar seduced her father-in-law. Both appear to have been abandoned by the father of their sons and had to manage on their own. God became their husband and provided their needs.

Single parents are not a new societal phenomenon, but they do represent a burgeoning segment of our population. The largest percentage of single parents are women. In 1970, 85 percent of children under eighteen lived with their fathers. By 1988, the latest year for this statistic, 72 percent lived with two parents (natural or step), while 21 percent lived with their mothers and 2.9 percent lived with their fathers.[23]

According to a Gallup organization survey in 1989, 35 percent of single households (whether divorced, death, separated, or never-married) were headed by women, and the majority of those families lived below the poverty level.[24] According to a 1990 study generated by the California Social Services Department, no-fault divorce, instituted in the 1960s, can be directly blamed for this sad statistic.[25] Absent fathers often ignore child support requirements. The courts are, unfortunately, too full to be bothered to prosecute these errant parents.

Divorced Parents. Divorce is an accepted part of life today, and approximately 70 percent of single households are headed by a female.[26] Many problems result from divorce: the presence of the ex-mate, children and child support, conflicts with former in-laws, property settlements, visitation rights, holidays, medical care, the list goes on.

Widowed Parents. The death of a parent brings finality to a relationship. The permanence of the loss can create severe hardship on the family's financial future. Rarely does one have adequate time to prepare for the death of a spouse, so the emotional stress is acute for some time. However, recovery can be quite successful since the source of the pain is not present, unlike a divorce; therefore, it forces surviving family members to learn how to cope.

Separated Parents. This situation results from a number of sources: the military, incarceration, or business. Even living parents are often absent for extended periods of time. In effect, the remaining spouse (usually the wife) operates as a single. Certain stresses related to these situations will be quite different from either a divorced or widowed household.

Single Never-Married Parents. This growing group is almost always female. More and more women, who believe their biological clocks are running down, have a child by artificial means. Also, quite a number of girls become pregnant out-of-wedlock and decide to keep their children. But this group is changing. Today we see young fathers suing to keep the children they fathered, rather than have them destroyed by abortion. Each group of single never-married parents creates a separate set of problems.

Ministry Opportunities

The church can do so much to help these parents. First of all, we can be a living demonstration of real love. Church members can help these struggling parents realize that God loves them because His people love them (Jer. 29:11; Phil. 4:8-9). The church can:

1. provide child care during the day for preschoolers;
2. design after-school care for children while parents work;
3. offer baby-sitting, especially evenings;
4. plan retreats and seminars for single parents (topics could include discipline, preparing for adolescence, coping with finances, handling grief, dealing with relationships);
5. invite single parents with children on family outings;
6. provide camping, or other out-of-doors activities;
7. create an adopt-a-kid program.

CONCLUSION

Despite the increase in the number of singles today, the church still stumbles over how to meet the needs of this segment of its congregation. Those of us engaged in church ministry must answer some key questions:

1. How are single adults and single parents received when they walk through the doors of your church?

2. What provisions will you make to care for the needs of the singles in your congregation?

3. What are the future goals and plans for ministry to single adults in your church?

4. How does your church handle the tough problems that some younger singles bring (homelessness, AIDS, sexuality, child care, commitment)?

5. How will your church enable single adults to attain their full potential for God?

God has a plan for each life, singles included (Jer. 29:11). The mission of the church is to assist all members to find and fulfill God's plan for their lives. When we do so we strengthen and enhance the entire body of Christ.

Notes

1. David Elkind, *All Grown Up and No Place to Go* (San Francisco: Harper and Row, 1984), 73.

2. Barbara Okun, *Working with Adults: Individual, Family, and Career Development* (Monterey, Calif.: Brooks/Cole, 1984), 57.
3. H. Norman Wright, *Premarital Counseling* (Ventura, Calif.: Regal, 1977), 23.
4. Okun, *Working with Adults,* 54.
5. Douglas C. Kimmel, *Adulthood and Aging,* 2nd ed. (New York: Wiley, 1980), 55.
6. Bernice L. Neugarten, "Time, Age, and the Life Cycle," *The American Journal of Psychiatry* 136 (July 1979): 887.
7. Okun, *Working with Adults,* 75.
8. Daniel Levinson, *Seasons of a Man's Life* (New York: Knopf, 1978), 91.
9. George E. Vaillant, quoted in Okun, *Working with Adults,* 76.
10. James W. Fowler, *Stages of Faith* (San Francisco: Harper and Row, 1981), 185.
11. Roger Gould, *Transformations* (New York: Simon and Schuster, 1978), 219.
12. Bernice L. Neugarten and D. Gutmann, "Age-sex Roles and Personality in Middle Age," in *Middle Age and Aging*, ed. Bernice Neugarten (Chicago: Univ. of Chicago Pr., 1968), 72.
13. Charles Wachler, *San Francisco Chronicle,* 16 July 1991.
14. Okun, *Working with Adults*, 198.
15. Neugarten and Gutman, "Age-sex Roles," 71–87.
16. Okun, *Working with Adults*, 201.
17. Kimmel, *Adulthood and Aging*, 223.
18. J.E. Birren, "Aging in America: Roles for Psychology," *American Psychologist* 83 (1983), 298–300.
19. Okun, *Working with Adults*, 308.
20. Ibid., 310.
21. Neugarten and Gutman, "Age-sex Roles," 890.
22. *Statistical Abstract of the U.S.,* Washington, D.C.: U.S. Department of Commerce, National Data Book 1988, 38–47.
23. Ibid.
24. George Barna, *Single Adults in America* (Glendale, Calif.: Barna Research Group, 1987), 85.
25. *American Journal of Public Health* (September 1991).
26. Barna, *Single Adults*, 87.

For Further Reading

American Journal of Public Health, September 1991.

Barna, George. The Frog in the Kettle. Ventura, Calif.: Regal, 1990.

_____. Single Adults in America. Glendale, Calif.: Barna Research Group, 1987.

Boyce, Mary I. "Female Psychosocial Development: A Model and Implications for Counselors and Educators." *Counseling and Human Development* (February 1985): 1ff.

Elkind, David. *All Grown Up and No Place to Go.* San Francisco: Harper and Row, 1984.

Fagerstrom, Douglas L., ed. *Singles Ministry Handbook*. Wheaton, Ill.: Victor, 1988.

Fowler, James W. *Stages of Faith*. San Francisco: Harper and Row, 1981.

Gould, Roger. *Transformations.* New York: Simon and Schuster, 1978.

Haan, Norma, Elaine Aerts, and Bruce A.B. Cooper. *On Moral Grounds: The Search for Practical Morality.* New York: New York University Press, 1985.

Kimmel, Douglas C. *Adulthood and Aging.* 2nd ed. New York: Wiley, 1980.

Levinson, Daniel. *Seasons of a Man's Life.* New York: Knopf, 1978.

Miller, Patricia H. *Theories of Developmental Psychology.* San Francisco: W. H. Freeman, 1983.

Neugarten, Bernice L. "Time, Age, and the Life Cycle." *The American Journal of Psychiatry* 136 (July 1979): 887ff.

Neugarten, Bernice, and Gutmann, D. "Age-sex Roles and Personality in Middle Age." In *Middle Age and Aging*, edited by Bernice Neugarten. Chicago: Univ. of Chicago Pr., 1968.

Okun, Barbara. *Working with Adults: Individual, Family, and Career Development.* Monterey, Calif.: Brooks/Cole, 1984.

Peterson, Randy, and Anita Palmer. *When It Hurts to Be Single.* Elgin, Ill.: David C. Cook, 1988.

Richards, Sue P., and Stanley Hagemeyer. *Ministry to the Divorced*. Grand Rapids: Ministry Resources/Zondervan, 1986.

Smith, Harold Ivan. *A Part of Me Is Missing.* Irvine, Calif.: Harvest House, 1979.

_____. *Fortysomething and Single*. Wheaton, Ill.: Victor, 1991.

Smoke, Jim. *Growing Through Divorce.* New York: Bantam, 1978.

Swindoll, Lucy. *Soloing: Experiencing God's Best As a Single Woman.* Old Tappan, N.J.: Power/Revell, 1985.

Vaillant, George E. *Adaptation to Life.* Boston: Little, Brown, 1977.

Welsh, Krista Swan, ed. *Successful Single Adult Ministry*. Cincinnati: Standard, 1987.

Wright, H. Norman. *Premarital Counseling.* Ventura, Calif.: Regal, 1977.

SEVENTEEN
THE "CRITICAL YEARS" OF YOUNG ADULTHOOD

Richard E. Butman

In the past twenty years, the sheer number of students in higher education in this country and abroad has risen dramatically. A college education has become a necessity in many job markets. Anyone teaching in a representative academic setting today knows how much more a heterogeneous group they are than even a generation ago. Unfortunately, most of us formulated our notions of the "collegiate experience" at a time when fewer people went to college, and the majority of these persons were residential students at selective educational liberal arts colleges.[1]

The bulk of the educational research on these "critical years" (i.e., a potential "make it" or "break it" period for most individuals) of young adulthood likewise reflects this same bias.[2] That realization alone should make us exceedingly cautious in formulating broad generalizations about students in any particular collegiate setting.

Clearly, more research needs to be done on this increasingly diverse and representative population if we are committed to improving our awareness and effectiveness as Christian educators. In particular, we need to learn more about the setting that shapes the character of young adults,[3] the intellectual and interpersonal implications of the potential changes that occur at the cognitive, psychosocial, and/or spiritual levels,[4] and how these might impact our attitudes and practices as exemplars of the Christian virtues.[5] In this chapter I explore several themes that have direct relevance for Christian educators as they attempt to improve their effectiveness with this challenging and often demanding group during their "critical years."

RELEVANT THEMES FOR CHRISTIAN EDUCATORS

The Need to Familiarize Ourselves with the Context of Contemporary Higher Education

If we are going to impact college students deeply I believe it is imperative for us to regularly enter into their world. Every year that I teach college students, the harder it is for me to fully appreciate and understand their responses to the institution in which I serve. I find it tempting to make generic assumptions and formulate stereotypes about "where my students are" in their own maturation process.[6] Not only do I get distracted by my own personal and professional issues, but I am increasingly finding what a sacrifice it can be to listen attentively and respectfully to students as they try to make sense of their milieu.[7]

To be effective as Christian educators we should be willing in word and deed to "identify with the people." Many college students confront substantive institutional issues on a daily basis which directly impact their well-being. It may be far too easy for us to stress personal "choice" and "responsibility" when we have a strong sense of efficacy in our own lives. Our work with college students will be significantly impaired if we never stand with them as their advocates, especially in the local church setting. At the most basic level, this requires us to at least begin to hear their "voice."[8]

The Need to Familiarize Ourselves with the Potential Changes That Occur Cognitively in the Collegiate Years

There is a rich literature on adult cognitive development which has great relevance for us as Christian educators.[9] Probably the most familiar study approach is the developmental or stage perspective (e.g., Jean Piaget's formal or postformal thought or William Perry's levels of cognitive and ethical development). Other approaches include the psychometric perspective and the information processing perspective.[10] Despite the differences in these strategies, a number of themes emerge.

Rather dramatic changes may occur in how efficiently or effectively college students process new information, how they integrate it with previously learned material, or how deeply and broadly they explore those matters that most directly concern them. Ideally, adult thinking is less self-centered and reflects a much higher degree of personal choice, integration, and deep-felt commitment.[11] Obviously, this is not always the case. There are certainly striking differences in both "raw ability" (e.g., IQ or ACT/SAT scores) and/or achievement (college grades or other performance-based criteria).

Importance of Life Application. Information and problem-solving are absorbed largely to the extent that the individual perceives them to be related to the particulars of his or her own life. Knowledge is no longer acquired in a relatively indiscriminate manner—it is much more goal-directed or achievement-oriented (Does it *really* matter to me in terms of my personal or professional objectives?). Consequently, the Christian educator who doesn't stress immediate life application is probably doomed to failure.

College students are most likely looking for someone who can help them articulate an adequate theology that provides for constructive and immediate behavior change. We must be exceedingly careful not to teach theological content without specific directions on how to work out that content behaviorally or emotionally.[12] College students are probably not looking for another formula on how to experience the "abundant" or "deeper" life, but they are vitally interested in immediate and direct "concrete relevance" of what they hear or read for their immediate lives.[13]

Diverse Intellectual Skills. Formal thinking can be a very powerful problem-solving tool for the college student. Unfortunately, not all young adults have developed this capacity. It presupposes certain academic and maturational competencies that may be rather unevenly developed in certain people. Suffice it to say that the Christian educator needs to recognize the diversity of intellectual skills or "learning styles" represented in any given audience of college students. Obviously, this raises pedagogical concerns: What to teach? How best to teach? Whom to teach?

But a deeper tension may emerge for the Christian educator. The formal operational thought so deeply valued in the university setting tends to be best suited for use in a "closed system." Under restricted conditions we can deal with a finite number of variables that can be analyzed, synthesized, or critically evaluated. In contrast, most of the problems that the college student confronts outside of the classroom reflect the relatively "open systems" of roles, responsibilities, and relationships. These tend, in contrast, to be characterized by "ambiguity, partial truths, and an infinite number of variables, many of them unknown."[14] For most college students, this is simply an overwhelming realization. It requires them to become more flexible and adaptive and to more effectively integrate their thinking processes and experiences.

Personal Experience. Christian educators will likely discover that many college students place a rather high value on subjective feelings and personal experience. They are perhaps less impressed by a more traditional emphasis on an objective and logical approach to problem-solving. According to Labouvie-Vief,[15] they struggle with how best to appreciate and reconcile both objective and subjective approaches to particular problems, often resulting in multiple perspectives that can prove to be rather threatening to the Christian educator.[16] What may appear to us to be rather "relativistic" may in fact be their effort to integrate their beliefs and experiences with the apparent contradictions and inconsistencies they encounter. It is no small development task for college students to make firm commitments when they have an increased capacity to acknowledge the rather inconsistent, open, and subjective nature of the human experience.[17]

The Need to Familiarize Ourselves with the Potential Changes That Occur Psychosocially in the Collegiate Years

Extended Adolescence. In a complex civilization like our own, college students must struggle to become adults. Few of us would disagree that adolescence is artificially extended well into the twenties and beyond—or that there are any clearly defined rites of passage. Indeed, the exact definition of "adulthood" is a focus of much discussion and debate in the developmental literature.[18] Realistically speaking, adolescence probably ends when an individual is able to be an "independent, self-supporting, self-directing member of society."[19] Consequently, it would probably be safe to assume that most college students are "almost grown" in that they have not yet assumed full adult responsibilities.

When adolescence is prolonged or protracted, which is usually the case, there is the increased risk of "aimlessness, boredom, indulgence in pleasure and resultant self-hate or guilt, self-destructive tendencies and several other psychological mishaps, especially for those who have suffered scars in childhood."[20] Far too many young adults are "dysfunctional" or seriously "wounded" at some level.

Problems in Living. We should remind ourselves that the presence of psychological problems in somebody's life does not invalidate or even cast doubt on his or her Christian commitment.[21] Indeed, we are all fallen creatures living on a fallen planet; Paul reminds us that "the whole creation has been groaning as in the pains of childbirth right up to the present time" (Rom. 8:22). Further, the doctrine of sin implies the utter impossibility of perfection. As Jones and Butman have observed,[22] it is certainly not inappropriate to expect that Christian commitment brings with it the possibility of enhanced emotional and spiritual well-being. But it certainly does not guarantee it, since we can never tell for sure what "raw material" one brings into his or her Christianity. The Christian educator oblivious to the reality of pain (or even serious psychopathology) in the lives of college students will certainly be less than effective in communicating the "good news." Once again it is imperative that we "know our audience."

Many college students struggle with developing a clear sense of self.[23] Without a clear identity, they find it difficult to devote much energy to meeting their needs for "affiliation" (love, belonging, or intimacy) or "achievement" (competence, esteem, or success). Many college students are simply bewildered by the many options available to them. Perhaps in no time in human history have young adults been as free to choose their own developmental path. This comes with a price, which certainly includes greater internal and/or external pressures.

The Need to Familiarize Ourselves with the Potential Changes That Occur Spiritually in the Collegiate Years

A major task of the Christian educator should be assisting students in developing a more mature faith. Consider the words of psychologist Gordon Allport in his highly influential *The Individual and His Religion:*

> We may then say that the mature religious sentiment is ordinarily fashioned in the workshop of doubt. Though it is known intimately as the "dark night of the soul" it has decided that theoretical skepticism is not incompatible with practical absolutism. While it knows all the grounds for skepticism, it serenely affirms its wager. In doing so it finds that the successive acts of commitment, with their beneficient consequences, slowly strengthen the faith and cause the moments of doubt gradually to disappear.[24]

College students, like all adults, need help in achieving a mature religious vision. Specifically, we can help them to develop a comprehensive and unifying worldview, centered on Jesus Christ, and one that "serenely affirms the wager." Further, we can assist them as they seek to develop more mature religious strivings. Helping them to see beyond themselves, developing more autonomous and effective motivation for service, and a greater willingness to serve others seems crucial. Providing effective structures to channel their creative and constructive energies seems imperative, along with the needed support and guidance to attain these objectives.

Honesty and Spiritual Growth. All of this presupposes, of course, that we are honest with ourselves and each other. If we are truthful, we must admit that the church has not always been an easy place to be honest, especially in those settings where "the truth" has been used as a club instead of a comfort.[25]

We, as Christian educators, must be willing to acknowledge what we do not like or respect in ourselves, or what we suspect others will disparage.[26] If we deny and distort the inner realities of our own states of consciousness before God, we can never fully grasp what it means for God to love us—or others.[27] "Our life with God will thrive only to the extent that we purpose in our hearts, sincerely and relentlessly, to reckon with truth—about Him, about others, about ourselves."[28] Certainly this is a "tall order" for us as Christians, but it seems especially important in our work with college students, who often seem distrustful of those they assume are less than fully candid.

This kind of honesty is essential for helping students to "internalize" or "own" their faith.[29] College students, not unlike adolescents, seem especially vulnerable to peer pressure or social conformity. As Fowler has warned, there appears to be a significant risk in the possible overconformity to others' wishes and too intense a reliance on other persons who may betray such trust (i.e., one's faith has to be more than people-pleasing or social convention).[30] Rather, we should encourage the critical capacity to reflect on identity (self) and on outlook (ideology), necessary prerequisites for developing a more personal faith.[31]

Heart of the Gospel. A further struggle for many college students has to do with their attempt to separate the core tenets of their "faithing commitment" from the potential cultural and/or subcultural overlay. Young adults today are probably much more aware of "cultural evangelicalism"[32] than they were a generation ago. They are often unusually perceptive about the ways in which the proclamation of the Gospel has become a message "cluttered with qualifications and corrupted by footnotes and appendices."[33] We as Christian educators must be careful not to add our inherited or otherwise acquired cultural or social convictions to the truths of Scripture that we have received by divine revelation. College students can provide for us some keen insights on what we have added to the "essence" of the Gospel message. "Rediscovering" those core truths can be liberating for young adults,[34] especially when the heart of their Christian experience has been fear or despair, rather than the good news of forgiveness and love.

The Importance of Pain/Loss. Young adults can be passionate and intense people. We need to communicate to them in word and deed how to link that with compassion for the pain and agony of others. George Regas has remarked:

> The older I get, the more convinced I am that passion—the deepest, strongest, most alive feeling—is linked with compassion. Maybe the greatest lovers are those who care deeply about the pain and agony in their brothers and sisters in the world, who choose to bear some of those burdens and transform the pain. . . . The world might think it absurd, but Christians have a way of believing that if we give our lives away for the healing of the world, happiness and joy and fullness of life will come along in the parentheses.[35]

In short, we need to assist college students in deciding how best to improve the world as well as enjoy it. Both are certainly part of the human struggle to live an authentic life.[36]

COLLEGE MINISTRY: SOME SUGGESTIONS

Teaching College Students

"Passion, hope, doubt, fear, exhilaration, weariness, colleagueship, loneliness, glorious defeats, hollow victories, and above all, the certainty of surprise and ambiguity—how can one begin to capture the reality of teaching in a single word or phrase?"[37] This passage from *The Skillful Teacher* summarizes many of my own thoughts and feelings about the risks and responsibilities inherent in the role of being a Christian educator with contemporary college students. My primary task as a Christian educator is to find the best ways to build the church and improve society worldwide by promoting holistic development in my students. To be effective in that task, I need to know what the options are. This presupposes, of course, that I know my audience, my subject matter, and myself.

There is a large literature on the subject. The American Educational Research Association has contributed a massive volume summarizing research on teaching.[38] Perhaps more accessible are the wonderful treatments on the subject by McKeachie, Timpson and Tobin, and Weimer.[39]

This information suggests that we need to develop a vision for our teaching, acquire knowledge about curriculum design and implementation, develop the ability to creatively present material, facilitate discussion, and carefully assess the effectiveness of our efforts.

Effective teaching assumes that changes will take place in all participants. Change, therefore, is influenced and mediated by a relationship with a teacher. Likewise, the teacher must have a flexible repertoire of techniques and the timing, tact, and sensitivity to know when to use them. Further, change is not likely to take place unless there is a commitment on all parts to grow intellectually and/or interpersonally. We might do well as Christian educators to discern the difference between those who truly want to grow and those who are "going through the motions" for whatever reasons. Unless there is a shared responsibility, even the most creative efforts appear doomed to failure. Finally, I am deeply convinced that there must be a commitment to a set of values which will guide and direct the overall educational process.

In my twelve years of full-time collegiate teaching, I have come to increasingly recognize the formative and substantive value of modeling and relevant life experiences. The outcome data on "direct teaching" are not nearly as impressive as those for alternative strategies. Despite the humanistic overtones of the assertion, I have come to see that my "being" is more important than my "doing." In other words, what we are in relation to each other is more important than what we accomplish. Christian community forms the backbone of all church life. It is the foundation on which all worship, Christian fellowship, evangelism and discipleship, and social compassion and justice should be built. It logically follows, then, that responsible education must be highly incarnational and interpersonal.

Whether the "classroom" is in the collegiate or church setting, several concerns deserve special attention. We must be willing to ask in a collaborative and non-adversarial manner whether or not a particular teacher has knowledge of the subject? Is he well-organized? Does she have clarity of expression? Is there sufficient opportunity for teacher-student interaction? Was the presentation made with sufficient passion and compassion? Did the students appear to be involved and invested in the material presented?[40] Depending on the response to any or all of these stimulus questions, we are in a much better position to measure teacher effectiveness, or to recommend suggestions for improvement or remediation. We would be wise to realize as Christian educators that certain personalistic and situational variables greatly impact the overall learning process with college students in the "critical years." Christian persuasion is both an art and a science.[41] Knowledge of effective communication strategies is simply imperative.[42]

"Mountaineers" and "Mentors"

I am deeply convinced that the effective teacher is not a pleader, not a performer, not a huckster, "but a confident, exuberant guide on expeditions of shared responsibility."[43] In short, he or she is most like a mountaineering guide. Nancy Hill, a colleague at the University of Colorado, has written:

> The mountain guide, like the true teacher, has a quiet authority. He or she engenders trust and confidence so that one is willing to join the endeavor. The guide accepts the leadership role, yet recognizes that success (measured by the heights scaled) depends on the close cooperation and active participation of each member of the group. He or she may have crossed the terrain before and is familiar with the landmarks, but each trip is new and generates its own anxiety and excitement. Essential skills must be mastered; if they are lacking, disaster looms. The situation demands keen focus and rapt attention; slackness, misjudgment, or laziness can abort the adventure.[44]

Christian educators must never lose sight of the magic and majesty of the learning experience; nor should we forget that good teaching is a self-eradicating process. Rather, it must be a highly active and interactive task of shared responsibilities and risks.

As good as the analogy may be, it may never capture the power of the teacher to serve as a mentor or spiritual guide. Ideally, the "mountaineer" should also be willing to bring her passion and compassion into the community of faith, in order that the Spirit may transform lives.[45] Many college students today long for a context in which to begin formulating and implementing a "dream." For some, those persons may be found in a local church.

Good mentors are willing to engage in a mutual and reciprocal relationship with the expressed purpose of facilitating holistic development. They see themselves as co-participants in life and are willing to be honest and flexible with regard to roles and expectations. Good mentors in the collegiate setting assist students in the process of making and keeping commitments[46] and are willing to serve as catalysts or facilitators of meaningful and significant change. In word and deed, they demonstrate their trust and confidence in others and voluntarily share their struggles as they attempt to become more authentic and honest in everyday Christian living.

College Students: Some Keys to Effective Ministry

Their Diversity. The local church concerned about making an impact on the spiritual lives of students needs to recognize that there are more female students today, a greater percentage from lower socioeconomic statuses, more ethnic minority and international students, a larger percentage of older students, a striking increase in part-time students, and a sustained interest in more specific "career-based" or "vocational" curricula rather than the more traditional liberal arts focus.[47] Obviously, this presents a tremendous challenge to Christian educators as they design and implement meaningful and significant programs for college students today.

The Need for Structure and Support. Responsible education in the "critical years" is full of risks and shared responsibilities. It has the potential to powerfully impact nearly every measure of adult cognition. Generally speaking, college students become more tolerant, flexible, and realistic. The task for Christian educators, then, is to determine how best to provide the structure and support that will enable and empower students to forge strong commitments while remaining open-minded and prepared for the inevitable changes of life. We need to recognize that most college students struggle with how best to learn, how best to think, or how best to judge.[48] These vital "critical thinking skills" need to be challenged and nurtured if we sincerely desire to help young adults more clearly articulate their control beliefs or worldviews, the essential cognitive attitudes and beliefs that can potentially shape their character.[49]

Dependency Prone. Ideally, the college years should be a time for making preliminary choices for adult life. As Christian educators, we need to be sensitive to how difficult it is for many young adults to make good decisions about what we might judge to be some of the rather trivial or superficial aspects of life (e.g., style of clothing or choice of entertainment). Especially for students who come from overly protective or authoritarian homes, such decisions may seem to be agonizingly difficult. Becoming "surrogate" parents is probably an unwise role to adopt, despite what may appear to be sincere requests for "help." Without some initial successes in these areas, it seems hard to imagine how the more abiding aspects of life—such as choice of career or marital status—can be effectively decided. Once again, young adults need someone who can be available to them, to really listen, to hear and to receive. Even well-meaning "advice" has the potential to foster an unhealthy dependence on external authority figures. Young adults need to make these tough choices themselves. It is our responsibility to "help them help themselves." There is a world of difference between "imposing" values and "exposing" them.[50]

Address Relationship Issues. Practically speaking, the church has much to offer young adults who are in this potentially difficult period of transition. It is wise to address the initial choices being made in love, occupation, friendship, values, and life-style. College students often need practical help in dealing with personal issues such as anxiety, loneliness, depression, anger, guilt, and shame.[51] Exploring singleness-marriage issues in the context of their intimacy struggles is certainly worthwhile, especially if the biblical insights are made "concretely relevant." Others need specific help in breaking away from excessive dependence on their parents, or guidance in career selection or planning. There will always be a need for a relevant and concrete discussion of the richness and complexity of human sexuality from a solid biblical, psychosocial, and sociocultural perspective.[52] At the level of the local church, it would be especially helpful to select educators who can empathize with students' failures in these areas as well as their successes.

Struggle to Find Meaning. Meaning and purpose in life can be hard to find in the current North American context. With uncertainty about the future, an acute awareness of the pressures to succeed in all one's life tasks, an increased recognition of the many injustices in the world, or a strong sense of personal anxiety that can result from living in an age of extreme subjectivism and relativism, the college student of today often finds it difficult to have the "courage to be."[53] Indeed, "lack of closure" on important existential or religious questions appears to be the norm or even desired end-goal in the contemporary collegiate context.[54]

Integrity. As committed Christians, we are called to accountability in our communities, not to independence and autonomy. Integrity is more than mere ethical compliance.[55] "Being ethical" is not an attempt to surround ourselves with a fence that barely constrains us, but a willingness to explore the frontiers of integrity and honesty in all that we do and say.[56] Christian educators should be exemplars of that kind of integrity and honesty. As in nearly every dimension of our lives, it is simply impossible to take another person any deeper than we have been willing to go ourselves.[57] Jesus reminds us of this truth in the words which follow the parable of the blind man leading the blind: "A student is not above his teacher, but everyone who is fully trained will be like his teacher" (Luke 6:39).

A FINAL COMMENT

I am fully cognizant that what I have said might be construed as "idealistic" or "unrealistic." I humbly admit that I speak better than I act.[58] Nevertheless, faith is, in the final analysis, more intention than performance. Fortunately, I too am a sinner saved by grace through faith (Eph. 2:5). Thank God that the Holy Spirit works through us—and in spite of us!

But it is good to remind ourselves regularly of our intentions, our convictions, and our dreams. I can think of few groups in the Christian community that have as much promise and potential as contemporary college students. If we are willing to be with them, identify with them, or serve with them "until justice and peace embrace," I suspect that they will continually prompt us to take our own emotional, interpersonal, and spiritual well-being more seriously.

Notes

1. Kathleen S. Berger, *The Developing Person through the Life Span,* 2nd ed. (New York: Worth, 1988).
2. Ernest T. Pascarella and Patrick T. Terenzini, *How College Affects Students* (San Francisco: Jossey-Bass, 1991).
3. Ernest L. Boyer, *College: The Undergraduate Experience in America* (New York: Harper and Row, 1987).

4. Sharon Parks, *The Critical Years: The Young Adult Search for a Faith to Live By* (San Francisco: Harper and Row, 1986).
5. Arthur F. Holmes, *Shaping Character: Moral Education in the Christian College* (Grand Rapids: Eerdmans, 1991).
6. There are certainly articulate spokespersons that have attempted to describe the contemporary collegiate setting. Ernest Boyer, a deeply committed Christian, is President of the Carnegie Foundation for the Advancement of Teaching and Senior Fellow at the Woodrow Wilson School of Public and International Affairs, Princeton University. His very accessible *College: The Undergraduate Experience in America* (1987) is must reading. Wheaton College's Arthur F. Holmes has done a good job of describing the particulars of the religious setting in his *The Idea of a Christian College* (Grand Rapids: Eerdmans, 1975). Most recently, the rather controversial but extremely thought-provoking Page Smith, *Killing the Spirit: Higher Education in America* (New York: Viking Penguin, 1990), is highly recommended.
7. William Miller and Kathleen Jackson, *Practical Psychology for Pastors* (Englewood Cliffs, N.J.: Prentice-Hall, 1985).
8. Carol Gilligan, *In a Different Voice* (Cambridge, Mass.: Harvard Univ. Pr., 1982).
9. See Pascarella and Terenzini, *How College Affects Students.*
10. See Berger, *The Developing Person.*
11. K. Warner Schaie, "Towards a Stage Theory of Adult Cognitive Development," in *Readings in Adult Development and Aging,* ed. K.W. Schaie and J. Geiwitz (Boston: Little, Brown, 1982).
12. Lawrence J. Crabb, *Inside Out* (Colorado Springs, Colo.: NavPress, 1988).
13. James R. Dolby, "Cultural Evangelicalism: The Background for Personal Despair," *Journal of the American Scientific Affiliation* (September 1972): 91–101.
14. Berger, *The Developing Person,* 414.
15. G. Labouvie-Vief, "Intelligence and Cognition," in *Handbook of the Psychology of Aging,* 2nd ed., ed. James E. Birren and K. Warner Schaie (New York: Van Nostrand Reinhold, 1985).
16. Parks, *The Critical Years.*
17. James Fowler, *Stages of Faith* (San Francisco: Harper and Row, 1981).
18. Parks, *The Critical Years.*
19. Benedict J. Groeschel, *Spiritual Passages* (New York: Crossroad, 1989), 47.
20. Ibid.
21. Clinton McLemore, *The Scandal of Psychotherapy* (Wheaton, Ill.: Tyndale, 1982).
22. Stanton Jones and Richard Butman, *Modern Psychotherapies: A Comprehensive Christian Appraisal* (Downers Grove, Ill.: InterVarsity, 1991).

23. W. Kaufman, *Shame: The Power of Caring* (Rochester, Vt.: Schenkman, 1985).
24. Gordon W. Allport, *The Individual and His Religion* (New York: Macmillan, 1950), 72.
25. Clinton McLemore, *Honest Christianity: Personal Strategies for Personal Growth* (Philadelphia: Westminster, 1984).
26. Ibid., 12.
27. C. Stephen Evans, *Sören Kierkegaard's Christian Psychology* (Grand Rapids: Baker, 1990).
28. McLemore, *Honest Christianity*, 12.
29. Parks, *The Critical Years*.
30. Fowler, *Stages of Faith*.
31. Ibid.
32. Dolby, "Cultural Evangelicalism," 91–101.
33. Horace L. Fenton, *The Trouble with Barnacles* (Grand Rapids: Zondervan, 1973), 14.
34. Vincent J. Donovan, *Christianity Rediscovered* (New York: Maryknoll, 1978).
35. G.F. Regas, *Kiss Yourself and Hug the World* (Waco, Texas: Word, 1987), 15.
36. Crabb, *Inside Out*.
37. S.D. Brookfield, *The Skillful Teacher* (San Francisco: Jossey-Bass, 1990), 1.
38. American Education Research Association, *Handbook of Research on Teaching*, 3rd ed. (New York: Macmillan, 1986).
39. Wilbert J. McKeachie, *Teaching Tips: A Guidebook for the Beginning College Teacher*, 8th ed. (Lexington, Mass.: D.C. Heath, 1986); W. Timpson and D. Tobin, *Teaching as Performing* (Englewood Cliffs, N.J.: Prentice-Hall, 1982); M. Weimer, *Improving College Teaching* (San Francisco: Jossey-Bass, 1990).
40. See Weimer, *Improving Teaching*, 210–12.
41. Em Griffin, *The Mind Changers: The Art of Christian Persuasion* (Wheaton, Ill.: Tyndale, 1976).
42. Cf. Em Griffin, *A First Look at Communication* (New York: McGraw-Hill, 1991).
43. Nancy K. Hill, "Scaling the Heights: The Teacher as Mountaineer," *The Chronicle of Higher Education* (16 June 1980): 48.
44. Ibid.
45. Evans, *Sören Kierkegaard's Psychology;* Parks, *The Critical Years*.
46. Lewis Smedes, *Caring and Commitment* (San Francisco: Harper and

Row, 1989).

47. American Council on Education, *Fact Book on Higher Education* (New York: Macmillan, 1984).

48. Cf. William G. Perry, "Cognitive and Ethical Growth: The Making of Meaning," in *The Modern American College,* ed. A.W. Chickering (San Francisco: Jossey-Bass, 1981).

49. Arthur F. Holmes, *Shaping Character: Moral Education in the Christian College* (Grand Rapids: Eerdmans, 1991).

50. McLemore, *Scandal of Psychotherapy*.

51. Cf. Gary R. Collins, *Christian Counseling: A Comprehensive Guide* (Waco, Texas: Word, 1980).

52. E.g., Lewis Smedes, *Sex for Christians* (Grand Rapids: Eerdmans, 1976).

53. Paul Tillich, *The Courage to Be* (New Haven, Conn.: Yale Univ. Pr., 1952).

54. M.J. Donahue, "Psychology of Religion: Problems and Premises" (Paper presented at the annual meeting of the American Psychological Association, San Francisco, August 1991).

55. Jones and Butman, *Modern Psychotherapies*.

56. Ibid., 412.

57. McLemore, *Honest Christianity*.

58. Cf. H. Newton Malony, *Integration Musings: Thoughts on Being a Christian Professional* (Pasadena, Calif.: Integration, 1986).

For Further Reading

Boyer, Ernest L. *The Undergraduate Experience in America*. New York: Harper and Row, 1987. Helps the reader to appreciate the contemporary context of higher education in this country from the perspective of a national spokesperson who is also a deeply committed Christian.

McKeachie, Wilbert J. *Teaching Tips: A Guidebook for the Beginning College Teacher,* 8th ed. Lexington: D.C. Heath, 1986. Probably the best available guide on the craft of college teaching in a pluralistic context.

Parks, Sharon. *The Critical Years: The Young Adult Search for a Faith to Live By.* (San Francisco: Harper and Row, 1986). Sensitively and compassionately describes the struggles of many college students as they seek to deepen their "faithing commitments." Written from a broad religious perspective.

Pascarella, Ernest T. and Patrick T. Terenzini, *How College Affects Students.* San Francisco: Jossey-Bass, 1991. An outstanding synthesis of the available research on the many factors that facilitate or retard development in the "critical years."

EIGHTEEN

FAMILY LIFE EDUCATION

James R. Slaughter

In the beginning when God desired to fill the earth with a visible manifestation of His image and presence, He created a family (Gen. 2:4–4:2). God brought the man and woman and their children together into this unique relationship, older than the church, more ancient even than the nation of Israel. Through family God would fulfill specific purposes for the world and for humankind.

God would use family to bring Jesus Christ to accomplish the work of redemption (a theological purpose, Isa. 7:14; 9:6; Matt. 1:1-16; Luke 1:26-38; 3:23-38; Gal. 4:4-5). He would use family to portray in their relationships with one another the same love and grace He shows for His people (a demonstrational purpose, Hosea 1:1–2:1, 14-23; Eph. 5:22-33). God would use family as the primary instructional agency for teaching children spiritual truth (an educational purpose, Deut. 6:4-9; Eph. 6:4), and He would use family as a safe environment for the development of a person's mental, physical, spiritual, and social health (a "nutritional" purpose, Luke 2:51-52). It would be difficult to overestimate the importance of family in God's global work and in the preparation of men and women for the service of Christ.

Sadly, many families today experience what Chandler calls "nuclear family fusion," that is, the disruption of primary family units or the formation of "non-family" households.[1] "Family" describes a group of two or more persons related by birth, marriage, or adoption who live together; "non-family" refers to such household arrangements as unmarried heterosexual couples, homosexual couples, and friends who "intentionally" live together.[2] Chandler reports that "non-families" will eventually receive legal recognition as "families" in every state in America.[3] The very definition of "family" appears blurred today.

Cohabitation has become more prevalent than ever before. Statistics demonstrate the changes in our culture. Half of all adults under the age of thirty will live with someone before they get married.[4] Sixty percent of recently married adults indicate they lived with their new spouse before getting married.[5]

Commitment in marriage today often is contingent on self-fulfillment. People remain "committed" to one another only as long as they make each other happy. Balswick and Balswick contend the focus in marriage has shifted from an emphasis on commitment to an emphasis on the individual's right to personal happiness.[6] As a result, the incidence of divorce has increased, even in Christian households, and may continue to do so. Barna warns that a life spent with one partner eventually will be considered both unusual and unnecessary. He predicts:

> We will continue our current moral transition by accepting sexual relationships with one person at a time—"serial monogamy"—to be the civilized and moral way to behave. But we will not consider it at all unusual to be married two or three times during the course of life.[7]

In spite of this "serial monogamy," Barna foresees that by the year 2000 it is likely more than half of all children will spend part of their lives in single-parent homes.[8] In fact, the tendency is growing for unmarried women to make the calculated and intentional decision to bear and raise a child single-handedly. These women may choose to have sexual relations with a selected partner, or may become pregnant through artificial insemination by a known or unknown donor.[9]

The church must address the family crisis brought about by such conditions as these. To do so it must enable people to understand the biblical characteristics of a Christian family; such characteristics as spiritual training with consistency (Deut. 6:4-9; Eph. 6:4), love with commitment (Gen. 2:24; Matt. 19:1-6), discipline with dignity (Heb. 12), Holy Spirit guidance and control (John 14:13, 16-17, 26; Gal. 5:22-23), prayer (1 Thes. 5:17), and mutual respect (Eph. 5:22–6:9; Col. 3:18-25; 1 Peter 2:18–3:7). In addition, the church must take advantage of every opportunity to become a center for the development of friendships and a source of insight into practical skills in personal relationships and communication. It must become an avenue for celebrating successful, working examples of marriages and family and solving tough issues in family relationships.[10]

Schaller and others have pointed out that though the structure of family today has become diverse, church attenders are attracted to local fellowships which can "deliver on the promise that their distinctive role is to strengthen the family."[11] Christians not only recognize and acknowledge their need for a strong family, but they plead with the church to help them achieve that goal through the teaching of healthy patterns of living. Families desperately feel the need for the church's help in developing spiritual maturity, strong family ties, and the skills to live life wisely. Family ministry in the church focuses on these spheres of family relationships and growth and is divided into two tasks:

(1) "Family Life Education" (Christian education *of* the home)
(2) "Family Nurture" (Christian education *in* the home)

Family life education, while eventually ministering to the entire family, and ultimately to the family of the church, is essentially a ministry to adults. Therefore, it demands an andragogical philosophy emphasizing content, ministries, and methods which address the needs of the adult learner. For a church to be strong it must be filled with strong, healthy families. What more important service can there be than the work of strengthening families spiritually, physically, mentally, and socially for the service of Christ in the context of church ministry? This is the work of family life education.

When the church makes family life education a priority, individual families grow strong and so does the congregation. There exists a mutual relationship, a spiritual symbiosis in which the church nourishes the family. The family, in turn, ministers to the growth and spiritual health of the local fellowship. Strengthening the family strengthens the church.[12]

Rather than an addition to the existing ministry of a local church, family life education (the church's ministry to families) needs to be integrated into the life of the entire church. As Charles Sell notes, this integration can happen by emphasizing family life in existing programs, and by improving the quality of church life so that educational programs, organization, and style of leadership conform more to the family life character of the New Testament teachings.[13]

THE PHILOSOPHY OF FAMILY LIFE EDUCATION

An adequate philosophy of family life education must be both biblical and andragogical. Family ministry must provide biblical solutions to problems encountered by husbands and wives, parents and children, in daily family living. Such a ministry will prepare and enable couples to live together in marriage according to biblical principles. It will also teach parents how to raise and relate to their children as Christian parents should. In addition, family life education will motivate and teach Christian parents to lead their own children to Jesus Christ, and to follow Him as disciples.

Biblical Foundations

The Bible argues consistently and convincingly from beginning to end that God gives leaders the responsibility for equipping parents to train their own children in spiritual truth. Before the conquest of Canaan began, Moses reminded Hebrew parents of their duty when they would settle the land. Of utmost importance would be their own passion for the Lord and their obedience to His commands. Having nurtured their own relationship with God, these parents were to impress His commands on their own children. The process of impression would take place as they talked with their children about the Lord and His laws throughout the common experiences of everyday living (Deut. 6:4-7). The Proverbs provide frequent examples of fathers training their children through observation, object lessons, and firsthand experiences (e.g., 4:1ff; 5:1ff; 7:1ff).

The Apostle Paul teaches fathers to raise their children "in the training and instruction of the Lord" (Eph. 6:4). Nor is the training of children the private domain of fathers. King Lemuel reflects on the crucially important principles, literally, "the weighty thing," his mother taught him (Prov. 31:1-9). All these references reveal that the bulk of family life education ministers to adults. Church leaders train parents who, in turn, train their own children to know Christ and to follow His precepts.

No environment provides a more natural opportunity for training children than the home. The home represents a relating fellowship in which parents and children enjoy one another's company over a period of years. Being together consistently affords a wide variety of occasions for the education of children to take place. The nurturing environment of a healthy Christian home invites talking openly and honestly, feeling deeply, and trusting completely. These characteristics, modeled consistently by parents who encourage their children to follow their lead, help insure a sense of security which enables the child to learn more effectively.

No teacher or minister will have the luxury of spending as much time collectively with a child as will the child's parents. Christian education of children happens best in the home which forms a truly nurturing environment. The duty of the family life educator emerges in the ministry of teaching parents how to create a healthy home environment and how to teach their own children spiritual truth. The "how to" will include both content and methods.

Andragogical Implications

In addition to being biblical, an adequate philosophy of family life education must be andragogical. Because family life education involves the training of adults, it must understand the attitudes, motivation, and behavior of adults and, in response, address issues and use methods which serve an adult audience. Knowles has described the primary ways adults learn differently from children.[14] Essentially adults are more self-directed in the learning process. They also want to participate in an educational endeavor by sharing examples from their own experience. Adults learn because they feel a need to know how to accomplish a particular task and thus seek to solve problems in the learning experience. For effective learning to take place, adults must be convinced of the immediate dynamic relevance of what they study. The family life educator should keep these characteristics in mind in establishing goals, selecting a curriculum, and choosing a method of instruction for the adults served.

THE CONTENT OF FAMILY LIFE EDUCATION

When family life educators ask the question, "What should I teach?" they need to remember that their focus on adults requires need-based learning. Curriculum development must be a function of felt needs within the congregation. A family life curriculum should be need-oriented, practically relevant, and immediately useful. The family needs felt by adults in the church will fall broadly into two spheres: (1) developmental needs and (2) crisis needs.

Developmental family needs arise out of the various endeavors of family members as they move through one stage of life to another. These family stages or "seasons" characterize the development of most families and give rise to a person's readiness to learn different things at different times. The following diagram[15] shows the basic seasons through which a family progresses.

The numbers in each pie segment below represent the average number of years a person devotes to each season of life (e.g., six years with each child in elementary school, six years during junior and senior high school, and so on).

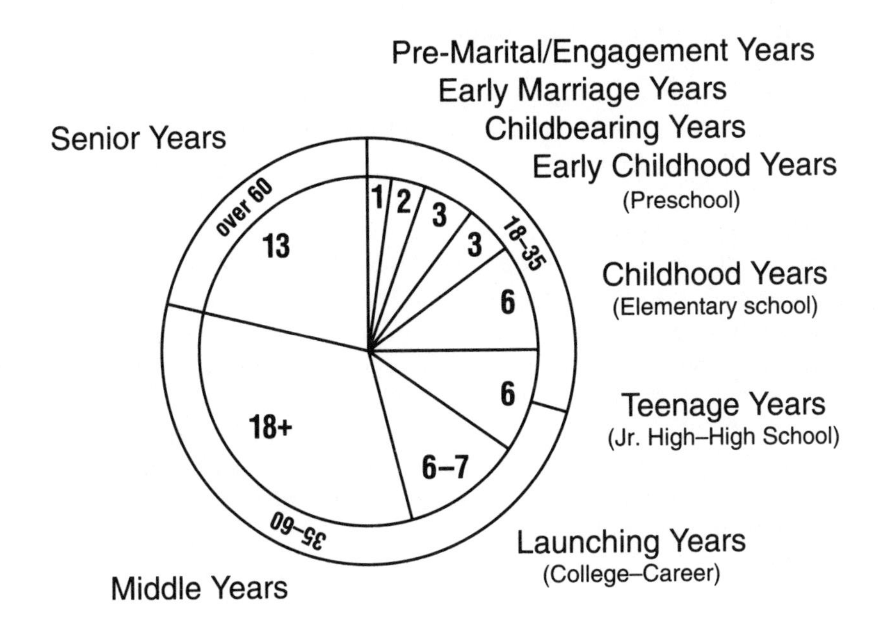

Figure 18.1

Premarital/Engagement Years

The eighteen-to thirty-five-year-old group represents six seasons of family life beginning with courtship and engagement and ending with the parenting of teenagers. During the premarital years young adults will need to understand how to appreciate and relate to people of the opposite sex. Engaged couples (represented by the first pie segment in the figure above) will be getting to know each other well. They must investigate their compatibility spiritually, emotionally, intellectually, physically, and vocationally. Once they have decided to marry they need to understand the biblical foundations of marriage, roles and responsibilities in the home, biblical sexuality and their own sexual relationship, as well as other family matters such as financial management and having children. The family life educator helps prepare the couple through a thorough, biblical program of premarital instruction.

Early Marriage Years

In the early marriage years (about the first two years of married life) couples are still getting to know each other and enjoy a time of high romantic involvement. They are trying to adjust to life with another person and begin to discover potential problems in their marriage. What at first produced a wonderful attraction now presents possible disillusionment. The premarital counselor now serves as a resource person, a friend to whom the couple will turn for direction in marriage and for help in solving problems.

Childbearing Years

The childbearing years become a time of high commitment to parenthood. Young couples, thrilled with the expectancy of a new life, search out a proven childbirth education program to help through pregnancy, labor, and delivery. With the birth of the baby comes the need for adjustment from the life-style of a couple to that of a family. Disruptions become commonplace; visiting friends seems almost to take as much effort as moving cross-country. Family life education aids a young couple in making this adjustment to parenthood, and helps them understand the biblical principles of parenting.

Early Childhood Years

The early childhood years represent the preschool years in the life of a family. During this time parents need help learning to communicate verbally with their children, learning the children's personality types, and helping children begin to understand their roles as members of the family. Parents will need to know how to begin channeling the child's will with the use of repetition in the learning process and with the exercise of patient endurance. Parents will seek advice about biblical approaches to disciplining children.

Childhood Years

Childhood, or elementary school years, involves the blending of children into the family in a more integrated way. Parents will need to continue building personal relationships with their children and will encourage children to assume responsibility by assigning household chores. Parents will begin to see the impact on their children of significant people outside the home such as church and scout leaders, teachers and coaches. Knowing how to challenge youngsters, how to discipline them lovingly, and how to teach them spiritual truth will be continuing needs of couples in this season of life. A well-organized family life education ministry can answer practical questions, enabling couples to be more effective parents.

Teenage Years

The teenage years include families with junior and senior high school students. Many changes take place during these years. In this season of life the unique opportunity exists for parents to begin relating to their children as young adults. In this phase of life parents need help knowing how to encourage independence in their children, how to help their teens deal with success and failure, and how to cope with sweeping fluctuations in adolescent emotions. They will need encouragement to continue the use of sound communication skills with their teenagers. That communication will involve intellectual exchanges in which children may take a view different from their parents. Parents may need help understanding the importance of allowing their young adult children the freedom to think independently and to take responsibility for their own decisions.

Launching Years

The second major category of family seasons consists of those families with people in the thirty-five to sixty-year-old group. People in this age-group often have teenagers in the home and face the same developmental tasks as those in the previous category. Parents in this category whose children are in college or who have begun a career find themselves in their launching years—the time children begin to leave home. Most parents find it extremely difficult to let their adult children go, to allow them full independence, and to provide counsel when asked but avoid advice-giving. They themselves may need counsel about how to relate to their fully adult children and how to adjust to the "empty nest" by refocusing attention on their marriage partners. During these years the church's ministry of marriage enrichment helps couples rediscover the joy of married love.

Middle Years

The middle years, from the time the last child leaves home to retirement, constitute a family season characterized by high career productivity. Couples in this phase of life need help channeling their resources and using their talents and gifts in the service of Christ. They may need help avoiding midlife crisis by developing a realistic view of life including the achievement of proper objectives and goals. They may turn to the church for an interpretation of life from a Christian perspective.

Senior Years

The third major category of family seasons includes one phase only: the senior years, including those people over sixty. People in this season of family life often need help accepting the physical and emotional conditions of aging. They have more time to use for Christian service and need to be challenged toward continued productivity. Normally they will be able to use their vast experience to assist others and will enrich the church through their ministry. During this time senior adults will be arranging their estates and contemplating their own passage into eternity with Christ.

The tasks listed below represent the developmental needs of American adults as they mature through the seasons of family life:[16]

Early Adult Years (18–35)

Courting
Understanding children
Selecting a mate
Preparing children for school
Preparing for marriage
Helping children in school
Family planning
Solving marital problems
Preparing for children
Managing a home
Raising children
Managing money

Middle Adult Years (35–60)

Helping teenage children become adults
Letting adult children go
Relating to one's spouse as a person

Adjusting to aging parents
Planning for retirement

Senior Adult Years (60 and over)
Adjusting to reduced income
Establishing new living arrangements
Adjusting to the death of a spouse
Learning to live alone
Relating to grandchildren
Establishing new intimate relationships
Putting the estate in order

These tasks serve well as a basis for curriculum development in the ministry of family life education. They create felt developmental needs in adult family members, preparing them to learn and making them eager to apply what they learn to the work of problem solving. Therefore, topics addressed in family life education grow out of the issues and tasks faced by families in the congregation. Based on the previous list of developmental tasks, church leaders might include the following themes in a family curriculum:

Christian Marriage
Preparation for Christian Marriage
Dating
Engagement
Pillars of Christian Marriage
Biblical foundations (Gen. 2:18-25)
Mutual commitment
Marriage roles and responsibilities
Meaningful communication
Conflict resolution
Sex and sexuality
Birth control and the Christian
Family finances
In-law relations

Christian Family
Priorities of Christian Family
Principles of parenting children
Principles of parenting teenagers
Discipline in the home
Family nurture—fostering emotional security

Building Christian convictions
Setting Christian standards
Worshiping as a family
Launching young adults
Feathering the empty nest
Marriage enrichment
Relating to adult children and their children
The task of grandparenting

These developmental family life themes addressed biblically, relevantly, and applicationally touch the felt needs of congregation members. Christian adults welcome instruction based on these topics because such teaching can help them stand successfully against the stormy winds of family seasons.

In addition to developmental needs, families in the congregation experience crisis needs. This category includes such crises as physical, sexual or emotional abuse, divorce, drug dependency (including alcoholism), emotional dysfunction, physical or mental disability, dying and death. For families suffering the trauma of these experiences, help comes when the family life educator deals with affective (feeling) as well as with cognitive (knowing) implications.

Along with biblical teaching about divorce, death, or drug dependency, the church must make an effort to meet the emotional, physical, and social needs of husbands, wives, and children ravaged by divorce. The church reaches out to comfort and encourage members who grieve for a loved one who has died; it offers understanding, prayer, and proactive support for one struggling to retrieve his life from control by alcohol.

Other crisis needs which families in the congregation may encounter include such trauma as teenage pregnancy, eating disorders, severe depression, Chronic Fatigue and Immune Deficiency Syndrome, homosexuality, infertility, miscarriage, rape, runaway children, and compulsion disorders.

The church must be alert to the host of crisis needs which plague families today. Family life educators must be able to identify such needs, seek to understand why they exist, and then aid the affected family through the recovery process.

To summarize, adherence to an andragogical philosophy of family life education necessitates the use of a need-based learning curriculum. The content of family life education arises out of developmental needs families experience as they move through seasons of life, or out of crisis needs they feel as they endure the pain of a serious family emergency. To serve families effectively, ministers (including pastors, directors of Christian education, and directors of adult education) must know their congregations, be acutely aware of the family seasons represented in their flocks, and understand the crises which threaten the lives of their people.

To discover where families currently find themselves in their journey through the seasons or in their struggles in crisis, the minister may use a congregational survey. Well constructed, relevant questions, answered and returned anonymously, provide a congregational profile which gives insight into practical curriculum development.

THE MINISTRIES AND METHODS OF FAMILY LIFE EDUCATION

Just as an andragogical philosophy dictates content selection in family life education, so also does it prescribe the ministries and methods used to communicate that content. Ministries of family life education fall into three basic categories: (1) teaching ministries; (2) counseling ministries; and (3) support ministries.

Teaching Ministries

Teaching ministries may include the preaching of family texts and themes. But for the sermon to achieve andragogical objectives it must compensate for one way dialogue by emphasizing relevance and offering suggestions for immediate application of practical biblical truth. These characteristics must be present if the sermon is to meet adult needs.

Robinson argues that application gives preaching purpose. A shepherd must relate "to the hurts, cries and fears of his flock. Therefore he studies the Scriptures, wondering what they say to his people in grief and guilt, doubt and death."[17] This concern can make preaching an andragogical ministry because it deals with practical, current needs and crises experienced by the congregation, and because it suggests immediately applicational principles from Scripture. Biblical texts addressing family themes include:

Genesis 2:18-25	Biblical foundations of marriage
Ephesians 5:22-33	Roles and responsibilities

1 Peter 3:1-7 1 Corinthians 7:1-7	in marriage
Song of Songs Proverbs 5	God's view of love in marriage; faithfulness in marriage
Deuteronomy 6:4-9 Proverbs 22:6 Ephesians 6:1-4 Colossians 3:18-21 2 Timothy 1:5	Teaching in the home; parent-child relationships
Hebrews 12:1-11	Discipline in the home
1 Timothy 5:3-8	Responsibility to care for family members

These texts and a plethora of others relating family experiences and principles from the time of Creation to the New Testament era provide a biblical context in which the Christian educator may speak to family issues.

Another andragogical teaching ministry takes the form of adult Sunday School electives. Allowing adult learners to select classes which best address their needs supports an andragogical approach to education. Such classes must provide a great deal of discussion time in order to fit an adult educational model. Small group Bible studies, family conferences, seminars, and family workshops all have a place as teaching ministries in family life education. Panel discussions and family forums provide an opportunity for open, productive interaction.

Counseling Ministries

Counseling makes up the second category of family life educational ministries. The pastoral staff and other trained people in the congregation or community will want to provide a premarital counseling program for couples preparing for marriage. In addition, they will need to consider offering marriage counseling for couples who need help working through problems in their relationship. Family counseling involves ministry to the family as a whole, helping to solve problems within such dynamics as parent-child relationships and sibling relationships and rivalry.

Support Ministries

The third category of ministries in family life education may be referred to as support ministries. It includes such relation-building experiences as support groups, prayer groups, family camps, and retreats. Family clusters and intergenerational events[18] round out this category of ministries for family life education.

Methods of family life education include those teaching techniques which most consistently allow adults to contribute to, and benefit personally from, the learning process. Adults learn best when they participate in educational experiences as part of a resource pool. What God has taught them through past successes and failures will be shared to help others in the group learn and/or solve problems. Interest in what they learn heightens as they help guide the direction of the discussion and interact verbally and nonverbally with their friends.

For an educational method to meet the needs of adults it must move the student from passive learning to active participation. Discussion achieves this very purpose[19] and for this reason will form the backbone of most techniques. Jesus often used discussion-oriented approaches in His teaching ministry. He would use object lessons, pose problems to be solved, ask questions, and invite conversation.[20] Such andragogical methods involve the learner as a participant in the educational process; they are as useful to the family life educator of today as they were to the Master 2,000 years ago.

Notes

1. Russell Chandler, *Racing Toward 2001* (Grand Rapids: Zondervan, 1992), 91.
2. Ibid., 92.
3. Ibid.
4. George Barna, *The Frog in the Kettle* (Ventura, Calif.: Regal, 1990), 67.
5. Ibid.
6. Jack O. Balswick and Judith K. Balswick, *The Family: A Christian Perspective on the Contemporary Home* (Grand Rapids: Baker, 1989), 81.
7. Barna, *The Frog,* 72.
8. Chandler, *Racing Toward,* 92.
9. Ibid., 96.
10. Barna, *The Frog,* 65.

11. Lyle E. Schaller, "Where the Family Is Going?" *The Lutheran*, September 1990, 14.
12. Ibid., 256.
13. Charles M. Sell, *Family Ministry: The Enrichment of Family Life Through the Church* (Grand Rapids: Zondervan, 1981), 15.
14. Malcolm Knowles, *The Adult Learner: A Neglected Species* (1973; reprint, Houston: Gulf, 1984), 55–59.
15. Adapted from Evelyn Millis Duvall, *Family Development* (Chicago: J.B. Lippincott, 1957), 13.
16. Knowles, *The Adult Learner,* 146–47.
17. Haddon W. Robinson, *Biblical Preaching* (Grand Rapids: Baker, 1980), 26.
18. See the excellent discussion of intergenerational experiences and family clusters in Sell, *Family Ministry,* 230–52.
19. Kenneth E. Eble, *The Craft of Teaching* (San Francisco: Jossey-Bass, 1982), 54.
20. Herman H. Horne, *The Teaching Techniques of Jesus* (1971; reprint, Grand Rapids: Kregel, 1974; 1st ed., 1920 under the title, *Jesus, the Master Teacher*).

For Further Reading

Curran, Dolores. *Traits of a Healthy Family.* Minneapolis: Winston, 1983.

Duvall, Evelyn M. *Family Development.* Chicago: J.B. Lippincott, 1957.

Eble, Kenneth E. *The Craft of Teaching.* San Francisco: Jossey-Bass, 1982.

Gangel, Kenneth, and Elizabeth Gangel. *Building a Christian Family.* Chicago: Moody, 1987.

Gangel, Kenneth O., and Howard G. Hendricks. *The Christian Educator's Handbook on Teaching.* Wheaton, Ill.: Victor, 1988.

Hendricks, Howard G., and LaVonne Neff, eds. *Husbands and Wives.* Wheaton, Ill.: Victor, 1988.

Horne, Herman H. *Teaching Techniques of Jesus.* 1971. Reprint. Grand Rapids: Kregel, 1974. First edition 1920 under original title of *Jesus: The Master Teacher.*

Kesler, Jay, and Gilbert Beers, eds. *Parents and Teenagers.* Wheaton, Ill.: Victor, 1984.

Kesler, Jay, Gilbert Beers, and LaVonne Neff, eds. *Parents and Children.* Wheaton, Ill.: Victor, 1986.

Knowles, Malcolm. *The Adult Learner: A Neglected Species,* 3rd ed. 1973. Reprint. Houston: Gulf, 1984.

Rekers, George. *Family Building.* Ventura, Calif.: Regal, 1985.

Money, Royce. *Building Stronger Families.* Wheaton, Ill.: Victor, 1984.

Olson, Richard P., and Joe H. Leonard, *Ministry With Families in Flux*. Louisville: Westminster/John Knox Press, 1990.

Sell, Charles M. *Family Ministry*. Grand Rapids: Zondervan, 1981.

Swindoll, Charles R. *Growing Wise in Family Life*. Portland, Ore.: Multnomah, 1988.

NINETEEN
ADULT EDUCATION WITH PERSONS FROM ETHNIC MINORITY COMMUNITIES

Robert W. Pazmiño

Adult educators must consider the place of multicultural education in their work with persons who may be identified as ethnic minorities. Multicultural education is a type of education that is concerned with creating teaching settings in which students, adults in this case, from all ethnic and cultural groups will experience educational equity. Educational equity is defined in terms of access to educational resources, respect of difference, space to be heard, appropriate role models, and shared power to make educational decisions. This is modeled for us in both the New Testament churches at Jerusalem and Antioch. The question of equity is also important in relation to the dominant cultural approach of andragogy in adult Christian education.

BIBLICAL EXAMPLES OF MINORITY EDUCATION

In exploring adult education with persons from ethnic minority communities, Christian educators should first consider some biblical insights. The New Testament Book of Acts helps in this exploration as it describes the churches at Antioch and Jerusalem. Acts 11 and 13 describe the church at Antioch which was a multiethnic and multicultural community. This is evidenced by the diversity of its leadership noted in Acts 13:1. Simeon was black. Lucius was Greek. Manaen was Jewish. An African, an Asian, and a Palestinian were leaders in this congregation.[1] In addition, Barnabas and Saul are named. Barnabas was a Levite and a native of the island of Cyprus as identified in Acts 4:36. Like Saul of Tarsus, he was a Jew of the Diaspora and a Hellenist. This church at Antioch had a significant missionary outreach through the commissioning of Saul and Barnabas. Acts 11:26 notes that at Antioch the disciples were first called "Christians." Thus the church at Antioch provides one model for the inclusion of persons from ethnic minority groups and the importance of ethnic leaders as models for the wider community. It is noteworthy that such a multicultural congregation became a vehicle for the global outreach of the Gospel.

In addition to Acts 11 and 13 which describe the church at Antioch, Acts 6 describes the church at Jerusalem and a conflict which arose between distinct ethnic groups. The Grecian Jews or Hellenists from outside Palestine complained against the Hebrews or Aramaic-speaking Palestinian community because their widows were being overlooked in the daily distribution of food. Ethnic tensions existed in New Testament times concerning the distribution of resources just as such problems exist today. This problem was resolved through the appointment of new leadership. It is noteworthy that the seven leaders had Greek names and were likely Hellenistic Jews. This suggests a strategy for adult education with persons from ethnic minority groups. That strategy is to equip and empower ethnic leadership to serve their own communities.

But even prior to the formation of the Christian church itself at Jerusalem and Antioch, the very setting of Galilee suggests that Jesus Himself lived and ministered in a multiethnic and multicultural world. Galilee, literally denoting a ring or circle, referred to a region comprised of Gentiles and foreigners, of persons with diverse ethnic backgrounds. It was a region that was constantly experiencing infiltration and migration. At various times in its history, Galilee was controlled by Babylon, Persia, Macedonia, Egypt, Syria, and Assyria, and thus was a center of diverse cultural currents.

In the first century, Galilee with a population of approximately 350,000 persons had a large slave population and about 100,000 Jews who were largely Hellenized. The primary language at this time was Koine Greek, although Jews primarily spoke Aramaic along with Hebrew in their synagogue participation.[2] Thus it was in the multicultural context of Galilee that God chose to be incarnated in the person of Jesus of Nazareth. Yet this very multicultural nature is so often ignored in considering the Christian education of adults who represent ethnic minority communities. For the end of the twentieth and beginning of the twenty-first centuries the recognition and affirmation of multicultural diversity in Christian education looms essential.

In the light of these New Testament insights, Christian educators in the United States are challenged. Adult education with persons from ethnic minority communities is a challenge because of the history of racism and discrimination that impacts upon the lives of individuals whose ethnic heritage is not identified as being Anglo. In such a societal context the Christian church must advocate and model an alternative community that embraces the Gospel's radical demands to love our neighbor as ourselves. Today that neighbor may not only be a member of an ethnic minority group, but also a Christian sister or brother and a member of one's local church. With the nationally recognized "browning of America," Christian educators confront a host of issues that were just not apparent when Anglo conformity, assimilation, and separate education were acceptable norms. These were norms not only for the wider public, but also for the Christian church on Sunday mornings. Another norm has been the approach of andragogy.

ANDRAGOGY AND MINORITY EDUCATION

In the area of adult education the approach of *andragogy* has been popularized in both the public and Christian communities with the work of educators such as Malcolm Knowles.[3] *Andragogy* opts for a focus upon learning rather than teaching and emphasizes four major assumptions among others: the adult self-concept; the role of experience; a need-based readiness to learn; and a concern for immediate application.

It is helpful to consider adult education with persons from ethnic minority communities in relation to the approach of andragogy. This approach to education focuses upon one of the three elements that I identify as being crucial to understanding education in general. I define education as the process of attending to or sharing content with persons in the context of their community and society. This definition identifies the three primary elements of content, persons, and the context of community/society.

Whereas andragogy emphasizes adult learning, I contend that teaching is at the heart of education. Learning and teaching need not be in conflict, but clarification and distinction are needed. A focus upon learning emphasizes the place of the individual person and one's needs and interests. Such an emphasis provides a welcome change from the earlier or current neglect of the individual. But it can too readily lead to a destructive individualism that distorts the essential place of the wider community and the act of passing on the content of the Christian faith.

Robert Bellah and his associates described this destructive individualism in the work *Habits of the Heart.*[4] An emphasis upon teaching includes not only a concern for learning, but a commitment to share content and to represent and form the community beyond a narrow interest upon the individual. An exclusive emphasis upon learning in andragogy can become a cultural bias for ethnic communities that stress the greater importance of the community and the essential task of passing on the content to future generations.

Whereas andragogy focuses upon the persons of adults and their unique individual needs in education, both the content and the community/society or context of teaching must also be seriously considered. This broader consideration balances any preoccupation with the persons of the adults for effective education to be practiced. Content considerations are foundational if one is to effectively share the Gospel of Jesus Christ in the Christian education of adults and challenge them with the demands of discipleship.[5] Content includes not just cognitive content, but affective and life-style content so that a head, heart, and hand response to the Gospel is fostered with adults.[6]

Contextual considerations are foundational if one is to transfer learning beyond individual parameters and see the adult person within the web of community and social relationships in which life is experienced. For adults from ethnic minority communities the consideration of the context is of primary concern because the context may or may not support one's very identity, survival, or full participation in the Christian community with an ability to give as well as receive. In the Hispanic community, personal advancement is not set as a higher goal than familial and communal connection and loyalty.

I will argue below that a narrow focus upon andragogy may not address the particular dynamics of adult education with ethnic minorities by considering its four central assumptions. I approach this subject as a North American-Hispanic Christian educator concerned about the adult education of all ethnic minority communities.[7] My effort is to suggest alternative ways of viewing the task without claiming to speak for a wide diversity of persons and communities whose perspectives need to be heard.

THE ADULT SELF-CONCEPT AND MINORITY CULTURES

Andragogy assumes that a person's primary source for identity is one's individual life and the various roles and tasks which one assumes. The focus is primarily upon the present and secondarily upon the future. This stance does not recognize that for a number of cultural and ethnic minority persons one's identity is closely tied with the family and community understood in extended and connected terms. For such persons identity is also tied in a much more direct way with the past and with the retention of one's rootedness to one's people and even one's land. In the United States this awareness has emerged in relation to the "unmeltable ethnic" peoples who do not opt for assimilation, but retain or restore their distinctive identities. The costs of such affirmation of one's distinctive ethnic identity is viewed by some as being counter to any effort to find a common identity amid a sea of diversity. But the challenge for persons from ethnic minority communities is how to balance dual identities in being North American and Hispanic, or African and American, or Asian and American and represented by the use of the hyphen between the two sources in the formation of a self-concept. This has been such a challenge historically because of the terms by which one was to become an "American." To become an American meant to leave one's previous ethnic distinctives as a member of a new society and to embrace an identity primarily based upon a Northern European Protestant heritage. This process was complicated if one's skin color or accent did not fit the norm or if one's values and commitments were other than the dominant culture.

In Christian education with adults, the challenge is not to allow the larger cultural agenda to exclude difference as a deficiency in relation to welcoming the full participation of persons from ethnic minority communities. The additional challenge is to avoid judging others who understand themselves in relation to interdependent relationships with their families and communities and not exclusively in individual terms. It is often assumed that if a person affirms and celebrates one's ethnic identity that an immature and isolationist stance has been taken.

While the dominant culture currently decries the lack of a sense of community among persons who embrace a radical individualism, persons from ethnic minority communities may have much to offer in understanding the nature of a commitment to be in community. The affirmation of ethnic and cultural heritage does not have to be at the expense of seeking for a wider unity that binds humanity created in the image of God and the new humanity offered through the redemptive work of the Lord Jesus Christ.

THE ROLE OF EXPERIENCE IN MINORITY EDUCATION

This second assumption of the role of experience can be affirmed from the perspective of educational practice with persons from ethnic minority communities. Such an assumption allows the space needed for ethnic persons to name their realities and to share their experiences. But andragogy might limit the place of reflection upon experience as a vital component of the educational process with adults. This occurs when the focus is upon learning and its facilitation to the relative exclusion of teaching. An exclusive focus upon experience can result in pooled ignorance if content considerations are not present. Christians can share the wisdom that has accumulated over time which is at the disposal of the teacher and students. The assumption of experience as central may actually limit the depth of dialogue possible if the terms and foundations for discussion are not clarified and shared by all adult participants.

In relation to ethnic communities, the sharing of experience may only be possible if the content includes a variety of perspectives initially presented by the teacher or teachers. This initial presentation can indicate the willingness to hear different voices and engage in genuine conversation. This conversation includes adult participants themselves who serve as teachers to one another as they share in areas of their relative expertise. Andragogy affirms the possibility of dialogue and interaction among adult participants. This does not assume that the content shared was imposed upon adults, but offered to them as a necessary catalyst for their thought and response.

Foundations in content are needed before they can be built upon, revised, or questioned. Foundations in content are needed before they can be explored in relation to personal and corporate experience. Andragogy may focus on personal experience to the relative exclusion of the corporate experience. For the Christian community, the corporate experience that honors the wisdom embodied in the community's treasured heritage is essential.

In the teaching of adults, educators must recognize that content in itself can become mere verbalism divorced from life. But we must also recognize that experience in itself can become mere practice or activism. The challenge is to wed both content and experience. This wedding enables adults to gain perspective in relation to the connections between their faith and their personal and corporate life. The content and experience wed together must represent the ethnic and cultural diversity that characterizes the global village at the end of the twentieth century.

MINORITY EDUCATION AND A NEED-BASED READINESS TO LEARN

The common educational wisdom affirmed in the approach of andragogy is to plan one's educational program or event in relation to the felt needs of the participants. This wisdom assumes that volunteer adult participation is dependent upon tapping into the motivation of persons. This motivation in relation to human psychology stresses the identification of needs and the design of programs and events to meet those very needs. But problems may emerge in relation to the very identification of needs and the identity and legitimacy of those persons who name the needs. In the case of ethnic minority communities and persons, the need for survival in a culturally alien and discriminatory society may set the terms for Christian education of adults. Survival may then be dependent upon gaining the essential resources and perspective to explore alternatives and to maintain hope despite the history of exclusion and oppression.

The emphasis upon needs themselves may also be problematic. Abraham Heschel warned of the tyranny of needs that characterizes modern life. This emphasis may fail to address the demands of God upon persons and the place of human responsibility in relation to God.[8] Needs beyond survival are often determined by cultural norms and expectations which must be questioned in relation to Gospel values and norms. This is not to deny the place of genuine human needs. But in identifying such needs, educators must exercise careful and deliberate discernment. They must also be open to the discovery of essential demands and needs that are not initially considered in educational planning.

For example, one particular need not readily named in the

dominant culture is the need for celebration and worship in life. Often persons in an urbanized and highly technological society do not reserve time for worship, time to gain a sense of wonder and awe in relation to God's multifaceted creation. In Hispanic culture the place of fiesta reserves this space for celebration.

MINORITY EDUCATION AND THE CONCERN FOR IMMEDIATE APPLICATION

This fourth assumption of andragogy reflects a preoccupation in the dominant culture of the United States with pragmatic and practical concerns. Heschel reflected upon this practical interest by comparing this modern concern with the Greek and Hebrew heritage. Heschel pointed out that the Greeks learned in order to comprehend, the modern person in the United States learns in order to use, but the Hebrews learned in order to revere.[9] The place of immediate application is to be affirmed, but not at the expense of learning for the inherent value of understanding and discerning the truth.

A comparison of cultural values points up the essential role that they play in the thought and practice of adult education. Adults from ethnic minority communities will have distinct values from the dominant culture in the United States, which places a high priority on the practical and immediate application of learning.

But such a pragmatic approach in the dominant U.S. culture may fail to recognize that which has been too readily forgotten. Forgotten values have often been nourished in a subculture or alternative culture. In fact, an ethnic minority community may retain a value essential to the Gospel which the Christian community has neglected in accommodating to the dominant culture. This is the case in the emphasis on time restraints to the relative exclusion of the importance of persons in some adult educational designs as ethnic persons interface with the dominant Anglo culture.

A CALL FOR CULTURAL AWARENESS

In order to educate adults from ethnic minority communities, Christian educators must first strive to understand the particular ethnic culture. The Apostle Paul described this effort in 1 Corinthians 9:19-23 where he sought to become like a Jew to win the Jews and like a Gentile to win the Gentiles. Clifford Geertz, a cultural anthropologist, describes a culture in terms of a worldview and an ethos. A worldview is the picture one has of the way things are in actuality, the most comprehensive idea of order. The ethos of an ethnic group is the tone, character, and quality of its life.[10] In order to understand both the worldview and ethos of a particular ethnic group, Christian educators must spend adequate time in the community with a variety of persons and develop trust.

A CALL FOR CULTURAL ANALYSIS

Christian educators must also compare and contrast the worldview and ethos of the particular ethnic group with the Christian faith. This assumes that one has critically analyzed one's own culture in a similar way. From such a comparison Christian educators will be able to discern areas in which the values and perspectives of the ethnic culture confirm, complement, and contradict the Christian faith.[11] The stress should be made upon areas of affirmation before any questions or criticisms are raised. This comparison requires the extensive cooperation with leaders who represent the particular ethnic community. In areas of confirmation and complementarity, the effort is to preserve and celebrate the culture. In areas of contradiction or conflict, the effort is by the grace of God to redeem and transform the culture wherever it is possible. Such discernment is best done by those who are native to a culture which again implies the equipping of ethnic leadership.

A CALL FOR CULTURAL COOPERATION

Christian educators must develop some working principles and guidelines for practice that uniquely address the worldview and ethos of the particular ethnic group. These principles and practical guidelines must draw upon biblical, theological, and philosophical foundations, but also make use of insights gained from the social sciences. The articulation and implementation of all that is developed must be done with careful cooperation with the leaders and adult persons of the ethnic community itself to avoid the ever present danger of cultural imposition that has characterized too much of Christian education.

CONCLUSION

This chapter has considered the adult education of persons from ethnic minority communities in relation to the four central assumptions of andragogy. The issues raised are appropriate for not only such communities, but the larger Christian community in its effort to educate adults. While recognizing the distinct needs of persons from ethnic minority communities, Christian educators should not advocate an approach that huddles these adults together on the basis of ethnic identity and does not allow for a multicultural mix which characterized the churches at Antioch and Jerusalem. The call to minister in a multicultural world requires the creative sharing and full participation of persons across the cultural walls that have too readily fragmented the work and witness of the Christian church across the centuries.

Notes

1. Thom Hopler describes the church at Antioch in *A World of Difference: Following Christ Beyond Your Cultural Walls* (Downers Grove, Ill.: InterVarsity, 1981), 109.
2. K.W. Clark, "Galilee," in *The Interpreter's Dictionary of the Bible,* ed. George A. Buttrick. Nashville: Abingdon, 1962, 344–47.
3. Malcolm Knowles, *The Modern Practice of Adult Education: Andragogy Versus Pedagogy* (New York: Association Press, 1970).
4. Robert N. Bellah et al., *Habits of the Heart: Individualism and Commitment in American Life* (Berkeley: University of California Press, 1985). Bellah's research itself does not adequately sample ethnic minority communities in relation to the themes he considers.
5. For a discussion of foundational issues in Christian education see Robert W. Pazmiño, *Foundational Issues in Christian Education: An Introduction in Evangelical Perspective* (Grand Rapids: Baker, 1988). Also see Robert W. Pazmiño, *Principles and Practices of Christian Education: An Evangelical Perspective.* Grand Rapids: Baker, 1992).
6. James Michael Lee makes this distinction and a host of others in his work *The Content of Religious Instruction: A Social Science Approach* (Birmingham, Ala.: Religious Education Pr., 1985).
7. For a fuller discussion on multicultural Christian education see Robert W. Pazmiño, "Double Dutch: Reflections of an Hispanic-North American on Multicultural Education," *Apuntes* 8 (Summer 1988): 27–37.
8. Abraham J. Heschel, *Between God and Man: An Interpretation of Judaism from the Writings of Abraham Heschel,* ed. Fritz A. Rothschild (New York: Free Pr., 1959), 129–51.
9. Ibid., 35–54.

10. Clifford Geertz, *The Interpretation of Cultures* (New York: Basic Books, 1973, 126–27.

11. Lawrence A. Cremin uses these terms "confirm, complement, and contradict" to describe the interaction between different educational influences in the lives of persons. See Lawrence A. Cremin, *Traditions of American Education* (New York: Basic Books, 1977), 128.

For Further Reading

Banks, James A. *Multiethnic Education: Theory and Practice.* 2nd ed. Boston: Allyn and Bacon, 1988.

Earl, Riggins R., Jr. ed., *To You Who Teach in the Black Church: Essays on Christian Education in the Black Church.* Nashville: National Baptist Publishing Board, 1972.

Foster, Charles R., ed. *Ethnicity in the Education of the Church.* Nashville: Scarritt, 1987.

Garcia, Ricardo L. *Teaching in a Pluralistic Society: Concepts, Models and Strategies.* New York: Harper and Row, 1982.

Goodwin, Bennie. *Designing Curriculum for Urban and Multiracial Christian Education.* Grand Rapids: CSI Publications, 1981.

Pazmiño, Robert W. "Double Dutch: Reflections of an Hispanic-North American on Multicultural Religious Education." *Apuntes 8* (Summer 1988): 27–37.

Tiedt, Pamela, and Iris M. Tiedt. *Multicultural Teaching: A Handbook of Activities, Information, and Resources.* 2nd ed. Boston: Allyn and Bacon, 1986.

Wyckoff, D. Campbell, and Henrietta T. Wilkinson. *Beautiful Upon the Mountains: A Handbook for Church Education in Appalachia.* Memphis: Board of Christian Education of the Cumberland Presbyterian Church, 1984.

TWENTY

ADULT SUNDAY SCHOOL

Harold J. Westing

A few decades ago, church and Sunday School attendance in American evangelical churches ran almost parallel. Today, according to the Institute for Church Development, only 76 percent of those who attend evangelical churches show up for Sunday School.[1] This does not mean adults have given up learning about their faith. Church consultant Lyle Schaller reports that more adults attend Bible studies today than twenty years ago, if you count the thousands who attend home Bible studies.[2] Many have chosen this format over the Sunday morning classes because they enjoy the informality, intimacy, and relevance they didn't find in Sunday School. Therefore, some church growth leaders claim that the percentage involved in Sunday School will continue to drop radically in the next decades.

The home cell model will take precedence over the Sunday School model in megachurches. A great influence over this change will be the churches' inability to build a sufficient number of classrooms for all the adults who attend churches larger than 2,000 adults. In smaller churches most adults will quite likely continue to attend adult classes during the Sunday morning hour. Other churches classifying themselves as "visitor-friendly" or more evangelistic in their Sunday morning services will no doubt opt for a midweek Bible study hour or move to the home cell model as well. This shift began in the early '90s and will continue into the next century.

The future will challenge church leaders to be far more creative in their approach to adult education. We call this the post-Christian era because Americans don't reflect the same values they did a few decades ago. They don't think of church and Sunday School as a normal part of American life-style as adults did in the past.

Adult Sunday Schools will take on a new face and a new format. The winners understand the ultimate function and goal of Christian education; the losers will be hung up on the form. For too long, church leaders have expected adults to come to Sunday School without giving them life-related, need-meeting instruction, but individualistic adult Baby Boomers will not attend out of habit. They insist that Sunday School be done in a quality fashion that meets their needs.

In a wonderful essay,"This Little Light of Mine," Tim Stafford describes the many changing goals of the Sunday School movement and the influence those major goal changes had upon its growth. The first American Sunday Schools, started in the 1790s, offered the illiterate, urban poor a basic education using the Bible as a textbook. In the 1860s and 1870s Sunday Schools operated in almost every large city. These schools, located in poor neighborhoods, were large and service-oriented. However, by the late nineteenth century, Sunday School structure and strategy had become more like what we would recognize today. Stafford quotes Jack Clark: "Sunday School is one of the most stable institutions that there is. People know what Sunday School is. It has an identity. That's one reason it's so hard to change."[3]

As we move into the decade of the '90s that axiom will be challenged. Already we have seen some major shifts in Sunday School structure and purpose. No doubt this familiar structure will keep its roots intact. But in our ever-changing pluralistic society, Sunday School, like many other institutions, will have many different faces.

PRINCIPLES AND STRUCTURES

In studied observation it appears that schools which yet have strong roots portray similar structures and principles. They are seldom all found in one school, but a strong majority of the following seem common to growing schools which strive to create an atmosphere of spiritual formation. Creative leaders arrange a mix of various principles in a unique fashion to fit their own environment. The model below pictures how the various ingredients can be built into a master plan. Most of these ingredients can be used in a creative fashion to fit any particular church.

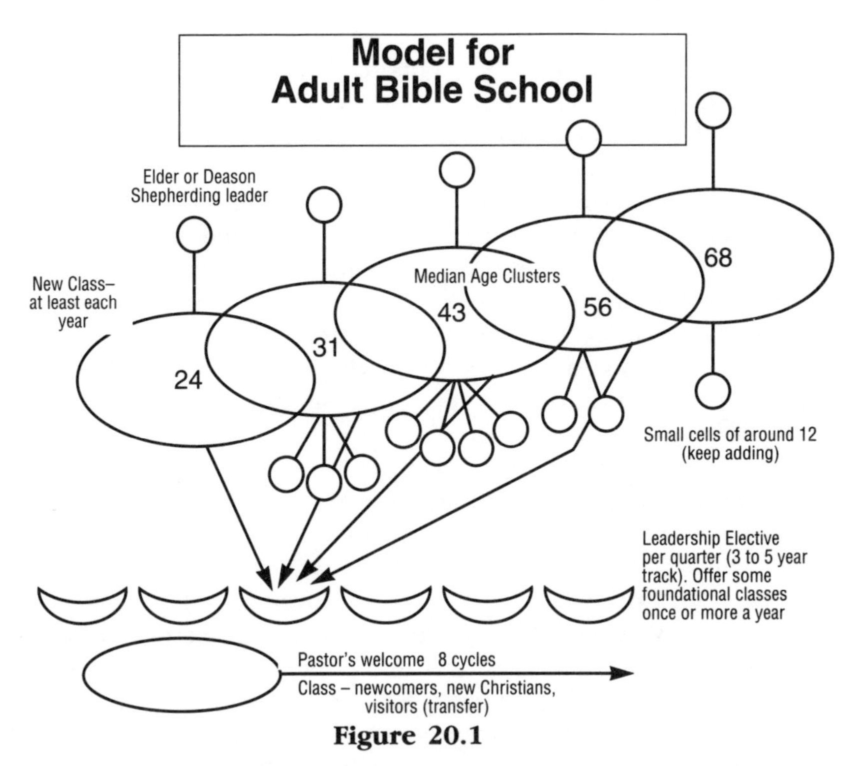

Figure 20.1

Adults Groups According to Life Stages

Daniel Levinson has identified the fact that as adults move from one stage of life to another, they engage in new cycles and each cycle accentuates a new time for learning about life. "Industry and other work organizations, government, higher education, religion and family—all of these must take account of the changing needs of adults in different eras and developmental periods. What is helpful in one era may not be in another."[4]

Because adults learn best when they face common conflicts, growing churches offer opportunities for people to study with others in like stages of life (singles, young marrieds without children, young marrieds with children, parents of elementary school children, parents of teens, empty-nesters and retirees). Parents of babies obviously need different learning than parents whose teens are "puberting" all over them. When adults come to class with such strong needs, they are far more ready to interact with God's Word in the context of others who face the same struggles.

Keep in mind that we need to learn God's Word "all over again" when we reach one of those new stages of life. If that isn't clearly in focus, teachers seem to get into a truth-dispensing style of teaching which causes students to feel no need to attend. The Word of God provides a guide for life and every time we take a turn in life's road, we need to get a new perspective for the journey.

The model above pictures classes grouped according to median ages rather than terminal ages. This gives married adults a chance to select a class that best fits the median year of their marriage. This has become increasingly important since so many second marriages tend to have a greater distance between the partners' ages than do first marriages. "In andragogy, therefore, great emphasis is placed on the involvement of adult learners in a process of self-diagnosis of needs for learning."[5]

As visitors come to the church they need to see some printed brochure or bulletin board announcing available classes so they can make that meaningful choice. This way we need not tell people which class to attend, but rather what classes are available. Some adults may choose classes far removed from their age-group because they desire to study with people in that particular group.

The adult elective system became popular back in the '60s and continued to grow in popularity for the next twenty-five years. The more American society became mobile, the less effective that structure seemed. Although it created a learning environment which many enjoyed, electives did away with meaningful ways to build relationships because people moved from class to class.

In general, people require four to nine months to feel sufficiently comfortable and become genuinely involved in a learning experience. Of course, some transfer members and other socially aggressive people make the transition much faster. The Sunday School often serves as the means of assimilating people into the congregation, perhaps an objective equally important with the study of the Word of God.

Classes with Common Goals

For too long, church leaders have expected adults to come to Sunday School without giving them specific direction. Teachers worked with broad and unmeasurable goals of helping people become more "spiritual" or allowing them to meet other believers in the church.

Several denominations, including the Christian Missionary Alliance, the Mennonites, and the Church of God, have formulated three-to-five-year training programs conducted during the Sunday School hour. Such classes become miniature Bible schools in which teaching helps prepare adults for leadership positions.

Some megachurches have begun to see their Sunday School hour in the same way and have designed training institutes for their own ministries. Other churches have taken that approach for either the midweek or Sunday evening time slots. Still other churches use that historic hour for special discipleship training programs, such as the Navigators' "Two Seven."

Congregations have even gone to closed groups in order to build in more learning accountability and allow for more specific training. One church used some Sundays as training sessions for evangelistic visitation. They not only found more people at home Sunday mornings, but the often-heard excuse, "I go to church someplace else," was no longer valid.

Classes Ought to Build In Fellowship Settings

Fellowship is a major purpose of the adult Sunday School. However, few classes take steps to see that intimacy and personal caring actually happen. A certain amount of that will occur naturally, but dynamic classes need to be proactive in seeing that it does happen. Most of these classes have a person in charge of this area to plan monthly or bimonthly activities. One church developed the following approach: when people enter their class, they find coffee available, but no chairs in place. The staff noted that people come in and sit down if chairs are set up, and then they are reluctant to mingle, especially with those they don't know. Without chairs, people will more likely interact. A cup of coffee can aid a friendly conversation! At the given time just enough chairs are set up in a semicircle for all those present. Now the "full class" has a friendly atmosphere to facilitate good learning.

Newcomers to the class must be made to feel welcome. One of the class leaders needs to gather the pertinent information about newcomers so they can be introduced to the class later.

As class members share common experiences, those experiences tend to create a community of memories and then those memories tend to build a sense of commitment to the community. Again, class members ought to have some say in the events which build that community of memories, and these events ought to happen often enough to expedite that sense of belonging.

Cell Groups Build Intimacy

Most adults in our busy society can relate intimately with only one group of people. Many churches have discovered this when they start cell and study groups during the week with groups different from their Sunday School classes. Adults tend to choose one group or the other.

Each cell group should function as an outgrowth of the Sunday morning Bible study. In this way, members can identify with both the Sunday morning class and the cell group during the week. When adults come on Sunday they will have built a certain amount of bonding with some members in the group. Each class can have numerous cells which meet at different times during the week. The Sunday morning experience allows for a broader acquaintance.

One rarely finds a church in which more than 60 percent of the congregation is actively involved in the church's cell or small group program. The Institute of Church Development database shows the average congregation can expect to have around 25 percent of the congregation in cells. Some cells are support groups, others feature discipleship training, and some center on evangelistic purposes.

A wise church conducts a variety of groups throughout its program. Remember, new groups should be started on a regular basis. Someone in the church's leadership team should oversee the various group ministries to make sure they meet needs and stay with their intended purposes.

Constantly Start New Groups

According to Dick Murray, one of the greatest myths of the Sunday School claims, "Adult classes can stay young (while their members grow older)." He goes on to say:

> By and large, adult classes attract persons only a few years younger than the youngest charter members, and nearly all ongoing adult classes die within a few years following the death of the last charter member. This is emphatically true of couples' classes and is somewhat less true of singles' classes and men's Bible classes, although they die, too. The significance of this is: the efforts of existing classes to block the starting of new classes of younger persons "because they will take our prospects," are a waste of time. These younger persons are, in fact, not *real* prospects for the present class."[6]

So why not launch out and start new classes? This keeps new life and excitement in the adult Sunday School, but more significantly the church will continue ministering to far more adults. If a church doesn't start new classes, it may find major blocks of certain adult age-groups missing in the makeup of the congregation. A church demographic chart may show a whole block of middle-age adults missing because ten years earlier it established no ministry for what was then a group of singles or newly married couples.

Offer Welcome Classes

When visitors "look over" a church, they seek answers to three questions:

- "Will my needs be met?"
- "Can I make friends?"
- "Where do I fit in?"[7]

When Don Bubna pastored in Vancouver, British Columbia, he led the Pastor's Welcome Class during the Sunday School hour. He discovered he could answer these nagging questions, and at the same time help assimilate newcomers into the church, by offering a continuous cycle of eight lessons. If adults enter at lesson three, they are free to leave when the class comes back to lesson three. The class devotes approximately half its time to the getting-acquainted process.

The welcome class is based on two major principles. Adults who have attended a church for a long time frequently have no room in their lives for newcomers. Therefore, unless a church has an appropriate way to assimilate newcomers, only the aggressive ones will become involved members of the congregation. Don's second observation grows out of the first. He saw that three groups of people—visitors, new converts, and transfers—all had the same friendship need and could be integrated into his Sunday morning Welcome Class. They also became immediately acquainted with the pastor. Those three groups of people were ushered into the class each Sunday and quickly assimilated into the life and ministry of the church.

A couple people who have a strong gift of hospitality need to be present weekly to introduce weekly newcomers to the class. They can also play a major role in ushering people into an established class when they have completed the cycle of lessons. They will be watching to see if perchance there might be the nucleus for the beginning of a new class. Of course, the adult department must constantly train new teachers who will be ready to launch that new class.

Offer Periodic Electives

Offering periodic electives in addition to continuing age-group classes makes it possible to meet the double needs of adults—to belong to a social group while at the same time having a choice of subjects to study. As we offer new classes each quarter throughout the year, people can leave their respective groups to be a part of those classes. At the conclusion of the class, they go back to their groups.

Some churches offer special training sessions for church leaders, teachers, and other workers during the Sunday School hour. This approach allows for selectivity on the part of students while at the same time giving them a chance to build deep and meaningful relationships.

CURRICULUM GUIDELINES

The potpourri approach to curriculum and format will become the norm for those who want to meet the educational needs of their adult congregations. It will be extremely essential for adult superintendents to keep in focus the following objectives as they plan adult education programs.

1. *Adults don't attend Sunday School primarily to study the Bible; their first and primary objective is fellowship.* "The ongoing adult Sunday School class must realistically be thought of as a church-organized social group, which incorporates to some extent all the ministries of the church."[8] Therefore, we need to make sure that the structure and format allow for people to build fellowship opportunities at which people know and are known and where intimacy, transparency, and accountability can help develop spiritual maturity. As adults have that kind of relationship they are far more apt to deal honestly with their spiritual growth and development in the weekly Bible studies.

2. *Teachers will need to practice genuine skill in plowing new cognitive ground, not just covering what seems to be attractive at the time of curriculum selection.* The great evangelical network fanned by Christian media and book publishers seems to promote universal themes for churches. Those curriculum choices may be right to study, but they rarely deal with the full context of Scripture. Unfortunately, adults prefer comfortable ground rather than plowing through more difficult topics when the choice is theirs to make. Who wants to study about the wrath of God when we can

study the nearness and protection of God in the Psalms? Of course, both are important and necessary. Curriculum must provide a comprehensive overview of Scripture and a full range of theology.

3. *Teachers must guide students in interacting rationally, not just emotionally, and with a high sense of responsibility to the full counsel of God.* I would guess that about half the students have a tendency to make decisions emotionally rather than rationally. Competent teachers will make sure they offer a balanced approach to both the affective and rational learning domains in their students. They must keep in mind that God's Word is propositional and demands a cognitive as well as a behavioral response.

4. *Efforts must also be made to get students to internalize the Scriptures.* This is best done as students verbalize the Word of God. When adults learn to verbalize God's Word in a Christian context, they can do the same in a secular setting. Astute teaching will be required when the class exceeds twenty students so that all class members can participate in some fashion. Teachers can use couple buzzers, panels, open debates, and other formats so that all students will interact with the main theme of Scripture before they leave the classroom each Sunday.

5. *Enriching curriculum for adult Sunday Schools will move people from the fantasy world of their perceptions into the reality of the eternal Word of God.* Students must be forced to exchange the nostalgia of the past or the fantasy of the future for the complex present. God's Word expresses reality and adults must be encouraged to willingly face the world and their lives from God's viewpoint. This will take some very practical study by teachers who can then get their students to deal with God's reality as it impacts their own lives. Of necessity, churches need good dialogical learning in their classrooms.

6. *Students must be encouraged to develop new spiritual skills and habits.* Godliness comes as believers learn the disciplines of the Christian life. The classroom becomes a training center, not just a place for interacting around some theological information. The classroom only provides the incubator for these spiritual habits, and therefore, the lessons will need to have some built-in accountability about how students disciplined themselves as a result of the lessons taught in the classroom.

7. *The genuine art of andragogical teaching is all based upon one central theme.* The enterprising teacher will serve as a facilitator, encouraging adults to decide for themselves from the truth of

God's Word what the Lord would have them do with the truth they have studied. According to Levinson, adults must "participate in decision-making" if they are going to give their energy to the learning process.[9]

Growing an effective adult Sunday School doesn't happen by accident—it takes godly, dynamic leadership. Adult departments can expand rapidly and greatly increase effectiveness if leaders give creative supervision and apply these principles and structures. God has gifted people for leadership just as He gifted others to teach. Both gifts must be applied to adult education. Spiritual nurture can happen in the adult Sunday School. It is worth all the time and effort our churches can give.

Notes

1. The Institute for Church Development is a church consulting organization affiliated with Denver Seminary.
2. (Source unknown) Lyle Schaller is the director of the Yokefellow Institute.
3. Tim Stafford, "This Little Light of Mine," *Christianity Today*, 8 October 1990, 30.
4. Daniel J. Levinson, *The Seasons of a Man's Life* (New York: Ballantine, 1979), 237.
5. Malcolm S. Knowles, *The Modern Practice of Adult Education* (New York: Cambridge Univ. Pr., 1980), 47.
6. Dick Murray, *Strengthening the Adult Sunday School Class* (Nashville: Abingdon, 1984), 30–31.
7. Harold Westing, "Comeback in the Classroom," *Moody Monthly*, July/August 1987, 28.
8. Murray, *Adult Sunday School Class,* 26.
9. Levinson, *Seasons,* 67.

For Further Reading

Bellah, Mike. *Baby Boom Believers.* Wheaton, Ill.: Tyndale, 1988.

Brown, Beth E. *When You're Mom No. 2.* Ann Arbor: Servant, 1991.

Fagerstrom, Douglas L., ed. *Singles Ministry Handbook.* Wheaton, Ill.: Victor, 1988.

Fowler, James W. *Becoming Adult, Becoming Christian.* San Francisco: Harper and Row, 1984.

Larson, Knute. *Growing Adults on Sunday Morning.* Wheaton, Ill.: Victor, 1991.

Murray, Dick. *Strengthening the Adult Sunday School Class.* Nashville:

Abingdon, 1984.

Parks, Sharon. *The Critical Years: The Young Adult Search for a Faith to Live By*. San Francisco: Harper and Row, 1986.

Peterson, Gilbert A., ed. *The Christian Education of Adults*. Chicago: Moody, 1984.

Richards, Lawrence O. *You and Adults*. Chicago: Moody, 1974.

Sell, Charles M. *Transitions Through Adult Life*. Grand Rapids: Zondervan, 1985.

Smith, Harold Ivan. *Fortysomething and Single*. Wheaton, Ill.: Victor, 1991.

Stubblefield, Jerry M., ed. *A Church Ministering to Adults*. Nashville: Broadman, 1986.

Wolterstorff, Nicholas. *Educating for Responsible Action*. Grand Rapids: Christian Schools International/ Eerdmans, 1980.

TWENTY-ONE
PROGRAMMING ADULT EDUCATION IN THE LOCAL CHURCH

Stanley S. Olsen

Richard Smithson, Jaci Thomas, and Ed Bottoms, the Associate Pastor, were meeting to discuss the coming year in Adult Education at Overview Church. "What we need this year, Ed, is a series of high powered seminars dealing with life needs," declared Richard. "More and more of the people I hang around with are anxious to receive practical training of this sort."

"But, Dick," broke in Jaci, "what about our commitment to biblical teaching on a systematic basis? Shouldn't we continue to make that our primary objective? After all, people can get all those self-help classes in the community education program!"

"Yes, I know what you mean, Jaci. We have made biblical instruction our standard in the past, but our Adult Sunday School classes seem to be losing their attractiveness to many of our adults," sighed Ed.

"But is running a series of seminars going to meet the needs of our adults any better? And what about the cost? Where's the money going to come from?"

The discussion between Richard, Jaci, and Pastor Ed is not untypical in many churches today. Many churches find their current approaches meet the needs of their clientele. They are looking for new directions in order to keep the programs going. Unfortunately, all too many churches are attempting to redesign by discarding fundamentals and replacing them with popular ventures that seem attractive for the moment.

The solution to this committee's dilemma is multifold.

1. They should develop a plan for adult education built upon the mission statement of the church, or at least the mission state-

ment of the adult education ministry of the church.

2. They must realize it is important to maintain balance between instruction, fellowship, and support.

3. They need to understand adults have varying needs at different times in their lives.

4. They must allow for variety and choice in the program.

5. They must go through the process of evaluation regularly and honestly, discarding those programs or events that no longer meet needs and draw adults.

Programming the local church for adult education can be a time-consuming and frustrating task. In the midst of creating a series of quality events that both attract adults and meet their needs, comes the problem of maintaining balance. Three underlying questions must be addressed before we can achieve balanced adult education programming:

1. Do the activities/events meet the mission statement and objectives of the church?

2. Will various church groups church be happy with the choices?

3. How difficult will it be to staff the event?

Underlying these questions is the natural tension that exists between instruction, fellowship, and support. Which is more important? Is transmitting biblical and other Christian principles the most important? What about the need of adults to be built up within the body through fellowship and support through the sharing of mutual concerns? Each has a part to play. Each needs to be in balance to the other. Each contributes toward the vigor of an excellent adult program.

The purpose of this chapter is to provide a view of programming for local church adult education that is both balanced and attractive, one that will intentionally tolerate tension between fellowship, support, and instruction.

FIRST STEPS

Developing a plan of adult education for a local church takes patience, observation, and evaluation. Researching the interests and needs of your adult population is imperative. Plan electives and course material with the goals and objectives of the church in mind. Thoughtful consideration of resources including money, time, space, and personnel available to validate the plan guarantees achievability.

Adult Interests and Needs

Some form of needs analysis should be considered when formulating a plan. All adults have interests and needs. These are the motivators that cause them to participate in adult education programs. Adults appear to find life's meaning "in the things for which people strive, the goals which they set for themselves, their wants, needs, desires, and wishes."[1] Needs do motivate adults! In other instances, peer pressure or association with others facing common concerns motivate participation.

Whatever the motivational force that ultimately causes an adult to participate in a program, some form of survey instrument should be used to assess needs and interests of your clientele. However, do not try to substitute surveys for true educational leadership. Get to know your people, but catering only to felt needs can lead to programs that ignore the deeper issues from which the need comes.

Please check the topics that would most interest you if offered during Adult Sunday School.

___ Parenting
___ Adult Children
___ Preschoolers
___ Adolescents
___ Infertility
___ Survey Study of PROVERBS
___ Inductive Study of MARK's GOSPEL
___ Biblical Views of Stress and Stress Management
___ Prayer
___ Financial Management
___ The 12 Steps in Biblical Perspective

Please indicate your status:
married _____ single _____ parent _____

Figure 21.1

People's needs and interests shift as they enter various phases of their life cycles. A person's preferences of one year do not necessarily remain constant throughout life. Expect needs and interests to change and be prepared to meet them with relevant and interesting activities and events. "Acknowledge the fact that people are interested in short bursts of activity. Programs that feature teachings, sports, entertainment, or other activities that last for hours on end (or for weeks and weeks) will lose people quickly."[2]

Whatever the reasons, adults today expect and demand the right to make choices based on their interests, needs, or inclinations. A wisely designed master plan for adult education in the local church will consider this reality and respond to it.

The Mission Statement

All organizations should have some type of purpose statement. This statement should spell out the heart of the organization's purposes for existence as well as identify the key objectives for its operation. Most churches do what they do based upon either formal or informal statements of purpose. In some instances they also identify strategies to accomplish their missions.

The plan for adult education in the local church must use the church's mission statement as the filter through which it evaluates its plan for action. The plan will be sure to include both cognitive and affective classes, seminars, events, and activities that help to fulfill the objectives of the church. This will ensure meaningful and responsible adult Christian education in that local church.

> The mission statement for Overview Church is *To Know Christ and Make Him Known.* This is further implemented by the strategy of five T's: Time, Talent, Testimony, Treasure, Togetherness. The church seeks to fulfill its mission by exalting Jesus Christ in the wise use of time; equipping people to serve Jesus Christ by the use of talents; engaging people to follow Jesus Christ by means of personal testimony; funding ministries through giving; and encouraging fellowship in Jesus Christ by means of togetherness.
>
> The mission statement for the adult program of Overview Church is to provide activities and events for adults that meet their needs, teaching them about scriptural truths and enabling them to grow spiritually and further understand Time, Talent, Testimony, Treasure, and Togetherness.

Resources

Always consider the implications of the resources necessary to complete the plan. In some instances, it is the amount of money available to purchase materials, pay honoraria, or rent facilities. What space is necessary to complete the plan? This is an ongoing issue, especially in growing churches, and needs to be considered. More often than not, the existing space available is allocated to children and students/youth before consideration is given to adults. So be mindful of this important commodity.

And then there is the question of time. How much time will the activity consume? How long will a series run? How much preparation is necessary to participate? What obligation will the participant have to do in follow-up? All of these are time considerations.

Futurist George Barna has done extensive research in what Christians need to know about life in the years to come. His conclusion is that time will increasingly be a major factor in people choosing to participate in activities and events.[3] Being aware of this increasing reality in the lives of adults may be a major factor in the success or failure of your plan.

PROGRAM PLANNING SHEET

Type of Activity	Leadership	Date/ Duration	Space Needs	Cost
Grief Seminar	Dr. N. Lackey	9/5-6	Room 227/ Food	$200
Parenting Adolescents	Roth	13 weeks	Rooms 125-127	$7@
Proverbs Study	Smith	13 weeks	Room 115	$3@
Fall Festival	Paul Brown, chair	9/29 (4-7 pm)	Church grounds	$1500

Figure 21.2

Teachers and Leaders

Last on our list of criteria is the critical issue of personnel. Who will do the job, teach the class, lead the group, motivate the troops? Adults are discriminating and do deserve the very best. Trends today indicate adults are making choices based on their perception of quality, name recognition, or demonstrated excellence.[4] This simply means the leaders who serve in local church adult programs need to meet some of the same standards existing in the secular arena.

Every church, large and small, can strive to seek the best qualified and best trained persons to lead and teach in their programs. Have expectations that include training and preparation as normative. Be prepared to supply resources and some type of orientation to all your personnel. Find teachers who can spark imagination, stimulate productive interaction, and win the respect of their students. If the teacher or leader cannot meet these expectations, in all likelihood, the event will fail. No longer will adults attend just because the church puts it on.

Putting the plan together is the starting point. After it is completed, the joyous task of programming can begin. Making use of the plan as the guide for all program development and administration is another. Resist the temptation to do whatever seems most convenient. Use the plan as a type of filter through which all adult activities are screened. Remember there will always be some tension between instruction, fellowship, and support. Remember to provide balance between these three and encourage the integration of these components in adult opportunities.

Instruction is the act of knowledge and experience being presented so that others may access it for themselves. It is both a cognitive and affective process. It is done in conjunction with fellowship and support.

Fellowship is the act of friendship. It is social encounter. It is adult to adult interaction that produces affection and body life.

Support is the act of adults supplying mutual love and concern for each other. It is the act of sharing one another's burdens. It is the act of discovery through encounter together.

A BALANCED ADULT PROGRAM

The balanced church program of adult Christian education looks for at least six different types of endeavors: the Adult Sunday School (sometimes called Adult Bible Fellowships), seminars and workshops, an organized system of small groups, a system of discipleship and/or mentoring, a calendar of fellowship events, and a church library/learning resource center.

Adult Sunday School

Most local church adult programs will have some type of Bible teaching program, commonly called Sunday School. While the format may vary, the approach is to transmit scriptural truths through instruction. Adult Sunday School classes should contain three ingredients that meet adult needs: *instruction, fellowship,* and *support.* Gathered together around some theme, we adults are enabled to develop spiritually. Sunday School classes provide a point of connection on a weekly basis. They become an entry into the adult culture of any local church. In a large church, the Sunday School class becomes a family for its adults.

Topics taught in the Sunday School setting should be approached from a biblical, life-centered and practical perspective. In all instances, adult classes must recognize the need for making choices, interacting with principles, and determining commitment. Sunday School should provide for natural groupings determined by age or characteristic or groupings developed out of interest in an instructional topic. Classes should strive to provide continuity over a lengthy period of time. Classes should have opportunity to develop service or ministry projects. Classes should provide adults with a safe haven from their normal environment.

Seminars and Workshops

Adults of the '90s are looking for substantive, practical workshops and seminars that speak to their interests and needs. They are intensely interested in delving into subjects that will profit their life-style, parenting ability, breadth of knowledge, or skill level. They are eager to join with others, especially if the session is of a short duration, in learning about something new. The two words that characterize these types of entities are excellence and relevance. Adults of this era look forward to investing themselves in sessions that deal with major causes of the day. This is especially true for adults in their twenties, thirties, and forties.

As in the case of Sunday School programming, seminars and workshops cannot demand long-term commitments. It is important to craft offerings that can be completed in short time periods. The success of ventures such as these will demand qualified expertise in leadership and well-developed and presented curricular materials.

Small Groups

Small groups are the wave of the present and future. The adult of today desperately needs a small (six to eight) cluster of other adults with which to build deep relationships. Adults need to practice *koinonia* with other believers as they grow in their relationship to the Lord and to one another as part of the body of Christ. Roberta Hestenes, well known small group expert, has described small groups as a place of opportunity for personal exploration of the content, meaning and application of the Christian faith.[5] Small groups provide a place to know and be known in a supportive environment. They offer an ideal environment for individual adults to struggle with themselves, experience change in a supportive atmosphere, and commit to decisions that will be life-changing. Small groups provide a point of vitality and growth for adults.

Discipleship and Mentoring

Every adult program needs an organized system to train key people. The purpose may be spiritual growth or simply skill acquisition. Discipleship is normally a process of providing a long-term relationship between experienced and inexperienced leaders. By means of demonstration, directed reading, and practicing of applications, learning occurs. Adult programs need opportunity for new believers to be discipled into spiritual growth by mature believers. This can be done through an organized curriculum, or it can happen as two persons link together with a common commitment to see learning and growth occur.

An organized mentoring program will recruit highly trained and qualified leaders and match them with adults who have demonstrated potential for ministry. This process allows for advancement on a timetable that meets the individual needs and ability of the one trainee. This is a fine way to raise up future leaders and teachers in any church.

Fellowship Events

All churches, regardless of size, need to provide social outlets for their adults. A good adult program will plan to offer a variety of activities that will allow:

- recreation,
- intergenerational interaction,
- cultural exposure, and
- family programs.

It is wise to provide one fellowship activity for each 200 adults in the membership of the church. This means the church calendar will offer one additional fellowship event each time the membership increases by another 200 adults. All adult programs should have a minimum of two all-church fellowship events each year. Then, as the membership grows, add to the quantity using the formula above.

Library/Learning Resource Centers

The church library has long been a depository of good books for the adult population of the church. Now, however, adults need other resources such as tapes and videos from the church library.

Many forward-looking churches want their libraries to be more than merely depositories of theological treatises. They are aggressively seeking materials that speak directly to real-life needs with a Christian distinctive. They are turning libraries into media centers filled with Bible study materials as well as good entertainment for the entire family. Some churches see their libraries as partners in adult continuing education. They are actively seeking to provide materials that will support investigation and research into a wide variety of subjects. They are making their libraries very user-friendly, supplying good reading, furniture, attractive decorating, and places to connect with other adults.

WRAPPING IT UP

So what is the secret to good adult programming in the local church? The basics include:

- good planning;
- good evaluation of interests and needs;
- varied choices of learning opportunities;
- sensitivity to the needs of the moment;
- careful calculation of resources; and
- a desire to genuinely serve the adults in your church.

"Why haven't we ever put together a plan for our adult programming before this? We could have saved ourselves so much grief and kept the peace among the generations so much better," exclaimed Jaci.

"Yeah, I agree," echoed Richard, "if only we had done some foundation-laying before we bulldozed ahead."

"Well, the lesson has now been learned," declared Pastor Ed.

"Let's get going and finish a plan for the church as we see it today. We've got a lot of ground to cover if we're going to balance our program and be ready for the opening adult events of the first of September."

Notes

1. Dr. Edward C. Lindeman's remarks are found in Raymond J. Wlodkowski, *Enhancing Adult Motivation to Learn* (Jossey-Bass, 1985), 105. This seminal text deals with all aspects of adult motivation.
2. George Barna, *The Frog in the Kettle* (Ventura, Calif.: Regal, 1990), 94.
3. Barna, *The Frog*, 39.
4. Ibid., 44.
5. For more information see Roberta Hestenes, *Using the Bible in Small Groups* (Philadelphia: Westminster, 1985).

For Further Reading

Cross, K. Patricia. *Adults As Learners.* San Francisco: Jossey-Bass, 1982.

Getz, Gene A. *Sharpening the Focus of the Church.* Chicago: Moody, 1974.

Hestenes, Roberta. *Using the Bible in Groups.* Philadelphia: Westminster, 1983.

Knowles, Malcolm S. *The Modern Practice of Adult Education.* New York: Association Press, 1980.

Wlodkowski, Raymond J. *Enhancing Adult Motivation to Learn.* San Francisco: Jossey-Bass, 1985.

TWENTY-TWO
MENTORING AND DISCIPLING
Allen D. Curry

Discipling programs exist in many churches and the shelves of Christian bookstores are filled with books about discipleship. Some experts claim that discipleship provides the primary tool the church should use to train adults.[1] Because of the proliferation of discipleship materials and programs, one can easily think that everyone knows all there is to know about this approach to adult education.

Clearly discipleship programs set out one of the most effective ways to encourage adults to grow in their Christian walk. However, most discipling programs can be improved and made more effective. An understanding of the biblical foundations of discipleship and of contemporary mentoring programs in business and education offers help in making a good church ministry better.

TYPES OF DISCIPLESHIP PROGRAMS

Discipling frequently takes one of two different forms. The first, sometimes called *follow-up,* deals with new converts. When someone embraces Christ in faith, he or she needs to begin the process of learning how to be a follower of the Savior. The follow-up approach concentrates on getting individuals to use the means of grace, particularly Bible study and prayer. When new converts develop facility in prayer and Bible study, some assume that they are discipled. They have the tools that will enable them to grow in grace and serve the Lord. From this point on the new Christian should be able to develop in a variety of ways through other available programs in the church.

The second form of discipleship, one that emphasizes *reproducing,* seeks to equip believers to lead other new Christians in the process of being conformed to the image of Christ. This approach builds on the first but assumes that people should not be designated disciples until they are able to lead others to the place at which they can take over a similar ministry. Consequently, training in evangelism and teaching are important aspects of a reproducing approach to discipleship.

WHAT IS A DISCIPLE?

The Bible describes a disciple as one who follows Jesus. Knox Chamblin further defines a disciple as a learner who follows and obeys Jesus, exercises loyalty, willingly sacrifices, and engages in works of service.[2]

Discipleship in the New Testament means adopting a life-style patterned after the life of Jesus. This life-style results from a changed heart rather than mere behavioral changes. As Fernando Segovia explains:

> First of all, belief in Jesus the Christ emerges as the very ground of discipleship: it is faith that constitutes the basic presupposition and point of departure for all Christian discipleship. . . . In the second place . . . belief implies and entails a very definite style of life on the part of the believers. Furthermore . . . such a way of life is, quite often, distinctly patterned on or modeled after the life and ministry of Jesus.[3]

This brief description of a disciple raises an important question. How do we enable adult believers in Jesus Christ to observe a life-style patterned after His, characterized by learning, obeying, serving, sacrificing, and loyalty? The Scriptures give us a clue where to begin. The original disciples acquired these characteristics as a result of following Jesus. They adopted His overall life-style of service, prayer, Scripture study, meditation, and worship. After they were taught by the Lord, they proceeded to encourage others to develop these attributes.

Paul's words to Timothy, "And the things you have heard me say in the presence of many witnesses entrust to reliable men who will also be qualified to teach others" (2 Tim. 2:2), provide a pattern for us to follow. Disciples are made by reliable followers teaching others how to be like Jesus. A congregation can help individuals acquire these characteristics by providing a program in which learners expose themselves to people and learning situations where the characteristics of a disciple are embodied and explained.

DISCIPLING AND THE LOCAL CHURCH

Sometimes discipling takes place exclusively within an individualistic framework, and misses incorporating the new convert into the body of believers. By examining the way business and education use mentoring, the practice of linking experienced practitioners with newcomers for the purpose of developing a relationship, we can learn how to pass on a more wholesome appreciation for the Christian community, the body of Christ. Our individualistic society sometimes produces church members who only see the church as an institution that exists to benefit them. Mentoring helps people make a personal connection with the institution, and this leads to institutional loyalty. Strong churches will cultivate a similar institutional commitment, so that members will work hard to improve the entire congregation.

Discipleship ministry enables the church to follow up on new converts, help people continue to grow in the grace and knowledge of the Lord, and strengthen their appreciation for the community of believers.

Three Characteristics of a Discipleship Program

Discipling has three key features: (1) leading people to follow Jesus and to pattern their lives after His; (2) providing personal examples of what it means to be like Jesus; (3) designing a church context for fostering discipleship.

The prime candidates for this kind of activity are adults. Adults have sufficient experiences to identify a life-style and live it. In their social and cultural milieu, adults are able to learn how to obey, sacrifice, serve, and be loyal. They are more attracted to teaching strategies that recognize and personalize their unique situations.

For convenience' sake, look at the discipling process as beginning after the initial work of grace in the heart of an adult. Initially, the person must believe in Jesus and what He has done for sinners in His substitutionary death on the cross. This entails a recognition of the impossibility of making oneself right before God, and receiving Jesus by faith as He is offered to us in the Gospel. Changing a person from a rebellious sinner to a believer in Jesus Christ is the work of the Holy Spirit. God uses the manifold evangelistic endeavors of the church to bring about conversion.

The discipling should begin quickly after a person professes faith in Jesus Christ. Chamblin points out that Jesus taught all those who followed Him and did not always make a distinction between members of the crowd and those who were clearly His disciples.[4] Therefore, nothing is gained if we postpone the discipling process until a convert shows some initial development in the Christian life.

DISCIPLESHIP AND THE MEANS OF GRACE

Historically, the church used three means to encourage people to grow as followers of Jesus. The means of grace—the Word, prayer, and the sacraments—have been the crucial ingredients in building disciples from the New Testament era until the present time (Acts 2:42).

The vast literature on discipleship clearly emphasizes the necessity of using the first two of these tools for Christian growth. Almost all programs of discipleship include Bible study and prayer as two necessary practices for developing mature followers of the Lord.

As a first step in the discipling process, the adult educator should help the new Christian recognize the value of Bible study and to acquire some facility in it. From what the Bible teaches, there can be no doubt that Christian growth requires knowledge of the Word. The pages of the Bible provide the only access for the believer to learn about Christ.

Prayer plays an equally important role in fostering growth in grace. Following Jesus and His way of life can only come through communion with the Father through the Son under the direction of the Spirit. Prayer characterized the practice of Jesus in His earthly ministry. After the Ascension, Jesus continues to intercede for His people at the right hand of the Father in heaven. Therefore, those who desire to be like Him must follow His pattern. In true prayer one exhibits the essential attributes of a disciple—

obedience, service, sacrifice, and loyalty.

Adult Christians will grow in prayer and Bible study by seeing others use these means of grace. Adult learners respond to modeling. They are also more inclined to use the tools of growth when other adults encourage them and hold them accountable for their stewardship of the tools.

Historically, the sacraments have played a crucial role in developing the character of a disciple. In the Lord's Supper one confirms one's belief in the efficacy of Christ's death—"This is My body, which is for you; do this in remembrance of Me . . . For whenever you eat this bread and drink this cup, you proclaim the Lord's death until He comes" (1 Cor. 11:24, 26). In this sacrament the believer confesses sin and gains assurance that God forgives sin for Jesus' sake.

In a similar way, the sacrament of baptism demonstrates that one belongs to Christ. Baptism can be likened to bearing the mark of God's ownership. Every time believers see a baptism, they should remember that they belong to the Lord and that He will never leave nor forsake His own. It is a concrete reminder of what Christ has done and that the believer is united to Him. It should encourage all believers to imitate Christ and to persevere in discipleship.

Both of these sacraments serve a pedagogical function for the adult being discipled. Each of them provides a sign of God's grace that enables the believer to grow in his or her relationship with the Lord. These two sacraments also seal or affirm for Christian adults that God's grace can and does benefit them. As followers of Christ use these means of grace, they can grow to be more and more like the Savior who gave these gifts to the church.

Both of the sacraments have immediate benefit for adult learners. The confirming function of the sacraments assists many adults who doubt the efficacy of their faith.

DISCIPLESHIP IS A LIFELONG PROCESS

Even though one has begun to use the means of grace, that does not complete the discipling process. On the contrary, it is still in its infancy. A growing belief in and understanding of Jesus and what He did forms a continuing part of the Christian life. The loyal practice of obedience, sacrifice, and service for Christ's sake never ends in the earthly existence of the believer.

Historically, the church has looked at what we refer to as discipleship training under the rubric of sanctification, the process of becoming holy, even as God is holy. The acquisition of holiness continues as a lifelong activity.

If a believer continually tries to learn about Jesus and to pattern his or her life after Him, especially in the areas of obedience, sacrifice, service, and loyalty, what process should the church use in making disciples? If the process of disciple-making requires two tiers (follow-up on new converts and development of servants committed to reproducing), where should the church start to develop this ministry?

One of the best ways to begin is to put the new follower of Jesus into contact with someone who increasingly possesses the characteristics of a disciple. Jesus Himself set the pattern when He lived with His disciples as their teacher, mentor, and model. In his classic text on discipling, *The Training of the Twelve,* A.B. Bruce examined the process that Jesus used with His disciples. He concluded, "by far the most important part of that training consisted in the simple fact of being with such a one as Jesus."[5]

Contemporary discipling cannot improve on the method of Jesus. Those who follow the Lord now need to see the life of Jesus lived out in the life of another believer. Discipling or mentoring simply requires the personal demonstration of the qualities that one hopes to see in the disciple and the willingness of the discipler to explain the reasons for his or her actions. A godly life, a clear explanation, and a glimpse at the passions of one's heart are keys to discipleship.

We should not forget that the church provides the context for discipling. Discipling fosters maturity in the church and affects every aspect of it. As Carl Wilson suggests, "a program in a church aimed at building disciples should become the catalyst to spark greater interest in the church school and in the worship services . . . it should be the nucleus to guide the understanding and direction of thought and activities of the entire church."[6]

MENTORING AND THE ASPECTS OF ADULT LEARNING

Mentoring and discipling take advantage of certain characteristics common to the adult educational enterprise. Each addresses the concerns of adults in a way compatible with what we know about adult education. The church can learn from the mentoring programs of business and education about how to develop specific characteristics in individuals within the context of an organization. Their programs provide a model for inculcating values that the institutions prize. The parallels with discipleship programs in the church open up many avenues to further our understanding of how we should conduct adult education in the church.

A well established principle of adult learning maintains that for adults, "time perspective changes from one of postponed application of knowledge to immediacy of application."[7] In a discipling program the disciples funnel all learning through the perception of what they need to know. When the discipler recommends a procedure, the disciple has the option of ignoring the suggestion and the trainer needs to come back to it again.

The principle of immediate application in adult education grows out of need-based learning. Adults "become ready to learn something when they experience a need to learn it in order to cope more satisfyingly with real-life tasks or problems."[8] A discipling program will only involve adults when they perceive a need for this type of nurture. It will be almost impossible to recruit individuals into a discipling program if they don't want it or don't think they need it. Mentoring programs in education have demonstrated these two principles. In reflecting on his relationship with his mentor, Forest Parkay points out that mentoring "provides the student with a curriculum that is truly 'individualized' and therefore maximally growth promoting. . . ."[9]

Mentoring and discipleship programs provide opportunities for the adult to use experience in the learning process. "As people grow and develop they accumulate an increasing reservoir of experience that becomes an increasingly rich resource for learning. . . . Furthermore, people attach more meaning to learnings they gain from experience than those they acquire passively."[10] In fact, most mentoring programs depend on both the experiences of the mentor and the protégé. Burke and McKeen describe mentoring in business as a program that "involves setting explicit goals and practices for linking less experienced and more experienced managers, and encouraging mentoring by 'arranging' relationships that serve developmental purposes for both individuals."[11]

This developmental aspect of mentoring that Burke and McKeen mention also addresses another characteristic of the adult learner, namely, the unique adult self concept. "It is a normal aspect of the process of maturation for a person to move from dependency toward increasing self-directedness, but at different rates for different people and in different dimensions of life."[12]

MENTORING SOME INSIGHTS FOR DISCIPLESHIP

Most adults learn primarily within the context of ordinary life settings. The school no longer serves as the primary teacher of adults; common everyday living supersedes the classroom. Therefore, it stands to reason that adults can better learn what it means to be a disciple and emulate the life-style of Jesus in ordinary life situations.

Business frequently uses mentoring programs to help new employees, particularly young executives, to master the corporate culture. Burke and McKeen point out that a formal mentoring program can improve "the career development process for all young managers by facilitating their acculturation to the organization. . . . "[13]

In a church filled with disciples of Jesus, new believers can benefit from mentors. The business model suggests precisely how the church can improve its work of making disciples.

Some of the research on mentoring provides insight as to how to set up and carry out a discipleship program. Zimpher and Rieger point out that mentoring programs in education address a number of issues that parallel those in discipleship programs in the church. A mentoring program must determine the role of a mentor, whether the program will be formal or informal, what are the best conditions for the mentor and protégé to work together, what makes a program effective, and how to match mentors and protégés.[14] Church discipling programs wrestle with the same concerns.

The role relationships "range from buddy teacher to clinical teacher, suggesting on one end of a continuum a far more personal relationship, and perhaps at the other end a more studied, scientific, and analytic relationship of one teacher to another."[15] The relationship between discipler and disciple has an equally broad range. Sometimes a disciple needs the encouragement of a buddy who understands what one is going through. At other times the discipler may need to explain how one goes about understanding complex topics in the Bible or to show how one uses the resources of the Holy Spirit in fighting temptation.

Functionally, mentors deal more with the development of professional skills. When mentors and protégés are paired, a common notion of the teaching-learning process provides the most important shared characteristic.[16] In the church we are not as concerned about professional skill, but we do want to help people develop deep and meaningful relationships with the Lord. We can cultivate these relationships whenever mature believers encourage younger Christians and together they study the Bible, pray, and celebrate the sacraments. Both parties should share a common commitment to the benefits of the means of grace and how to use them to promote spiritual growth.

Business and education use both formal and informal mentoring programs. There does not seem to be any conclusive evidence that one works better than the other. Formal programs have the advantage of the support of the leadership of an organization. In the church such encouragement may be necessary for a discipleship program to maintain long-term effectiveness. Some businesses have found that an informal program of mentoring works best. Women, in particular, seem to benefit from informal programs.[17] Church discipleship programs should be sensitive to the ways in which men and women differ in responding to formal and informal programs. Perhaps formal programs will attract men while women will do much better in informal programs.

Mentoring programs work best where the mentor makes himself available to the protégé, keeps open lines of communication, allots sufficient time, shares expertise, and gives support.[18] All of these fit well with the notion of discipleship described above. If one expects to help a disciple grow in the Christian life, one must be available, communicate freely about the issues of Christianity, and provide the necessary support when the disciple struggles with growth. Without these a discipling program probably will not work.

Establishing and maintaining an effective program requires that one carefully match mentors and protégés. Levinson claims an eight to fifteen year gap provides the ideal difference in age between mentor and protégé. Anything outside this range creates problems.[19] Mentors should be able to recognize unique traits and talents in the protégés and then motivate them to open up new ways to view themselves and others. In effective mentoring programs there exists a sense of spiritual kinship between mentor and protégé.[20] Notice the way in which these elements of effective mentoring programs coincide with what the church frequently expects to see in discipleship programs.

In churches that use discipling programs, paying attention to age differences may lead to more effective results. When churches train individuals to function as mentors in discipling, the mentors should be shown how to recognize the talents of those with whom they work. All concerned will benefit when people from different age-groups realize that others have gifts from the Spirit. Discipleship programs using these research findings should enable church members to learn to appreciate the way that the differences in the church reflect the manifold wisdom of God (Eph. 3:10).

Church leaders will no doubt continue to use discipling in adult education, and the literature on mentoring programs promises to provide helpful new insights into how to improve a biblical model of education.

Notes

1. Lawrence O. Richards, *A Theology of Christian Education* (Grand Rapids: Zondervan, 1975).
2. J. Knox Chamblin, "Following Jesus According to the New Testament" (Th.M. thesis, Columbia Theological Seminary, 1969), 70ff.
3. Fernando F. Segovia, ed., *Discipleship in the New Testament* (Philadelphia: Fortress, 1985), 17–18.
4. Chamblin, "Following Jesus," 40.
5. A.B. Bruce, *The Training of the Twelve* (Grand Rapids: Kregel, 1971), 544.
6. Carl Wilson, *With Christ in the School of Disciple Building* (Grand Rapids: Zondervan, 1976), 73.
7. Malcolm Knowles, *The Modern Practice of Adult Education* (Chicago: Follet, 1980), 45.
8. Ibid., 44.
9. Forrest W. Parkay, "Reflections of a Protégé," *Theory into Practice* (Summer 1988): 196.
10. Knowles, *The Modern Practice*, 44.
11. Ronald J. Burke and Carol A. McKeen, "Developing Formal Mentoring Programs in Organizations," *Business Quarterly* (Winter 1989): 76.
12. Knowles, *The Modern Practice,* 43.
13. Burke and McKeen, "Developing Mentoring Programs," 76.
14. Nancy L. Zimpher and Susan R. Rieger, "Mentoring Teachers: What Are the Issues?" *Theory Into Practice* (Summer 1988): 175.
15. Ibid., 176.
16. Ibid., 180.
17. Murray Reich, "The Mentor Connection," *Personnel* (February 1986): 55.

18. Marsha A. Playko, "What It Means to Be Mentored," *NASSP Bulletin* (May 1990): 29.
19. Daniel J. Levinson. *The Seasons of a Man's Life* (New York: Knopf, 1978), 98.
20. Beverly Hardcastle, "Spiritual Connections: Protégés' Reflections on Significant Mentorships," *Theory into Practice* (Summer 1988): 206–7.

For Further Reading

Bruce, A.B. *The Training of the Twelve.* Grand Rapids: Kregel, 1971.

Coleman, Robert. *The Master Plan of Discipleship.* Old Tappan, N.J.: Revell, 1987.

Davis, Ron L. *Mentoring: The Strategy of the Master.* Nashville: Oliver-Nelson, 1991.

Eims, LeRoy. *The Lost Art of Disciple-Making.* Grand Rapids: Zondervan, 1978.

Hull, Bill. *The Disciple-Making Pastor.* Old Tappan, N.J.: Revell, 1988.

Kidd, J.R. *How Adults Learn.* New York: Association Press, 1973.

Kincaid, Ron. *A Celebration of Disciple-Making.* Wheaton, Ill.: Victor, 1990.

Knowles, Malcolm. *The Modern Practice of Adult Education.* Chicago: Follett, 1980.

Kuhne, Gary W. *The Dynamics of Discipleship Training.* Grand Rapids: Zondervan, 1978.

Levinson, Daniel. *The Seasons of a Man's Life.* New York: Knopf, 1978.

McKenzie, Leon. *The Religious Education of Adults.* Birmingham, Ala.: Religious Education Pr., 1982.

Segovia, Fernando, ed. *Discipleship in the New Testament.* Philadelphia: Fortress, 1985.

Shell, William. *Come Follow Me.* Philadelphia: Great Commission Publications, 1988.

Wilbert, Warren. *Strategies for Teaching Christian Adults.* Grand Rapids: Baker, 1984.

Wilson, Carl. *With Christ in the School of Disciple Building.* Grand Rapids: Zondervan, 1976.

Wlodkowski, Raymond. *Enhancing Adult Motivation to Learn.* San Francisco: Jossey-Bass, 1990.

TWENTY-THREE
SEMINARS AND WORKSHOPS

James A. Davies

This chapter addresses the use of seminars and workshops in church adult Christian education and training. It is written primarily from the perspective of the program planner. It will define and review the uniqueness of the seminar and workshop formats, discuss their current place in church life, and provide guidelines for improving the use of these designs for adult Christian education.

UNIQUENESS OF THE SEMINAR OR WORKSHOP FORMAT

Terminological Problems

The terms "workshop" or "seminar" are widely used and abused in contemporary church life. They appear almost interchangeably, without any consideration as to the distinctiveness of each. In addition, anyone who reads program ads or brochures quickly realizes that many events represented as workshops or seminars are something else entirely.

Workshops and seminars are actually only two of a closely related cluster of short-term instructional formats. Other formats most likely to be confused with workshops and seminars are the institute, clinic, conference, session, program, and the short course. Perhaps the words themselves, or their marketing appeal, cause planners to prefer them over other, more accurate labels.

Definition and Uniqueness

What's unique about a seminar or workshop when compared to

other teaching formats? There is no consistency of use in the terms for the church ministry field. This chapter uses workshop as a "relatively short-term, intensive, problem-focused learning experience that actively involves participants in the identification and analysis of problems and in the development and evaluation of solutions."[1] A seminar, however, is a session or series of sessions in which a group of experienced people meet with one or more knowledgeable resource persons to discuss a given content area. Information and experience are exchanged. But it is "not expected that either problem solving, action, or planning will necessarily result from the meeting."[2]

Although they share some characteristics with other teaching formats, seminars and workshops are solidly based on common andragogical assumptions. Both assume that good adult learning is self-directed, need-based, participatory, and draws deeply from life experience. They are short-term, intensive, problem-centered, and experience-based.[3]

There is one significant difference between these two formats. The workshop places stronger emphasis on the development of competencies and the immediate application of the learnings, while the seminar assumes each adult learner is capable of applying the shared content independently. This distinction may seem like a slight nuance, but it is especially significant when designing the learning experience. Having highlighted this distinction, the term "workshop" will be used for both workshops and seminars throughout the remainder of the chapter.

Advantages and Limitations

Every instructional format used in adult religious education has advantages and limitations. The workshop format provides both structural and individual advantages. Due to its short-term nature, the format allows for many people to participate. The workshop is very flexible. It can be repeated several times, in different locations, and at different hours. When well-designed, this format provides an opportunity to watch the process as well as learn content. It affords an opportunity to see an expert resource person in action. A final structural advantage pertains to the physical setup. Workshops require few if any changes in room arrangement or equipment. With careful advance planning and flexible facilities, there is little need to reorganize the facilities and the equipment once they are in place.

Personal advantages include plunging the participant into a

unique learning atmosphere. He or she is temporarily removed from day-to-day concerns and distractions. A certain amount of this kind of environmental "baggage" always accompanies learners to workshops. But removing learners from their natural settings for the time of the program isolates and enables them to concentrate on the problem at hand. Interest tends to remain high because learning is packed into a concentrated time period. In a workshop individuals have time to practice and make mistakes. Practicing a skill or applying knowledge at a workshop is a low-risk way to gain confidence and experience in it.

Application of the results can be immediate without having to wait the many weeks that it takes for a longer program to conclude. Finally, the intense nature of the workshop forces people to genuinely interact with one another. The personal relationships that emerge among participants can develop into a support system or friendship network.

Limitations to the workshop format cluster into two basic areas. *Pacing* difficulties include the potential for information overload, individual fatigue of the participants or staff, and having little opportunity to correct problems that arise. Equipment failures, sessions that last longer than expected, and meals or snacks that are served late can become critical events. *Participation* difficulties develop when those in attendance do not possess the level of communication and small group skills needed for program effectiveness. The intensive learning experience of the workshop provides little time to take corrective action if an individual lacks the necessary interpersonal skills. Awareness of the advantages and limitations can enable the Christian educator to design impactful workshops which maximize the former and minimize the latter.

Guidelines for Selecting the Workshop Format

This section presents basic issues to be considered by the Christian educator when deciding whether to use the workshop format. The workshop format should be used:

1. In situations where the learning objectives emphasize problem-solving.

2. For solving difficulties that are relatively complex and generalized and that require intensive analysis.

3. In situations where the necessary resources are available and where they can be effectively incorporated into workshop activities during a concentrated period of time.

4. In situations where it is important to remove participants

from their "natural" environment.

5. Only if skilled leadership is available.

6. Only if the participants come with, or can be provided with, the group process skills that they need to engage in effective problem-solving.[4]

PLACE IN CHURCH LIFE

When searching for words to describe the place of workshops in contemporary adult Christian education, the adjective "omnipresent" comes to mind. Almost all churches use the format at some time or another—for new member orientation, missions education, teacher training, marriage enrichment, leadership development, or to address life concerns and issues.

Two ways of using workshops dominate the contemporary church scene. Each way is different in terms of degree of use and in philosophy of ministry. First, many select a *complete immersion* pattern. Such churches have deliberately chosen to deliver all the formal education and training needs using only the workshop format. Demographically these churches tend to be in greater urban areas and have younger congregations. Leadership believes the workshop design is the most culturally viable format for their people. It is user-friendly and need-oriented. It can be relevant. It carries with it the potential for almost instant results and "consumer gratification." As the Baby Boomers move into their forties and fifties, more and more churches will choose the complete immersion approach.

Servicing all the training and educational needs of the church through the workshop format is a relatively new development. It represents, for some, a radical departure from the historic educational position of the evangelical church (that of gradual change into a Christian world and life view through broad-based, systematic biblical instruction).

A church should address several questions before adopting an educational philosophy which follows a workshop-only delivery system. Is a smorgasbord approach (which allows people to pick and choose what they want) the best way to present training in all areas of the Christian life? Does the format excessively feed a consumer-oriented and individualistic approach to education? What are the long-term benefits and dangers of allowing people to select based only on current need? What lasting gains come about when using an intensive, short-term format? Is that really how people change? What provision is made for follow-up, including such features as accountability, mentoring, and loving support?

Occasional offerings is the second way workshops are used in church life. This category represents churches which sometimes use the workshop design. They offer workshops in addition to the normal, ongoing educational programs. Some plug into the workshop format only when a special speaker, a "hot topic," or a unique media series comes along. Other churches follow a more topical approach, such as when a special missions conference or leadership development emphasis creates a weekend integrated with the ongoing ministries. In either case, the use of workshops is not the dominant means by which Christian education is practiced at that site. It is viewed as an enrichment to the already full educational programming. Almost all evangelical churches have used workshops in this way.

GUIDELINES FOR IMPROVING SEMINARS AND WORKSHOPS

Planning and Managing Workshops

The managerial process is often undervalued in workshop delivery. Applying the tools of planning and management to workshops will increase the likelihood of producing the desired results. This section provides an overview of the components in workshop planning. It highlights key information, pitfalls for the unwary, and considerations born of experience in planning hundreds of workshops. The elements are not linear, even though they are presented here in logical fashion. In reality each component depends upon the others; change in one influences the rest. A planning checklist is provided at the end of the chapter.

Determine Needs. One undertakes a needs assessment to collect enough data about the learning needs of a particular group. By doing this the program planner and the workshop presenter can eliminate as much guesswork as possible in developing workshop goals, objectives, and design. A needs assessment is an effective and appropriate way of raising awareness about gaps in knowledge or skill. It also serves as a basis for persuasion to a funding agency, department, or even the learners themselves.

Some Christian educators do needs assessment intuitively; others practice it by "keeping a listening ear" to their staff; still others regularly send around anonymous survey-response sheets. Whatever method you use, remember that poorly conceived assessments can fail to yield useful planning information. When engaging in informal needs assessment, be sure to talk to people representing several segments of the church population. Too many assessments have not discovered genuine needs because those responsible chose to talk only to a close circle of friends. Furthermore, people often do not accurately diagnose their own needs. Also important is the fact that acknowledgment of the need is not a commitment to attend a program that addresses that need.

Select the Workshop Presenter. This key component requires the Christian educator to match the workshop participants with the most appropriate presenter. A workshop presenter is an individual with expertise in the subject area, brought in to lead and facilitate the workshop experience. There are five prerequisite qualifications for such an individual. Without these, the success of the workshop is uncertain.

Prerequisites for Workshop Presenters

1. Knowledge of the subject matter
2. Ability to teach/facilitate using proper adult education principles
3. Personal style that respects adults as learners
4. An approach that rapidly allows learners to become engaged in the learning process
5. Enthusiasm for the subject and for helping others learn about it

Figure 23.1

The biggest pitfall in selecting the workshop presenter lies in choosing an individual who has credentials in the subject matter but whose skills are not adaptable to the format or who treats participants in ways inconsistent with their expectations. To avoid this dilemma, one should: check the qualifications (usually done by requesting a résumé), personally contact the person (a face-to-face meeting, a telephone conversation, or correspondence, in descending order of desirability), and seek information about the potential presenter from respected others.

Develop the Plan. The planner generally sets the overall goals of the workshop and sometimes consults with the presenter to develop specific learning objectives. Both parties can act as a team to develop the workshop design, although more commonly this task is undertaken by the presenter alone. Christian educators must assume responsibility for the design. It is prudent to ask for a detailed workshop plan far enough in advance that adjustments or major changes can be made if required. Pfeiffer and Ballew's *Design Skills in Human Resource Development* is a useful sourcebook of suggestions and principles to follow when designing workshops. Workshop plans that feature variety, involve participants actively, give opportunities to apply new content or information, and provide participants with feedback are hallmarks of effective designs.

Experienced workshop leaders discuss the agenda, learning objectives, and methods at the beginning of the session so that the design is clear. They allow time for participants to ask questions and provide input into the course design. This ensures that the trainer and the participants have the same expectations. It is often helpful to take a few minutes for participants to write down their individual objectives for the workshop. These can be kept strictly as a personal guide or may be shared in small groups or with the entire class. Encourage participants to take full advantage of the learning opportunities. Let them know that you expect them to take responsibility for their learning by asking questions and interacting meaningfully.

Encourage participants to build networks. Many are likely to have similar interests and learning needs. Use learning methods that provide an opportunity to make some good contacts, get to know one another better, and share information together. The design should build in time at the end of the class for participants to plan how they will use the knowledge or skills they have developed. Five or ten minutes provide sufficient time to develop a rough action plan with target dates. Finally, encourage participants to meet with their department head or team leader and discuss their plans for using their new skill and knowledge.

Design difficulties include mistaking an agenda or subject outline for a workshop design. Planners should insist on knowing the specific activities, techniques, devices, and exercises that will be used to meet the agreed upon objectives. Workshop designs also err in crowding too much content into the time available at the expense of both problem-solving and learner participation. Generally speaking, it is better to concentrate on three or four learning objectives than it is to deal superficially with a great deal of material.

Select a Location. The ideal room for a workshop is spacious, carpeted, well ventilated, and versatile. It should have natural lighting, good acoustics, movable tables, and comfortable chairs. Other considerations are convenience for participants, ease in locating the selected site, and parking. In most cases, telephones should be adjacent to, but not within, the workshop meeting area so that participants can receive and respond to important messages. Advance information should clearly indicate the procedure to follow if someone wishes to get in touch with a workshop participant during the program.

Planners who do not personally inspect the selected location for a workshop take an unnecessary risk. Inspect familiar sites, such as a room at the church, as close to the date of the workshop as possible but still in time to make other arrangements if necessary. More than one church training session has suffered because coordination with maintenance personnel was lacking and the curtains necessary for showing the video had been removed for cleaning. Planners should also be certain that the facility has not booked unduly noisy programs in adjacent rooms.

Budget Considerations. The cost of the following items should be considered when developing the budget expenses: the presenter's time, the workshop site, workshop materials (including books, papers, instructional media, and other learning aids), marketing, participants' meals and/or coffee breaks. Accommodation, transportation and hospitality costs, staff time for professional and support services (such as graphic artists, secretaries, and registration personnel), and needs assessment and evaluation costs may also be included.

The greatest dangers in budgeting include underestimating of the actual costs of items and failure to anticipate all the items needed. Reaching agreement with the workshop presenter about the fee can also be a source of frustration. In general, budget planners should consider it appropriate to negotiate fees with presenters (i.e., treat the figure named as the usual per diem as an opening position only). Influential factors to keep in mind when negotiating fees are the publicity the presenter will receive from the marketing efforts, the opportunity for contacts from workshop participants, the financial circumstances of intended participants, credibility and drawing power of the person's reputation, the size of the market for a particular subject area, the prestige factor of working with certain agencies or groups, and the availability of other resource persons for particular workshops.

Publicity. Three critical decisions are necessary. The first concerns the choice of publicity and advertising approaches. Planners should select the approach(es) they believe will bring in the desired number and type of workshop participants. Promotional strategies should be developed from among several options. These include: notices in newsletters and bulletins, creative announcements on Sunday morning and at departmental meetings, posters and brochures, and mailings to a select target audience. Advertisements in newspapers or on radio or television can be helpful if the workshop is designed to meet the needs of the general community. In general, the most cost-effective marketing tool is a brochure sent to a carefully compiled list of prospective participants.

The second critical set of decisions involves the length of time that elapses between the date on which potential participants receive information about the workshop and the date on which the workshop begins. For local church work a minimum of six weeks is recommended. The length of time should be increased if expense, absence from work, or special travel arrangements are involved.

Who should do the marketing is the third critical decision. This refers to the organization of people and resources to produce effective, efficient, and timely marketing. The best decision depends on a number of situational factors which may point to anything from a brochure produced on an office copier to a four-color glossy product designed with the assistance of a copywriter. For something like the latter, planners would be prudent to allocate eight weeks or more for the production.

The wise Christian educator knows that unexpected delays are a routine fact of life. Planners relying on someone else's services should make it a practice to monitor progress weekly and build in time for inevitable delays.

At the Workshop. Conducting successful workshops requires meticulous attention to detail. Because of the short time frame, there is little opportunity to correct oversights or make changes. It helps to have a staff person on hand during the entire workshop whose sole responsibility is to solve problems that develop during the program. If that is not possible, the planner should try to be present at the beginning and the end of the workshop and at break times. Participants will leave more well-disposed if they have had a chance to express any dissatisfactions to the planner, particularly when that individual expresses gratitude for the feedback.

Enhancing Participation

A number of factors inhibit or facilitate participatory group-interaction and task-oriented learning environments. The topic of the workshop should be centered around a current life need of the target group. Learner motivation and involvement is higher when the problem is complex and one with which the participants have experience.

Group size should be small. Working with two to seven participants is good for group dynamics but may result in too few points of view being presented and lack the sheer number of ideas required for creative problem solving. Seven to fifteen participants is recommended. This size is ideal for the decision-making and discussion central to the workshop format. Groups of this size are complex enough that their task needs to be clearly structured. They function best with a facilitator and a recorder for each group. Experienced workshop leaders divide larger groups into subgroups of less than fifteen. In cases of large audiences a good technique to use is one which limits the discussions to group representatives selected by their peers.

Heterogeneous groups are more successful than homogeneous groups in solving problems. Consequently, the workshop leader should aim for groups composed of members with diverse abilities and backgrounds. Maximize diversity in the groups.

Collaborative learning is increased when there is an atmosphere in which a free exchange of ideas, opinions, and feelings occurs. Such an environment allows members to feel that they can trust one another with their opinions and remain free from attack. Active participation does not imply equal participation by all members. The contributions of some members will always be more valuable than those of others. Wise workshop leaders work at developing a warm, caring climate in which authentic interpersonal communication can occur. But they are careful not to violate the personhood of each adult by forcing participation.

The best workshop group *clerk* I've ever seen was Sarah Henley; she was a member of a church in which I served as educational pastor. She always volunteered to be a group clerk; she just loved the role. After conducting several training workshops in which she was a participant, I noticed there was something different about how she fulfilled her role as group recorder-secretary. She did all the technical things right—like providing a concise written summary of what participants had to say or decide—but she did something else. She listed the ideas mentioned in the group without attributing them to the contributor. When I asked her about it, she said, "I want the group to be free to talk to one another without fear, competition, or embarrassment. I try to be the mother hen who encourages each member, keeps them on track, and lists the ideas. If I listed the contributor, some might feel their ideas are not as good as others and keep quiet." Sarah was an expert at promoting a nonthreatening group atmosphere while helping track her group's accomplishments.

A second role is equally important in establishing a positive group climate. The group *facilitator* is a neutral servant who focuses group energy on the common task, suggests alternative methods and procedures, protects individuals and their ideas from attack, and encourages individual members to participate. It is important that the facilitator clearly understands his or her role. This includes the tasks of being sensitive to the group dynamics, "boomeranging" problems back to group members, and encouraging one another while avoiding talking too much.

Often the facilitator is a member of the group who has been selected at random ("The person whose birthday is closest to. . . . "). I wonder if facilitators selected in such a manner truly understand the multiple responsibilities they have undertaken. For this reason many workshop leaders prefer to work with a group of preset facilitators whose task has been explained to them before the beginning of the learning experience.

Some workshop leaders routinely rotate the task of clerk among group members. Others ask for volunteers. In either case the group facilitator and scribe must work closely together. If one group member dominates the conversation, the wise facilitator will give the recording task to that person and periodically ask the individual for a two or three sentence summary. This keeps the dominator busy with a significant task while freeing time so others can participate. Closely related to both the facilitator and clerk roles is group leadership. In a way, leadership touches all the other factors and either minimizes or maximizes their impact on group productivity. If the group is to be effective, leadership must perform two major functions. Task functions involve facilitating and coordinating group efforts to solve problems. Equally important are the group maintenance functions. These involve member activities that help to make the relationships among group members satisfying. Leadership behaviors that meet these important socio-emotional needs include the following:

providing warmth, friendliness, conciliating, resolving conflict, relieving tension, providing personal help, council, encouragement, showing understanding, tolerance of different points of view, showing fairness and impartiality.[5]

For some adult participants (Houle suggests up to one third), this sociability is the primary reason for attending. Workshop leaders and facilitators recognize this need and strive to make the group experience mutually satisfying and positive. Good leaders help groups to be both enjoyable and productive.

Fostering Transfer of Learning

The purpose of a workshop is to produce change. Lewin reminds us that changing is using new information to develop new responses.[6] This involves a cognitive redefinition through the acquisition of information. It also involves practicing the new competence within the workshop environment. In the successful workshop, learners are given the opportunity to understand and observe the performance that is the object of the workshop experience and to practice it until they master it. Participants also need opportunities to evaluate their performance in this controlled setting. Effective workshops include exercises that demonstrate how new knowledge, skills, or behavior can be applied to life.

Three guidelines help establish a link between successful performance in the workshop with the adult learner's volunteer ministry. Taken together, this trio can be used to successfully overcome obstacles to the transfer of learning. *First,* workshop planners and facilitators should investigate the value orientation, goal structure, and the power and authority relationships within the learner's setting. A church's organizational structure and process, both formal and informal, can create an environment that is either conducive or resistant to the application of new behaviors. Some churches are open to innovative ways of doing things; others are hesitant because they've "never done it that way before." These values and structural underpinnings need to be realistically explored with workshop participants.

Second, problems that can block the transfer of learning to the ministry environment should be simulated as part of the workshop's formal activities. For example, if a church has tension between the weekday Christian day school setup and the setup required by the Sunday School teachers on Sunday morning, those difficulties should be simulated in the workshop. Simulation is a powerful tool for isolating the learner's first frustrating and confusing encounter with conflicts raised by attempts to introduce new or altered performance into the ministry.

Third, it is important to follow-up on learners after the workshop. Periodic follow-up from one to three months is not inordinate. Follow-up after the conclusion of the workshop complements the concern to improve competence and performance.

Evaluating Workshops

Both planners and participants make judgments about the value of every workshop; the issue is not whether workshops should be evaluated, but what type of evaluation is most helpful in providing needed information. For some, evaluation means determining whether people enjoyed a program by using so-called "happiness"/satisfaction indicators. Others test people to determine if gains have been made in knowledge of skill levels. Still others observe people's performance after a program is completed.

Six categories of evaluative questions may be used to determine the workshop's overall effectiveness.[7] These six categories can be grouped into two main clusters: Implementation questions are useful for determining what happens during the workshop. Outcome questions explain what happened as a result of the workshop. See Figure 23.2.

Categories of Workshop Evaluation

1. IMPLEMENTATION QUESTIONS
   —Workshop Design and Implementation
   —Learner Participation
   —Learner Satisfaction
2. OUTCOME QUESTIONS
   —Changes in Knowledge, Skill, and Attitude
   —Application of Learning
   —Impact of Application Learning

Adapted from R. Cervero, "Evaluating Workshop Implementation and Outcomes," in *Designing and Implementing Effective Workshops*, ed. T.J. Sork (Jossey-Bass, 1984).

Figure 23.2

Figure 23.3 lists each category heading. It gives sample questions that can be asked and suggests which designs are most appropriate to collect the answers.

Workshop Evaluation Grid

CATEGORY	SAMPLE QUESTIONS	APPROPRIATE DESIGNS
WORKSHOP DESIGN & IMPLEMENTATION	Was there deviation from the design? In what ways? Should the adjustments be incorporated into future designs?	General questionnaire. Interviews & observations.
LEARNER PARTICIPATION	Quantitative: How many? How compare to expectations? Qualitative: How involved were participants? Did they stay for the entire workshop?	Resource person or select participants write narrative statement after the workshop.
LEARNER SATISFACTION	Were topics adequately covered? Did the sequence promote effective learning? To what extent was the instructor organized?	Anecdotal response by a representative sample or end-of-workshop anonymous questionnaire.
LEARNER KNOWLEDGE SKILLS & ATTITUDES	Did participants develop an understanding of the topic? Did learners change their attitudes? To what degree? To what degree have learners developed techniques/strategies to use the new understandings?	Pre- and post-test analysis, follow-up interviews.
APPLICATION OF LEARNINGS	In what ways are the newly acquired understandings, reflected in the adults' behavior at work/home/church?	Self reports days or weeks after the workshop, observation.
EXTENDED IMPACT	Do family members sense a difference because of the participants' attendance at the workshop? Do students feel more positively about their Sunday School classroom experiences now because their teacher attended the workshop?	Self reports days or weeks after the workshop, observation.

Adapted from R. Cervero "Evaluating Workshop Implementation and Outcomes," in *Designing and Implementing Effective Workshops*, ed. T.J. Sork (Jossey-Bass, 1984).

Figure 23.3

Workshop Design and Implementation is important because the actual workshop may be quite different from its design on paper. It includes factors related to quality, such as the activities of the instructor and the nature of the teaching-learning transaction. Three groups—participants, instructors, and program planners—possess a unique vantage point on this category. Questionnaires, interviews, and observations can be used to gather data from each group. If the workshop is being offered for the first time, the adult educator might wish to be a participant observer. Interviewing participants at the close of the workshop is another strategy for collecting the same information. Generally, these strategies require a small amount of effort, yet they tend to produce quite useful data.

Learner Participation. This evaluative category has both quantitative and qualitative dimensions. The quantitative aspect is embodied by the most common evaluative questions: How many participants? How many were expected? The qualitative dimension includes physical and psychological components: Did participants stay for the entire workshop? How involved were the participants? Collection designs appropriate to these questions are relatively simple. A sign-up sheet provides the actual attendance. It is easy to compare that total to the projected attendance. The qualitative aspect can be measured by asking the resource person and/or select participants to write a narrative statement at the end of the workshop.

Learner participation is often overemphasized in judgments of workshop quality, but it is important for three reasons: First, a minimal level of participation is often required to justify offering a program. Second, the number of participants can affect its quality. Third, the extent to which participants are actively engaged in the workshop can influence its effectiveness.

Learner Satisfaction. This segment examines how the workshop is subjectively judged by the participants. The information required in this category is often collected anecdotally. One method involves selecting a representative sample—usually between three and five people—at the beginning of the workshop. This strategy is most effective if participants are allowed to select their own representatives. Another method is the end-of-workshop anonymous questionnaire in which participants respond to a series of open-ended or fixed response questions. It is relatively inexpensive. But the validity of the data depends largely on the quality of the questionnaire's construction.

Learner satisfaction data should be interpreted cautiously. It is often unrelated to achievement. Further, the method is so overused that participants are likely to give little thought to their answers. On the positive side, these evaluative questions are important in revealing the variety of reasons why adults participate and differing preferences in learning format.

Learner Knowledge, Skills, and Attitudes. This category focuses on changes in the learner's cognitive, affective, or conative competence. Frequently used designs include pretest and post test analysis and follow-up interviews. Taken together, these methods can provide a balanced assessment for this aspect of the workshop.

Application of Learning after the Workshop. This category addresses the degree to which learnings made during the workshop are applied in the learner's natural environment—job, home, church, or area of service. This type of information can be collected only after the workshop. Self-reports and observations are the commonly used designs. Observations of volunteer adult church workers may be accomplished in one of three ways. Leaders may note each time a learner demonstrates a behavior, count the frequency of specific effective and ineffective behavior, or evaluate the appropriate use of a desired behavior using a Likert scale.[8] A sample is shown in Figure 23.4 below.

Sample Observation Scale

The teacher demonstrated the level of giving positive affirmation to student's comments.

1	2	3	4	5
Poor	Less than Sufficient	Sufficient for the Situation	More than Sufficient	Excellent

Figure 23.4

The use of collegial accountability teams or ongoing mentoring by an experienced worker increases tremendously the degree of learning transference among volunteer adult workers in the church.[9]

Impact of Application of Learning. This category focuses on "second-order effects"[10] (i.e., the workshop's secondhand impact on other people or institutions). The data collection methods listed in the previous section can be used here. This category of evaluation is potentially very significant. Yet, answers to such questions can be hard to obtain. Most difficult is the problem of whether the effect can be attributed directly to the workshop.

Any evaluation should be planned so that its results can be used. To increase the likelihood of this, the evaluator should determine who would use the information and what kind of information those persons would need. There are five important groups of information users: workshop participants, the workshop resource person, the program planner, administrators of the sponsoring institution, and those who financed the learner's attendance (church or department scholarship). Each group can have different information needs. For example, the instructor may want to know whether learners were satisfied with the workshop, the program planner may be concerned primarily with the attendance, while those who financed the learner's attendance may want to know how much of the learnings were transferred. Wise evaluators select questions that are most significant for the targeted information group.

CONCLUSION

Workshops and seminars are used by almost all churches who engage in adult Christian education. The format is well-suited for lifelong learners. Its short-term length and need-based focus is attractive to members of contemporary society, as is its emphasis on participatory learning. When done well these vehicles can be effective tools to impact hundreds of adults for Christ.

CHECKLIST FOR WORKSHOP/SEMINAR PLANNING

1. Identify problems or discover needs of the particular target group.
2. Determine subject areas.
3. State objectives in such a way that they imply changes in knowledge, skill, and behavior of individuals.

4. Determine the criteria for selecting the instructional staff.
5. Select instructional staff.
6. Determine the overall design and methods to be used.
7. Select the instructional materials.
8. Construct a budget.
9. Arrange for facilities and services to be rendered.
10. Establish fees (conference and/or registration).
11. Develop pre-workshop activities (such as a suggested reading list, study materials, assignments).
12. Develop multi-track public relations strategies/promotion with specifics and time lines.
13. If attendance is limited, select and inform prospective participants.
14. Develop evaluative instruments to measure the effectiveness of the program in light of stated objectives.
15. Orient instructional staff to the program.
16. Orient participants to the program.
17. Observe the participants at work and troubleshoot. Watch for continuing concerns of the adult learners and the many dynamics of group endeavor.
18. Insure evaluative instruments are administered.
19. Develop post-program activities (such as home study, readings, assignments, or individual follow-up).
20. Analyze the program (knowledge gained or skills and behaviors acquired, opinions on the changes in attitude, strengths and weaknesses of the program).
21. Prepare a final report on the program including financial statement.
22. Analyze and report the results of the evaluation.
23. Follow up the program to test the long-range effects of the experience.

Notes

1. Thomas Sork, ed., *Designing and Implementing Effective Workshops* (San Francisco: Jossey-Bass, 1984), 5.
2. L.E. This, *The Small Meeting Planner*, 2nd ed. (Houston: Gulf, 1979), 50.
3. Malcolm S. Knowles, *The Modern Practice of Adult Education* (Chicago: Follet, 1980), 50, 135.
4. Adapted from Sork, *Effective Workshops*, 9–10.
5. T. Newcomb et al. *Social Psychology* (Fort Worth, Texas: Holt, Rinehart and Winston, 1965), 481.

6. Kurt Lewin, *Field Theory in Social Science* (New York: Harper and Row, 1951), 132.

7. Ron Cervero, "Evaluating Workshop Implementation and Outcomes," in T.J. Sork, *Designing and Implementing Effective Workshops* (San Francisco: Jossey-Bass, 1984), 55–68.

8. Dana Robinson and James Robinson, *Training for Impact* (San Francisco: Jossey-Bass, 1988), 197–201.

9. James A. Davies, "Factors Contributing to Successful, Long-term Laity Care Ministries" (Ed.D. diss., The Univ. of Georgia, 1989), 110–35.

10. Anthony Grotelueschen, "Program Evaluation," in A.B. Knox and Associates, *Developing, Administering, and Evaluating Adult Education* (San Francisco: Jossey-Bass, 1980), 248.

For Further Reading

Bard, Ray, et al. *The Trainer's Professional Development Handbook.* San Francisco: Jossey-Bass, 1987.

Boone, Edgar J. *Developing Programs in Adult Education.* Englewood Cliffs, N.J.: Prentice-Hall, 1985.

Brookfield, Stephen D. *Understanding and Facilitating Adult Learning.* San Francisco: Jossey-Bass, 1986.

Cross, Patricia K. *Adults As Learners.* San Francisco: Jossey-Bass, 1981.

Davies, James A. "Factors Contributing to Successful, Long-term Laity Care Ministries." Ed.D. diss., The Univ. of Georgia, 1989.

Grotelueschen, Anthony D. "Program Evaluation." In A.B. Knox and Associates, *Developing, Administering, and Evaluating Adult Education.* San Francisco: Jossey-Bass, 1980.

Houle, Cyril O. *The Design of Education.* San Francisco: Jossey-Bass, 1972.

Knowles, Malcolm S. *The Modern Practice of Adult Education*, 2nd ed. Chicago: Follett, 1980.

Lewin, Kurt. *Field Theory in Social Science.* New York: Harper and Row, 1951.

Margolis, F.H., and Chip R. Bell. *Understanding Training.* San Diego: University Associates, Inc., 1989.

McLagan, P.A. *Getting Results Through Learning: Tips for Participants in Workshops and Conferences.* St. Paul: McLagan and Associates, 1983.

Merriam, Sharan B., and Phyllis M. Cunningham, eds. *Handbook of Adult and Continuing Education.* San Francisco: Jossey-Bass, 1989.

Miles, M.B. *Learning to Work in Groups: A Practical Guide for Members and Trainers*, 2nd ed. New York: Teachers College Press, 1981.

Newcomb, T. et al. *Social Psychology* (New York: Holt, Rinehart, and Winston, 1965.

Pfeiffer, J. William, and Arlette C. Ballew. *Design Skills in Human Resource Development.* San Diego: University Associates, Inc., 1988.

Robinson, Dana G., and James C. Robinson. *Training for Impact.* San Francisco: Jossey-Bass, 1989.

Rosow, Jerome W., and Robert Zager. *Training—The Competitive Edge.* San Francisco: Jossey-Bass, 1988.

Sork, Thomas, ed. *Designing and Implementing Effective Workshops.* San Francisco: Jossey-Bass, 1984.

Wilson, Marlene. *The Effective Management of Volunteer Programs.* Boulder, Colo.: Johnson, 1976.

Wlodkowski, Raymond J. *Enhancing Adult Motivation to Learn.* San Francisco: Jossey-Bass, 1985.

TWENTY-FOUR

ILLUSTRATIONS OF EFFECTIVE CHURCH EDUCATION WITH ADULTS

Michael S. Lawson

Illustrations of effective church education with adults are not hard to find.[1] Many evangelical churches offer a wide variety of educational options for adults.[2] As never before, church adults pick and choose those ministries they feel will help them most in their spiritual journeys. They experience this educational smorgasbord in a holistic way rarely anticipated by planners of adult curriculums.[3]

If we carefully examine what churches offer, seven major pieces to the adult education puzzle consistently appear. Each piece makes a significant and unique contribution to a comprehensive approach toward adult education in the church.

1. The Sunday School still represents the central piece in the adult education puzzle.
2. The Sunday morning and evening services appear significant due to the sheer numbers of people who attend.
3. Music ministries involve numerous participants and recipients.
4. Wednesday evening studies attract adults when the church offers concurrent children and youth programs.
5. Weekday morning and evening home Bible studies, support groups, and intensive programs of every shape and size have become standard offerings.
6. Camps, seminars, retreats, trips, and fellowships fill special niches in the puzzle bypassed in the week-to-week format.
7. Personal enrichment through Christian radio, television, books, periodicals, tapes, videos, or individual Bible study complete the puzzle.

These categories may not surprise anyone, but Christian education specialists have creatively combined these pieces of the puzzle with the four central assumptions of andragogy. The remainder of this chapter describes what churches actually offer adults in each category and how andragogical assumptions have been integrated.

THE ADULT SUNDAY SCHOOL

The church does not presently have a more important tool for carrying out her teaching ministry (see chap. 19). "More people attend Sunday School today than lived in our country in 1865."[4]

The adult Sunday School must address the broadest range of needs within the church's adult community. Yet every evidence indicates that Sunday Schools respond well to this spectrum of adult needs. Today many such schools flourish under the sound leadership of a growing group of professionally trained educators adept at translating complex adult learning theory into meaningful programs.[5] These sophisticated practitioners within the church have enabled the Sunday School to change with culture in a very fluid and flexible way which bodes well for its future success.

For instance, one church wisely decided that adult curriculum decisions should be made at the local rather than the national level. This makes sense because church needs vary geographically, economically, socially, and in many other ways. The leadership followed a systematic four-step research process.

1. They studied and synthesized secular authors of learning theory.
2. They questioned all the adults in the Sunday School concerning their needs.
3. They interviewed twelve Christian education specialists outside their denomination.
4. They talked to those who did not attend Sunday School.

From this, they developed a fifty-page handbook and a five-person ministry team implements their new philosophy for the adult Sunday School.

Our survey uncovered other indicators that the adult Sunday School, at least in these churches, can keep pace with sound andragogical theory. These Sunday Schools offer:

1. Some form of electives where adults choose from multiple offerings.

2. Life stage classification of adults.

3. Teachers called "facilitator" or "selector of activities and guide to exploration" in the promotional material.

4. Need-oriented studies such as "parenting," "marriage," "loneliness in top management," "marriage to an unbeliever," "dealing with peak performance for high achievers."

One church quit measuring its success by numerical attendance in Sunday School. They removed the statistical straitjacket by offering the same variety of subjects on Sunday morning, Tuesday evening, and Wednesday morning. An adult with a temporary schedule conflict could easily attend the same session at a different time that week. For those who had strong group allegiances, they simply returned to the preferred time and group the following week.

The Sunday School can, should, and does carry a significant, perhaps disproportionate load because of its convenient time next to the morning worship service. Simultaneous education for children and youth also makes the Sunday morning package more attractive. However, the church should not make the same mistake with the Sunday School that society makes with the public school. The Sunday School cannot cure all adult educational ills.

Although the Sunday School cannot bear every load put on it, two seem to emerge as consistent with its goals: instruction and fellowship. But here we have a problem: *those who plan adult Sunday School often focus on instruction while those who attend frequently come for fellowship.*

SUNDAY WORSHIP

Interestingly, not one of the Christian education specialists surveyed lists the Sunday sermon as a piece of the adult education puzzle. Perhaps they did not include it because they bore no responsibility for its supervision. But, the Sunday sermon must be included.

The pastor certainly plays a major role in adult education. More people consistently listen to the pastor than any other single teacher in the church. In the future, pastors may wish to integrate their sermon series more thoroughly with the overall adult education package. They might even see themselves as one part of a comprehensive plan and coordinate their material with all church ministries for adults. Some Sunday School curriculums provide substance and structure for this approach. One publisher developed a wide range of materials with correlated study books for the pastor and the teachers.[6]

Many churches have given up on their evening services. People apparently do not feel the need for another sermon. However, we should not conclude they do not feel the need for Bible study. With the slow demise of the Sunday evening service, a number of creative alternatives appear. Many people apparently still set aside time on Sunday evening for programs that meet their needs. One church has moved its entire Sunday School to the evening; another offers family enrichment seminars; a third involves adults in six- to eight-week electives on Sunday night.

The many small group ministries indicate a strong felt need exists. These ministries, scattered through the week, might take on more substance and power if they (1) moved into the Sunday evening time slot, and (2) combined with coordinated children's and youth ministries. If Sunday-evening-at-church experiences a renaissance, it will come from innovative approaches like these that appeal to specific interests within the adult community.

MUSIC MINISTRY

Three Christian education specialists specifically mention music as a major tool in adult education. They perceive the preparation and performance of the music as equally important. The proliferation of musical groups within those churches evidence their philosophy. The standard adult chapel choir was surrounded by handbell choirs, singing groups, instrumental ensembles, and special musical mixtures of all kinds.

Modern church music has drifted toward simple praise choruses with their focus on the worship aspect of the service. A blend of the educational and worshipful in music would seem very desirable. More churches should envision music educationally. The enormous popularity of Christian music should alert us to an undervalued opportunity. One publisher has capitalized youth's affinity for music by offering a youth curriculum centered on the lyrics of contemporary Christian music.[7] No one has yet tapped into the adult market. Music along with the lyrics attaches itself easily to the mind. Adding theological substance and study makes a powerful educational device. Perhaps adults should study the words used in praise choruses to give a similar effect. In any case, music deserves much more premeditation and consideration in the adult church education.

WEDNESDAY EVENING GROUPS AND STUDIES

Of all the times mentioned by the Christian education specialists in this survey, this one fared the poorest. Over half ignored this time slot altogether. Very little of substance appears on Wednesday night. Of the few churches who provided something, the standard approaches of prayer, Bible study, and choir rehearsal occur most frequently.

Three notable exceptions to this disappointing trend stood out with shocking clarity. First, one church offered what it describes as a seminary level program for training adult teachers. Since the quality of an adult ministry largely depends on developing teachers and leaders, this emphasis seems very healthy. Although the other churches did not provide detail on when they train adult workers, any successful adult ministry must pay considerable attention to training.

A second church provides special support groups on Wednesday night. They specifically mention a Twelve Step Recovery group and a Grief group. This whole idea seems very wholesome since the church can demonstrate its caring in a tangible way.

The third church caught a vision for expanding the fellowship side of the Sunday School on Wednesday night. Their Shepherding program, though organized around the adult Sunday School, holds many of their small group meetings on Wednesday evening. One would certainly expect anyone attending Wednesday evening to belong to a Sunday School class. In addition, they offer special fellowship groups for men and women. Of the seventeen women's groups, two meet on Wednesday evening; of the five men's groups, one meets on Wednesday evening. And of the sixteen shepherding groups, three meet on Wednesday evening.

These illustrations hardly constitute a trend. But perhaps they point the way. The fabric of American society continues to unravel at every relationship. Does the church need to focus major time commitments and energy in helping people heal and strengthen their primary relationships? Christians need permission to meet and discuss the concerns of Christian living outside the context of formal Bible study. Wednesday evening may provide a desirable time slot especially when simultaneous programs for children and youth occur.

WEEKDAY STUDIES, GROUPS, AND PROGRAMS

If we assume that the major pieces of the adult education puzzle appear only on Sunday or Wednesday, we might draw some false conclusions. For instance, we might infer that anemic adult program offerings on Sunday or Wednesday indicate declining interest in church or spiritual things by American adults. That would be an erroneous conclusion.

If skimpy Sunday evening and Wednesday offerings afford bad news for adult church education, the good news comes in the incredible array of offerings at every other conceivable time. The proliferation of programs reflects a growing adult appetite for spiritual things offered on their terms.

Categorizing and classifying the almost endless assortment of group meetings provides quite a challenge. For analysis' sake, consider the following categories which we will expand.

1. Bible study groups
2. Support groups
3. Prayer groups
4. Service groups
5. Recreation groups
6. Peer groups
7. Fellowship groups
8. Skill development groups

Bible study groups include national favorites such as Precepts, Bible Study Fellowship, and Navigator 2:7. The offerings expand from these to almost every imaginable combination. Sometimes an unsupervised teacher decides the subject; at other times, the group chooses its own leader, members, curriculum, and schedule. Churches promote everything from formal instruction to self-guided studies.

Interestingly enough, home Bible studies seem to be following the history of the Sunday School. Only a few decades ago, home Bible studies started outside the supervision of the church. Many pastors considered them dangerous since the leaders were theologically unsophisticated. But almost irresistibly these studies moved within the church's teaching ministry. Now they show up as integral parts of an overall strategy for church education of adults.

The list of *support groups* reflects the groaning of a needy society. Which church prophet of twenty years ago would have predicted the following list of support groups within the church? The mere listing of these ought to alert us to the fact that no one program could ever possibly meet all the Christian education needs of adults. You may even find yourself grieving as you read the list.

- Career recovery
- Divorce recovery
- Single parenthood
- Eating disorders
- Physical or emotional abuse
- Substance abuse
- Children of adult alcoholics
- Codependency
- Parenting support
- Dysfunctional families
- Homosexuality
- Caring for aging parents
- Grief groups for widows/widowers

In the past, people with these kinds of needs were isolated cases and clearly in the minority. Today, hardly any family escapes from one or more of these distressing problems. Churches that rightly address these needs rightly include caring as a part of Christian education.

The idea of *prayer groups* certainly does not strike us as novel. Yet, it represents the kind of group that ought to survive and receive more attention in adult education circles. Prayer remains one of the fundamental Christian disciplines. These groups do best when they revolve around the most pressing concerns of life. One unique group of women with school-age children meets to pray for the twenty-seven area elementary schools.

Service groups range from women's missionary groups to caring for the needy within the church family. Some represent the visitation arm of the church while others offer ministry to the deaf. Obviously, service groups can take on any size and shape. It's refreshing to see educators view service as an integral part of adult education. Sometimes adult education preoccupies itself with expanding the adult's Bible database and loses sight of other significant educational experiences.

Recreation groups include a less than surprising list of women's aerobics, bicycling, golf, softball, and volleyball. These seem to be a low priority in adult education since only two churches mention them specifically. Perhaps the evangelical church remains somewhat skeptical about how play really fits into adult Christian education. If developing relationships moves high on the adult education agenda, recreation will move with it. People need time to work and play together.

The *peer group* phenomenon appears among singles, senior adults, and mothers of preschoolers (MOPS). The mere listing of these groups hardly reflects the extensive activity and multiple offerings of ministry to them. No church surveyed ignored either the singles or the senior adults. Though popular, MOPS was not universally offered like the other two. No doubt this reflects the growing statistics among the general population and the desire of adults to group themselves into life stage categories. Adults obviously (though not exclusively) prefer to associate with people in similar circumstances.

Fellowship groups typically extend the Sunday School's shepherding/caring ministry. The whole concept of extending pastoral care through the Sunday School has gained popularity. But, due to the time constraints of the Sunday School hour, the care groups often meet separately for fellowship. In the future, the American church must give more attention to this area. Too often, people think of Christian education only in terms of individual learning. But, Christian education involves helping people live wisely in the context of homes, communities, and society at large. Deepening fellowship capacities does not come naturally in our disconnected society. Adults will follow quality leadership in this area. We have many experts on church growth and exposition, but where are the experts in fellowship?[8]

Skill development groups offer adults the opportunity to explore areas such as lay counseling, evangelism, teaching, personal budgeting, gift discovery, and much more. Here we find churches training the leadership necessary to staff the growing list of ministries to adults. Obviously, the more adults take responsibility for their own programs, the more they feel the need for training. Conversely, if the pastor is the only one doing evangelism, he is the only one who needs training.

The sheer existence of this many categories and kinds of groups cries out for explanation. They probably reflect the most determined andragogical outcry in the history of the church. Clearly, the adult small group is a permanent addition to the overall adult education puzzle within the church.

CAMPS, RETREATS, SEMINARS, TRIPS, AND FELLOWSHIPS

Up to this point, the categories of adult ministries represent ongoing weekly kinds of opportunities. Whether adults come together on Sunday morning, Sunday evening, Wednesday evening, or sometime during the week, the meetings normally occur on a week-by-week basis. This category represents occasional ministries that supplement all the others. Singles, seniors, couples, and families all receive special treatment, though not in equal proportions.

As mentioned previously, every church offers some ministry to senior adults. Social or activity oriented events dominate the list. Weekly fellowship meals and short trips are among the most popular offerings. Clearly, senior adults call upon their churches to provide more than the standard weekly services. They want to be with their church friends more as retirement frees up their personal time.

Every church also reported additional offerings for singles. This growing segment of the population receives special attention in some churches which provide a minister to exclusively coordinate their activities. Solutions to their unique problems require creativity. For instance, one church offers a retreat for single parents to which the children are invited. The retreat provides college-age coordinators of activities for the different ages of children at certain times during the day. At other times, they plan activities that involve single parents with their children.

The growing emphasis on women's ministries has resulted in numerous special offerings especially for women. Retreats and conferences with special speakers or particular agendas seem to be very popular. Some progressive churches add women to their staff to supervise and promote ministries to women.

PERSONAL ENRICHMENT

In modern America, "feeding the sheep" is no longer the sole prerogative of the pastor. In fact, his sheep will most likely graze in several different pastures. Whether pastors like it or not, they may be only one voice among many to whom their people listen.

Only two churches specifically mentioned individual development programs for their adults. Nevertheless, one church's provision was exceptional enough to deserve special mention. Its extensive video offerings support eight categories of training. They describe their adult educational opportunities in a forty-seven page document published quarterly.

The growth of media centers within churches has largely gone uncelebrated as a major andragogical device for training adults. Yet nothing short of counseling provides such instant servicing of personal needs. The information explosion has literally put the finest biblical thinking at the fingertips of the Christian public. All you ever wanted to know about solving problems from a Christian perspective is available for the listening or reading. Or, if you prefer, any number of quality periodicals can be mailed directly to your home.

Seeing all these adult ministries as a composite helps explain how these churches address four central assumptions of andragogy. Reexamining the results of the survey in light of these assumptions provides yet another perspective on adult education in the church.

1. How do these ministries address the adult self-concept? Adults identify with care groups, support groups, and peer groups whether within normal church hours or during weekday meetings. Contact with other adults in similar circumstances addresses their sense of isolation in the midst of life's problems and their feeling of belonging to a group of fellow strugglers.

Different courses offered by the church affect the adult self-concept. As adults acquire additional skills in Bible study, evangelism, teaching, or parenting, they approach life in general with more confidence. When the church affirms and celebrates the Christian service of her adults, those adults sense accomplishment, satisfaction, and worth to others.

2. How does the church utilize the vast reservoir of experience represented by her adults? Sunday Schools organize their adults by life stages, children's ages, or marital status because these adults share common life experiences. Leadership teams made up of a class leader, curriculum leader, outreach leader, social leader, and assimilation leader represent and plan for the class. They bring their experiences to the planning process.

More and more, churches describe their teachers as selectors of activities and guides to exploration. When teachers function in that capacity, the life experiences of the adults in the class become a major resource in the teaching-learning process.

Numerous support group ministries draw almost exclusively on the experiences of their members to address the current needs of those facing similar struggles. The senior adult ministries utilize hobbies and interests of the participants more extensively than any other group.

3. How are the adult ministries of the church addressing the adult need-based readiness to learn? Many adult classes choose their own curriculum with approval from church leadership. Choosing what they will study virtually assures a level of interest and need. In addition, almost every church provides some variation of the elective system. The beauty of electives lies in the adults' ability to register their needs or interests with their attendance. Loyalty to class members is temporarily set aside. Courses with low attendance are usually not repeated.

Certainly the proliferation of home Bible studies enables adults to select what they choose to learn. Growth in these areas may indicate that adults are more concerned with their spiritual development than we give them credit for.

The church's collection of tapes, books, and videos also offers a powerful tool to motivated adults. More than any other educational agency, this resource addresses adults' needs precisely when they feel it.

4. How does the church answer the adult's concern for immediate application? Almost every congregation offers special classes such as single parenting, marriage building, childrearing, or caring for aging parents. In addition, they promote the notion of life-related studies of the Bible in even the most traditional settings.

One Sunday School brought all the adult classes together every quarter to share both what they learned and how they had applied what they learned. The emergence of support/recovery groups speaks to the immediate need of adults to deal with life-damaging problems.

Most of the leadership training opportunities were conducted on the job. Whether the adult had assumed a leadership role in the Sunday School or wanted to develop lay counseling skills, the immediate pressure of accomplishing an assigned task stimulated the training process.

Other ministries which appeal to immediate application involve everything from prayer chains to visitation teams which call on newcomers the same Sunday they attend the church.

Without question, the churches surveyed have developed broad and effective adult ministries. However, no one offered a planning/reporting grid to assist adults in evaluating how each item contributes to their development as disciples of Jesus Christ. That task still lies before us. Churches wishing to move toward a more thorough approach to adult education may wish to consider the following procedure:

A PROCEDURE FOR DEVELOPING A COMPREHENSIVE ADULT MINISTRY

1. List each category of ministry available to the adults of your church along with each specific offering.
2. Identify the single or dual focus of each ministry, for example, instruction/fellowship for Sunday School.
3. Decide exactly how each piece should fit into the whole adult education puzzle.
4. Lay out a dual agenda: one from leadership's perspective and one from the adult student's perspective. Decisions about content, fellowship, emotional support, spiritual ministry, and personal enrichment among others should be made here.
5. Acquire a resource inventory of adult curricular materials from various publishing houses to make available at all times. Purchasing these over time spreads out the cost.
6. Look at the actual teaching time for each year along with general attendance patterns for each program.
7. Lay out an evaluation device that will help adults keep track of everything they read, study, attend, or listen to.
8. Leave open windows in adult programs so the curriculum remains flexible as needs and interests change.
9. Consult adults often in the process to be sure the overall plan maintains a correct focus.
10. Educate the church about the cost of quality training for adults.

Remaining objective about the ministries provided for adults in these twenty-three churches is almost impossible. All of us in Christian education should take pride in the efforts exhibited by the specialists who work week by week and year by year to keep the church on the cutting edge. Although no one church can do everything, all of us can probably do more by learning from one another and allowing adults to take more responsibility for their own Christian education.

Notes

1. However, defining "effective church education with adults" is not easy. I allowed Christian education specialists to define it through the Ministry Idea Network of PACE.

   The MIN surveys PACE members to find the two or three ministries they supervise which seem to be flourishing. These are cataloged by subject and person, published annually, and provided as a networking device for the membership. PACE can be contacted by writing: PACE, 8405 N. Rockwell, 5 Plaza Square, Suite 222, Oklahoma City, OK; (405) 841-1712.

2. The following information summarizes the demographic data provided by twenty-three Christian education specialists.

   Survey Results

   *The survey reflected ministries from 14 different states:
   5 from California
   3 each from Texas and Illinois
   2 from Michigan
   1 each from Connecticut, Pennsylvania, Kansas, Florida, Ohio, Oregon, Minnesota, Georgia, Michigan, Washington and Arizona

   *A total of ten different denominations were represented:
   5 Baptist
   4 each from Christian and Evangelical Free
   2 each from Congregational, Community, and Bible
   1 each from Methodist, Lutheran, Friends, and Alliance

   • The attendance in church services ranged from 150 to 1,800. According to Lyle Schaller's scale, these churches represent every congregation between the Small Church and the Mini-denomination. His smallest size labeled "Fellowship" understandably did not appear. Lyle Schaller, *The Multiple Staff and the Larger Church* (Nashville: Abingdon, 1980).

   • The total Sunday School attendance ranged from 128 to 2,200. Some churches furnished Sunday School enrollment figures which were consistently much higher. This discrepancy may indicate a shadow market of readily available students for the Sunday School. Some research on this group might reveal ways to draw them into a more consistent attendance pattern.

   • Consistently, more people attended the morning worship service than Sunday School.

   • Three churches reported exceptions to this pattern with more people attending Sunday School than church. The first had church attendance of 625 and Sunday School of 652. The second with 800 in church had 900 attending their Sunday School. The third had church attendance of 1,800 and 2,200 in Sunday School.

   • Although more people consistently attended the morning worship service, the percentage of people attending Sunday School compared to morning worship varied over a wide range. One church had 20 percent of those attending morning worship in Sunday School while another had 122 percent of morning worship in Sunday School. Sunday School attendance averaged 81.6 percent of morning worship with a median of 80 percent.

   • The average adult Sunday School program ran 48.4 percent of total attendance. The median Sunday School had 47.6 percent adults. The

Sunday School with the smallest percentage of adults reflected a church only a year and a half old with limited facilities. That church, however, has a whole range of adult ministries in the planning stage. The largest percentage of adults in a Sunday School was 60.8 percent.

• Most of the Sunday School attendance figures did not indicate how they calculated adults staffing children's and youth classes. If these churches failed to include those teachers, the total number of adults involved in Sunday School (both teaching and attending) could creep closer to 50 percent.

• The most popular class size seemed to fall somewhere between thirty and forty. Classes in this size range clearly outnumbered anything larger or smaller.

3. This oversight justifies the churches' appointing some person to specifically coordinate the overall educational effort. For a full development of this proposition see chapter 1 in Michael S. Lawson and Robert J. Choun, *Directing Christian Education* (Chicago: Moody, 1992).

4. *Celebrate Sunday School: 4 Million Teachers Strong.* (Elgin, Ill.: David C. Cook, 1988), video.

5. Two adult ministries reflect programs designed and implemented as part of doctoral dissertation research. Several church ministries were supervised by practitioners with earned doctorates.

   This chapter reflects the collective wisdom and extensive ministries supervised by twenty-three members of the Professional Association of Christian Educators. We are in their debt.

6. Lyman Coleman and Richard Peace, *Mastering the Basics* (a series of Bible book studies), available from Serendipity House, Box 1012, Littleton, CO 80160.

7. *Spectrum,* David C. Cook Publishing, 850 N. Grove Avenue, Elgin, IL 60120.

8. The proliferation of small group material and emphasis in the church indicates the depth of the felt need in this area.

List of Participating Churches

1. Bethel Bible Church
   Tyler, Texas
   Cecil R. Price, Associate Pastor

2. Black Rock Congregational Church
   Fairfield, Connecticut
   Douglas G. Christgau, Minister of Christian Education

3. Huron Hills Baptist
   Ann Arbor, Michigan
   Mark Struck, Co-pastor

4. Crescent Park Baptist Church
   Odessa,Texas
   Reggie Bowman, Minister of Education

5. Crossroads Baptist Church
   Belevue, Washington
   Dave Glass, Christian Education Pastor

6. Evangelical Free Church of Huntington Beach
   Huntington Beach, California
   Douglas J. Denne, Director of Christian Education

7. West Shore Evangelical Free Church
   Mechanicsburg, Pennsylvania
   Skip Lewis, Associate Pastor of Christian Education

8. First Evangelical Free Church
   Wichita, Kansas
   Bill Beahm, Associate Pastor of Adult Ministries

9. First Christian Church
   Centralia, California
   Greg Ishmael, Minister of Education

10. First Christian Church
    Phoenix, Arizona
    Roy Reiswig, Assistant Administrator

11. First Christian Church
    Largo, Florida
    A. Leon Langston, Minister of Nurture and Development

12. Granada Heights Friends Church
    LaMirada, California
    Wes Rylander, Director of Christian Education

13. Ginghamsburg United Methodist Church
    Tipp City, Ohio
    Lou Walthall, Minister of Education & Discipleship

14. Grace Baptist Church
    Newhall, California
    J. Michael Broylas, Associate Pastor of Christian Education

15. Immanuel Lutheran Church
    Arlington Heights, Illinois
    Tim Hetzner, Director of Adult Education and Social Ministries
    (response courtesy of Patrica Paulson)

16. Christ Community Church
    Glendale, Michigan
    Doug Swank, Pastor to Adults

17. Paramount Terrace Christian Church
    Amarillo, Texas
    Bob Schroeder, Minister of Christian Education

18. Salem Alliance Church
    Salem, Oregon
    Don Sappington, Pastor of Christian Education and Adult Ministries

19. Sierra Madre Congregational Church
    Sierra Madre, California
    Larry Mills, Minister of Christian Education

20. South Suburban Evangelical Free Church
    Apply Valley, Minnesota
    Edgar J. Bender, Christian Education Pastor

21. Stone Mountain Community Church
    Stone Mountain, Georgia
    Andy Chappell, Pastor of Christian Education

22. The Western Springs Baptist Church
    Western Springs, Illinois
    Daniel B. Holmquist, Minister of Christian Education

23. Wheaton Bible Church
    Wheaton, Illinois
    Gary Dausey, Associate Pastor

For Further Reading

Barnard, Thomas. *The Adult Class in Action.* Kansas City, Mo.: Beacon Hill, 1970.

Clark, Robert E., Lin Johnson, and Allyn K. Sloat, eds. *Christian Education: Foundations for the Future.* Chicago: Moody, 1991.

Coleman, Lucien E. Jr. *Understanding Today's Adults.* Nashville: Convention Pr., 1983.

Cooper, Polly. *How to Guide Adults.* Nashville: Convention Pr. 1982.

Dyer, James T. *Getting Through to Adults.* Denver: Accent, 1980.

Gangel, Kenneth O., and Howard G. Hendricks. *The Christian Educator's Handbook on Teaching.* Wheaton, Ill.: Victor, 1988.

Journal of Adult Training 1, no. 2, Evangelical Training Association.

Journal of Adult Training 2, no. 2, Evangelical Training Association.

Journal of Adult Training 4, no. 1, Evangelical Training Association.

Marlowe, Monroe, and Bobbie Reed. *Creative Bible Learning for Adults.* Glendale, Calif.: Regal, 1977.

Sell, Charles M. *Transition: The Stages of Adult Life.* Chicago: Moody, 1985.

Stubblefield, Jerry M., ed. *A Church Ministering to Adults.* Nashville: Broadman, 1986.

CONTRIBUTORS

Dr. Warren S. Benson (Ph.D.) is Vice President of Professional Doctoral Programs, Director of the Doctor of Ministry Program, and Professor of Christian Education at Trinity Evangelical Divinity School, Deerfield, Illinois.

Dr. Richard E. Butman (Ph.D.) is Professor of Psychology at Wheaton College, Wheaton, Illinois.

Dr. Samuel L. Canine (Ph.D.) is Professor of Pastoral Ministries at Dallas Theological Seminary, Dallas, Texas.

Dr. Gregory C. Carlson (Ph.D.) is Professor of Christian Education at Grace College of the Bible, Omaha, Nebraska.

Dr. Patricia A. Chapman (Ed.D.) is Professor of Christian Education at Simpson College, Redding, California.

Dr. Allen C. Curry (Ed.D.) is Academic Dean and Associate Professor of Christian Education at Reformed Theological Seminary, Jackson, Mississippi.

Dr. James A. Davies (Ed.D.) is Professor of Christian Education at Simpson College, Redding, California.

Dr. John M. Dettoni (Ph.D.) is President of Chrysalis Ministries, San Clemente, California.

Dr. Duane H. Elmer (Ph.D.) is Professor of Christian Education at Wheaton College, Wheaton, Illinois.

Dr. Robert E. Fillinger (Ed.D.) is Professor of Christian Education and Senior Program Associate at Gordon-Conwell Theological Seminary, South Hamilton, Massachusetts.

Dr. James C. Galvin (Ed.D.) is Vice President of the Livingstone Corporation, Carol Stream, Illinois.

Dr. Kenneth O. Gangel (Ph.D.) is Academic Dean, Vice President for Academic Affairs, and Professor of Christian Education at Dallas Theological Seminary, Dallas, Texas.

Dr. Edward L. Hayes (Ph.D.) is President of Denver Theological Seminary, Denver, Colorado.

Dr. Malcolm S. Knowles (Ph.D.) is Professor Emeritus of Adult and Community College Education at North Carolina State University, Raleigh, North Carolina.

Dr. Michael S. Lawson (Ph.D.) is Professor of Christian Education at Dallas Theological Seminary, Dallas, Texas.

Rev. Stanley S. Olsen (M.A.) is Executive Pastor at Hillcrest Covenant Church, Prairie Village, Kansas.

Dr. Richard Patterson (Ph.D.) is the retired President of Evangelical Training Association, Wheaton, Illinois.

Dr. Robert W. Pazmiño (Ed.D.) is Professor of Religious Education at Andover Newton Theological School.

Dr. James R. Slaughter (Th.D.) is Associate Professor of Christian Education at Dallas Theological Seminary, Dallas, Texas.

Dr. Catherine Stonehouse (Ph.D.) is Professor of Christian Education at Asbury Theological Seminary, Wilmore, Kentucky.

Mr. David R. Veerman (M.Div.) is Executive Vice President of the Livingstone Corporation, Carol Stream, Illinois.

Dr. James C. Wilhoit (Ph.D.) is Associate Professor of Christian Education at Wheaton College, Wheaton, Illinois.

Dr. Harold J. Westing (D.D.) is Associate Professor of Pastoral Ministries and Dean of Students at Denver Seminary, Denver, Colorado.

Dr. Wesley R. Willis (Ph.D.) is Administrator, Vice President of Academic Affairs, and Dean of Academic Studies at Philadelphia College of the Bible, Phildelphia, Pennsylvania.

Dr. Fred R. Wilson (Ph.D.) is Academic Vice President, Dean of Faculty, and Professor of Christian Education at Canadian Theological Seminary, Regina, Saskatchewan, Canada.